PRAISE FOR
THE BILLIONAIRE'S APPRENTICE

"I couldn't put it down; it's a true story that reads like a thriller."
—William D. Cohan, bestselling author of
The Last Tycoons, House of Cards, and *Money and Power*

"THE BILLIONAIRE'S APPRENTICE is that rare work of nonfiction that follows an ambitious hero as he climbs to the pinnacle of power inside the top boardrooms of corporate America, gets seduced, and falls in a spectacular insider trading scandal. This is a modern-day Greek tragedy that plays out among the upper echelons of Wall Street, Silicon Valley, and the global business elite. Doggedly reported and utterly compelling."
—Bryan Burrough, bestselling author of
Barbarians at the Gate and *The Big Rich*

"Thanks to author Anita Raghavan's intrepid reporting, THE BILLIONAIRE'S APPRENTICE combines the drama of the federal government unraveling an insider trading ring with the historical sweep of immigrants rising from nothing to the corridors of power."
—Bethany McLean, bestselling coauthor of
The Smartest Guys in the Room and *All the Devils Are Here*

"I've always wondered how Indian-Americans came out of nowhere to become a force in the business establishment. THE BILLIONAIRE'S APPRENTICE explains that meteoric rise, but it is also a page-turning cops and robbers story set against the backdrops of Silicon Valley and Wall Street."
—Adam Lashinsky, bestselling author of *Inside Apple: How America's Most Admired—and Secretive—Company* Really *Works*

THE
BILLIONAIRE'S APPRENTICE

THE RISE OF THE INDIAN-AMERICAN ELITE AND THE FALL OF THE GALLEON HEDGE FUND

ANITA RAGHAVAN

BUSINESS PLUS

New York Boston

Grand Central Publishing
Hachette Book Group
1290 Avenue of the Americas
New York, NY 10104

www.HachetteBookGroup.com

Printed in the United States of America

RRD-C

Originally published in hardcover by Hachette Book Group
First trade edition: June 2015
10 9 8 7 6 5 4 3 2 1

Grand Central Publishing is a division of Hachette Book Group, Inc.
The Grand Central Publishing name and logo are trademarks of Hachette Book Group, Inc.

The Hachette Speakers Bureau provides a wide range of authors for speaking events. To find out more, go to www.hachettespeakersbureau.com or call (866) 376-6591.

The publisher is not responsible for websites (or their content) that are not owned by the publisher.

LCCN: 2013932397

ISBN 978-1-4555-0401-5 (pbk.)

To my loving parents
for making their journey

Brightest and best of the sons of the morning,
Dawn on our darkness and lend us Thine aid.

—Opening line from an epiphany hymn
by the Right Reverend Reginald Heber,
Anglican bishop of Calcutta, 1823–1826

CONTENTS

CAST OF CHARACTERS

In September 2009, as Wall Street recovered from the worst financial crisis since the Great Depression, an insider trading case was brewing...

The Leading Actors

The Guptas

Rajat K. Gupta—former three-time head of McKinsey and board member for Goldman Sachs, Procter & Gamble, and AMR

Anita Mattoo Gupta—his wife

Geetanjali, Megha, Aditi, and Deepali Gupta—his daughters

Ashwini and Pran Kumari Gupta—his parents

Kanchan Gupta—his younger brother

Jayashree Chowdhury—his younger sister

His Lawyers

Kramer Levin Naftalis & Frankel

Gary P. Naftalis—Gupta's lead counsel; a former federal prosecutor turned A-list criminal defense attorney who has represented everyone from former Walt Disney CEO Michael Eisner to Wall Street legend Kenneth Langone

David S. Frankel—longtime litigation partner of Naftalis, who represented New York State Liberal Party leader Raymond

Harding in an inquiry by New York attorney general Andrew Cuomo

Robin Wilcox

Alan R. Friedman

The Kumars

Anil Kumar—McKinsey consultant who was Raj Rajaratnam's classmate at Wharton and Gupta's protégé at McKinsey

Malvika Kumar—his wife

Aman Kumar—his son

His Lawyers

Morvillo Abramowitz Grand Iason & Anello

Robert G. Morvillo—Kumar's lead counsel; he represented domestic goddess Martha Stewart

Gregory Morvillo—his son, who after his father's death would start his own firm and represent Level Global cofounder Anthony Chiasson

The Rajaratnams

Raj Rajaratnam—head of the Galleon Group

Asha Pabla Rajaratnam—his wife

Rengan Rajaratnam—former head of Sedna Capital and Raj's youngest brother

Ragakanthan Rajaratnam—Galleon portfolio manager and Raj's middle brother

His Lawyers

Akin Gump Strauss Hauer & Feld

John M. Dowd—Rajaratnam's lead counsel; a feisty ex-marine who also served as special counsel to three commissioners of Major League Baseball in the investigation of Pete Rose and others

Terence J. Lynam

Samidh Guha

Patricia A. Millett

The Sheriffs of Wall Street

The Securities and Exchange Commission

George S. Canellos—director, New York office

David A. Markowitz—former assistant regional director, New York office

Sanjay Wadhwa—assistant regional director, New York office

Jason E. Friedman—senior staff attorney

John P. Henderson—senior staff attorney

The FBI

B. J. Kang—special agent who was one of the arresting agents of Bernie Madoff and also worked the Galleon case

The US Attorney's Office, New York

Preetinder S. Bharara—US attorney, Southern District of New York

Reed Brodsky—assistant US attorney

Andrew Z. Michaelson—special assistant US attorney on loan from the SEC

Jonathan R. Streeter—assistant US attorney

The Galleon Circle

The Galleon Group

Michael Cardillo—portfolio manager

Kris Chellam—former Xilinx executive turned Galleon portfolio manager

Caryn Eisenberg—Rajaratnam's executive assistant

Tom Fernandez—Rajaratnam's Wharton classmate and head of investor relations

Michael Fisherman—analyst

Ian Horowitz—trader

David Lau—Rajaratnam's Wharton classmate and Asia chief

George Lau—chief compliance officer

Ananth Muniyappa—trader

Gary Rosenbach—portfolio manager

Richard Schutte—chief operating officer

Leon Shaulov—portfolio manager

Adam Smith—Harvard Business School graduate, former Morgan Stanley investment banker, and portfolio manager at Galleon

Other Traders

William J. Lyons III—former Sedna trader with a weakness for instant messaging

Matt Read—Lyons's cousin and instant-message partner

Frank "Quint" Slattery—manager of Symmetry Peak Capital

Around the Galleon Ring

Sunil Bhalla—Polycom executive

Danielle Chiesi—New Castle Funds consultant

Rajive Dhar—executive at Arris Group

Rajiv Goel—Wharton classmate of Raj Rajaratnam and Intel Treasury executive

Shammara Hussain—former investor relations associate at Market Street Partners

Roomy Khan—former Intel marketing employee and former Galleon trader

Deep Shah—credit analyst at Moody's Investors Service

Apjit Walia—RBC Capital Markets analyst

Goldman Sachs

Lloyd C. Blankfein—chief executive

Gary D. Cohn—president

John H. Bryan—board member

William W. George—board member

Gregory K. Palm—general counsel

Steven R. Peikin—Goldman's outside lawyer at Sullivan & Cromwell

John F. W. Rogers—Blankfein's chief of staff and secretary to the Goldman board

Byron D. Trott—Warren E. Buffett's banker

David A. Viniar—chief financial officer

Jon Winkelried—former president

McKinsey

Dominic Barton—managing director

Marvin Bower—former managing director (1950–1967)

D. Ronald Daniel—former managing director (1976–1988)

Ian Davis—former managing director (2003–2009)

Frederick W. Gluck—former managing director (1988–1994)

Herbert Henzler—former chairman of McKinsey Germany

David Palecek—McKinsey consultant

Anupam "Tino" Puri—former managing director of McKinsey India

Paresh Vaish—former engagement manager on Hindustan Motors project

Donald C. Waite III—former head of McKinsey's New York office

Adil Zainulbhai—chairman of McKinsey India

Harvard Business School

Walter J. Salmon—Gupta's professor

John V. Carberry—Gupta's suite mate

David Manly—Gupta's late friend

THE
BILLIONAIRE'S APPRENTICE

The Twice Blessed

It was Tuesday, November 24, 2009, and Rajat Kumar Gupta was headed to the White House for the first state dinner hosted by President Barack Obama and his wife, Michelle, the most glamorous political couple since the Kennedys. Six years had passed since Gupta had stepped down as the three-term global managing director of consulting giant McKinsey & Co., but at sixty, he was busier than ever. He sat on a handful of corporate boards—Goldman Sachs & Co., Procter & Gamble Co., and American Airlines, to name a few. His wife, Anita, had hoped his retirement from the top job at McKinsey would slow him down, but he was in the throes of building his own private equity company from scratch. Jetting from continent to continent, living out of a suitcase, he was as intent on being a game changer in private equity and philanthropy as he had been during a storied career in consulting.

Dressed in a black Nehru suit, with a red handkerchief tucked in his pocket, Gupta made his way to the white tent on the South Lawn from the gilded East Room, which served as the staging area for the dinner. At every turn, he ran into friends. He chatted with Deepak Chopra, the new age physician, who was wearing his signature gem-studded eyeglasses for the glittering gala. He mingled with Preeta Bansal, a top lawyer in the new administration, and caught up with Bobby Jindal, a former McKinsey consultant and now the Republican governor of Louisiana. Jindal, whose given name is Piyush, was born in Baton Rouge; his parents migrated to America from the Indian state of Punjab six months before he was born.

Jindal was typical of the guests at the White House that night. While the ostensible purpose of the evening was to honor the Indian prime minister, Dr. Manmohan Singh, the event also served as a barometer for how far and how fast an immigrant group had risen. In one generation Indian-Americans had vaulted from geeky outsiders to polished players in all facets of American society.

If Gupta wanted to make small talk in the security line with a Fortune 500 CEO, he could approach either GE's Jeffrey Immelt or Indra Nooyi, the CEO of PepsiCo, who was born and bred in Chennai. If he wanted to bask in the reflected glow of a TV presenter, he could chat with Katie Couric or the Mumbai-born Fareed Zakaria. Hollywood was represented at the event. Both Steven Spielberg and the Indian director of *The Sixth Sense*, M. Night Shyamalan, whose birthplace is Pondicherry, were in attendance that night.

As one of the pioneering Indian success stories in the United States, Gupta knew almost all the Indian invitees and, as a McKinsey legend, their non-Indian counterparts too. He had worked with many and served as a mentor to others. When Neal Kumar Katyal, the principal deputy solicitor general, was in high school and getting pressure from his Indian parents to study medicine, Gupta advised him to follow his dreams. Katyal's position in the Justice Department as one of the chief attorneys representing the government before the US Supreme Court was a testament to the heights to which Indians had risen in American society.

"As you looked around the room that night, it was breathtaking to see the diversity and depth of talent," says Timothy J. Roemer, at the time the US ambassador to India. "There were CEOs and entrepreneurs, there were doctors, hotel owners, and writers. There were aspiring office seekers and office holders. There were people who had grown up poor in India but now they were the CEO of the company. You could feel how alive the American dream was in that room," exults Roemer.

Gupta and the other Indian-American luminaries were either part of or the children of a generation that academic Vijay Prashad has dubbed the "twice blessed." The first blessing was to be born after India had achieved its independence from Great Britain at the stroke of midnight on August 15, 1947. The blessing of this freedom was not just political; it was cultural too. The end of the Raj made educational and social advancement possible to a young nation throbbing with 340 million people.

The second blessing was the culmination of the civil rights struggle in the United States and the passing in 1965 of the now largely overlooked Hart-Cellar Act into law. The act—an outward-looking follow-up to the 1964 Civil Rights Act—did away with long-standing isolationist policies that severely restricted Indian immigration to one hundred people each year. Hart-Cellar meant that future immigrants would be allowed into America based on their skills and not just their countries of origin, race, or ancestry. For a generation of Indians weaned on a strict diet of education, it was a momentous breakthrough with far-reaching implications.

In the wake of the act, Indian immigration into America grew from a trickle to a torrent. Unlike the previous waves of huddled masses who took several generations to make their way from digging ditches to holding office in the statehouse, Indian immigrants were highly educated and brimming with ambition. "There is an immense, immense selectivity in the pattern of Indian migration to the United States," says Professor Marcelo M. Suarez-Orozco, an expert on immigration and dean of UCLA's Graduate School of Education and Information Studies. The average Indian in the United States is "ten thousand times more likely to have a doctorate" than the average Indian in India. In other words, the Indians who come to America are by and large the country's "brightest and best," an observation borne out even today by hard facts.

Of the 3.2 million Indians in the United States, 70 percent have bachelor's degrees compared to just 28 percent nationally. Their median annual household income of $88,000 is almost twice what most Americans earn each year and 33 percent higher than the average income of Asians in the United States. Most of the overachievers are immigrants. In the new millennium, Gupta and other Indian-born natives were ubiquitous in every sphere of American life. They were among the country's most promising doctors and engineers and its most successful bankers and lawyers. Some ran or were poised to run the nation's biggest corporations—Citigroup and MasterCard. Others were contenders for top jobs at all-American companies like Warren Buffett's Berkshire Hathaway.

None of this would have been possible had it not been for the path staked out by the likes of Rajat Kumar Gupta. He was the most accomplished representative of an entire generation of strivers. He cleared an eight-thousand-mile path to the United States for hardworking Indian émigrés. Through his exemplary career—and without ever consciously choosing to do so—he broke down America's prejudicial business barriers and served as a model not only for his peers but for their sons and daughters too.

In the weeks before the White House dinner, there was much handicapping about who would be asked and whether previous guests to state dinners with Indian prime ministers would be asked again. In the bruising politics of the Beltway, the drop-offs were more widely publicized than the invitees and the absences—the most notable being Citigroup chief Vikram Pandit—talked about in hushed, funereal tones.

There was never any question that Gupta would be invited. He was one of the few Indians in America who waltzed through vastly different worlds, business and philanthropy, in India and America, without ever losing a step. He was friends with almost all the Indian businessmen accompanying Dr. Singh on his trip to the United States. He was close to Mukesh Ambani, the head of the powerful Indian conglomerate Reliance Industries, who viewed Gupta as one of India's most treasured exports, someone who had reached the pinnacle of corporate and public life in the United States but had never lost his affection for his homeland. He knew Ratan Tata, often described as the David Rockefeller of India. Tata, whose holdings run the gamut from cars—Jaguar Land Rover—to hotels—Mumbai's iconic Taj Mahal Palace hotel—had worked early on to help Gupta turn his dream of an Indian business school into reality.

But Gupta's most important relationship—one that certainly helped secure an invitation that evening—was his friendship with the guest of honor, Dr. Singh. Gupta was one of the few Indian executives in America who could get the Indian prime minister on the phone on short notice. Despite McKinsey's prominence in India, the two were not acquainted in the early 1990s when Gupta was a rising star at McKinsey, and Singh, then a little-known finance minister in a previous Indian government, was the architect of a fusillade of economic reforms that dismantled the Red Tape Raj and ushered in an era of entrepreneurial freedom. But when India prospered in the wake of Singh's moves, McKinsey thrived, advising a raft of Indian companies on restructuring moves and playing a pivotal role in building "Offshore-istan."

It was during Gupta's time as managing director that McKinsey opened its groundbreaking "Knowledge Center" in a suburb of New Delhi, hiring a fleet of Indian researchers, many with MBAs, to analyze important trends such as cellular phone penetration for McKinsey consultants.

When the McKinsey Knowledge Center turned out to be a huge hit, Gupta went global with the idea. He preached the sermon of offshoring to American companies eager to cut costs and pushed them to send more and more of their back-office and support work—corporate research, legal transcription, and financial analysis—to India. Clients were thrilled, and in India, Gupta was a corporate rock star, just as recognizable in Mumbai as Jamie Dimon is in New York.

It was no small irony, then, that one of his dinner companions at the White House that evening was labor leader Andy Stern, the president of the country's second-largest union (the Service Employees International Union). Stern, whose organization spent the most money supporting Obama, sat between Gupta and his wife, Anita, at a table sumptuously decorated with gold charger plates and purple and magenta arrangements of roses, sweet peas, and hydrangeas on green-apple tablecloths. Over a dinner of green curry prawns, collard greens, and coconut-aged basmati rice, Stern took the opportunity to nudge a key party some consider responsible for the fading prospects of the American worker. He pressed Gupta on why companies like Goldman, whose investors include public pension plans, didn't have more regard for the worker. In his soft-spoken but firm way, Gupta insisted they did. They gave a lot of money away to needy organizations. But Stern had something more radical in mind—profits more broadly distributed to rank-and-file employees.

Overhearing the debate were Gupta's dinner companions Treasury secretary Timothy Geithner and North Dakota senator Kent Conrad. It was heady company. If anyone had told Gupta back when he was a little boy in Calcutta that he would someday work at—let alone run—McKinsey & Co. and be invited to the White House for dinner, they might have had an easier time convincing him that he would walk on the moon. The heights he had attained would only serve to make the events that followed all the more unfathomable.

* * *

Seventeen days later, as Gupta rushed through airport security with his carry-on in tow, his cell phone rang. The caller on the morning of Friday, December 11, 2009, was Gregory K. Palm, the general counsel to Goldman Sachs & Co. Gupta had been a board member since 2006, and at least once a quarter, he would hear from Lloyd Blankfein, Goldman's chief executive. Blankfein considered it a key part of his job to post his board of directors on the quarterly goings-on at the bank. But it was rare for Gupta to hear from Palm alone.

At Wall Street investment banks, general counsels are often among the most powerful (yet invisible) members of the leadership team. They are the keepers of secrets. They know where the corporate bodies are buried. Palm was extraordinarily discreet. Even though he was one of the firm's most influential and highest paid executives—since 2002, Goldman had awarded him stock and options worth $67.3 million—Palm kept a very low profile. Many of the bank's thirty-three thousand employees didn't even know who he was.

Like Blankfein and Gupta, Palm came from modest means, a case study in American meritocracy. He was an electrician's son who won the National Science Foundation fellowship award at the

Massachusetts Institute of Technology. After MIT, Palm headed to Harvard, where he enrolled in its joint JD/MBA program. He was actually in Gupta's class at Harvard Business School. (The two were in different sections and didn't know each other.) In 1992, after a decade working for Goldman's outside legal counsel, the whitest of white-shoe firms, Sullivan & Cromwell, Palm joined Goldman.

When Palm reached Gupta, his tone was unusually serious; he said there was something important he wanted to discuss with the respected Goldman director.

The night before, Palm had been sitting in his corner office overlooking the Statue of Liberty, on the thirty-seventh floor of One New York Plaza, wrapping up for the day. It was dark and most of his colleagues had left when Goldman's outside lawyer from Palm's old firm, Steven R. Peikin, called. Like many before him, Peikin worked for nearly a decade in the US attorney's office for the Southern District of New York. He rose to head the Securities and Commodities Fraud Task Force before moving to Sullivan & Cromwell, where he now guarded the interests of one of the banks he used to scrutinize. Peikin told Palm that he had learned through the legal grapevine that there was evidence floating around that could draw Goldman director Rajat Gupta into an insider trading case.

The next morning, as Gupta prepared to catch a plane, Palm went to brief his boss at the bank's headquarters, then at 85 Broad Street. Blankfein was surprised to hear what Palm had to say. Gupta had impeccable credentials and a sterling reputation. "We need to figure this out," Blankfein told Palm. Goldman was under considerable scrutiny after the 2008 financial crisis. More bad press was the last thing the firm needed. "This is something that is obviously serious, but we don't know a lot here.

"[Whatever you do], let's make sure we don't ruin Gupta's reputation."

PART ONE

Discovery

CHAPTER ONE

"Who Will Show Me the Way in the World?"

Ever since he was born, Rajat Kumar Gupta was likened to his father. He was as handsome as his father, with the same strikingly chiseled jawline that gave both men a distinguished air, a sense they belonged to a secret world of privilege that went beyond wealth, intellect, or bloodline. In a society where skin color was a defining force, both Rajat and his father, Ashwini, were fair-skinned, a clear advantage that afforded them a natural superiority. Both were known for their generosity of spirit—an obliging way that over the course of their lives would win them steadfast friends and loyal followers. But beneath the surface the similarities ended.

Unlike his son, Ashwini Kumar Gupta came of age in an occupied country, seemingly fated by his birth in 1908 to live in deference to an imperial power. As a descendant of one of India's oldest bloodlines, Ashwini was also, ironically, one of the chosen ones. He would be tapped and trained to deny his Indianness and perform like a faux Englishman, all in the service of India's emperor, His Majesty the king. While he would receive a proper British education like the other esteemed members of his family, Ashwini Kumar Gupta rejected intellectual servitude.

When the British East India Company first settled in India in 1612—in hot pursuit of black pepper and cinnamon—few expected that England would one day turn its adventure in commerce into a chapter in conquest. Other European nations—France, Portugal, the

Netherlands, and Denmark—were already well ensconced in the critical trading territory of India's northeastern Bengal. It was not until the tail end of the seventeenth century, when Job Charnock, an enterprising agent of the East India Company, pitched stakes on the banks of the Hooghly River, a fast-flowing tributary of the mighty Ganges, that England began its rise to power.

Under the East India Company's aegis, Calcutta grew into a thriving commercial hub, a hive of trading in spices and the other riches of the East: opium, jute, and muslin. Along with commerce, the English imported their way of life. Besides gin and tonics and golf (a sport that arrived in Calcutta in 1829, some sixty years before it reached New York), they introduced English education. Offering formal higher education to natives did not come from a sense of altruism; rather, as Thomas Babington Macaulay, a member of the Supreme Council for India, put it: "We must at present do our best to form a class who may be interpreters between us and the millions whom we govern; a class of persons, Indian in blood and color, but English in taste, in opinions, in morals, and in intellect."

With Macaulay's urging, Governor-General William Bentinck introduced English as the official language for Indian higher education, a move that would have momentous consequences a hundred years later.

As of 1858, though, the educated Indian class had not fully embraced their inner Englishman. While receiving the finest Western tutoring elevated their social position, education did not bestow an economic advantage. Poverty and scarcity were the norm for Indian natives, regardless of academic proficiency. After a bloody native Indian uprising—called the Sepoy Mutiny by the British and the First War of Indian Independence by the native nationalists—the Crown relieved the East India Company of rule and took complete control of India. Queen Victoria ultimately became the empress of the South Asian jewel.

Fifty years later, when Ashwini Gupta was born, the British Raj was firmly in control, and Ashwini's birthplace—Bengal—was its seat of power. At the vanguard of almost every major social, intellectual, political, and economic movement in India, Bengal was New

York, Paris, London, and Hong Kong all rolled into one. So powerful was its sway that one Indian National Congress leader quipped, "What Bengal thinks today, India thinks tomorrow."

The Guptas were an old and distinguished Bengali family who counted themselves among India's English-educated elite, a rarefied group at the turn of the century, representing less than 0.1 percent of the country's total population. Their roots lay in Goila, a village then part of East Bengal, now Bangladesh. Despite their education, the Guptas struggled financially. They settled in North Calcutta, colloquially known as "Blacktown" because it was the domain of the city's dark-skinned natives. South Calcutta, which the English appropriated, was labeled "Whitetown." For native Indians, shut off as they were from economic opportunity, learning, not lucre, conferred status. And the Guptas were very learned. Education for them was a vocation, not just a profession.

Given the family's intellectual pedigree, Ashwini Gupta was expected to have a celebrated academic career too. He did not disappoint. He had a fine mind and was a "brilliant student" at Calcutta University, where he received a master of arts in economics. But even though he was raised and educated as a fluent English speaker, Ashwini Gupta did not aspire to become a British dandy. He was a fiery Bengali at heart. He thought like one, lived like one, and even dressed like one.

"Like all Bengalis at the time, he was a leftist," says the journalist Inder Malhotra, who got to know Gupta when he was in New Delhi in the 1950s. In the bitterly cold winters commonplace in Delhi, Gupta donned a khadi dhoti—a garment popular among Bengali men. It was a rectangular piece of white cloth that wrapped around his waist and stretched to his feet and was made of khadi— a coarse fabric woven from hand-spun yarn. Gupta was rarely seen without it.

Khadi was one of the most powerful visual symbols of the burgeoning freedom movement. It was the cloth of choice for hard-core Indian nationalists. First championed by an English-educated Indian barrister named Mohandas Karamchand Gandhi, who urged Indians to boycott foreign cloth in favor of khadi, it soon became the leitmotif of the pro-independence Congress Party. It happened to be a cloth that meshed perfectly with Gupta's political sensibilities.

Ashwini was one of India's fervent freedom fighters who stridently rejected the native "interpreter" role he had been born into. He longed to stand out among the hundreds of thousands of khadi-wearing nationalists. In 1929, while studying in Calcutta, he joined the All-Bengal Students' Association, an innocuous-sounding group that on its face had seemingly little to do with India's struggle for independence. In reality, it was an organization brimming with revolutionary resolve.

Ashwini Gupta immersed himself in the association, often skipping classes to attend its meetings. His close friend Apurba Maitra, whose roll call number was next to his at the university, would cover for him, pretending to be Gupta at the customary call-outs at the start of each class. Maitra viewed his friend Ashwini, then all of twenty-two, as something of a senior statesman among student activists.

On January 26, 1932, Maitra was studying law at Calcutta University when an edict was imposed forbidding students from flying the Indian national flag in any university building. If they did, they would face "unpleasant consequences." At that time, Calcutta's police commissioner, Sir Charles Augustus Tegart, was notorious for torturing political prisoners (even young students) and for his uncanny ability to avoid assassination. But patriotic Indians viewed January 26 as the country's show-your-colors day: were you an independent Indian or a pawn of the British Empire? Two years earlier the Indian National Congress had passed a resolution fixing the day for countrywide protests in support of complete independence. For khadi wearers, kowtowing in fear of British retaliation was ignoble and cowardly. For them, flying the flag separated the truly possessed from the poseurs.

Overcome with nationalist fervor, Maitra and nineteen of his friends flew the flag and then signed a declaration of opposition as required by the university. Not long after, while Maitra was at the university cricket field, an envelope addressed to him arrived at his dormitory. It was marked "On His Majesty's Service."

The terrified men, disregarding their collective code of conduct respecting individual privacy, tore open Maitra's letter. Inside they found a summons demanding that Maitra appear before the powerful chief secretary to the government of Bengal at the Writers' Building in Dalhousie Square, the seat of British power in Calcutta.

They hatched a plan: they would accompany Maitra to Dalhousie Square, but he would go in to see the British official alone while they waited for him outside. Knowing that the meeting could lead to swift imprisonment, the activists set aside their indispensables—sleepwear and books—so that they could grab them if the police van arrived to round them up and make arrests.

When Gupta overheard their plan, he chided them: "You idiots, if you go to Dalhousie Square en masse, the plain-clothes 'spies' around the Writers' building will suspect you are supporters of Benoy Basu and his gang." (Gupta was alluding to an incident from two years earlier when Basu and two accomplices shot and killed the British inspector general of prisons, a brute of a man who condoned torture.) Since the attack, a spree of assassinations had shattered the peace in Bengal. The province became such a hotspot for terrorists that word of its growing violence reached Buckingham Palace in London. In 1932, King George V, apparently befuddled by the reports he was receiving from Bengal, beseeched the provincial governor, "What is *wrong* with Bengal?"

One of Ashwini Gupta's strengths was his skill as a versatile strategist and tactician. "Don't go," he advised. "Let Apurba [Maitra] go alone with the letter."

Maitra obeyed. When he arrived at the Writers' Building, he was escorted into the imposing office of Sir Robert Niel Reid.

"So, young man, you know the very bad position [you] are in?"

Maitra quickly confessed his crime. He and his friends were ready to accept any punishment for their flag-hoisting caper, but they would not apologize on any account.

"You are mad," Reid said before explaining that the summons had nothing to do with flying the flag. "This anonymous letter has shaken your bones, you are talking incoherently. Have courage. This may not happen."

Maitra was flummoxed. "Why courage?"

Reid informed Maitra that his father, a native serving the British as a magistrate, was a target of terrorists. "Imagine yourself with your widowed mother and her five children, you are the eldest," Reid intoned. "You may be doomed and ruined."

To ease his father's anxieties, Reid suggested that Maitra quit his legal studies and accept a post as a warden in the Bengal prison system, a steady job with steady pay.

"Sir, if I do not accept it?" he queried.

In case Maitra forgot, Reid reminded him that round-the-clock armed police, provided at the discretion of His Majesty's government, protected his father.

Reid didn't need to say any more. Maitra agreed to the prison posting.

On the day Maitra's train was set to depart to a prison high up in the rolling green hills of Darjeeling, Ashwini Gupta entered his compartment and took his hand, gently pulling him away from his well-wishers. Somehow Maitra had been found out. Through his vast network, Gupta knew Maitra wasn't going to Darjeeling as a political prisoner, but as a guard.

"So, Apurba," he said. "This little ovation of friends on the platform, a few bunches of flowers on your berth speak of our old love for you, but do you feel what you are carrying in your luggage?"

Maitra lowered his head.

"Our eternal hatred for you. Eternal hatred."

Then, overwhelmed by emotion, Gupta drew his sash over his eyes and exited the train.

For the rest of the 1930s, Gupta and Maitra lived very different lives. Maitra, a warden at a small jail in Darjeeling, surrounded by acres of sprawling tea estates, spent his days guarding petty criminals and prominent freedom fighters. He looked upon his time as a young activist with some nostalgia, but he knew it was far behind him now. Ashwini Gupta, meanwhile, stayed in Calcutta. For a brief time, he lectured in economics at what was then known as Ripon College. But teaching was only a day job. In his off-hours he forged ties with prominent leftist leaders.

Gupta and Maitra would have never crossed paths again had it not been for Gupta's participation in the militant Quit India movement in 1942. Gupta was among the tens of thousands rounded up and arrested in Bengal and sent to Presidency Jail in Calcutta. Maitra, by now an officer at Presidency Jail, was stunned when he saw his old friend Gupta.

"So, Ashwini," said Maitra, placing his hands on Gupta's emaciated shoulders. "You are all skin and bones...how?"

"Tuberculosis; one lung bleeding, fever every night, twenty pounds weight lost...Apurba, don't come so near to me, you may catch it."

Weakened by a multitude of beatings fighting for India's independence and stricken with tuberculosis years before antibiotics, the thirty-four-year-old Gupta was as good as dead. But that evening, Maitra signed out from the prison under the pretext of going to see a movie. Then he visited a prominent local doctor and pleaded with him to treat his old friend.

After two weeks, an ambulance arrived and Maitra watched as the withered Gupta was led inside. He was in the hospital for six months, and after multiple surgeries, Gupta lost several ribs, but he regained a modicum of health and his familiar smile was back.

Maitra cared for Gupta upon his return to jail, and while censoring his inbound and outbound mail, he discovered that Ashwini had a "wife in the making...a nice non-Bengali girl."

Gupta had vowed not to marry until India won its independence. But before his final internment, he fell in love with Pran Kumari, a Bethune College student whom he tutored. Their courtship transcended traditional barriers.

The two came from different parts of India—one the cultural capital of the country, the other its breadbasket. Ashwini was a quintessential Bengali. Though his wife, Pran Kumari, grew up in Bengal, her family originally came from Punjab, which, because of its position on the flank of India, bore the brunt of constant assault from a series of invaders. The violence marred the natural beauty of Punjab's rolling fields of wheat, barley, corn, and sugarcane. If the Bengalis were considered the soul of India, the seed of its cultural and intellectual heritage, the Punjabis were its body, literally tilling the land to feed India's people.

Their love flourished in censored letters during Gupta's years in prison. In early 1947, at the urging of friends and before India's independence, Ashwini Gupta married Pran Kumari. The two belonged to different Hindu reform groups, but they were too progressive to care. The wedding took place on the campus of Bethune College. It was a modest affair. The Guptas were not showy people. Besides, though few knew it at the time, Ashwini Gupta's incarceration had left the family in dire financial straits.

Soon after marriage, Ashwini and Pran started a family, eager to make up for lost time. Their first child, a daughter, was born in 1947. Thirteen months later, on December 2, 1948, came Rajat; his pet name was Ratan, meaning "gem." Then, after two years, the Guptas welcomed another daughter. The family of five squeezed into a three-room flat on a busy main road in North Calcutta, around the corner from Ashwini's brother's green-shuttered house on Rajendra Lal Street.

* * *

On the morning of Thursday, November 5, 1964, Apurba Maitra—now a citizen of an independent India—unfolded his morning newspaper to find a photo of Ashwini Gupta on the front page.

Earlier on that same muggy morning in November, Ashwini's eldest son, fifteen-year-old Rajat Kumar Gupta, dressed himself, carefully draping his best white dhoti over his body. Growing up in a close-knit Indian family of four children, two girls and two boys, the youngest born after the family moved to New Delhi in the 1950s, Rajat was accustomed to shouldering responsibility. He and his older sister were always looking after their younger siblings. By economic necessity, his parents were a two-career couple long before it was in vogue. His mother taught at the local Montessori school, and upon his release from prison, Ashwini took up journalism as a means to support himself and his family.

His old revolutionary ties to the leaders of a newly free India helped him rise. After India's independence, he was dispatched to start the Delhi edition of the *Hindusthan Standard*. He was a frequent visitor to Rashtrapati Bhavan, the official residence of the president of India, and it was well known among the Delhi press corps that the country's first prime minister, Jawaharlal Nehru, called him by his first name. So trusted was Gupta by government ministers that they would often seek his counsel on how to deal with the press. Born as a British subject, Ashwini Gupta, through hard work and sacrifice, became an insider in modern India.

Rajat then steeled himself and walked into the anteroom of his uncle's Calcutta home at 19C Rajendra Lal Street to say farewell. Shrouded with heaps of roses, marigolds, and fragrant jasmine, his father lay in a coffin. As was customary, the body was washed in purified water and dressed in a white kurta (a loose-fitting shirt) and a white dhoti.

When he'd arrived at the hospital the previous day, he was told his father was dead. But as he stood at the entrance to his father's room, he saw a plastic bag, still attached, bubbling with air from his father's last gasps. For a moment, he thought the doctors had made a mistake. But the years of struggle and incarceration had taken their toll. At fifty-six, Ashwini Gupta was dead of kidney failure.

In the months leading up to his father's death, young Rajat had spent a lot of time with his father, accompanying him on long walks and listening to stories of his time in the freedom movement. He learned that his father had been intentionally exposed to TB in prison, which ultimately cost him the use of one lung. The ragged two-foot-long scar on his back came from his skin being split open over and over again during one particularly brutal interrogation. Yet in spite of it all, the father he knew was kind and obliging to everyone. He would later recall, "He never spoke ill of anybody, and I would have thought he would have a lot of resentment built into him, but it wasn't true. [This attitude] was true of most of my father's generation...They were quite extraordinary in terms of simple living and high thinking and not thinking ill of other people."

This morning, in front of Rajat's uncle's house, a crowd gathered; neighbors, friends, and admirers descended like pilgrims on a sorrowful journey. Door-to-door launderers (dhobi-men) and their donkeys watched as a coffin was placed into a glass-topped hearse parked in front of the redbrick house with the green shutters. In tribute, the dhobi-men nudged their donkeys away from the mourners and solemnly cleared a path for the procession.

At 9 a.m., the hearse, closely followed by cars carrying the immediate family, departed. As the throng approached the top of the street, Rajat could make out a small shrine to Shiva, the Hindu god of destruction. After a stop at the offices of his father's employer, the newspaper group *Anandabazar Patrika*, he led the crowd to Whitetown.

On the other side of town, Maitra raced to catch one final glimpse of Ashwini Gupta. He ran to a crematorium known as the Nimtollah burning ghat, then south to the Keoratola funeral parlor, to no avail. On his last guess, he found the right destination. Clenching a fistful of flowers, he elbowed through a crowd of hundreds of friends, family, and admiring strangers and made his way beyond the row of bodies stacked in a line to be cremated.

At last, after pushing his way past Ashwini Gupta's brother, the former prison guard made it to the coffin. Ashwini Gupta's teenage son, Rajat, was just completing the final death rite. In the silence that followed, Maitra was able to place what was left of his bunch of lotus flowers on the feet of his fallen friend. Rajat Gupta then helped roll the stretcher holding his beloved father's body into the orange flames of Calcutta's electric crematorium.

Overcome with grief, Maitra muttered a prayer to his dead friend, Ashwini: "Pray not a grain of hatred remains mingled in your ashes. I tried to atone for my sin." If he hadn't been awash in his own sadness at the premature death of one of India's unsung heroes, Maitra might have heard another voice—the tender voice of Rajat Kumar Gupta quietly beseeching a higher power:

"Who will show me the way in the world?"

CHAPTER TWO

"I Respectfully Decline to Answer the Question"

It was three days before Christmas when Rajat Gupta, dressed in a gray pin-striped suit and flanked by his three lawyers, arrived at the visitors' reception on the fourth floor of the US Securities and Exchange Commission's New York headquarters. His white shirt was perfectly pressed and his black hair, tinged with touches of gray, impeccably groomed. He and his lead counsel, Gary Naftalis, looked like they had stepped out of a regional theater production of *The Odd Couple*. Naftalis was the absent-minded professor, his suit rumpled and his white hair flying. Gupta, solemn and distinguished, had the presence of a dignified head of state. Never in his wildest dreams did he expect at his age—he'd turned sixty-two a few weeks earlier—and with all his accomplishments, to be embroiled in the kind of matter that prompted his sit-down with the SEC on this morning in December 2010. Surely this must be a misunderstanding that could be resolved.

A year had passed since Goldman Sachs's head counsel had first told Gupta that he was being drawn into a government investigation. He had spent much of the time in the dark, frustrated by the swirling innuendos but powerless to quell them. Privately and publicly, he denied that there was anything to this nascent blemish on an otherwise spotless career. Now, with one of the country's most prominent criminal defense attorneys by his side, he would be meeting with the government's lawyers for the first time. He was to be deposed in the matter of Sedna Capital Management LLC, a little-known and now defunct New York hedge fund.

For four full years, the investigation into Sedna had consumed Sanjay Wadhwa, the deputy chief of the SEC's Market Abuse Unit. It already had produced the biggest case the SEC had ever brought against a New York hedge fund manager. Now Wadhwa was preparing to build a new, possibly even bigger case. After much maneuvering and countless delays, he and his team of SEC lawyers were finally going to interview the most respected Indian executive in America, the man who had blazed a trail that younger Indian-Americans like Wadhwa followed.

Despite flecks of white in his jet-black hair and graying sideburns, the forty-four-year-old Wadhwa looked a decade younger. He was trim, wore wire-rimmed glasses, and had a deceptively benign, contemplative face. Born in New Delhi, Wadhwa came to the United States when he was nineteen years old. A tax lawyer by training, he is a Punjabi Indian who was raised to revere pioneers like Gupta who had shown a younger generation the pathway from India's backstreets to America's corridors of power. The stops along Gupta's journey—the Modern School in Delhi, the hypercompetitive Indian Institutes of Technology, Harvard Business School—were well known in the Indian-American community. Wadhwa's story was a less familiar but equally emblematic one.

Wadhwa's father, Arjun, was born in January 1937 into a working-class family in Lahore, then a city in northwest India that owed its splendor to a succession of invaders. The Mughals gave Lahore beautiful gardens and much of its inspiring architecture. The British, who followed the colorfully turbaned Sikhs as rulers, endowed the city with enduring administration buildings, styled after the Victorians' architecture.

Sanjay's mother, Rashmi, was born just a year and a half later in Sargodha, a city one hundred miles northwest of Lahore on the way to Afghanistan.

Before India's declaration of independence, both Lahore and Sargodha were part of Punjab Province, a collection of 17,932 towns and villages with 15 million Hindus, 16 million Muslims, and 5 million Sikhs. Despite the hodgepodge of religions and a history of bad blood between them, the Hindus, Muslims, and Sikhs managed to live in relative peace under the British. The time-tested philosophy "The enemy of my enemy is my friend" held fast.

At first, Arjun Wadhwa's family, like other Hindus, mingled freely with Muslims. The children attended school together and parents socialized. Lahore was held up as a model of tolerance, a place where Hindus, Sikhs, and Muslims lived for centuries with little rancor.

Political expediency changed that.

India's independence from Britain in 1947 required Partition, as the division of India was known. To quell Muslim unrest and accelerate the departure of British forces in India, the Indian Independence Act of 1947 split two of the country's most distinctive provinces, Punjab and Bengal. Parts of both formed the Islamic Republic of Pakistan. West Bengal was part of India, but East Bengal became Pakistan. Similarly, part of Punjab went to Pakistan and half stayed with India.

For Wadhwa's family, as for many Punjabis, Partition meant starting over. In June, Arjun, his two sisters, his two brothers, and their mother boarded a train to Haridwar, a holy city for Hindus that was expected to remain in India after Partition. His father stayed behind.

As they were leaving Lahore, ten-year-old Arjun Wadhwa was struck by the desperation. Whenever the train made stops, "people would try and get into the compartment—they would try and sit in the vestibules," recalls Wadhwa. "Even if they didn't have a ticket they would get on the train—they wanted to save themselves." Around the same time, on a separate train, Arjun's future wife and Sanjay Wadhwa's mother, eight-year-old Rashmi, left Sargodha, where her family owned vast swaths of land and her father, a government contractor, was well connected, even friendly with the Muslim police commissioner. He was so tied to Sargodha he would stay in his ancestral home until August 14, making the trek to Delhi like thousands of other displaced Punjabis only after it was clear that Sargodha would go to Pakistan.

Partition triggered a mass migration of people, with about 7.2 million Hindus and Sikhs moving to India from the newly created Pakistan and an equal number of Muslims making the reverse migration. One million lives were lost along the way, many victims of brutal sectarian violence.

Stemming bloodshed as a result of Partition was just one of the goals on the new republic's political agenda. Independent India's first leader, Jawaharlal Nehru, invited the country's masses to fulfill their "tryst with destiny" and "awake to life and freedom." In his maiden speech to the young republic, he vowed to end "poverty and ignorance and disease and inequality of opportunity." But by the time Arjun and Rashmi Wadhwa welcomed young Sanjay into the world in October 1966, none of Nehru's promises had come to pass. The country stagnated in an economic swamp that deepened in the 1970s under Nehru's daughter and India's leader, Indira Gandhi.

For ordinary Indians, life was a hard slog. Food was scarce. Essentials such as sugar and rice were rationed and queues were common. Even though wheat was abundant in states like Punjab, the roads were so poor it could not be delivered quickly to India's starving masses. Installing a private phone took months or even years. It helped to secure a letter from a member of Parliament to get a second line or a gas cylinder.

Alarmed by rampant corruption and worried about soaring unemployment, Arjun Wadhwa fretted about the future—not so much for himself but for his teenage son, Sanjay, and his two daughters. Inspired by the success stories of men like Rajat Gupta—the Calcutta boy who headed to Cambridge, Massachusetts, in 1971—many, including Arjun's own brother, left home looking for opportunity. If Wadhwa didn't join soon, his family could be sucked into India's vortex of despair. In 1985, he took his brother up on his offer to sponsor him for a green card.

At the age of forty-eight, Arjun Wadhwa left his wife and children in Calcutta to start a new life for them in Lake Worth, Florida—a coastal city on the Atlantic Ocean. Despite his years as a seasoned business manager in India, he began at the bottom. He joined a Florida drugstore chain as a management trainee. After just a year, he sent for his family. Soon he was promoted to assistant store manager.

Arjun's wife and three children left their home with only a few suitcases in hand. Sanjay's mother had just $100 cash—a reminder that despite the depth of their sadness, they were doing what was necessary. In an effort to conserve India's perilously low currency reserves, the government restricted the amount of money each person could take out of the country.

In America, it proved difficult to support a family of five on an assistant manager's salary, so the Wadhwa children worked their way through college. Sanjay focused on accounting and got a bachelor's degree in business administration from a tiny, little-known college (Florida Atlantic University). He picked it because it was the only school with a decent accounting program within driving distance of his parents' home. There was no way he could afford to live on campus. Even with a full course load, he worked fifty hours a week as a stockroom boy and cashier in a local drugstore, earning the tuition he needed for the next semester. After graduating, he received his JD from the South Texas College of Law. Then he headed to Manhattan.

He had always dreamed of working in New York, sensing that his father, who had an MBA, might have had more opportunities in America if he had landed in New York rather than Florida. But he also knew there was little chance of him being hired by a white-shoe firm in New York without a degree from a top-tier law school, so he did what pragmatic Indians did. He went back to law school and graduated among the top of his class with a degree from New York University in tax law. If there ever was a guarantee of steady employment, it was a graduate degree in tax law.

Recruited directly out of NYU by the prestigious firm Cahill Gordon & Reindel, Wadhwa navigated the grueling law associate gauntlet and later moved on to the even tonier Skadden, Arps, Slate, Meagher & Flom. The work proved intellectually challenging but soul crushing. The hours he spent helping investment banks like Merrill Lynch and Goldman Sachs design esoteric financial products to peddle to pension funds for ordinary Americans left him queasy.

Wadhwa knew his mother and father hadn't left their comfortable life in India just so he could collect a big check protecting corporate greed. They raised him to value public service, not material wealth. Wadhwa's uncles went to Oxford and Cambridge and then headed straight back to India to teach at Indian universities. Once he paid off his law school loans, Wadhwa was ready for a change.

Just as Rajat Gupta rode out his nine-year tenure as global managing director of McKinsey, in July 2003 Wadhwa joined the Securities and Exchange Commission in New York as a staff attorney. David Markowitz, a branch chief in New York for the SEC, introduced Wadhwa to his first case by taking him into a war room in the Woolworth Building—the SEC's temporary digs in Lower Manhattan after 9/11. Before the terrorist attacks, the SEC was housed in the World Trade Center. Hundreds of thousands of files were destroyed in the attacks, along with accompanying cases. The windowless room in the Woolworth Building was stacked from floor to ceiling with bankers boxes containing a vast assortment of documents. Markowitz pointed around the room and said, "Someone in these seventy-two boxes is a violation." And then he left.

Wadhwa spent two years digging through the material. But he found the perpetrator and his violation and, in April 2005, brought his first major insider trading case at the SEC. It was a complaint against a former managing director of SG Cowen, the US brokerage arm of French bank Société Générale. Another case soon followed—bigger than the last. It was the discovery of an insider trading ring involving a retired seamstress working at an underwear factory in Croatia who netted $2 million in profits on a two-day investment in Reebok International. Behind the seamstress was a cabal of Wall Streeters who were swapping information in the Winter Garden Atrium of the World Financial Center complex, where Wadhwa often went to grab a cup of coffee. It was galling to Wadhwa that insider trading was so rampant that it was happening on the SEC's doorstep. Little did he know that the perseverance required for the Société Générale and Reebok wins was a dress rehearsal for his next case, an assignment that hit very close to home.

At 10 a.m. sharp on December 22, 2010, as he pored over the case records in his office yet again, Sanjay Wadhwa heard the ping from an email sent by one of his colleagues, Jason E. Friedman. "Just got a call from reception," Friedman wrote. "They're here."

* * *

Testimony Room 419 at the SEC's New York headquarters is a small, narrow space with yellow walls scuffed by the stacks of bankers boxes routinely pressed against them. At the corner of the room stood an American flag, and at one time, a photo of the sitting president had hung at eye level on one of the walls. But when former president George W. Bush was in power, his photo started disappearing from testimony rooms. It was not uncommon for a prominent New York lawyer with liberal leanings to tilt a rare one remaining askew. By the time President Obama took office, there were so few rooms with presidential photos that the practice fell by the wayside.

A guard showed Gupta and Naftalis and his two associates into the testimony room. Despite his rumpled appearance, Naftalis is one of the most celebrated white-collar defense attorneys in New York. The *Wall Street Journal* referred to him as "the Zelig of the white-collar bar: He's everywhere." He has represented everyone from former Walt Disney Company chief Michael D. Eisner to Wall Street hotshot Kenneth Langone. Like many defense lawyers, Naftalis spent six years at the US attorney's office for the Southern District of New York (the district that made Rudy Giuliani's career). He rose to be deputy chief of the Criminal Division before going into private practice. Naftalis had accompanied clients to interviews like this one innumerable times. He knew the script by heart and was a skilled performer inside a conference room, a pro's pro.

A few minutes after Gupta and his legal team settled in the room, Sanjay Wadhwa, Jason Friedman, and another SEC attorney, John Henderson, entered. Wadhwa was a little taken aback to find Gupta and his lawyers already seated. Typically, the SEC attorneys arrived before the witnesses to control the order of seating. Witnesses being deposed are usually ushered to seats facing the window so they can relax and be more loquacious. Having a guard escort the group in earlier, the wily Naftalis instructed his client to sit next to him with their backs to the window.

Naftalis greeted Henderson warmly, asking the young SEC lawyer about his holiday plans and his two-and-a-half-year-old son. Before joining the SEC, Henderson, a Yankees fan, had worked at Naftalis's law firm, Kramer Levin Naftalis & Frankel. He'd sat three hundred yards from Naftalis, a big Mets fan. After the usual introductory pleasantries—Gupta gave Wadhwa a half smile when they shook hands—the witness was sworn in. Wadhwa found Gupta controlled and inscrutable. If he was irritated by the SEC's invitation to testify, he didn't let on. As Henderson launched into the SEC interrogation, Wadhwa kept an eye on Gupta to see if he was showing signs of nervous body language or looking shifty. He didn't betray a thing.

"Mr. Gupta, are you taking any medication or drugs that would affect your ability to recall events or answer truthfully?"

"No," Gupta replied.

Then Henderson drilled into the heart of the case. He first asked whether Gupta reviewed any documents in preparation for his testimony.

"Upon advice of the counsel, I respectfully decline to answer the question at this time based on my right under the United States Constitution not to be compelled to be a witness against myself," Gupta replied.

"There are different ways to formulate that," Henderson said. He spoke formally yet awkwardly, clearly surprised by Gupta's response. He told Gupta that if he wanted to assert his privilege against self-incrimination, "you need merely state that you refuse to answer on the grounds that it may incriminate you. In other words, you are not compelled to answer questions if you believe that a truthful answer to the question would tend to show that you committed a crime, and you wish to assert your privilege against self-incrimination."

Henderson asked Gupta if he understood what he was telling him. Gupta fell back on the elaborate response he'd offered moments earlier, one that the savvy Naftalis had coached him to give.

Naftalis then asked to go off the record.

A few minutes later, Henderson summarized the point of discussion for the stenographer on the record: "For the sake of efficiency...we can agree that if you say 'I take the Fifth,' or 'Five,' it will mean 'Based on my Fifth Amendment privilege against self-incrimination I decline to answer the question." Henderson looked to Naftalis. "Gary, is that an acceptable formulation for you?"

"I don't like that formulation." Naftalis understood how damning "I take the Fifth" would be for Gupta in the public record. Headlines like "Gupta Takes the Fifth" could destroy him. Wadhwa suspected it was the reason Naftalis and his client Gupta had been pushing to delay the SEC testimony until after the Rajaratnam trial. Naftalis said his preference was for Gupta to "say 'same answer' or something like that."

Jason Friedman jumped in. He wanted to make clear that "same answer" referred to the response Naftalis so clearly did not want his client to articulate. "Can we agree that the representation, that the formulation he read before into the record is an invocation of his Fifth Amendment privilege against self-incrimination?"

"Yes," replied Naftalis.

So over the next fifteen minutes, Henderson asked Gupta fifty-three questions. His response to all fifty-three questions was a weary "same answer."

As Wadhwa watched Gupta during the absurd exercise, he saw his facial expression change from that of the implacable stoic to a more human one. He seemed far away, lost in a great sadness. It was as if Gupta was internally reviewing his life story and thinking, *I can't believe I am sitting here.*

* * *

As Rajat Gupta grew up, there was a sense among friends that he would be as remarkable as his *baba*. "He got the brilliance of his father," says Udayan Bhattarcharyya, who lived in the same compound in New Delhi as the Guptas.

When "he decided on something, it had to happen," says his cousin, Damayanti Gupta-Wicklander. One time when the family was setting off on an outing in New Delhi, young Rajat decided to climb onto the car hood and lie flat on his stomach. Repeated efforts at coaxing and cajoling failed to bring him down, so the family finally resorted to the one inducement that always seemed to work: sweets. They—along with bananas—were a great weakness of his and he quickly succumbed.

When Rajat was five years old, his father, Ashwini, was given a tall task, moving to the nation's capital and founding the Delhi edition of Bengal's English-language paper, the *Hindusthan Standard*. It was a difficult assignment because at that time people tended to read local newspapers.

Despite the challenge, the Guptas' early years in Delhi were among the family's happiest. They enjoyed a comfortable, middle-class Indian life, living in a twelve-hundred-square-foot company flat housed in a big enclosed compound not far from the old Delhi Railway Station. It was a protected world, a self-contained city with its own soccer field. On weekend nights, Ashwini Gupta and friends walked to Connaught Place, a business district in the center of Delhi, to catch one of the English-language movies coming out of Hollywood. Sometimes the men would play bridge while the boys kept busy with chess, a game Rajat quickly mastered.

At the time the Guptas moved to New Delhi, there were two elite schools in the city. One was St. Columba's, a Catholic boys' school, and the other was the Modern School on Barakhamba Road, not far from Connaught Place. Founded at the height of the British Raj, the Modern School married Indian ways of education with modern pedagogy. It was "'the' school in those days," recalls Mukul Mudgal, the retired chief justice of the High Court of Punjab and Haryana.

Students from the 1950s and 1960s tell long tales of how they got a place at Modern. Some used money or influence; others who had neither resorted to determination. It is not known if Ashwini Gupta used his connections to get young Rajat enrolled at Modern. It didn't matter. Rajat quickly showed that he deserved as much as anyone else to be at the school. He was a living embodiment of the school's motto, a Sanskrit saying that translates into English as "Self-realization cannot be achieved by the weak-willed."

Like his father, Rajat worked hard, often putting in long hours to overcome deficiencies in subjects such as written English. Once when a classmate scored a perfect mark on a pop quiz in physics on the topic of momentum, the young Rajat insisted on sitting next to the classmate to examine the work he did. He later borrowed the classmate's paper to review the work further. That was the first and last time the classmate got the top marks in Rajat's class.

Modern's virtue was that it brought together students from all walks of life. A classmate of Rajat's was a maharaja from a princely state who lived near the school but sometimes showed up in a fancy chauffeur-driven car. Young Rajat, by contrast, traveled to school on the creaky, often overcrowded buses of Delhi Transport, the public bus system, with a pack of close friends, carrying khaki knapsacks.

Within the walls of Modern, the differences between the high and mighty and the hoi polloi were imperceptible. Boys all came dressed in a uniform of blue shirts and gray-blue shorts. Almost every interest was nourished—riding horses, playing soccer, and bowling on a cricket pitch with a grass wicket, the type favored by professionals. Rajat soaked it up, acting in plays, reciting poetry, and studying Sanskrit. Often, during the lunch break, he and his friends would take to whacking a tennis ball along the walls of the assembly hall, playing a game akin to handball.

By the time Rajat was a teenager, he was a force. His nickname was Gaju Gupta—a moniker that fit him well. It rhymed with Raju and was a play on the Hindi word for "carrot." With his hair close-cropped at the base and rising straight up, he looked like a flattened carrot top. Well liked, he was a standout student and succeeded in securing a place for himself in Section D—a group of high achievers focused on the sciences, a sure path to future success in India. "People were in awe of him because of his intensity," says a classmate. One year, he prepared so hard for a public speaking contest that involved the recitation in English of a passage from an Indian religious tract that he won the first prize in the competition. What was impressive was that he unseated a classmate who was widely regarded as a shoo-in because he'd spent his early years in England.

* * *

After his father died in 1964, friends noticed a new seriousness sweeping over young Rajat, who applied himself more vigorously than ever to his studies.

Few knew it, but Rajat had no choice but to be strong and focused. His mother was frail; she had been diagnosed with incurable heart disease. It fell to him as the eldest son to hold the family together and to be a father figure to his younger brother, Kanchan, who was only seven years old when his *baba* passed away, and his younger sister, Jayashree.

Every morning, Rajat woke up at the crack of dawn to help his younger brother pack his schoolbag and get dressed, even seeing to it that his tie was properly tied. At night, he supervised homework. One time when Jayashree came back crying from school after having to shoulder her heavy schoolbag on the public transport system, Rajat patiently wiped away her tears and consoled her, assuring her that the difficult times would soon pass.

It wasn't clear they would, though. One of Rajat's responsibilities as the eldest son was to manage the family's finances. Faced with mounting expenses, he, like his father, started tutoring young children to earn extra money.

Debasish Bhattacharya, who grew up with Gupta in Delhi, says that Rajat may have coped admirably with his father's death because he had no choice. "He did not come from a big family that showered him with money," says Bhattacharya. After their father died, the Guptas realized "they had to make something of themselves."

Rajat quickly showed he had every intention of doing exactly that. In his final year at Modern, he placed fifteenth in the national entrance examination for the Indian Institutes of Technology, then a little-known collection of state-sponsored universities that in twenty years would be harder to get into than Harvard or Yale.

CHAPTER THREE

A Family Affair

Rajat Gupta's and Sanjay Wadhwa's paths might never have crossed if not for the brief that landed on the SEC attorney's desk on August 22, 2006.

On that late summer afternoon four years before Gupta would plead the Fifth, John Moon, an in-house lawyer working in New York for Swiss bank UBS, paid a visit to Wadhwa and his boss, David Markowitz, at their office at Three World Financial Center. He had come to inform the SEC about a tiny hedge fund called Sedna Capital.

Moon's firm, UBS, is a significant player in a highly profitable business on Wall Street known as prime brokerage. Banks provide back-office support, IT, office space, and custody services to independent hedge funds and earn money by lending cash and stock to the funds. For most of its history, prime brokerage was an unsexy business and not much of a moneymaker for investment banks. At some white-shoe firms like Morgan Stanley, prime brokerage departments were relegated to Brooklyn, where the back-office services were. But in the late 1990s, as hedge funds exploded onto the investment landscape and multiplied like weeds, Wall Street rediscovered prime brokerage and dressed it up. In a sign of the times, Morgan Stanley moved its department that serviced hedge funds to Manhattan.

After its acquisition of ABN AMRO's prime brokerage unit in 2003, UBS inherited a thriving business catering to small hedge funds. These funds were lower-tier grinders, ignored by behemoths like Goldman Sachs. UBS's John Moon had come to see Wadhwa and Markowitz about one grinder UBS serviced, an off-the-radar hedge fund called Sedna Capital. A heady thirty-five-year-old money manager named Rajarengan Rajaratnam ran it.

After graduating from the University of Pennsylvania in 1992, Rengan, as he was known to friends, bounced around Wall Street, working at investment bank Morgan Stanley and at hedge fund SAC Capital Advisors. Rengan lasted at SAC, named after its enigmatic founder, Steven A. Cohen, for only eight months. One day, Cohen asked Rengan why SAC was not involved in telecommunications equipment stocks, which were rallying at the time. Rengan, who covered the sector, said he'd traded the stocks a few months before. "How come we are not involved now?" Cohen asked. Before long, the discussion devolved into a screaming match, with Rengan yelling about his pay and Cohen about Rengan's performance. When it was all over, Cohen told Rengan, "If you don't like it, leave."

The word on Wall Street was that Cohen then preemptively called Rengan's influential brother, billionaire and hedge fund impressario Raj Rajaratnam, to break the news. "Someone came up to me on the floor and he was complaining about something, so I fired him," Cohen said. "The bad news is that it was your brother."

In May 2004, Rengan Rajaratnam and a trader whom he shared an office with at SAC started Sedna Capital, plowing in "every single dime we've ever earned" and raising some money from a couple of investors who like Rengan had gone to Penn. The two created a stable of funds that were supposed to be run on an equal footing, with trades distributed proportionately to all funds, and by mid-2006, Sedna's assets under management had swelled to $80 million. During a family vacation that summer to Gila, New Mexico, Rengan, while chatting with his big brother Raj, floated the idea of creating a high-risk fund that would deliver big returns. Raj was encouraging, and in July 2006, Rengan opened a new fund, the Sedna Strategic Opportunities fund, an investment pool for friends and family. When he hit up the small circle for money, he didn't sugarcoat the risks: "Listen, give me as much money as you are willing to lose."

The new entity was seeded with $700,000 of Rengan's savings. Investing in it was a family affair. Rengan's sister, Vathani, threw in $50,000 and his middle brother, R.K.—the nickname of their brother Ragakanthan—forked over $25,000. Rengan's father declined to invest because he thought the fund was too risky. But Rengan's older brother Raj put in $1 million, making him the single largest outside investor.

The new fund raised eyebrows at UBS almost as soon as it began. Its performance seemed too good to be true. Between late July 2006, when the fund started trading, and late August 2006, it doubled its money. Two million dollars ballooned to almost $4 million in a month—a stunning 100 percent return in the span of thirty days, all because of Rengan's investing "prowess." Behind the big gains were ten trades—every one of which was a winner. There was another irregularity: after a blockbuster first month, Rengan forced investors to redeem some of their money. Typically, investors like to keep their money in a fund that is beating the street, but in late August Raj Rajaratnam got back half his cash after his brother distributed the funds to investors.

UBS first noticed the fund's heady success after it executed a trade on July 26 in the stock of Arris Group, selling "short" $1.4 million worth of shares, the maximum allowable position in the friends and family fund. Short selling, a sign an investor is bearish about a stock, is a method of trading in which an individual sells borrowed shares at one price on the hope of buying back the stock later at a lower price and repaying the loan with the cheaper shares. A profit is made when the borrowed stock is replaced with less expensive shares. For instance, selling one borrowed share today for $20 and replacing it later when the stock is then trading at $19 allows the trader to pocket a $1 profit.

After saying he wanted to be "long into numbers"—Wall Street–speak for taking an optimistic view about a stock ahead of a company's earnings—Rengan Rajaratnam switched course and bet heavily against Arris Group in the friends and family fund and the main investment pool. It was a prescient move. On July 27, the company's stock fell 20 percent after Arris, a communication equipment maker, reported second-quarter earnings that fell short of expectations. "The timing [of Sedna's trade] was impeccable," Moon remarked.

Sedna overall made more than $1.1 million on the Arris trade alone, and Rengan, the only investor in the friends and family fund at the time, personally netted $270,000 overnight. It was such a home run that even his older brother Raj noticed and gave him a backhanded compliment.

"U r my heroine...u da man...keep the streak alive," Raj messaged Rengan on July 27, 2006, at 9:21 a.m.

Raj did not have to say so. They both knew that in the Rajaratnam family he was always the hero and Rengan always the heroine. This made for a fractious relationship. At one point, Rengan worked for Raj, but word was his big brother threw him out of his company, the Galleon Group, after a falling-out. They never stayed mad at each other for long, though. Raj was always protective of his kid brother, much to the astonishment of associates, who considered Rengan arrogant. He had a way of making everyone around him feel small. One time Rengan asked an analyst at Galleon what he should do for his girlfriend for Valentine's Day.

Why not cook her dinner, the analyst suggested, adding that women often liked it when men showed their feminine side.

"I have a South Asian woman to cook dinner," he snapped back.

Rengan and Raj spoke several times a day, exchanging investment ideas over the phone. On weekends, Rengan often headed to Greenwich. He enjoyed hanging out with Raj and his family at their spacious McMansion in what's known as Back Country, Greenwich, an area that once housed sprawling horse farms and big estates. Set well away from the main road, behind a stone wall that stretches around the perimeter of the property, the Rajaratnam estate, with a long driveway leading up to the main house, was secluded just like a fly-below-the-radar hedge fund manager would want.

Unlike his brother, Rengan was a bachelor who freely confessed to having a hard time meeting the right woman. "It definitely feels like there are less quality women out there," he told FoxNews.com in 2001 for a feature the website was doing on the lack of young single women. Thirty-one years old at the time, Rengan said he was stressed about it. "It's like they've all gone away or someone snatched them all." Raj, the more successful of the pair, often helped out his kid brother, making introductions on his behalf for business and pleasure.

For a change, on the Arris trade it looked like Rengan was giving his older brother Raj a hand. On July 26, hours before Arris reported its poor earnings, two Galleon funds managed by Todd Deutsch, a socially awkward Galleon portfolio manager who reminded colleagues of the movie character Rain Man because of his astonishing ability to name the exact stock price of a thousand different stocks, sold more than $1 million of Arris stock. In an email sent at 11:17 a.m. the next morning, Deutsch, the manager of the Galleon Captain's Partners fund and the Captain's Offshore fund, said to Rajaratnam, "Arris [thank you] for getting us out." (Deutsch has not been charged with any wrongdoing.)

Unusual as the Arris trades were, for Wadhwa, the case offered little promise. Moon, the UBS lawyer, suggested that Sedna was engaging in a pattern of cherry picking, where a manager who runs several funds allocates the best investments to a preferred fund, in this case keeping the winners for an investment pool where all the investors are friends and family members. Cherry picking works like this: shares in a trade are allocated to different funds *after* a fund manager determines if a trade is profitable or not. Ordinarily, shares are supposed to be allocated to funds at the time of purchase, when it is unclear if a trade is a winner or a loser. Cherry picking is a violation of US securities laws, but it is hardly a sexy, headline-grabbing crime like insider trading. Few regulators, if any, have made their name on cherry-picking cases. And the hedge fund involved, Sedna, was minuscule. Was pursuing a case against Sedna the best use of the SEC's scarce resources?

The meeting concluded and Wadhwa went back to his office to investigate.

A quick search on Google revealed that Sedna was a speck on the hedge fund landscape, which by 2006 was a sprawling investment metropolis of more than sixty-five hundred hedge funds, mostly based in Greenwich and London, managing $1.1 trillion in assets. The only thing that distinguished Sedna from the hedge fund pack was that its founder, Rengan, was the younger brother of Raj Rajaratnam, the manager of the Galleon Group, a successful New York hedge fund managing some $5 billion in assets. As Wadhwa delved deeper, he found a trove of laudatory articles on Raj Rajaratnam that gushed about his stunning market-beating investment performance.

Jaded by his experience with other cases, Wadhwa took a more jaundiced view of Galleon's steady returns and the positive press surrounding Raj Rajaratnam. He wondered: was Rajaratnam truly a hedge fund savant as the articles portrayed, or was he simply a mere mortal with impressive connections?

CHAPTER FOUR

Drama at IIT

When Rajat Gupta arrived at IIT in 1966, he stood apart. Most of the boys in his class—and they were largely boys—were living away from home for the first time and found the small liberties of dormitory life intoxicating. Not Gupta, who at seventeen was mature beyond his age.

"Our adolescent hormones and new-found freedom formed a dangerous mixture and we were all 17 going on 14," says Harbinder Gill, who lived in the same dorm as Gupta. "We spent every waking moment on some insane prank or the other, which would today be considered sexist or even harassment. Except Rajat, who seemed to be 17 going on 30." While classmates would spend their free moments "gallivanting on the Delhi University's richly co-ed campus [a neighboring school to IIT], Rajat was busy volunteering his services around IIT," remembers Gill.

Unlike his classmates, Rajat could not afford the luxury of adolescence. Not long after he arrived at IIT, his mother died of a heart attack. Gupta and his elder sister were already in university, but his younger brother, Kanchan, and sister needed supervision. Rather than farming them out to various relatives, as was common at the time, Gupta arranged for an unmarried aunt to come and stay. And he took on the role of parent. Whenever he could, he would drop in on his younger brother's parent-teacher meetings at school so that Kanchan would not feel left out when the parents of other kids showed up. And every weekend, Gupta would leave his dormitory at IIT, which was then on the outskirts of Delhi city and was surrounded by thick forests teeming with wildlife. It was so out of the way that three-wheeled scooter taxis in the more crowded parts of Delhi were loath to ferry faculty and students to the campus. A trip home required changing buses a few times, not to mention missing out on campus socials. But Rajat knew that Kanchan eagerly awaited his visits, and he made a point of never disappointing. Whenever he returned home, he brought a small gift, such as a tin of jam, a rare luxury in 1960s India.

When the IITs, or the Indian Institutes of Technology, welcomed their first students in the early 1950s, many believed the grand experiment destined to fail. The country was struggling to feed its population, so how could it possibly build a network of MIT-like universities from scratch? But that is exactly what it did, in large part because of the vision of Jawaharlal Nehru. Even before independent India came into being, its first prime minister foresaw the need for technocrats who could design dams and build power plants and help shore up India's industrial base.

IIT Delhi, where Gupta was studying, was one of the last of the original IITs to be set up with the help of the British. Shashi K. Gulhati, who interacted with Gupta as the faculty advisor on extracurricular activities at IIT Delhi and is the author of *The IITs: Slumping or Soaring*, says, "Getting admission in the IITs was not always a dream come true." From time to time, he would get telephone calls from uncles who said, "Our son has been admitted to IIT Delhi. Should we send him there?" At the time in Delhi, IIT was far eclipsed by the more famous establishment school, St. Stephen's College.

Seeking to staff the schools with world-class faculty, Indian recruiters wooed native students like Gulhati, who heard of the IITs for the first time at a lecture at MIT. When he returned to accept a position at IIT Delhi, he found it underwhelming compared to MIT's state-of-the-art facilities. The campus "looked very bare," says Gulhati about his first visit in 1963. Unlike at MIT, "there was no imposing multistory block, library building, no auditorium with an eye-catching roof."

Today Gulhati gets calls ranging from outright appeals for help in getting a child into IIT Delhi to advice on the best crammer courses to prepare a child for the make-or-break entrance examination. The school's attraction is its long list of successful graduates, who credit their achievements to their time at India's engineering boot camp. "When I finished IIT Delhi and went to Carnegie Mellon for my masters, I thought I was cruising all the way through Carnegie Mellon because it was so easy relative to the education I got at IIT Delhi," said Vinod Khosla, the prominent venture capitalist and cofounder of Sun Microsystems.

Aside from Khosla and his fellow tech titans, many IIT alumni have worked their way to the tops of giant firms in mainstream corporate America. Victor Menezes, a former senior vice chairman of Citigroup, is a graduate of IIT Bombay; Rakesh Gangwal, the former chief executive of US Airways, went to IIT Kanpur; and Rono Dutta, the former president of United Airlines, graduated from IIT Kharagpur. They all may come from different IITs, but they generally have a one-word description of their time at school: brutal.

It is the IITs' focus on meritocracy that has made it a beacon of excellence in an India bedeviled by cronyism and back-scratching. Admission requires academic excellence, period. Narayana Murthy, founder of software giant Infosys, or India's Bill Gates, told *60 Minutes* that his son could not get into IIT to study computer science, so he had to go to his safety school, Cornell University, instead. Indira Gandhi, Nehru's daughter and later prime minister of India, also discovered that wealth and family connections would not ensure admission. Gandhi was very keen for her son, Rajiv, to attend IIT Delhi. "So Pandit Nehru invited us to tea," recalls Kanta Dogra, the wife of R. N. Dogra, the first director of IIT Delhi.

"Nehru was too uncomfortable to ask my husband for admission for his grandson, so he left the room," Kanta Dogra says. When Indira Gandhi broached the subject, "my husband told her simply, 'From his school records, he will not be able to get a place because it is very competitive. But I will get him a place in the Imperial College of London,' which he did." (Rajiv Gandhi attended both Cambridge University and Imperial College, but he did not receive a degree from either.)

Gupta was one of sixty-two students at IIT Delhi in the "Mech 71-ers"—the mechanical engineering class of 1971. From the beginning, he stood out less for his engineering abilities and more for his leadership skills. His earliest-known management role came when he was elected general secretary for the Recreational and Creative Activities Committee, a group that managed the extracurricular activities at IIT Delhi. As a young student leader, he made a name for himself during a tense time in IIT's early history.

In 1970, about one hundred students, spurred on by a couple of ringleaders, marched on the house of the IIT Delhi director, R. N. Dogra. The students were unhappy with what they believed was Dogra's oppressive way of running the institute and wanted to create a student union. Among other things, Dogra required 85 percent class attendance. If a student was just one class short, the student was expelled.

The protests got so impassioned that three students camped in the vestibule outside Dogra's office and went on a hunger strike. One of them was ultimately expelled, while others were kicked out of the institute for a year. During the tense days of the disturbances, Gupta worked with Dogra and the administration to restore order. "When Rajat got involved, he took the establishment standpoint," says Anjan Chatterjee, a classmate of Gupta's. At one point, at the peak of the foment, Gupta confronted Chatterjee, who was among the group of demonstrators. "We are not afraid," Gupta told him. "If you burn down the buildings, we will call in the fire engines and rebuild." Unlike his father, Rajat would not live a life falling on his sword for radical principles. His sympathy lay with the establishment.

Gupta had another passion beyond academic excellence. He was an actor. In another life, without his heavy responsibilities, he would have considered taking up acting as a profession. Like everything else at IIT, drama was serious business. Rehearsals began after dinner and often lasted until 4:30 in the morning. Costumes were elaborate, and the performances, which were staged in IIT's Seminar Hall, on the ground floor of IIT's main building, drew packed houses. As many as five hundred people would attend. VIP guests included IIT's director, Dogra, and his wife. The only room for many students in the audience was standing on the stairs.

It was the fashion at the time to adapt English and French plays and to then perform them in Hindi. Gupta was a convincing actor, versatile at playing a part, and prodigious; during his five years at IIT, he acted in seventeen plays, Hindi and English, modern and classical. But by far, his most remembered performance was his role in Jean-Paul Sartre's searing existential drama *Men Without Shadows*.

Men Without Shadows concerns five French resistance fighters during World War II who fail to liberate a village, resulting in the slaughter of many innocents. They've been arrested and are awaiting interrogation, locked in a communal cell. Throughout the play, the five characters contemplate how they will confront the inevitable torture coming their way. Will they cooperate and give up the location of their leader? Will they beg for their lives? Will they resist?

Gupta did not have to plumb the depths of his imagination to understand the dilemma. At one juncture in the adaptation of the play at IIT Delhi, the lone female character asks Gupta's character, "Do you have parents?"

"*Nahi*," Gupta replied, shaking his head sorrowfully and answering with the Hindi word for "no."

It was heartbreaking to watch. On the close-knit IIT campus, many in the audience knew of his mother's death after he arrived at IIT.

"You must have felt terrible knowing that she was going to die," Chatterjee remembers saying to Gupta.

"Think of how she felt knowing she was going to die and leave us alone," Gupta responded to Chatterjee. He further confessed to his schoolmate that there were "nights I can't stop the tears. It is not easy living without parents."

Few of Rajat's classmates had any sense of his personal travails. But in 1968, a quiet young woman from Srinagar, the beautiful summer capital of the northernmost Indian state of Jammu and Kashmir, arrived at IIT to study electrical engineering. Anita Mattoo was born into a prominent Kashmiri family of Brahmins, India's highest caste group, the priestly caste. The summer before Anita arrived at IIT, Anita's mother died in childbirth, leaving her father to care for four children, one a newborn.

Like Rajat, Anita felt the weight of family responsibility. Though she was a girl and not burdened with the same duties as a son in an Indian family, she was the eldest child, separated by many years from her younger siblings. She came from a close-knit family and grew up in a shared living arrangement, known as the "joint family system," that was common in India at the time and exists even today. Anita lived under the same roof as her uncles, aunts, and cousins. Family was as important to her as it was to Rajat.

The two met while performing in a one-act English play whose name Anita no longer remembers. The friendship between the two turned into something more when they appeared onstage in *Kanjoos*, a Hindi adaptation of the Molière play *The Miser*. Rajat and Anita, in full view of others, would share laughs together on the set. Gupta nicknamed Mattoo "Grandma" because she played an older woman in the play. Many young girls would have been turned off by the moniker, but Mattoo was unperturbed. She knew the handsome Gupta was a catch. He was one of the most eligible men on campus.

"I was the only girl in a graduating class of 250, shy, scared and still reeling from the sudden death of my mother," she recalled years later. "Rajat was a big man on campus, bright, talented, popular, head of the student government and very involved in all extracurricular activities...But I have never forgotten his kindness to the very shy, quiet, small-town girl who felt so out of place."

Friends in Mattoo's dormitory first sensed the depth of their feelings when they ventured downstairs into the common area of the women's hostel, Kailash, which was fittingly situated near the faculty residences. Often, they would find Gupta, who lived on the other side of campus, visiting with her. Men were not allowed in the women's rooms, so their friendship flowered into love in the visitors' area of Anita's dorm.

In 1971, when Gupta was set to graduate from IIT Delhi, he was at a crossroads. India's private sector was rudimentary. For the most part, it consisted of companies consigned to making inferior copies of Western goods—televisions, cars, drinks—and hawking them at discounted prices. Entrepreneurship was not considered an appropriate occupation for an Indian. A thriving bureaucracy of red tape, a veritable small business unto itself, strangled any economic ambition.

Moreover, India's hostile policies toward foreign investment succeeded in keeping non-Indian businesses at bay. In 1970, in a bid to "Indianize" foreign investment, the government moved to pass an act requiring corporations to dilute their shareholdings in Indian companies to 40 percent. Scores of Western companies quit India in the wake of the law. The best-known defector was the US soft-drink giant Coca-Cola, which, rather than comply with the law, up and left. For years after Coke's departure, bottles of Coke were smuggled into India clandestinely from Nepal and sold on the black market at stratospheric prices. Serving Coke rather than the local soft drink Thums Up came to be seen as a sign of affluence. To many, it was also an indictment of India after independence.

Inevitably, bright and hungry students like Gupta cast their eyes abroad. "All Rajat would talk to me about was getting to America and getting admission" to a US business school, says Subramanian Swamy, a well-known Indian politician who taught Gupta economics at IIT Delhi. At Gupta's behest, Swamy, who received his PhD from Harvard University and taught there before joining IIT Delhi, wrote Gupta a recommendation for Harvard Business School. Anita kept Gupta company at the campus coffee shop as he wrote his essays for his HBS application.

In his final year, Gupta was one of two students at IIT Delhi to get a job offer from ITC Ltd., the equivalent of Philip Morris in the United States, a prestigious company with pedigree beginnings in India dating to the time of the British Raj. When ITC started in 1910, it began operating under the name Imperial Tobacco Company of India Ltd. But as India changed overlords, ITC changed owners. After independence, the company's ownership increasingly fell into the hands of Indians and its name changed to reflect its new complexion—first it was christened India Tobacco Company and ultimately ITC.

Every year, ITC hired a number of students with postgraduate management degrees as trainees. It also took a few bright undergraduates straight into its management program. But the company is not without its prejudices. It has its own good old boy network. When students interview at ITC, as a running joke goes, they are asked not what school they attended but what house they were in. The company is filled with "Doscos"—men who went to India's preeminent boys' school, the Doon School.

Since its founding in 1935 by a moderate group of Indian nationalists led by an eminent Calcutta barrister intent on establishing an Indian version of England's venerable Eton College, the Doon School had been the preserve of India's privileged. The grandsons of independent India's first prime minister, Nehru; the late Sanjay Gandhi, who perished in a plane crash in 1980; and his brother, Rajiv, who was prime minister of India from 1984 until he was assassinated in 1991, attended Doon. Over the years, the school has milled bestselling authors including Vikram Seth and Amitav Ghosh, noted television interviewers such as Karan Thapar (the Mike Wallace of India), and titans of business such as Bhaskar Menon, one of the first Indians to rise to the top of a Western company, Britain's recording giant EMI Music Worldwide. Even ITC, the company that offered Gupta a position, was headed by a Dosco, Ajit Haksar.

In the India of the 1970s, a job at ITC was a ticket to the upper echelon of society. The tobacco company by then had branched out into packaging and was on the cusp of scaling other industries. In his ITC interview, Gupta impressed the panel of executives with his maturity and foresight. Though only twenty-two years old, he described a leader as "one who can motivate his colleagues and get things done without making his teammates feel that it was the leader who actually got the work done." He was not a Dosco, but he was perfect for ITC.

When Gupta declined the company's job offer, Haksar, ITC's then chairman, was stunned. He himself had gotten his start at the company as a trainee and was something of a rarity: he was one of the few men at the helm of an Indian conglomerate who could boast having an MBA. He'd earned it way back in 1948, the year Gupta was born.

Shocked by Gupta's chutzpah, Haksar asked the young man to explain himself—in person. He sent Gupta a plane ticket to Calcutta, where ITC's headquarters were located. Gupta jumped at the opportunity. "It was the first time I had been on an airplane," he would say years later. Besides, as he liked to joke, he had some good friends and relatives that he could visit in Calcutta. When Gupta met Haksar, he told him the dilemma he faced: "Either I can join you or I can go to Harvard Business School."

Haksar, an HBS man himself, didn't hesitate.

"Go to Harvard. It is the chance of a lifetime."

CHAPTER FIVE

Birdie Trades

"Let's get some boots on the ground," David Markowitz, the assistant regional director of the SEC's New York office, told his branch chief, Sanjay Wadhwa. As soon as UBS's John Moon left their offices, Markowitz and Wadhwa decided to dispatch an SEC examination team into Sedna. They knew that banks like UBS routinely reported misdemeanors like cherry picking at Sedna because they were required to and it helped them earn a goodwill chit from the SEC—nothing more. Still, why not take a peek at Sedna? An examination—a common check of a registered hedge fund to make sure it is complying with securities laws—would be the perfect cover to poke around Sedna. By sending in the exam staff, the SEC wouldn't ring any major alarm bells either.

Often, when a hedge fund learns that the SEC's enforcement staff is formally investigating it, instant messages and emails mysteriously go missing. Wadhwa and Markowitz didn't want to run that risk. Examiners didn't freak people out like enforcers did. Within two days of Moon's visit, an exam team decamped to Sedna.

Dispatching examiners also would get the regulatory ball rolling before a formal order of investigation was in place. In 2006, when Christopher Cox, a California congressman, led the SEC, enforcement lawyers often got pushback when they sought formal powers to probe. Cox believed that financial players like investment banks and hedge funds could be trusted to regulate themselves. During his time, the agency missed some stunningly huge fraudsters, such as Bernie Madoff, who ran a Ponzi scheme for nearly two decades. It also overlooked troubling practices such as collateralized debt obligations that led to the financial system's near meltdown in 2008.

For a month, the SEC's exam staff camped in Sedna's offices. They turned up instant messages and emails that seemed to point to something suspicious. What exactly was going on was less clear. On September 21, 2006, Wadhwa received an order of investigation captioned "In the Matter of: Sedna Capital Management LLC," giving the SEC the authority to subpoena documents and take testimony. Digging into the practices of a tiny hedge fund might not yield career-making headlines, but Wadhwa was intrigued and had a hunch it could lead to a bigger case.

One of Sedna's traders, a gregarious young man by the name of Bill Lyons, was a prodigious instant messager who liked to enliven his dull day with some cyberbanter with a cousin. Lyons, a political science graduate from Rutgers University, had bounced around a bit, working at a liquor store and attending a chiropractic college in Atlanta before he decided to start a career as a day trader.

As the exam's staff trolled through Lyons's IMs, they found a series of odd messages that came to be known within the enforcement staff as the "birdie trades" IMs. One in particular stood out. In late July 2006, just after Hewlett-Packard agreed to acquire Mercury Interactive, an Israeli technology company, for $4.5 billion, Lyons instant-messaged his cousin Matt Read, who was a trader at another firm, and told him that Sedna was "long"—or taking a bullish position—on 140,000 shares of Mercury Interactive, making a bundle on the trade. "You guys are on fire," Read messaged back, "shazamm... birdies are flying all over the place... duck."

In another IM exchange, after Lyons cautioned Read that Sedna's IMs were being logged, Read messaged back, "Does the SEC know what a birdie trade is; LOL." Though it sounded cryptic and vague, the frequent banter about "birdie trades" got the attention of the SEC examiners. They suspected a "birdie trade" was code for the fact that someone—a birdie—was tipping off Sedna to valuable inside information like news of Hewlett-Packard's acquisition of Mercury Interactive. In October, Wadhwa took testimony from Lyons. Neither he nor his cousin Read was ever charged with wrongdoing, but not long after Lyons visited the agency, Wadhwa brought in a new colleague to work on the Sedna case.

Andrew Michaelson joined the SEC in New York in October 2006, a month after he and his wife, an urban planner, had their first child. He was thirty-one years old and hoping to focus on corporate fraud. Growing up in Weston, Connecticut, he always knew he wanted to work in government. After graduating from Harvard Law School and clerking for a judge in New Orleans, he joined Boies, Schiller & Flexner, a small but prestigious firm known for big cases such as the landmark *Bush v. Gore*.

At the SEC, Michaelson hit the ground running. He combed through thousands of pages of trading records and emails, and it quickly became clear to him that the Sedna case was not just a case of cherry picking. There were two trades that first caught Michaelson's eye. One was the big and early wager the friends and family account made in Arris. Michaelson was struck by how Rengan was itching to make the trade in the personal fund. On July 25, the day he started accumulating a big short position, Rengan pressed his chief operating officer about whether the money he wired to fund the friends and family investment pool had hit the account.

"Please check to see if the money has reached us," Rengan instant-messaged his COO. "Check once every hour please; as I need to trade." The words "I need to trade" were highlighted in bold.

Unlike his brother Raj, Rengan's net worth was far more modest, about $4 million. To be so persistent and to be happy to wager his $700,000 investment all on one trade and all on one stock, Michaelson reasoned that Rengan had to know it was going to be a winner. The question was how. A possible clue lay in the thick stack of emails that the SEC obtained through a subpoena it issued Sedna on October 3.

Rengan sent several emails on July 17, shopping the résumé of Rajive Dhar, a corporate strategy executive at Arris. In one to the private equity firm Apax, Rengan described Dhar as someone who knows "telecom and cable industries cold." Dhar normally worked for Arris in California, but the week before the company's earnings were to be released, he was at its headquarters in Atlanta. It was un-usual for Dhar to know Arris's earnings before they were announced, but that quarter he was sent the draft earnings release because he was working on a corporate deal for the company. For the SEC, here was the first piece of the puzzle: a possible tie between Rengan and a company insider whose shares he was dabbling in. (Dhar says he spoke to Rengan but not in the context of earnings. He notes he has never been contacted by the SEC and has never divulged informa-tion specific to the company. He has not been charged in connection with the Sedna case.) To build an insider trading case against Ren-gan, the agency still had to show actual communication between him and Dhar about earnings, which proved harder than expected.

The second curious trade that stood out to Michaelson was a big bullish bet that the Sedna friends and family fund made in Advanced Micro Devices (AMD) call options—a bet that a company's stock price would rise. On July 31, 2006, Rengan's big brother Raj Ra-jaratnam wired his $1 million investment into the friends and family fund. Rengan deployed that money and all his capital and winnings from his trade before Arris's earnings into AMD call options. It was the only position in the fund, and it was a bold, gutsy gamble for a hedge fund manager with an ordinary track record.

To Michaelson it seemed like a sure-bet trade, and in this case, it looked like the information was flowing from Raj to his kid brother Rengan. Michaelson was convinced there was no way Raj would give Rengan $1 million to pour into one stock if he was not certain that the investment would be a winner. Rengan also would not risk his brother's money unless he was sure the trade was going to be a slam dunk.

That July 31 evening, at 8:32, Bloomberg News reported that Dell would start selling notebook computers with AMD processor chips as early as October. It didn't go unnoticed at the SEC that Rengan's order to buy AMD options was made just hours before the article hit the newswires. During the evening, the Bloomberg article was fol-lowed by a flurry of others. Shortly after midnight on the morning of August 1, the *Wall Street Journal*, citing Bloomberg, mentioned that IBM was "increasing its use of semiconductors" from AMD.

When the Rajaratnam brothers woke up the next morning, they

were pleased with themselves. Sometimes their trades—no matter how well constructed and planned—had a way of going awry. Whenever that happened, obscenities flew between the two—"fuckers... screwing my picture," Rajaratnam instant-messaged his brother Rengan once when an investment bank issued a research report that conflicted with his take on the company. "Sucks," replied Rengan.

But, on the morning of August 1, 2006, the Rajaratnam brothers took to high-fiving each other electronically.

"see the ibm/amd news; on wsj," Raj instant-messaged Rengan at 8:27 a.m.

"very nice; also did you see the digitimes? On Dell and amd?" Rengan replied.

"On Dell... yes," Raj wrote back.

A little over an hour later, Rengan wanted some advice from his brother on AMD.

"are you going to hold the amd?" Rengan instant-messaged Raj.

"y thru the 13th," replied Raj, using the shorthand "y" for "yes."

"cool, will do the same," said Rengan.

The reference to the thirteenth puzzled Michaelson; August 13 was a Sunday and it was rare for companies to make corporate announcements on a Sunday, aside from negative news or to unveil a breaking merger or acquisition. Since the bet that Sedna made on AMD was a bullish one, it looked like the news the Rajaratnam brothers expected was positive. In any case, the instant-message exchange buttressed a hunch that Michaelson had had all along. Unlike the Arris earnings intelligence, the information on AMD was flowing from Raj to Rengan.

Two weeks after the IM banter, Dell released its earnings and said it would unveil desktop computers with AMD processors. That same day, August 17, Sedna's friends and family fund sold the options for a gain of $2.8 million. At 11:34 a.m., Matt Read was back with his usual cyberbanter. He instant-messaged his cousin Bill Lyons at Sedna.

"AMD," Read said.

"story to tell you man; this weekend," Lyons said.

"Birdie," Read countered.

"Nothing big; talk on weekend," Lyons replied.

"dude you always do that," Read said.

On October 19, 2006, the SEC issued a subpoena for testimony from Rengan Rajaratnam. He was surprised to receive it. "I can't believe I am being asked to testify," he told his elder brother. Though Raj Rajaratnam had never been asked to give testimony to the SEC, he was used to dealing with regulatory inquiries. The agency had been investigating Galleon on and off since 2003. Invariably because of their prolific trading, hedge funds like Galleon often cropped up on regulators' radars. The probe consumed a lot of time and resources, but all the investigating had not amounted to much. In 2005, Rajaratnam paid a fine of $2 million to settle an SEC case over the alleged improper short selling of seventeen stocks just before the companies sold additional shares. By the time the Sedna investigation started heating up in the fall of 2006, all was quiet on the regulatory front at Galleon and business was thriving. In late 2006, Galleon moved into swanky new offices at 590 Madison Avenue. To ensure the move was auspicious, Rajaratnam's wife, Asha, organized a *puja*, or religious ceremony, in the new offices. A Hindu priest presided and offerings were made to the gods.

On December 20, 2006, five days before Christmas, Rengan Rajaratnam, flanked by his lawyers, strode into a testimony room on the fourth floor of the SEC's New York offices at Three World Financial Center. It was Michaelson's first deposition at the SEC, and he and his boss, Wadhwa, were eager to hear explanations for some of the curious trades and the chatter around them. From the time Rengan started giving testimony, Wadhwa was struck by his manner. He veered between extreme cockiness and moments of unease. His body language was nervous, and at times he seemed contemptuous of the SEC's line of inquiry. When asked if he consulted with his brother Raj before making the big purchase of AMD options because so much money was at stake, he said he didn't remember and then was dismissive of the question.

"First, let's frame this," he said, taking a didactic tone that the SEC lawyers found highly irritating, "a million dollars is irrelevant to my brother, absolutely irrelevant. He's worth several hundred million. So I don't think he cares."

A minute later, when Michaelson showed him the instant-message exchange in which he asks his brother Raj, "Are we going to hold AMD?" and Rajaratnam responds by saying that he would hold the stock through the thirteenth, Rengan said he did not know the relevance of the thirteenth and he could not think of any market-moving news, such as a merger, around that time that would impact AMD's stock. As hard as he tried, he still could not remember if he told his brother that he was buying AMD options. Sparking laughter among his lawyers, he explained that he forced his brothers to redeem their investments in the friends and family fund because he didn't want to get any flack from them if the fund floundered.

"Even though they're my brothers, if I am down 30 percent I am going to hear about it," said Rengan. "I don't need that. I just don't need that. Trading is a very psychological game. If someone gets in your head, it can really mess you up."

At other times, the SEC lawyers were struck by Rengan's high-handed manner and inflated view of his own intelligence. When discussing his move to short Arris's stock in July 2006, Rengan said he looked at the analysts' models and saw they were expecting a steep ramp-up in gross margin, or revenue minus costs of goods sold.

"Analysts, no offense to them but they tend to be somewhat lazy, they have a trend, they just draw a straight line," Rengan said. "They don't sit there and kind of really think is the mix shifting and what does that impact. They kind of take whatever the company says." His job, what investors are paying him to do, Rengan explained, was to take one more step and consider other factors that might bear on a stock's performance. Rengan was actually taking a page from his big brother's playbook. Expectations about a stock are set by analysts working for Wall Street securities firms—so-called sell-side analysts who are in the business of getting investors to buy shares—but money was made when these analysts turned out to be wrong. Raj always impressed on his buy-side analysts that their task was to figure out "the reality," or how on or off the mark a sell-side analyst was.

This "arbitraging of consensus" favored hedge funds. Unlike analysts at the banks, who are judged by the forward-looking accuracy of their calls and are slow to change estimates, hedge funds like

Galleon can be more fleet-footed, adjusting their assessments of a company and its prospects at will. And unlike mutual funds, hedge funds can take short positions, or have pessimistic views of a stock.

Even at times when Rengan was trying to seem humble he came off as arrogant. When asked whether the $700,000 he invested in Sedna was his risk capital, he replied, "I'm single. I am a bachelor. I live in the same apartment I lived in for five years, my rent is a couple grand. I don't spend money. If I lost it, it wouldn't touch my life."

The one item Rengan was prepared to make a concession on was the quality of record keeping at Sedna. He admitted to the SEC lawyers that Sedna kept poor records, failing to preserve emails as required by a hedge fund that registers with the SEC as a "regulated investment adviser." Not all funds seek the title. While it can give a fund an aura of legitimacy, it imposes strict reporting requirements that are expensive for small funds like Sedna. SAC Capital, run by Rengan's former boss, Steven Cohen, did not seek the SEC imprimatur until 2012, and Sedna got it only in January 2006, nearly two years after it was launched.

"This is kind of the mistake we made," Rengan told the SEC lawyers. He said at one time Sedna's analysts "used to actually burn the emails to the CD-ROM drive, take it home and keep it in Brooklyn, God forbid anything happened in New York." Wadhwa suspected Rengan's contrition was calculated and the allusions to a 9/11-type event deliberate. All too often an SEC lawyer, confronted with a hedge fund manager who can't produce the emails he is requesting, will charge the fund with a books-and-records violation—essentially a slap on the wrist. Wadhwa found it hard to believe that a manager like Rengan, who had worked at SAC Capital and who seemed well put together, was unable to lay his hands on all of Sedna's emails. At 4:57 p.m., after nearly seven hours of questioning, the deposition ended.

Rengan felt good about it. When his brother asked how it went, he said well. At the SEC, though, Wadhwa and Michaelson were left with a different impression: they had no doubt that Rengan was dissembling when he gave testimony.

CHAPTER SIX

Promises to Keep

In the fall of 1971, Rajat Gupta said good-bye to his college sweetheart, Anita, and boarded a KLM airplane from New Delhi, making the first leg in his journey to the United States. The flight was Gupta's maiden trip outside India. After a stopover in Amsterdam, where he and a friend marveled at the spanking-new Mercedes cab they hailed—nothing like the clunky Ambassador cars on the streets of Delhi—they landed in London. There they caught a play and Gupta bought a London Fog raincoat. Gupta and his friend quibbled over which coat to buy. In the end, Gupta wisely bought the more expensive one with a lining. Boston winters, he would discover, are brutal.

At Harvard, Gupta found himself in the company of accomplished men from pedigreed backgrounds who went to the best private schools, summered in Europe, and, through family ties, landed jobs at Fortune 500 companies or clubby Wall Street banks before even arriving at Harvard. They had an easy confidence and an aura of sophistication. Many, like Edward Shoen, a classmate of Gupta's, were part of an exclusive, moneyed club. Shoen would one day run U-Haul International, the company his father founded. For others, like Ray Dalio, the son of a jazz clarinet and saxophone player, Harvard would become a way station en route to founding one of the world's largest hedge funds, Bridgewater Associates.

If Gupta was intimidated by it all, he didn't show it. Instead he struck a balance between assimilating and retaining his Indianness. During the week, he absorbed American culture from his dorm mates, but on weekends, he often took to the campus of MIT to catch a Hindi movie or joined a married friend from Delhi for an Indian meal. He so missed the spicy food from home he kept a jar of hot pickles in his room.

His quiet confidence was all the more striking given that he was one of the youngest members of the HBS class of 1973 and one of three from India. Of the 768 students in his class, there were only 30 women and half as many Asian students. "There were a lot of Brits, Aussies, and an occasional Japanese student" at the school, recalls Grover T. Wickersham, a member of the class. "But in those days there weren't many foreign students from India."

Unlike a number of his peers, who worked on Wall Street or served in the military before making their way to Harvard, Gupta was a greenhorn, arriving in Allston, Massachusetts, straight from IIT Delhi. John Carberry met Gupta on his first day at Harvard at their dormitory, Morris Hall, which, like all the dorms at Harvard Business School at the time, was fittingly named after a leading figure in finance, in this case Robert Morris, who saw to the bankrolling of the Revolutionary War. "My immediate impression was what a nice guy this is," says Carberry. "There wasn't a cockiness about him. If anything there was a sweetness, a kindness about him—maybe a little naive but always upbeat, always pleasant."

Gupta and Carberry were part of the same "can group"; they each belonged to a set of four two-room suites connected to a can, the slang for "bathroom." Typical of his friends in his first year was David Manly, who was as provincial as Gupta was exotic. He came to HBS from a small town in upstate New York and was taken with Rajat's gracious manner and his roots in the "mysterious east." On his study table in his room, Gupta kept a tattered piece of paper. It read, "But I have promises to keep and miles to go before I sleep—Robert Frost." He had received the piece of paper from his father during his final days. Close to Nehru, Ashwini Gupta knew that the poem was a favorite of the Indian leader.

The eight members of the can were a tight group, often strolling into each other's rooms for help with cases or simply for a late-night chat to break the relentless grind. Every evening, they would make the quarter-mile trek to Kresge Hall for dinner, wending their way in the bitterly cold Boston winters through the underground tunnels that were a signature feature of the HBS campus. "All we ever did during those walks—and over dinner—was to go over the case discussions earlier that day or see if anyone started on the cases for the next day," says Carberry.

Operating along the lines of a top music conservatory, HBS culled the business-world equivalent of highly talented pianists and violinists who were yet to realize their full potential as concert-level artists. Like any good music school, Harvard recognized that talent itself was not enough to produce effective leaders. So the bedrock of its philosophy was practice, practice, practice. The view was, "You don't teach business by having people read textbooks; you teach business by having people make many, many decisions during their two years," says Fred Sturdivant.

Thirty-two years old and self-described as cocky, Sturdivant struck students as a youthful Professor Charles W. Kingsfield Jr., the exacting Harvard Law School professor immortalized in the 1973 movie *The Paper Chase*. Like in Kingsfield's law class, one of the key teaching devices at HBS was "cold calling," in which students were randomly selected to answer questions. Sturdivant kicked off by walking into the large amphitheater-style classroom "like a Gestapo officer," Carberry recalls. Without even looking up, and with his back turned, Sturdivant said, "Mr. Clarke, will you begin." Townsend Clarke, or Towney, was hardly a slouch. He was about six foot four and 240 pounds, with wispy blond hair and a square jaw. He was said to be the last all-American football player to graduate from West Point and arrived at Harvard fresh from his latest tour of duty in Vietnam. For fifteen minutes, Clarke offered a penetrating diagnosis of Hesper Silver, a case about marketing silver flatware. When he finished, Sturdivant, seeming singularly unimpressed, declared, "Mr. Clarke, if you can't do anything better than recite the case, I think we had better ask someone else."

It was no accident that Clarke was selected to be the first target of the new class. At a party the night before, Sturdivant said he was looking for a "strong student"—someone who could take the pressure of leading off on the first day. When students offered up Clarke's name, Sturdivant didn't quite appreciate what he was getting. "The minute I said, 'Mr. Clarke would you begin please,' the young man jumped to his feet, snapped to, and barked, 'Sir, yes, sir,' " says Sturdivant. "It scared the hell out of me. Everybody sat there traumatized, thinking, *Is this what I am supposed to do?*"

As Carberry and other students slogged through their first term at Harvard, Gupta appeared to cruise. "Rajat constantly just floated above all this," says Carberry. "We all got the impression that the academic challenges at Harvard Business School were not that much of a challenge for him." Even though Gupta had no experience working in the business world, he was as fluent at navigating an income statement as his classmates who'd held jobs at companies before coming to Harvard. Friends marveled at the ease with which he tackled problems, getting to the nub of cases so much faster than they did. "If you had a problem with a case, Rajat would gladly help you out," says Carberry. "He wouldn't give you the answer, but he would say, 'Have you thought about that?' He would open some doors for you."

Among the pride of alpha males at HBS, Gupta was distinctive in a very non-alpha-male way. In a picture that appears in the class prospectus, Gupta appears very reserved. "When you look at the guy, he is kind of a Nehru. Even without a jacket, he seemed like he had a high collar," says Wickersham. In study groups, students would often ask, "What is the deal with Rajat?" recalls Wickersham. Few really had a sense of what IIT was at the time except to know "it is three times harder than MIT. Everyone figured he got here so he is pretty smart. He did everything on a slide rule that everyone at MIT did with massive computers." Wickersham got the impression that Gupta came from a modest background—he wasn't the kind of guy who made it to HBS because he was born with a silver spoon in his mouth. "I looked at Rajat and used to think he's the guy who vindicates the system," says Wickersham. "It's the American approach of meritocracy. It doesn't matter who you are or what kind of family you are from. Rajat is the guy who should have gotten in if you believe in meritocracy. He, to me, was the shining light; he went the distance. If they made movies like *Rocky* about a business guy, he would be the guy."

During the first six weeks at HBS, Wickersham says, an engineer like Gupta thrived because the course work was quantitatively driven. But when the courses started having a more liberal arts flavor to them, Wickersham expected Gupta to struggle, like some of the math geeks did. He didn't. What was remarkable was that Gupta excelled even though he was reticent in class. It was well known that a large part of one's grade came from class participation, triggering a curious pattern of one-upmanship in class, with one student trying to outdo the next in the heated competition for airtime.

In later years, Gupta would acknowledge his silence as one of his personal shortcomings at HBS and would attribute it to his Indian upbringing, in which children were judged in school by their written work rather than their class participation. In the end, Gupta said he made a deal with three of the five professors who taught him; he would be judged on his written final exam rather than his contributions in class.

Despite his quiet way, Gupta was learning a lot at HBS—both inside and outside the classroom. At times, Carberry says, he would return home from the library at about eleven o'clock at night and find Gupta working on cases as he kept one eye on the television, often to watch *Monday Night Football.* Gupta proved to be a quick learner. By mid-November of his first semester at Harvard, he could carry on an intelligent conversation about the game, filling in Carberry on the strategy of a given team or how its players lined up. About two or three months after Gupta arrived in the country, he and Carberry were watching a football game in their suite. "I think it was the Vikings versus the Giants," says Carberry. "At one crucial point in the game, with the Vikings having the ball, Rajat says to me, "I think the Giants need to 'red dog' here." ("Red dog" is an old-school term for "blitz.")

At other times, Carberry would return to Morris Hall late at night and find his can mate Gupta watching Johnny Carson. "He was picking up on American culture," says Carberry as he thinks back on Gupta's first year in the United States. "He would say, 'What is Johnny Carson doing with Ed McMahon? Sometimes he is funny and sometimes he is not.'"

As eager as Gupta was to soak in American culture, he kept silent about one of the most salient features of life in America at the time, the Vietnam War. Classmate John Hook remembers sitting in a class next to Clarke, the celebrated West Point graduate, one day when "I proposed we stopped the bombing." The class was divided between students who served in the military and believed the bombing was necessary and appropriate retaliation for a North Vietnamese offensive that started in late March, and civilians in the class who adamantly opposed the escalation. What was clear was that when heated discussions like this flared up, "someone like Rajat would be silent through these debates," says Hook, who is now an adviser on global trends to hedge funds. "Rajat would not take controversial positions—I would say that is not his thing." Growing up in India, Gupta was always likened to his father; he shared his dad's brilliance and his breathtakingly good looks. But as he matured into a grown man in America, Gupta would stand apart from his father; over time, the similarities between the two would fade and be overshadowed by differences.

CHAPTER SEVEN

The Good Ship Galleon

At the tail end of January 2007, Wadhwa and Markowitz decided to dispatch a team from the SEC's examination staff to Galleon, Raj Rajaratnam's firm. Their antennae were raised by the curious instant messages between Rengan and his brother Raj about stocks around which the SEC suspected insider trading was occurring.

Even before the examiners arrived at Galleon's offices at 590 Madison Avenue, the 603-foot-high black stone skyscraper on Fifty-Seventh Street formerly known as the IBM Building, they knew what they were looking for. A couple of the staffers on the SEC's Galleon exam team were camped out at Sedna months earlier and were up to speed on the touch points between the two brothers' firms.

On the morning of Monday, February 12, 2007, four SEC examiners met with a team from Galleon—Lindi E. Beaudreault, Galleon's outside lawyer; George Lau, its compliance officer; and Tom Fernandez, its head of investor relations and a college buddy of Raj Rajaratnam's. At a welcome meeting, during which Rajaratnam popped in to say hello, Beaudreault painted a picture of a hedge fund operating in full compliance with US securities laws. She told the examiners that Galleon adhered to a very detailed policy on insider trading, which was reviewed every year with the hedge fund's one hundred employees, comprising largely portfolio managers, traders, and analysts. The SEC team smiled and nodded. This was not the first time they'd heard this speech.

The Galleon portrait Beaudreault painted eroded over the next few weeks as the team examined the emails and instant messages themselves. A couple of IM exchanges in particular piqued their curiosity. In one, on April 21, 2006, just a few days before Computer Associates, which trades under the stock symbol CA, unveiled quarterly earnings guidance, Rajaratnam chatted with Quint Slattery, the manager of Symmetry Peak, a fund in which Rajaratnam was invested:

> [Slattery] quintussf: what about our ca
> quintussf: u staying short?
> rajatgalleon: my guy has seen the press release
> rajatgalleon: yes
> quintussf: obviously I know you are kidding about that
> quintussf: for the record I think the ims here are logged...
> rajatgalleon: Oh shit
> quintussf: its no big deal
> quintussf: I am careful on im
> rajatgalleon: press relase [*sic*] about the Yankees releasing derek jeter
> quintussf: that is what I heard
> quintussf: though he might stay

The exchange was so ham-fisted that it was an insult to regulators. Did Rajaratnam really think they would buy that he was referring to a press release about the Yankees' star baseball player Derek Jeter? It demanded a response, but building a case from the casual chatter alone was difficult. When Michaelson delved into Galleon's records, he found that the hedge fund did trade Computer Associates stock around the time of the IM banter. But the name of Rajaratnam's source—the individual who Rajaratnam boasted had seen the press release and the indispensable link to build an insider trading case—eluded him entirely.

Michaelson checked the contacts in Rajaratnam's Microsoft Outlook folder, he reviewed all his IMs and emails and trolled through his copious phone records, but he came up empty-handed. He even reached out to Computer Associates, which sent a thick document detailing all the people at the firm and outside it who were briefed on its earnings, but the document did not help uncover the source. Besides showing that material nonpublic information has been divulged, to bring an insider trading case the SEC needs to demonstrate there has been a breach of duty when the information is given. But after weeks of digging, Michaelson couldn't turn up Rajaratnam's source. Without an informant, it was tough to allege a breach. As long as Rajaratnam had so many diverse sources of information—some of the tips he traded on came from middlemen, other hedge fund managers, for instance—the SEC could do nothing to dredge up his source.

From the beginning, Markowitz believed that the Sedna-Galleon case would be one the SEC referred to the criminal authorities. Unlike other insider trading cases that fell on his desk, many of them isolated instances of individuals trying to profit from corporate news they accidentally stumbled upon, there were early signs that trading on inside information at the two hedge funds run by the Rajaratnam brothers was widespread and that it rose to the level of criminal behavior.

But there was a downside to bringing in the big criminal guns. Whenever the SEC enlists their help, it can lose control of a case. The SEC is a civil body and typically has a lower threshold for cases than the US attorney's office, which lives and dies by the "beyond a reasonable doubt" yardstick. Many times, the SEC has to wait for prosecutors before it can bring an action. And prosecutors want "winners," which means building an unbeatable criminal case.

There was another issue. Wadhwa and Markowitz had got wind that a previous insider trading investigation into Rajaratnam in the late 1990s was squashed because a criminal probe into his possible involvement with a Tamil insurgent group had taken precedence. They didn't want to waste their time and have that happen again.

Despite the potential downside of bringing in the feds, Markowitz decided to refer the case to the US attorney's office for the Southern District of New York in March 2007. The office, dubbed the *Sovereign* District of New York because of its storied reputation for independence, covers the boroughs of Manhattan and the Bronx and has far more cases to choose from than it can handle. Wadhwa and Markowitz knew that they had to convince the criminal authorities that the developing case against Galleon was worth their time and effort. Markowitz was encouraged when the prosecutors said they would be willing to come to the SEC's offices for a meeting. Usually it was the SEC lawyers who made the trek across Lower Manhattan.

"This is our best shot at getting into hedge fund insider trading," said Markowitz. His subtext was *This is a headline-grabbing case.* The SEC lawyers shared with their criminal counterparts some of the suspicious instant messages the exam staff had uncovered. William F. Johnson, deputy chief of the Securities and Commodities Fraud Task Force, appeared intrigued. "Wow, that is good evidence," he said. Then Michaelson handed over a binder focused on trading in two stocks, AMD and Arris; two DVDs containing emails; and a CD containing a trade blotter and some instant messages. Soon after the meeting, the US attorney's office in Manhattan embarked on a criminal investigation. Wadhwa and Markowitz were thrilled; their pitch to the US attorney's office had worked.

At the same time, an anonymous letter arrived at the offices of the SEC. It was postmarked Queens, New York, and was addressed to the SEC's New York Regional Office director. "It is hedge funds like Galleon Group that create wealth for their shareholders and themselves at the expense of innocent investors," the letter began. The writer went on to say that the limited partners in Galleon "are industry executives...and Board Members of large public companies... They share quarterly results with the management of this fund prior to release to the public. In return the fund provides greater returns on their money."

The anonymous letter writer claimed never to have worked for Galleon but seemed astonishingly well-informed about the company's practices. "Faxes are delivered from companies containing financials, product mix data etc. on Galleon management's desk prior to release the next day." The letter's author waxed colorful when describing the corporate culture: "Prostitution is rampant for executives visiting Galleon. You will find that the superbowl [*sic*] parties for the executives, paid for by the Galleon Group, including [*sic*] prostitutes and other forms of illegal entertainment. In return, the executives provide Galleon the unfair edge that the fund leverages so well." The letter closed by throwing down the gauntlet to the SEC: "I'm sure you will not have to dig too deep to unravel the truth behind this manipulative hedge fund." It was signed "Seeking Integrity in Business," but its author, whom SEC lawyers suspected was a disgruntled employee, could not be found.

By April it was clear to Galleon's lawyers that the SEC was training its sights on Galleon rather than Sedna. At a deposition of a Sedna employee, the fund's lawyer Jerry Isenberg asked Wadhwa point-blank, "Is this an investigation of Galleon or an investigation of Sedna?"

The inscrutable Wadhwa did not answer. He was not required to respond. At Galleon, where Rajaratnam tended to cultivate silos, in keeping with his secretive management style, few except for a handful of Rajaratnam's closest lieutenants were aware of the escalating probe. But for anyone who cared to look, there were clues. Sedna Capital, Rajaratnam's brother's hedge fund, whose suspicious trading activity sparked the investigation into Galleon in the first place, suddenly closed, largely on account of poor performance. Tellingly, its employees were absorbed by Galleon.

As the SEC examination continued into spring, Galleon and its lawyers turned hostile. In April, Beaudreault telephoned Wadhwa and charged that it was improper for the SEC to be investigating Galleon under an order sanctioning a probe of Sedna. When Wadhwa failed to act, her colleague Isenberg telephoned Wadhwa's boss, David Markowitz, and claimed that the SEC was on a fishing expedition. Wadhwa was furious but Markowitz backed him, telling Isenberg that if he thought that kind of tactic was going to work, *he* didn't understand how things worked at the SEC.

On May 14, 2007, nearly nine months after the initial tip that Rengan Rajaratnam's Sedna Capital was engaging in some sketchy trades, the SEC issued a subpoena to Galleon for information on all trading activities, all trade blotters from September 2005 to the present, recording purchases and sales of securities, diaries, date books, and calendars, and all documents concerning specific securities such as AMD, the security that the Sedna friends and family fund made a killing on in 2006. They also issued a subpoena for Rajaratnam's testimony. Galleon fired back immediately, canceling a scheduled SEC interview with Tom Fernandez, Galleon's investor relations head, and effectively ending the exam.

"My team is getting kicked out," George DeAngelis, a branch chief in the SEC's Investment Adviser/Investment Company Examination Program in New York, told Wadhwa. (Members of DeAngelis's team are the beat cops who patrol broker-dealers, the hedge fund and mutual fund industry, and other large swaths of the country's financial infrastructure. If they spot troubling and pervasive activity, they can enlist Wadhwa and his enforcement group.)

"Don't worry," Wadhwa replied. By this time, he was comfortable that the SEC had enough strands of suspicious activity at Galleon to chase. It had a good idea, for instance, of the stocks Galleon made money on in 2006. One winning trade that stood out was a huge bet that Rajaratnam made on ATI Technologies, which was acquired by AMD. Surely the suspicious instant messages between Raj and his brother Rengan about AMD a few weeks later were not just a coincidence. The SEC could not prove it yet, but Wadhwa and Michaelson were just about convinced that Raj had an inside source on AMD and Raj was tipping off his brother.

The question the SEC lawyers now faced was whether to take testimony from Raj Rajaratnam immediately or subpoena more documents and then depose him. Ultimately they decided there was little harm in bringing him in straightaway. There was always a chance he might be able to offer a believable explanation for the suspicious threads the SEC lawyers were starting to tug at. After weeks of combing through emails and IMs, the SEC examination team had not nailed down any of his inside sources. In any case, if it needed to, the SEC could ask him to return, and there was always the possibility it could catch a break. Rajaratnam might say something that was provably false that could be used against him later. He might even slip and give up the name of a source, the indispensable element needed to build a case.

On the morning of June 7, 2007, as Wadhwa was walking with his colleague DeAngelis to take Rajaratnam's testimony, DeAngelis spotted an email on his BlackBerry. One of his staffers had found "some interesting" chatter in a stack of instant messages between Rajaratnam and a person using the IM handle "roomy81."

This was the first time Wadhwa and Michaelson had heard of roomy81. Not knowing the person behind the IM handle and wanting to do more digging, they filed the name away. They made a conscious decision not to ask Rajaratnam about the exchanges between him and roomy81. The last thing they wanted was for him to get the idea that they were going after roomy81. If he did, he could simply coordinate stories and cover up any impropriety. The less they appeared to know, the better. Walking to the deposition, they quickly devised a seemingly innocent way of asking Rajaratnam about the identity of the person behind the IM handle.

At 10 a.m., Raj Rajaratnam, flanked by the same two lawyers who had accompanied his brother Rengan six months earlier, walked into the SEC's Testimony Room 416. With windows looking out onto the World Financial Center's Winter Garden, Room 416 is rectangular, with a stained beige carpet. Rajaratnam wore a blue blazer and looked relaxed. Unlike his brother, he was smooth and understated. He explained the foundation for all his suspicious trades in a calm, matter-of-fact way, never losing his composure and never appearing arrogant or high-handed.

But, like his younger brother, he plied the SEC lawyers with half-truths. The SEC lawyers were not surprised. It was a tack they often encountered. When people are deposed by the agency, they have three choices. They can tell the whole truth, which could lead to the SEC bringing a case against them. They can invoke their right against self-incrimination and plead the Fifth Amendment, which the SEC could present to an SEC administrative law judge in any future civil case. Or they can lie. While invoking the Fifth Amendment can't be presented as evidence in a criminal proceeding, it is permissible in a civil action. Some executives take the gamble that lying under oath is better than invoking the Fifth Amendment in the event that the SEC brings a civil complaint and their pleading of the Fifth is used against them.

During the course of the seven-hour deposition, Rajaratnam tripped all over himself.

Michaelson, who had prepared meticulously to take Rajaratnam's testimony, spent most of the morning easing his witness into the process and getting him comfortable. He walked him through simple questions such as where and when he was born, what computers he used, and how he kept track of his appointments. Rajaratnam breezed through it all, rarely hesitating before replying. When he was asked if he had ever come into possession of material nonpublic information, he responded: "Me personally, no." Sometimes his answers were revealing. When Michaelson asked Rajaratnam about the hedge funds he invested in, he offered a variety of names. Some were start-ups like his brother's fund, Sedna Capital, and Slattery's Symmetry Peak. But others were old, established hedge funds like the Tudor funds, run by business chum Paul Tudor Jones, a renowned commodities trader; and Duquesne Capital, run by his good friend the legendary Stanley Druckenmiller. A protégé of George Soros, Druckenmiller masterminded one of Soros's most brilliant trades: making $1 billion in 1992 speculating on the devaluation of the British pound.

When Michaelson asked which investors in his funds were also directors and officers of public companies, he threw out a couple of names—Ken Levy of KLA Instruments, Charlie Giancarlo of Cisco, and Kris Chellam of Xilinx. But he failed to mention Rajat Gupta, who at the time sat on the board of Goldman Sachs and was an investor in Galleon's Voyager fund.

At 12:30, Isenberg requested a break. Rajaratnam was a diabetic, and his blood sugar was low.

When they reconvened after lunch, Michaelson started grilling Rajaratnam on AMD, asking him about the kind of information he relied on to buy the stock.

He said he acquired about $40 million of AMD stock between July 24 and August 11, 2006, because the stock was a bargain. AMD was unveiling a new product, Opteron, and it had a technological edge over Intel. He thought his source on the new chip may have been *PC Magazine* or industry buzz.

Galleon's investment decisions were built upon a hundred different variables—analysts' reports, money flows, Rajaratnam's view of the market, and his tolerance for risk, among others. The hedge fund had thirty-four analysts to whom Rajaratnam paid somewhere between $30 million and $60 million in total a year to keep happy. They drew on public announcements and articles, stock analysts' reports, trading patterns, and money flows to patch together winning investment ideas. When lawyers pressed him about whether he had any specific information that Dell or IBM was going to use AMD products in its computers, he said he had none.

Then Michaelson said, somewhat offhandedly, that he had a couple of quick questions before they recessed again.

"Are you familiar with a 'roomy81' instant-message address?" he asked.

"Yes."

"Who is that?"

"She worked at Galleon and then she left Galleon to start her own fund. I think she primarily manages her own money."

"What is her name?"

"Roomy...Khan," said Rajaratnam, spelling out her surname.

Michaelson asked Rajaratnam if he ever talked with Khan about Advanced Micro Devices.

"She may have given me information, but I can't recall."

Then Michaelson called the midafternoon break.

Rajaratnam's prevarication appeared to peak during the last hour, when Michaelson grilled him about an instant-message exchange on August 2, 2006, between him and an analyst with the IM handle APJITW. Apjit Walia, whose aim in life was to be a fighter pilot before becoming a securities analyst, worked at the investment banking unit of Royal Bank of Canada. Walia first met Rajaratnam when he and a colleague called on Galleon, a client of the bank. As often happens on Wall Street, a business relationship turned into a friendship. From time to time, Walia and Rajaratnam would have a drink, and on one occasion Walia accompanied Rajaratnam, an avid cricket fan, to Trinidad for an exciting match: India versus West Indies.

"AMD on August 1st, now 13th," Rajaratnam appeared to be messaging, writing "13eh" instead of "13th."

"Hey, for the tickets have to choose package B?" the analyst, Apjit Walia, shot back.

Michaelson wanted to know "what's going on in this IM exchange," clearly trying to figure out the link between package B and AMD, the ticker symbol for Advanced Micro Devices. ("A ticker" is Wall Street lingo for the symbol under which a public company's stock trades. Google's ticker symbol, for example, is GOOG.)

"We were going to see cricket in Trinidad," Rajaratnam responded. "We were talking about the cricket packages, the tickets we had to buy for the World Cup. There were different packages as to whether you could play in Barbados or Trinidad." (Walia, who has not been charged in connection with the Galleon case, also told the SEC in his voluntary testimony that his remark referred to the World Cup cricket.)

At first, it seemed like for every question Michaelson posed, Rajaratnam had a ready answer. Package B, he said, referred to accommodation and tickets packages that some tour operators were offering. When Michaelson followed up by asking which tour operator he was using, he retorted: "We decided to get our own house."

But then Rajaratnam was flummoxed.

"Did you buy package B?" Michaelson asked.

"Sorry?" Rajaratnam answered.

Michaelson asked the question again. For a moment, it seemed like the stories had caught up with Rajaratnam.

"What is package B?" Rajaratnam asked. Then, without missing a beat, he said package B, which he ended up buying, was unavailable to people who followed India in cricket.

The SEC lawyers were divided about the meaning of package B. Some, like Markowitz, were convinced that "package B" was a code word to buy a security. Rajaratnam denied it was. After the deposition, Michaelson spent hours Googling cricket packages to look at the various permutations. His gut feeling was that the exchange about package B probably was innocent, as Rajaratnam suggested. It just seemed too elaborate a way to telegraph the buying of a security.

What clearly was not innocent from Michaelson's perspective was the apparent shift in timing—"AMD on August 1st, now 13th." When Michaelson asked Rajaratnam about it, he claimed that he did not know the significance of the word "13eh."

"I know this is about cricket," he told the SEC lawyers. "I don't know. It's about cricket. I remember package B and the ticket, absolutely about the tickets. I don't know of anything else."

He said he was pushing Walia to choose tickets and now Walia was reminding him and so he called him a "rocket scientist." "We nailed the deadline," Rajaratnam said. "I don't know what the deadline was, the thirteenth or the fifteenth."

Seconds after the protracted discussion, during which Wadhwa and Markowitz jumped in, Michaelson showed Rajaratnam an IM exchange between him and his brother Rengan that took place the day before the chat with Walia.

"are you going to hold the amd?" Rengan asked.

"y through the 13th," Rajaratnam messaged back, using "y" as an abbreviation for "yes."

Again, Michaelson asked if Rajaratnam could tell the SEC lawyers the importance of the date, the thirteenth.

"I don't recall what the significance of the thirteenth was," Rajaratnam said.

In an effort to jog Rajaratnam's memory, Michaelson pointed to the two instant messages within twenty-four hours that seemed to refer to the thirteenth, one correctly and the other as "13eh." But before Michaelson could finish posing his question, Rajaratnam's lawyer Jerry Isenberg jumped in.

"Are you representing that '13eh' means the thirteenth?" Isenberg asked. "Do you have some secret knowledge that the rest of us don't have?"

The SEC lawyers persisted in their line of questioning, and Rajaratnam stubbornly stuck to his line of defense.

"It doesn't change my memory," said Rajaratnam. "I don't know."

Before the SEC wrapped up the deposition, Michaelson asked Rajaratnam how he paid for package B for the cricket match. Rajaratnam said he paid with his credit card.

The next day, June 8, 2007, the SEC issued a five-page subpoena to Galleon for his email and cell phone contacts, requests to identify his personal security and brokerage accounts, bank accounts, and investments in privately held companies, and handwritten notes concerning any securities transactions. Buried in the five-page subpoena was a request for Rajaratnam's credit card bills.

Then the SEC went dark—it issued no more subpoenas and asked for no more testimony from anyone at Galleon. As far as Rajaratnam was concerned, the investigation, which had cost him a lot of time, money, and headache, had ended. Now he could get back to one of his core businesses, trading on inside information.

PART TWO

Rising

CHAPTER EIGHT

No Ask Backs

Walter Salmon had just wrapped up a class at Harvard Business School in the spring term of 1973 when he noticed a defeated look in the eyes of one of his best students. Salmon didn't know Rajat Gupta socially. He sometimes had students over to his house in bucolic Lincoln, Massachusetts, for brunch or cocktails, but if it happened, it was generally in groups, not the kind of setting to get to know one student particularly well. As with most professors, Salmon's knowledge of Gupta came from his interaction with the young Indian's work. And that work was extraordinary. It was odd to see someone with such a bright future deflated.

Gupta was an amiable young man, even tempered and usually upbeat. Some of Salmon's colleagues considered Gupta quiet and reserved, but Salmon, a professor of retailing, did not share that impression. During the course of the semester, Salmon was struck by the quality of Gupta's insights in the elective class on retail marketing that he taught second-year students. He knew enough about him to tell that Gupta was not himself that day.

"What's going on?" Salmon asked Gupta as they stowed their notes and materials.

By the early 1970s, Salmon, a youthful red-haired professor with a penchant for chewing on rubber bands while in his office, was one of HBS's most influential faculty members. After getting his MBA from the school, he went into the Army for two years before returning to HBS as a research assistant in 1956. Three years later, in September 1959, he had his baptism at the front of the classroom. Since then, he had gained a reputation within and outside Harvard for his work in better understanding the profitability of particular lines of business and finding effective ways of motivating and compensating the management of retail organizations. Like many HBS professors, he matched academic research with experience in the real world. He didn't offer freelance consulting services because he preferred a more steady income stream, but he did sit on a number of corporate boards, among them Hannaford Brothers, a Scarborough, Maine, supermarket chain; and Stride Rite, a shoemaker.

Salmon was astonished by Gupta's news that he'd not received any "ask backs."

Recruiting at Harvard Business School is an important ritual whose structure is much like that of a senior prom. Every fall, America's biggest and most prestigious companies—Procter & Gamble, Goldman Sachs, McKinsey, and scores of others—appear on the Allston, Massachusetts, campus of HBS to interview the sharpest new business minds in the country. After one or two on-campus interviews, students jockey for "ask backs"—invitations to visit companies at their headquarters, all expenses paid. "Ask backs" are the equivalent of getting asked to the prom—a sign that firms are serious about hiring a student, so serious they are even willing to pay for a visit to their offices. Some students game the system. They accept "ask backs" from companies they are not particularly interested in joining simply because their headquarters are in a fun city—San Francisco or Los Angeles. Perhaps to reduce the risk of trips to New York by frivolous recruits, it was common in the 1970s for savvy Wall Street investment banks to take a small coterie of prospective hires to a fancy dinner at a then popular Boston eatery like Maison Robert. It was not quite an invitation to go steady, but it was an overture to start dating.

Back then, jobs on Main Street (manufacturing, retailing, energy), not Wall Street (trading and banking), were the traditional path to prosperity for MBAs. The markets wheezed and sputtered in the late 1960s, so much so that by mid-1973, when Gupta's Harvard class was set to graduate, the risk to stock investors of the three I's—interest rates, inflation, and the impeachment of President Richard Nixon—had risen exponentially. Harvard MBAs angled to land "residencies," much like medical residencies, at big, prestigious companies such as US Steel, 3M, Procter & Gamble, and General Mills. The traditional career path for the men—mostly white men and very few women or men of color—who came of MBA age in the 1970s was to start at the bottom of the corporate ladder and work to the top. Getting an MBA from Harvard allowed one to skip a slew of steps and offered the possibility of a country-club lifestyle after graduation.

At the same time, American business culture was in the throes of a quiet but seismic shift—the emergence of a kind of Harvard-after-Harvard career landing zone made up of business experts and advisers. Big, visible, brand-name companies were being usurped at the top of the "ask back" hierarchy by a new class of companies that were not in the business of selling goods. Rather, they sold advice. In the decades to come, the stock market and the companies that serviced it would mint a new class of wealthy individuals and become the most sought-after path to American success. The service industry to corporate America would emerge as the new driver of economic growth, drawing not just America's but the world's best and brightest with the allure of unimaginable wealth. Among the arrivistes on the American corporate scene were consulting companies, and there was no firm better known than McKinsey & Co.

The oldest consulting firm in the world, McKinsey had its roots in a company founded in 1926 by James O. McKinsey, a certified public accountant and University of Chicago professor. McKinsey saw an opportunity to counsel managers when he worked in the Army Ordnance Department and dealt with suppliers during World War I. After the war, he started his eponymous firm, specializing in accounting and in what was then known as "management engineering."

The name McKinsey would probably have been relegated to a footnote in history had it not been for the arrival in 1933 of a young Harvard Business School graduate named Marvin Bower. Over a career that spanned six decades, Bower single-handedly built a profession out of McKinsey and spawned what we now call management consulting or corporate problem solving. Initially, consultants helped CEOs chart out their companies' strategic course, but over time they have come to work with firms on more picayune problems, such as devising ways to cut costs and boost sales. One of Bower's first projects was a prototype of the kind of work consultants would routinely come to practice. In 1935, big Chicago department store Marshall Field & Co. hired McKinsey to perform a study of its entire business.

Bower and McKinsey recommended that Marshall Field focus on its department store business and jettison other assets. After the study, Marshall Field's board was so impressed that it offered James McKinsey the job of chief executive. Not only did McKinsey's acceptance secure Bower's control of the consulting concern; it was the beginning of a one-way revolving door that would become common among McKinsey consultants in later years.

During the course of sixty years at the firm, Bower saw consulting as an above-the-fray profession, not a profit-above-all-else enterprise. A career dedicated to helping companies solve problems for a fee would and did provide a comfortable living, but Bower firmly believed that to exploit a client was contemptible. As a graduate of Brown University, Harvard Law School, and Harvard Business School, Bower sought to find other men like himself to staff his company.

At the time Gupta was looking for a job, McKinsey was a bastion of Waspy, Ivy League–educated young men with lines into America's dominant families and businesses. A firm handshake and entrée into New York's Social Register set were more important than academic achievement. "BCG and Bain hired the 'best and the brightest' while McKinsey focused more on hale fellows well met," says Jeffrey Skilling, who joined McKinsey's Dallas office directly out of HBS in 1979.

As Skilling notes, McKinsey was not the only place an MBA from Harvard could find consulting work. Spurred by Bower's success, Bruce D. Henderson, a onetime Bible salesman and Harvard Business

School graduate, founded the Boston Consulting Group in 1963. It started with just two consultants and in its first month racked up just $500 in billings. Unlike McKinsey, which built a local-office-based model of client relationships, which amounted to spending considerable time at the country club, the Boston Consulting Group competed by offering "thought leadership"—consultant-speak for developing new and innovative ideas to win clients. It was known for its "fly in, fly out" expert-based consulting, which ate into McKinsey's market share.

By 1973, Boston Consulting had grown to 142 consultants, and like McKinsey, it had offices in London and Paris. Management consulting was so promising a profession that in that same year Bill Bain and a coterie of others quit BCG to found Bain & Co. The last of what came to be known as the big three, Bain relied on consultant star power and competed with the behemoths by cultivating big-name talent. It recruited the top 5 percent of the graduating Harvard Business School class, so-called Baker Scholars such as unsuccessful presidential candidate Mitt Romney. (Despite stellar grades in his first year, Gupta was not a Baker Scholar.)

Besides being intellectually challenging, consulting appealed to young HBS graduates like Rajat Gupta because it forestalled the important decision of what to do in life. As James McKinsey had demonstrated forty years earlier, it was a back door to jobs in corporate America. It allowed young men to mingle with corporate chiefs and forge close ties that they could later parlay into employment. A number of consultants at McKinsey—Harvey Golub, Michael Jordan, and Louis V. Gerstner Jr.—would leave over the course of the 1970s and 1980s and ultimately land top jobs at prestigious companies such as American Express, Westinghouse Electric, and IBM. In the years that followed, countless other McKinsey consultants trod similar paths, among them Jeffrey Skilling, who ran Enron; and James Gorman, a native of Melbourne, Australia, who succeeded the charismatic John Mack as the chief executive of Morgan Stanley. In 2008, a *USA Today* study calculated that the odds of a McKinsey employee becoming CEO at a public company were the best in the world, at 1 in 690. In

1973, for the young and undecided like Gupta, it was a great way of keeping one's options open.

Though he was one of two students in his class who was awarded perfect grades after his first term, Gupta struck out during his second interview with McKinsey—a setback that carried greater weight for him than for many of his peers. After graduating, Gupta planned to marry his IIT sweetheart, Anita. She thought when Gupta left India, that was the last she would see of him. Well-meaning friends had told her that people change when they go to America. But Gupta didn't forget her. He wrote long letters to her every day and waited for her missives back. In his wallet, he kept a five-rupee note that she had signed and a small photograph of her.

Anita's academic concentration was electrical engineering. She was a brilliant student who received the coveted director's gold medal at IIT, and Gupta liked to say that Anita was the smarter of the two. As modest and self-effacing as Gupta appeared to be, those who knew the couple tended to agree that in terms of raw intelligence, Anita Mattoo outshone Rajat Gupta.

To stay in the United States and to bring Anita over, Gupta needed a job. Straight out of the gate, Gupta hit a roadblock. Many corporations would not even contemplate interviewing job candidates on student visas. They told the HBS placement office that foreigners need not apply—no exceptions, not even standout students with stellar work experience.

The previous summer, Gupta had worked at a food-processing company in upstate New York. He got the summer job because his former suite mate David Manly's father was a senior executive at the company. During his summer stint, Gupta devised an innovative production planning system for jam and jelly making that is used even today at the company and is known as the "Rajat system." "It was a very professional piece of work for a young man," said Doug Manly forty years later.

But as Gupta prepared to graduate in 1973, none of that seemed to matter.

"If you didn't have a US citizenship or a green card you never got an interview," Gupta said years later. The one exception was the plum positions to be had at the big three consulting firms. In their gusto to expand overseas and outflank one another, they were keen to attract the right kind of foreign consultant.

Gupta had two back-to-back interviews with McKinsey. After the second interview, Bill Clemens, then head of recruiting at McKinsey, told Gupta that he had terrific credentials. But then with a subtle, yet time-honored, between-the-lines message, Clemens told him, "You're obviously very smart, but you need to go and work somewhere else for three or four years before we'll consider you."

"Nobody else is interviewing me so how would I go and work anywhere else?" Gupta asked pointedly. Clemens was unmoved. Gupta's rejection was curious, especially as both McKinsey and its archrival, Boston Consulting, vied every year to land the most Harvard B-schoolers. At one point, more than a third of McKinsey's consultants held a Harvard MBA. The consulting giant historically rolled out the welcome mat to top students like Gupta. When word got around the class that Gupta had been rejected by McKinsey, some students suspected an undercurrent of discrimination at play. Out of necessity, universities and hospitals had started integrating Indian intellectual manpower in the late sixties and early seventies. But opportunities for nonwhite immigrants in the clubby, largely Waspy world of corporate America and Wall Street were rare. When he was recruited to McKinsey in 1979, Anjan Chatterjee recalls meeting with a partner who said to Chatterjee: "You guys do great work and you are terrific consultants. The question is will our senior clients ever relate to you."

*　*　*

HBS professor Walter Salmon listened intently to Gupta's story of getting rejected by McKinsey because of his lack of experience.

"That surprises me given your work in my class," Salmon said. He was seasoned enough to know that Gupta was one of those very bright students who were few and far between. He also was acquainted with a number of McKinsey partners and had a good sense of the caliber of people the firm hired. In his view, Gupta fit the

McKinsey mold perfectly. He was quick at figuring out the core issues of an HBS case and was effective at delivering his analysis.

"He was exceptionally able and a very nice person," says Salmon today. Salmon told Gupta that D. Ronald Daniel, the head of McKinsey's New York office, was an old classmate of his. The two had been in the same section at HBS. Salmon would call him and suggest McKinsey reconsider its decision. It wasn't a step Salmon ordinarily took. In fact, Salmon says some forty years later that he doesn't recall ever making an overture like that before or since. "It rarely happened, if at all," he says.

When Salmon got a hold of Daniel, he didn't have to say very much. Salmon was a rising star at Harvard Business School; he was chairman of the marketing department, and in a year he would be elevated to the powerful position of associate dean of faculty affairs. Daniel knew that Salmon wouldn't be calling on just anyone's behalf. For Salmon to get in touch with him, he must have believed that the student McKinsey had just rejected for a job was extraordinary. "This is a bright student," Salmon told Daniel. "I think you should take a second look." Salmon spoke with characteristic understatement, but his message was clear. Shortly after the call, Gupta received a coveted "ask back." He was invited to McKinsey's New York office for a full day of interviews and then he was offered a job.

CHAPTER NINE

"The Tamil Tiger" of Wall Street

In the fall of 1983, a heavyset young man flashing a big white smile strode into Chase Manhattan Plaza to report for his first day of work. With his MBA ticket recently punched from the University of Pennsylvania's Wharton School of business, Raj Rajaratnam arrived on Wall Street with impeccable timing. He was selected from more than two thousand applicants to be one of fifty analysts in Chase Manhattan Bank's coveted credit program. After finishing it, many analysts left to take up enviable jobs at investment banks like Goldman Sachs and Morgan Stanley. The only Sri Lankan in his class, Rajaratnam would play the expected role of reserved math whiz. He started at a salary of $34,000.

After limping through the seventies, Wall Street got its swagger back thanks to President Ronald Reagan's personal and corporate tax cuts and his push to deregulate the American economy. In 1981 the markets began a long rally that except for one interruption, a terrifying one-day crash in October 1987, would rage almost unabated for nearly two decades. The boom and its unprecedented demand for people—brokers to sell stocks, bankers to help raise capital, traders to make money on all the dizzying market moves—transformed Wall Street, changing its complexion from a bastion of all-white men to a colorful mosaic of women, South Asians, and, to a lesser extent, African-Americans. The new arrivals added color and helped break down the barriers that had persisted for most of Wall Street's history, segregating Jewish banks like Goldman Sachs and Lehman Brothers from Wasp banks like Morgan Stanley and First Boston. The South Asians also formed tribes of their own.

For decades, long-standing client relationships had driven business to Wall Street securities firms. Investment bankers were men who had the talent and the social connections required to nurture and keep Wall Street's best clients. But the opening of the capital markets in the early eighties and the advent of technology that powered the way to the growth of complex mathematically driven trading strategies changed Wall Street. What securities firms needed most were financial wizards who actually had the brains to dream up newfangled products—derivatives and junk bonds—and sell them to an ever-increasing number of clients, savings and loans, pension funds, and high-net-worth individuals. It needed analysts who could understand the sophisticated products and technologies of the corporations they analyzed—and not simply swallow the spoon-fed and curdled explanations that companies served them. With their highly quantitative backgrounds, the new emigrants from South Asia were perfect for the job.

Men like Indian native Vikram Pandit, the former CEO of Citigroup, and Sri Lankan Raj Rajaratnam heeded the call. Others followed. Anshu Jain, today the co-chief of Deutsche Bank AG, joined Kidder, Peabody & Co. in 1985 as a research analyst after earning an MBA at the University of Massachusetts at Amherst. Arshad Zakaria, brother of journalist Fareed, started at Merrill Lynch & Co. in 1987, straight out of Harvard Business School, and rose to become the firm's powerful head of global markets and investment banking. Though the new recruits from South Asia were appreciated for their mastery of math and finance, there was little sign at the time that they would ever be respected for anything more.

"Wall Street was tough to get into for us," Rajaratnam would say decades later. "Not to be crude but there's a Jewish mafia, and a Wasp mafia, and an Irish mafia up in Boston...They hire their own; they socialize among their own." Rajaratnam understood how the system worked. If he couldn't get into anyone else's club, he'd build his own.

At Chase, Rajaratnam discovered that there were two hot industry groups that analysts were vying to join: electronics and petroleum. After completing the credit program, Rajaratnam was tapped for the electronics group, where he earned the nickname "HP Raj." Unlike his peers, he didn't need a Hewlett-Packard calculator to figure out mathematical computations; he could do complex calculations in his head.

Except for his acumen in math, Rajaratnam kept a low profile at Chase. He struck superiors as humble and deferential. One time, Rajaratnam was on a trip with a couple of colleagues visiting a client. The group was divided into two cars. Rajaratnam drove one, while a seasoned and more senior colleague drove another. The men from Chase were late for the meeting, but the gray-haired gentleman would not accelerate. Rajaratnam's colleagues gesticulated to him with hand signals to overtake them. Despite their frantic motioning, Rajaratnam lagged behind, refusing to pass. Quizzed about it later, Rajaratnam said he was not comfortable overtaking the older gentleman. In his mind, he said, it showed a lack of respect. His colleagues found his gesture charming; they didn't focus on the fact that among Asians the elderly were revered. All Rajaratnam was doing was behaving as he had been brought up to do.

Even though Rajaratnam thrived at Chase, colleagues sensed that his passions lay elsewhere. "Give me a Quotron," he often quipped, referring to the stock quotation machines once ubiquitous on Wall Street trading floors. He liked that the markets were unforgiving and that they humbled you. But most of all he loved the game and the thrill of winning. It was an energy that he infused into every part of his life. Whenever he played tennis, he would blast every ball. Years later, when he started his own company, he described his drive to compete: "After a while, money is not the motivation. I want to win every time. Taking calculated risks gets my adrenaline pumping." Soon he would be an adrenaline junkie.

In 1985, Rajaratnam quit Chase to join Needham & Co., a second-tier, scrappy investment bank specializing in technology and health-care stock trading. Founded by George Needham, a former investment banker at CS First Boston, the upstart firm challenged

Wall Street by filling its ranks with outsiders. "I hire one-legged men, and I beat the crap out of them," Needham liked to say. Employees were required to take red-eye flights on business trips and stay over Saturday nights if it saved the firm money. Needham himself was known to sift through the stack of FedEx slips every day to see which employees sent FedEx packages rather than using the cheaper and preferred Airborne Express. And he thought nothing about putting down his employees, calling his banking group an "island of misfit toys" and his analysts "hundred-thousand-dollar doorstops."

Amid Needham's hardscrabble culture, Rajaratnam flourished. He had vision and fortitude. When US semiconductor companies were struggling, battered by a flood of cheap Japanese computer chips, most research analysts gave up on the sector, thinking it a dead end. Rajaratnam decided to build a career out of it.

Boyish and dashing, he traveled to Silicon Valley and charmed an up-and-coming generation of technology executives with his folksy ways. He told them his first name meant "king" in Hindi and together with his last name, it made him the "king of kings." He mesmerized them, regaling them with larger-than-life tales. "He would tell about his experience with the Tamil Tigers," says Gerald Fleming, who covered chip equipment makers at Needham. Fleming remembers a trade group conference in Monterey, California, during which Rajaratnam captivated dinner companions by telling a tale of how "he went into training with the [Tigers] and one day a bullet whizzed past his ear, and that's when he decided to go and study in England." No one knew what to make of the story. (A spokesman for Rajaratnam told *Forbes* in October 2010 that the insurgent group Fleming refers to was not in existence when Rajaratnam left Sri Lanka.)

As Rajaratnam unleashed his natural charisma at social gatherings, in the trenches he was even more impressive. A cut above the typical analyst in the technology sector, then a Wall Street backwater, Rajaratnam displayed a prodigious knowledge of the industry and an all-consuming desire to learn about the companies operating at the cutting edge. "When you are presenting a highly technical story, it is not too often you get an analyst who really understands it," says Bob Anderson, one of the cofounders of KLA Instruments. "He clearly had the ability to understand what was going on."

Fortuitously for him, Rajaratnam arrived on Wall Street just as Silicon Valley was starting to see an influx of South Asians too. Rajaratnam forged multiple ties with Silicon Valley's small but growing community of Indian expatriates. One of his earliest contacts was Kris Chellam, a technology industry veteran who worked at Intel. A professional relationship between the two flowered into a friendship, particularly after Chellam joined Atmel Corp. in September 1991. Whenever Chellam came to New York City, Rajaratnam would rent a limousine and the two would head off to Atlantic City.

"Raj sort of had a South Asian mafia," says Fleming, the Needham analyst. There were people he could call and "get, for a number of companies, [their] earnings to a penny." Fleming recalls once sitting in Rajaratnam's office when he logged a call to Advanced Micro Devices. After some time, his secretary came in and said that someone with an Indian-sounding name had returned the call. Rajaratnam took the call, walked onto the trading floor, and announced the profit figure. "And he was right," says Fleming, astonished at the time.

As his clout at Needham grew, he shed his quiet persona and took on the bravado of a Wall Street wheeler-dealer. If a banker missed a piece of business and the treasurer of the company was a woman, Rajaratnam would inquire: "Why didn't you sleep with her?" At Needham, he was "pretty much the same guy you see now. He was bossy, he was loud, and not a particularly nice guy but he was a rainmaker at the firm," says Lisa Lettieri, who worked as a sales assistant at Needham in the mid-1980s. "He had to be on a beautiful woman's arm all the time. He wanted lots of [money]. It was money and women."

While playing the bon vivant at work, Rajaratnam was seriously dating a woman at the time. Asha Pabla was a quiet Sikh Punjabi woman who worked in the textile industry. She was as fair as he was dark. Even though he publicly denied it, his intimates knew that he had always had a chip on his shoulder about the color of his skin. Years later, when he catapulted to hedge fund stardom, he would often marvel at how he—a man with a black, ugly face—had gone from being an outsider, hovering on the fringes of Wall Street, to being a consummate insider. (Rajaratnam, through a spokesman, denied to *Forbes* that he ever mocked his own appearance.)

Rajaratnam told friends he fell in love with Asha at first sight, but it took her awhile before she was convinced that she wanted to settle down with him. Her parents were dead set against the union because they were from different communities, but Rajaratnam vowed that he would earn $1 million quickly and then ask her to marry him. In 1988, with Raj still far from the million-dollar mark, the two were married. Soon Rajaratnam was earning the big bucks.

Sometimes he did it by cutting corners. In the early 1990s, Novellus Systems learned that Rajaratnam, who covered their company at Needham, was courting its archrival, Applied Materials, for an offering of securities. Novellus was founded by a group of refugees from Applied Materials and the two companies were fierce competitors. When the Novellus executives found out that Rajaratnam won the mandate, they suspected he might have clinched the deal by discussing with Applied Materials some cutting-edge technology that Novellus had developed and previewed before him. Whether he had done so is not known. They were furious with Rajaratnam; after the incident, Novellus cut off Rajaratnam and Needham for a time from future investment banking business.

In 1991, George Needham, impressed with the deals Rajaratnam was winning, promoted him to president. As a boss, Rajaratnam drove employees—and himself—hard. One time, when an analyst returned home to take a nap after a red-eye flight, Rajaratnam chewed him out. "You don't show people that you are tired or you are beat," he told the analyst. Rajaratnam understood the importance of appearances. In later years, when he started his own hedge fund, he hired a fleet of analysts, openly calling them "window dressing." Having them around drove home to investors that he was serious about research even though he made most of his trading decisions without their input.

At Needham, pushing boundaries—both personal and professional —became a point of pride for Rajaratnam. One time, after Rajaratnam bragged to his colleagues that he could handle any kind of spicy sauce, a colleague decided to put his taste buds to a test. As a crowd looked on, Rajaratnam spread a bottle of habañero sauce called Armageddon onto two chicken wings. Within moments of tucking in, tears were streaming from his eyes and he was coughing. He rushed to the bathroom and went home early that day, a rare move on his part. Later, he chuckled about the episode.

By the beginning of 1994, Rajaratnam owned 17 percent of the small boutique bank—the second-largest equity owner after Needham himself, who owned 26 percent of the firm's equity. He was earning $1 million a year. Job offers from big investment banks were pouring in—a fact he reminded George Needham of all the time. To cement his power, he began building his own empire of loyalists—many of them from South Asia, including his old Wharton friend Krishen Sud. The hires were so blatant that at one point George Needham confronted him. Rajaratnam rattled off the names of the employees on Needham's trading desk. Most were Jewish.

Needham took the point… *If you have your tribe, I'll have mine.* On Fridays, Sud, Rajaratnam, and Ari Arjavalingam, another colleague, would head off to Bombay Palace, one of the oldest Indian restaurants in New York, for a long lunch. George Needham would needle the trio when they returned from their meal, remarking that they came back with extra vim and vigor because of the spicy food they ate.

For years, Rajaratnam was hankering to manage money, and in 1992, in a bid to capture more business from Silicon Valley technology companies, he started a small hedge fund at Needham. Many of the companies he served were going public, enriching their executives along the way. Rajaratnam figured the newly minted entrepreneurs needed a place to invest their new wealth. What better venue than a hedge fund managed by their investment banker? He quickly raised $250 million—a sizable sum of money at the time—from some of his best banking clients.

Rajaratnam was excited about the new fund, but not everyone at Needham shared his enthusiasm. A number of executives started fielding complaints from brokerage clients who were worried about the many hats Rajaratnam now wore: he was president of the company, he was a banker, and he managed money for the very same executives whose companies he covered as a banker. The risks were obvious. Rajaratnam was in a position to get information from his banking clients that he could then use to trade on for his hedge fund. To avoid any impropriety of this kind, it is common at investment banks for there to be a Chinese wall separating investment banking from trading; this forbids bankers who are advising companies on deals from discussing the transactions with colleagues on the trading floor.

Between 1993 and 1996, at least five Needham executives told George Needham that they were concerned about Rajaratnam's business practices. In November 1996, amid growing tensions between Rajaratnam and the firm he helped build, George Needham told employees, "I greatly regret that Raj Rajaratnam, my friend and partner," was quitting the firm.

Soon after Rajaratnam left, Theodore O'Neill, a semiconductor analyst, moved into Rajaratnam's old office. Along one wall, he found row after row of spiral-bound logs of inbound calls from tech executives all over Silicon Valley.

How do I get these guys to call me? O'Neill thought.

CHAPTER TEN

Up or Out at McKinsey

After arriving at McKinsey's offices in September 1973, Gupta by his own account struggled. He was assigned to share an office with Karl Wyss, who came to McKinsey with experience in the corporate world and an impressive résumé. The two could not have been more mismatched. Gupta was young and callow. Wyss was mature and wise to the ways of business. Gupta came to McKinsey fresh out of business school. By contrast, his office mate was a ten-year veteran of the computer giant IBM with the experience of managing two thousand people before becoming a consultant. Wyss advanced very rapidly. Within nine months, he started managing projects and was handed numerous responsibilities.

Gupta, meanwhile, was on a slow learning curve, simply treading water. At a company like McKinsey, which evaluates its consultants almost as rigorously as it does the companies it counsels, Gupta was constantly reminded of his shortcomings. In reviews, he was upbraided for being too quiet in team meetings, the routine gatherings of a group of consultants working on a specific project. Always the academic all-star, Gupta found the transition from carefully prepared written responses to off-the-top-of-the-head verbal statements difficult.

"I was sitting there and wondering, *Am I in the wrong place, am I really falling way behind?*" said Gupta years later. "I was very late in almost everything I did." Unlike his office mate Wyss, Gupta took four years of incremental progress before he managed his first project.

Whatever Gupta's own insecurities about his early time at McKinsey were, they slipped past his office mate, Wyss. "Rajat did not seem overwhelmed at all," says Wyss. Often, when he finished his work, Gupta would pack up and head home at 2:30 in the afternoon to be with his family. "He was his own man," says Wyss. "You could tell if someone asked him to do something he didn't want to do, he knew how to say no."

In the two years that Wyss and Gupta shared an office, Wyss remembers Gupta as being "very private," rarely divulging much over their morning coffee. Gupta never mentioned the death of his parents even though it would have been fresh in his mind. Then and to this day, "he is a hard guy to pull out," says Wyss. Though he left McKinsey before Gupta's real rise at the firm began, he saw in Gupta a quality that would help him climb in later years. "He was not a partner who made enemies," says Wyss. "He was a partner who tried to build bridges. If you know McKinsey from the inside, becoming managing director is a highly political process. Rajat was a good politician."

In his early years, while Gupta got solid reviews for his analysis of consulting problems, he was so quiet that he didn't stand out or make a serious impression. Tom Peters and Robert H. Waterman Jr. thought of Rajat as a "sweet little kid," recalls Waterman, the coauthor with Peters of the best-selling management bible *In Search of Excellence*. Waterman first encountered Gupta in the late seventies when Gupta attended one of the training sessions for the Excellence Project. "Rajat didn't strike me as more ambitious than any other McKinseyite," Waterman recalls. In fact, Waterman saw Gupta as "possibly less" ambitious because he was a "little bit shy and quiet at the time." His work, though, was fine—so quietly exceptional that his contributions earned him a spot as an "Excellence" trainer.

Gupta did not know it at the time, but he joined McKinsey during one of the most perilous periods in its history. "The 70s was a lost decade for McKinsey," says Jeffrey Skilling, who started at McKinsey in 1979 when it was emerging from its dark days. "After growing at breakneck speed through the 50s and 60s, the firm hit the skids in the 70s. The 'big ideas' of the 50s and 60s, divisionalization, product management and quantitative decision-making (the 'McNamara-like' whiz-kid thinking), had clearly run out of steam by the early 70s. The onslaught of Japanese competition in the 70s in some ways repudiated the American management model that was McKinsey's stock in trade. Probably even more threatening was the rise of BCG [the Boston Consulting Group] and its offshoot Bain."

The challenge McKinsey faced was that even as the market for the firm's product grew more saturated, "the new markets were blocked by the new guys [BCG and Bain]," Skilling recalled in a series of emails from federal prison in Englewood, Colorado. (He is serving a twenty-four-year sentence for his role in the collapse of energy giant Enron, a McKinsey client.) "Staff levels and number of offices actually DECLINED in the early 70's." Compared to fast-growing BCG and Bain, McKinsey was unattractive to new recruits. With little corporate growth, the chance for an associate to be elected into the partnership diminished dramatically.

Accustomed to the chaos and scarcity of India, Gupta was little bothered by the problems facing McKinsey. He was more excited by the array of new opportunities the firm offered its associates. Soon after joining the firm, Gupta met with Bud Miles, a Yale graduate and a McKinsey institution. Miles was the "staffing coordinator," who matched McKinsey consultants and their interests with the assignments that were flowing into the firm. Visiting Miles was like going to the candy store—there were all kinds of candies to be had, complex consulting jobs for some of the biggest companies in the world and small assignments that specialized in a certain arcane area, such as operations.

"You got this feeling that the world was there for you to pick and choose what you wanted to do," said Gupta years later. Most young consultants tried to latch on to important assignments for well-known companies that promised to burnish their careers. When Gupta met with Miles, Miles offered him about half a dozen assignments and gave him a few days to decide which ones he wanted to pursue. Gupta wasted no time in performing his due diligence. He talked to the partners responsible for some of the assignments in the hope of learning a little bit more. He tried to handicap which ones would be good for him and his career, and he tried to figure out what kind of experience he would get from working on each.

One day while he was mulling it all and pacing along the corridor deep in thought, a partner called him into his office. Gupta was toying with signing up for a study that the partner was about to launch. But it was clear to the seasoned partner that Gupta was swamped by the choices before him and could not decide which to pursue. He gave him some advice.

"You should just not worry about what is going to be good because you will never be able to tell," the partner told him. "I have been in consulting a long time, and whenever I try to figure out what is good for me, it always turns out differently." Projects you expect to learn the most from, the partner explained, often turn out to be disappointing, and assignments that have seemingly little promise can often turn out to be invaluable, offering a consultant a new insight or expertise. The important thing is to have "a learning mind-set" so that you learn from anything you do and everything you do, the partner advised.

The insight resonated with Gupta, a man who grew up in a land where deferring gratification was a way of life. While others jockeyed to get on teams that worked on what seemed like the most promising consulting projects, Gupta took a Zen-like approach to getting new assignments. Whenever he visited Miles, he would say, "Bud, I don't want to know what's available. Just tell me what I should do and that's fine with me."

One of the first big clients he worked for was the phone giant AT&T Corp., a relationship McKinsey owned because of a formidable consultant, Frederick W. Gluck. An electrical engineer by training, Gluck arrived at the firm in 1967 after a stint at Bell Labs, where he was program manager for the Spartan missile.

It was an era before people owned their phones. Rather, customers picked phones of their choice out of a catalog and paid AT&T a monthly fee to rent them. A persistent problem came with that system: disappearing phones. When people moved, they took the phones that AT&T provided. In one of its less glamorous assignments for AT&T, McKinsey was hired to figure out how to prevent AT&T from losing so many phones to its customers.

Gupta dived into the project, going on field visits with low-level AT&T employees to get a grasp of the issues. During one visit, Gupta got stuck with more than he gambled for. When he removed a phone from the wall, a swarm of cockroaches crawled out. "The whole place moved," says Chatterjee, Gupta's IIT friend and McKinsey colleague. The consulting firm's prescription was classic McKinsey: AT&T had defined the problem incorrectly. In many cases, it was spending more money to recover the phones than they were worth.

Despite its genteel bearing and ivory tower reputation, McKinsey is a notoriously competitive place. Gupta was keenly aware of its legendary "up or out" employment philosophy—either you moved up in the organization or you were asked to leave. Though McKinsey partners loathe describing the underpinnings of the company's philosophy this way, "up or out" is an intrinsic part of the firm's business model, a key ingredient to the profitability of the partnership. It allows the firm to stick to the bedrock of keeping the pay of its directors, or senior partners, as steady as its principles.

Every six months during Gupta's early years at McKinsey, a body called the Principal Candidate Evaluation Committee met to elect new partners. On average, it took about six years in the seventies for associates to make it to principal, the term McKinsey gives its junior partners. Some stars made it to principal far earlier; in the case of former head of McKinsey Germany Herbert Henzler, in just four and a half years.

As with almost everything in his early days at McKinsey, Gupta was characteristically late in being named a principal. Every time the partner elections took place, Gupta's friends would ask, "Oh, what happened? You didn't get elected." Gupta would try to shrug it off, saying, "I don't know." He watched as others in his class made principal before he did. It was a nerve-racking time, though Gupta didn't let on to anyone. In January 1980, after almost seven years at the firm, he was elected a junior partner.

Even as Gupta struggled to find his footing at work in the 1970s, home provided comfort. Gupta and Anita married in New Delhi in the summer of 1973. The newly wedded couple rented a studio apartment near Columbia University, where Anita had been accepted to study for her PhD. Gupta's annual salary of $25,000 was generous, but household finances were still tight. Like many immigrants from India at the time, Gupta scrimped and saved so that he could help support his brother and sister back home. He bought $2 shirts at Filene's Basement; he had only two, one to wash and one to iron for the next day. Within a year, he'd sent enough money to his siblings so they could build their own house.

Still, Rajat and Anita's first few years in Manhattan were among their happiest. Their apartment, while small, was perfect for the young couple to get to know each other. On weekends, the two took to the streets of New York, exploring the city together for the first time. Friends from India, who had also come to the United States to study, often visited on weekends, cramming into the Guptas' spartan accommodations. "I spent my first night in the US in that apartment," says Anjan Chatterjee, Gupta's IIT Delhi pal. When Chatterjee settled in Washington, DC, he and his roommate would often drive up on weekends to visit the Guptas. By day, the visiting friends toured New York City landmarks such as the Empire State Building and the Statue of Liberty. At night they camped on the Guptas' floor. Often they would while away the evenings smoking and playing bridge or Scrabble. It was a simple life among trusted companions, much like the one Gupta observed growing up in New Delhi among his parents and their friends.

When Gupta was first approached about going to work for McKinsey in Scandinavia, the assignment was billed as a single study. The hope, however, was that Gupta would find enough to like in Scandinavia that he would want to decamp for a while. Since McKinsey had opened its fledgling Copenhagen office in January 1972, it had lost money—not unlike most of McKinsey's overseas offices in the early years—but unlike the other outposts it hadn't entirely righted itself. Gupta worried that if he were sent overseas, he would be too far from New York, the center of McKinsey power. It was well known that McKinsey partners toiled in the hinterlands for years in the hope of getting to New York from the consulting firm's satellite offices.

Gupta was already in New York. Why would he take on a job that would move him away? It didn't make any sense. Nevertheless, Gupta said he would consider the Scandinavian opportunity, but, like the others before him, he had every intention of rejecting the overture, suspecting that his wife, Anita, would give him the corporate cover to turn down the job.

After finishing her graduate studies at Columbia, Anita took a job working at prestigious Bell Labs doing research at its Holmdel, New Jersey, complex. To make things easier on her, the Guptas bought a house and moved to New Jersey in March 1977. The $75,000 purchase in Middletown, New Jersey, was about five minutes away from her new place of work. When he wasn't at a client's offices, Gupta took the train every day into New York, commuting an hour and a half each way. A year after they moved, the Guptas had their first daughter, Geetanjali. In a nod to his Bengali heritage, they named her after the Nobel Prize–winning epic *Gitanjali*, written by the Bengali poet Rabindranath Tagore. After a short break, Anita returned to work. Her career was flourishing, but like many working women, she was having a tough time juggling it all, balancing the demands of her professional life with raising a child.

To his surprise, when Gupta told Anita about the opportunity to go to Scandinavia, she jumped at it. Since starting her job and having their first child, she felt tugged from all sides. It would be difficult for Anita to leave her job voluntarily; after all, she would be leaving a good company where she had a promising future. But when Gupta was offered the chance to go to Scandinavia, she thought it was an elegant way to quit Bell Labs.

Though he dreaded the transition at first, the more Gupta thought about it, the more he realized he had little to lose by going to Scandinavia. When his IIT friend Chatterjee, who by now had joined McKinsey too, asked if he had any choice about moving, Gupta replied, "I don't think I do." Then he said he thought it would be much harder climbing the ladder at McKinsey in New York. "Let's see what Copenhagen gives," he told Chatterjee.

Gupta approached his first big move since coming to the United States with little fuss or fanfare. McKinsey offered Gupta the chance to visit its Copenhagen office before committing. Gupta was amused. Why would he need to go see a McKinsey office? He knew what people at McKinsey looked like and what their backgrounds were. Visiting was an indulgence he didn't need or want. Why waste company money?

Just before the Guptas were about to move, though, he and Anita took up the firm on a house-hunting trip. They couldn't go for long because their daughter was still a toddler. After spending a day looking at a dozen houses, they realized they weren't going to be able to settle on anything before they left. In a move worthy of a seasoned psychologist—build trust by empowering others with a personal decision—Gupta asked his new colleagues in the office to make the final decision. "Here are the three best ones we like. You could get us either one of these or anything that is similar." One of his colleagues chose his house and, in 1981, the Guptas headed to Copenhagen to live in it.

Scandinavia was "a very homogeneous environment," Gupta would say years later. "When I went there, they had never seen anybody with dark skin and dark eyes, I don't think. It was a very closed environment."

In Copenhagen, the quiet Gupta finally got the chance to show his superiors his promise as a leader. For years, there were whispers about the head of McKinsey's Copenhagen office and his penchant for excessive drinking, but Gupta appreciated the seriousness of the problem only a year after arriving in Scandinavia.

"He was a brilliant guy but an alcoholic," said Gupta years later. "It was beginning to impact his work, and his relationships with clients and colleagues." At first Gupta and two of his peers in the office tried to cover for him and back him up at client meetings to make sure he was not an embarrassment. But "at some point in time, it became a very, very impossible situation," said Gupta. "And there were some very embarrassing incidents and client situations."

Gupta and his colleagues wrestled with the problem for weeks, offering different solutions and discarding them almost as soon as they came up with them. If Gupta raised the matter with New York, his boss would feel that it was a personal betrayal. It could also jeopardize his career. But the man needed help. "Office managers had a lot of power, and no one had the gumption to take him on," says Gupta's IIT friend Chatterjee. What Gupta did was to unite the other partners in the office and convince them that they had to take up the matter with Daniel, McKinsey's then managing director. Gupta built a coalition and then he led it.

Daniel happened to be in Paris for the firm's executive committee meetings when Gupta and two colleagues, a Swede and a Dane, visited him.

"We're having a big professional issue," Gupta told Daniel, and then he went on to explain the problem in the office. The next day, Daniel summoned the Copenhagen office manager to Paris, relieved him of his duties, and had him check into the Betty Ford Center, which treats individuals with drug and alcohol dependencies.

As Gupta expected, his boss was livid because he felt he'd been sold out. But only two years after the partner sought professional help, the two men reconciled. When he returned to Scandinavia after treatment, he invited Gupta and his two colleagues to dinner. They went with some trepidation, knowing that their last meeting had been filled with rancor. The partner, now a recovering alcoholic, was grateful to the consultants for what they had done.

"He had realized that we had saved his life," said Gupta years later, "and he came to thank us...because if he had gone on in the way he had gone on, he probably would not have lived for very long."

Some at McKinsey interpreted Gupta's humility and quiet manner as a sign of weakness. But McKinsey head Ron Daniel knew from his own experience that Gupta was every bit as much the go-getter as the next consultant. Daniel tapped Gupta, then age thirty-two, to run the Scandinavian business, making him one of the youngest consultants at McKinsey to hold the position of office manager.

Gupta turned his taciturn style into a powerful tool with clients. Christian Caspar, a McKinsey colleague, remembers Gupta's presentation of a change-management program for a large corporation. At a pivotal point, when the client wondered if the inevitable disruption was worth it, Gupta, rather than offering his opinion to the client, said nothing. "He just looked them right in the eyes," says Caspar. "A minute must have passed in silence. It was quite effective, because the client had to make the decision. It wasn't ours to make."

Gupta's rise coincided with Daniel's makeover of McKinsey. Daniel recognized that McKinsey needed to innovate and offer clients much more than a nearby regional office. Strategic, organizational, and operational expertise was required. McKinsey's best consultants were put in charge of developing new thinking in each area: Fred Gluck in strategy, Tom Peters and Bob Waterman in organization, and other stars from Cleveland and Germany in operations. "What a change," exults Skilling. "*In Search of Excellence* was researched and developed and the strategy effort came up with world-beating, actually BCG-beating ideas. Even the operations guys developed some powerful tools. Suddenly McKinsey was leading the thinking."

Unlike its rivals BCG and Bain, which had office scale, McKinsey's average office size was small, making it imperative that its managers embrace an office-to-office esprit de corps. Some of the old guard, the entrenched office managers protecting their power base, resisted the shift. But Gupta embraced it.

Skilling remembers being invited to speak to two of Gupta's clients. In one instance, in his role as head of McKinsey's natural gas practice, he talked to a Scandinavian energy company about the impact of deregulation. Another time, in his role as head of McKinsey's North American chemical practice, Skilling discussed the microeconomics of commodity chemical prices so that the client could figure out how to better model the economics of an acquisition. During the meetings, Skilling was struck by the "low-key, comfortable relationship" that Gupta had with the client executive. "He didn't ever try to show that he 'knew everything,'" Skilling says. "There was a lot of question asking and Rajat would ask a lot of questions—he was amazingly willing to show his lack of knowledge and uncertainty. He felt no need to be all knowing, something that a lot of partners had a tough time with."

The meetings Skilling had in Scandinavia with Gupta's clients were different from others he had with other offices. In those meetings, the local manager would act as a go-between, not a colleague. The office chiefs would dissociate themselves from their visiting McKinsey colleague until it was clear that their client was on board with the advice. "I could understand this posture since it gave the local people a second shot if something went wrong, but it was a bit cowardly," says Skilling. "Rajat didn't play that game. He was up front and transparent. The term 'trustworthy' often came to mind."

By the time Gupta was ready to leave Scandinavia in 1986, he had grown the McKinsey practice from 15 to 125 professionals, expanding its reach into Norway, *and* he had made it profitable. "To this day, our competitors find it hard to compete with us in that region," Daniel says of the historic strength of McKinsey's practice in Scandinavia. Skilling believes that Gupta's achievements there were profound and that his approach "probably foreshadowed McKinsey's phenomenal worldwide success in the late 80s and early 90s."

Gupta made plans to leave Scandinavia during the Christmas holiday. To say good-bye and mark his time in the office, Christian Caspar, his successor, hosted a farewell party, to which he invited all the partners in Scandinavia. Caspar arranged for children to sing Christmas carols. He even organized a Santa Claus for the occasion.

When Santa appeared, Caspar told Gupta that it fell to him to guess who Santa was. As hard as Gupta tried, he couldn't fathom the identity of Santa, who stayed mute. Gupta was about to give up when Santa finally spoke. The conscience of the company had flown four thousand miles to personally thank him.

Santa Claus was Marvin Bower.

CHAPTER ELEVEN

The Camera Never Lies

In the spring of 1998, Intel Corporation did something extraordinary. It installed a hidden video camera above a new fax machine at its Santa Clara, California, offices. By design, the fax feeder required that documents be laid faceup on the machine so that the overhead camera would capture an image of the document being faxed. Intel also installed a camera in a fabric divider panel to record the face of the faxer. And without the specific employee's knowledge, the semiconductor giant fixed a hidden camera above her desk and recorded her comings and goings. The time clock on the digital camera was synchronized with the clock on the fax so that there would be no dispute over when a specific document caught on camera was actually faxed.

After complaints two years earlier from investors, Intel resorted to these unprecedented measures to plug internal leaks of sensitive corporate information. Early investigations of its phone records turned the company's suspicions to a junior employee working in Intel's product-marketing area. The worker raised a red flag herself when she told a colleague that she had access to important data on computer chip sales. "If you sell this information, you can get real money for it," she remarked.

In the mid-1990s big institutional investors noticed that some of Intel's most sensitive financial data was leaking into the market before it was publicly released. Institutional investors—mutual funds, insurance companies, banks, hedge funds, and pension funds—invest large pools of money. They buy and sell hundreds of millions of dollars of stock in companies like Intel every day. They live and die on quarterly profit figures (publicly traded companies are required to report earnings or losses every three months) and make large bets in the stock market in anticipation of a company's earnings. If earnings exceed analyst expectations, a company's stock usually rises. If a company misses projections, the stock usually declines.

An investor who has an early bead on quarterly earnings can make a killing—and show up his rivals along the way. Those whose performance declines face the risk of losing customers. Knowing the earnings of a company before they are announced is the holy grail in the information-gathering game, but even nuggets like the number of computer chips a technology company like Intel sells and the price at which they are sold can be extraordinarily valuable. Production figures also provide a savvy investor with an astonishingly accurate tally of the company's revenue.

Many investors had come to believe that someone at Intel was divulging confidential information about the company before its earnings were announced. The recipient of the information was widely thought to be a fast-rising analyst at a boutique investment bank named Needham & Co. The information the Needham analyst Raj Rajaratnam was receiving was making its way into a must-read newsletter Rajaratnam published entitled *First Call*. The investors were livid over the leaks. Many of them competed with Rajaratnam for money to manage, and by 1998, Rajaratnam had gone from being a behind-the-scenes research analyst who produced reports for star traders like them to being a fearsome rival. He now trolled for money in the same investing waters as they did. And he was drawing a boatload of it.

Just a year earlier, in 1997, after a decade at Needham, Rajaratnam had struck out on his own. He had been chafing for some time, tired of his job as a manager dealing with mundane matters. "I was spending two or three hours a day as a shrink dealing with people issues, organizational issues and strategic planning issues," he remembers. He was also frustrated that the firm's owner, George

Needham, did not share his ambition to grow the company. Needham liked to say that he could see the face of every client on every dollar that the firm took in. Employees suspected Rajaratnam did not care one bit whose face was gracing the dollars flowing in. He just wanted to book more dollars.

In January, he and three lieutenants from Needham—Gary Rosenbach; Krishen Sud, his close chum from his days at Wharton; and Ari Arjavalingam—launched the Galleon Group. Galleon was yet another hedge fund, one of thousands of lightly regulated investment pools targeted to wealthy investors and institutions. The funds charge a small percentage of a client's assets as a managing fee, but they make the real money on profits, typically charging 20 percent on the dollar for any return they provide the client.

Few knew it at the time, but Rajaratnam's arrival would coincide with one of the hedge fund industry's greatest periods of growth. Within a decade after he set up Galleon, assets at hedge funds would swell to nearly $1.5 trillion compared to $257 billion in 1996, and the number of hedge funds would triple to a little over seven thousand from about twenty-four hundred. Along the way, the industry would mint a whole new class of billionaires. Unlike the tycoons of bygone times, who husbanded their money discreetly, the titans of the hedge fund world were all too ready to flash their cash. One of the most visible was Steven A. Cohen, the founder of SAC Capital Advisors, who ranked fortieth in 2012 on the Forbes 400 list of richest Americans. A Wharton grad, Cohen grew SAC from $25 million in assets in 1992 to $14 billion today. He lives in a massive 1920s estate in north Greenwich, Connecticut. Cohen bought the property for $14.8 million in 1998. He then added a twelve-thousand-square-foot annex with a basketball court, an indoor pool, and a movie theater that seats twenty. The palatial property houses Cohen's humongous art collection—an eclectic mix that includes masterworks of Cézanne, Picasso, Damien Hirst, and Jeff Koons.

When Rajaratnam started, he worked out of a cramped and shabby office on Lexington and Fifty-Seventh Street, about a block from his old company Needham, managing about $350 million that he cobbled together from close friends and family. His firm was called Galleon Group after the large ships that traded in spices and ivory with Sri Lanka, his birthplace, known long ago as the Isle of Serendip. Galleon stuck to its knitting. It drew on Rajaratnam's expertise, technology stocks. On the walls of his new office, he hung prints of galleons, and on the sides of the room he displayed models of ships. On his desk, he had a small flag signifying his support for the Tamil cause. To kick off his new venture, he reached out to the prominent Silicon Valley executives he'd cultivated over the years.

As an analyst, Rajaratnam had written copious research reports on their fledgling firms, which had long been neglected by big Wall Street investment banks. It was he who exposed their companies to institutional investors in the first place. Emboldened by the success he had managing their money in the small hedge fund he ran on the side at Needham, he went back to the same people to seed Galleon. Many of his early investors were familiar names in the tech space—men like Ken Levy of KLA Instruments, Neil Bonke of Electroglas, and Kris Chellam of Xilinx. Just as he did at Needham, he would rely on some of them, such as Chellam, to serve as his eyes and ears on the industry. He was not shy about the role they played in Galleon's success. In marketing tours and early pitch books, he highlighted the fact that around seventy-five officers of tech companies were also investors in Galleon.

Like many South Asians, Rajaratnam was close to his parents. Impressed by his hot streak, his father—a soft-spoken and conservative businessman who loathed risk—invested in his new hedge fund. He and his wife lived with their son and daughter-in-law in a postwar building at Sutton Place, a tony enclave of apartments overlooking the East River. At one time Marilyn Monroe lived at the address with her then husband playwright Arthur Miller, and today it counts among its famous residents former New York governor Mario Cuomo. When Rajaratnam first moved in, he was hardly a bold-faced name on Wall Street. Neighbors suspected his lack of stature accounted for his buying into one of the community's least desirable buildings. But that didn't stop him from making the most of his purchase. In 2000, when he moved to combine the two apartments he owned at 60 Sutton Place, he told city officials that he needed two kitchens for religious reasons. Typically, only one kitchen per unit is allowed. The reason cited in his application was "adherence to Jewish traditions," whch seemed a stretch for a Hindu. Rajaratnam liked to game the system—not just at work but even at home.

He could not have picked a better moment to pour money into technology stocks. The industry was on the cusp of an intoxicating bubble that would make brash young kids—the exuberant entrepreneurs of the tech world—wealthy overnight. The surge began on August 9, 1995, when Netscape, the brainchild of Marc Andreessen, then a twenty-three-year-old computer prodigy, went public. Netscape made Web browsers that ordinary people could use. It transformed the Internet, making it accessible to millions and millions of consumers. It spawned a virtual world with a revolutionary new business platform where in time hundreds of billions of dollars in commerce would flow. Between 1995 and 1999, 435 technology companies debuted on the stock market, start-ups including Yahoo!, Amazon, and Akamai Technologies, raising a little over $21 billion in capital.

Rajaratnam had a vision and the experience analyzing tech companies to understand the potential of the Internet. He believed it would eclipse the first revolution in tech—the personal computer—as an economic force. Many thought he was crazy, but his reasoning was sound. "It took the personal computer industry about six years to reach ten million users," Rajaratnam told Antoine Bernheim, the publisher of *Hedge Fund News*, in an interview in April 1997, just four months after he set up shop. By contrast, the Internet had 10 million users in only ten months.

He knew it was not enough to be investing in a hot area. If Galleon was to be huge, it needed cachet. So he stacked its board of advisers with impressive names including hedge fund titan Stanley Druckenmiller and Paine Webber chief Don Marron. Druckenmiller and Rajaratnam had gotten to know each other when Druckenmiller was at Soros and Rajaratnam was at Needham. Druckenmiller had a clutch of Wall Street analysts he trusted for insightful research, and Rajaratnam, the number one semiconductor analyst on the street, was one of them. When Rajaratnam launched Galleon, Drucken-miller and his mentor, George Soros, threw some money his way. He had made money for them as an analyst at Needham. They had no reason to believe he wouldn't make money for them again as a hedge fund trader.

Rajaratnam quickly moved to staff his new firm with analysts and portfolio managers from Wall Street's Ivy League, Goldman Sachs and Morgan Stanley. The Needham name was simply not going to bring in investor dollars, so he created his own A-team. He hired Prem Lachman, a health-care analyst from Goldman; David Slaine, a trader from Morgan Stanley; and, as Galleon grew, he brought on board Rick Schutte and Rick Sherlund, the Goldman software analyst who helped take Microsoft public.

On the surface, Galleon had the veneer of a respectable hedge fund whose returns flowed from Rajaratnam's undeniable expertise as a technology analyst. And Rajaratnam, its captain, exuded the aura of an upstanding money manager. After having breakfast with his family, he generally walked to his office on Fifty-Seventh Street, a short walk from his apartment on Sutton Place. Every day at 8:30 a.m. sharp, Galleon's analysts and portfolio managers and traders gathered to review the companies that were reporting earnings that day and discuss other market-impacting developments. Rajaratnam would sit like a general at the head of a long conference table and fire a barrage of questions. He was a stickler for punctuality. At a firm that shelled out multimillion-dollar bonuses every year, analysts and portfolio managers routinely tripped over each other to make it to the meeting on time to avoid Rajaratnam's $25 fine for latecomers.

Even as the firm grew, Rajaratnam made it a point to know if an analyst had recommended buying the stock of a company that later posted abysmal profits or selling a stock about to surge. Whenever that happened, Rajaratnam was legendary for his public floggings. He liked to reduce grown men to quivering sacks of jelly, but only when appropriate. A keen leader, Rajaratnam also knew when it was best to be ice-cold.

When Galleon's restaurant analyst predicted that McDonald's would report disappointing same-store sales only to watch in horror as the company posted better-than-expected sales and its stock price rose, Rajaratnam confronted the analyst: "Tell us what happened."

"People ate a lot of burgers this month," the analyst deadpanned. No one laughed.

Though it didn't appear that any Galleon funds had taken a position based on the analyst's call, Rajaratnam was livid. He couldn't believe the analyst had the nerve to make a joke about something so serious. Rajaratnam knew it was not the time for showing explosive rage. Displays of anger signaled a loss of control. Instead, a week later the analyst was let go in a collective culling.

Rajaratnam told prospective investors that the fund's returns were driven by "bottoms-up research" carried out by a team of analysts who visited more than three hundred companies a month. Analysts were urged to travel as much as they wanted and to visit as many companies as they could. Rajaratnam had only one requirement: at the end of the day, the analysts had to email or fax an explanation of what they learned during their company visit. If they didn't, their travel expenses were not reimbursed.

When Galleon started, eight of its ten analysts were engineers by training and worked in the technology industry. David Blaustein, the manager who ran Galleon's health-care fund for a time, got his start as an emergency room/trauma doctor at Yale University before arriving on Wall Street in the mid-1990s. Rajaratnam liked to boast that his analysts weren't "blindsided by the marketing hype." An engineer by training himself, he often said it was easier to teach an engineer how to pick stocks than to teach engineering to a stock picker.

Rajaratnam imbued Galleon with his playful and fun-loving personality. On Thursdays, employees could sign up for massages at the office. He would hold job interviews at the topless club Scores. And in the hothouse culture of the Galleon trading floor, he indulged his passion for pranks. Traders who made bets and lost would be required to spend the day wearing lingerie. He would offer $5,000 to anyone who would drink ten tequila shots or $1,000 if they could eat a whole loaf of bread without drinking a glass of water. Even as the firm grew and his stature rose, he acquiesced in the freewheeling culture.

In the summer of 2008, as the economy was quickly sliding into a recession, Rajaratnam gave a junior female employee an interesting assignment: he supplied her with a budget to buy clothes and accessories from retailer Lululemon Athletica. At the morning meeting, Rajaratnam, feigning sincere analysis, remarked that he thought few consumers would pay for the pricey gear in a recession. Then Rajaratnam pushed the woman to explain to the mostly male analysts and portfolio managers the reason the company's clothes resonated with consumers. As part of her presentation, she donned a black Spandex outfit and did a turn around the room. When someone suggested she should stand up on the conference table and model the outfit as if she were a fashion show runway model, Galleon's chief operating officer, Rick Schutte, pressed for the display to stop.

In many traditional ways, Rajaratnam conducted business at Galleon just as he had done at Needham. Like his mentor, George Needham, he pinched pennies, hounding assistants about the amount of money the office spent on essentials like paper. Employees were required to fly economy, and when they stayed in hotels they were not allowed to use the minibar. A budget for travel had to be approved before the trip was taken. He also adopted the fast-and-loose operating style that had worked so well for him at Needham. In early marketing materials, pitching his new fund to investors, he laid out his historic returns even though Galleon had come into existence only in January 1997. In making his claim, Rajaratnam relied on the performance he had generated at the small hedge fund he ran at Needham.

Deep analysis and a lean expense ledger were not the only core competencies at Galleon. Rajaratnam's secret sauce was that he was an expert manipulator. He knew just the right way to push corporate insiders to pass along confidential financial information long before it was publicly released. And with his own money riding on Galleon, he squeezed them harder than ever before.

James Bagley met Rajaratnam in the early 1990s when he was president and chief operating officer of Applied Materials, a Santa Clara, California, maker of silicon-chip-manufacturing machines. "He was always just a little bit slick for me," says Bagley. "He was always kind of pressing you for information." He wanted details about customers and other companies that Bagley declined to answer. Often, Bagley says, Rajaratnam would present him with a nugget of information and "then he would want you to confirm it." "Several times," particularly after Rajaratnam moved to Galleon, he would suggest trades of information, but Bagley says he stayed clear. "I didn't want to have anything to do with him," he says.

Not everyone felt that way. In his decade in the banking industry at Chase and then at Needham, Rajaratnam had developed close ties to Silicon Valley's expatriate South Asian community. Like Rajaratnam on Wall Street, many of them started in Silicon Valley in the early 1980s, when South Asians were rare. Segregated from their Wonder Bread colleagues, the new arrivals from South Asia bonded easily, forging intimate friendships in the workplace.

Unusual alliances arose—even between Hindus and Muslims—more often out of mutual need than real kinship. To get ahead, one needed connections. Besides the Atmel Corp. executive Kris Chellam, one of Rajaratnam's best "friends" in Silicon Valley was a thirty-nine-year-old product-marketing engineer at Intel named Roomy Khan.

Like other South Asians, Khan, who traced her roots back to New Delhi, came to America in the fall of 1982 to study. She was twenty-four years old, past the perfect age to find a suitable boy. But Khan had never been the kind to hew to convention. Even as a young girl, she was plucky, vivacious, and every bit as driven as the men around her—not exactly the best résumé for marriage in a country like India, where arranged unions were still commonplace. When Khan got a scholarship to study in the United States, she jumped at the opportunity. She told her parents that if they didn't give her the money for the plane ticket, she would borrow it and go.

Rajaratnam and Khan first got to know each other in 1995, when Khan was working in Intel's microprocessor group and Rajaratnam was still at Needham. As part of her job, Khan tracked expert analysts in the semiconductor industry, and there was no one as well regarded in the tech space as Rajaratnam. One day, Khan telephoned Rajaratnam about Advanced Micro Devices, Intel's rival in semiconductor production. The two hit it off and found they had a lot in common; Rajaratnam's wife, a Sikh, was from Punjab just like Khan. When the two women met some time later, they spoke in their native language, Punjabi.

"I wish I had spoken to you a few months ago," before joining Intel, Khan joked to Rajaratnam. Her dream, she confessed, was to work on Wall Street, not to be carrying out boring market research for a semiconductor company.

"Oh, you can still do that," replied Rajaratnam.

As it happened, when Khan approached him, Rajaratnam was in the market for a semiconductor analyst and Khan fit his hiring profile. She was highly educated—after Kent State, she got a master's degree in electrical engineering from Columbia University and an MBA from Berkeley—and, more important, she'd worked at a number of companies in the tech space, including the biggest player, Intel. Later in the year, Rajaratnam met her in Menlo Park and, just as he had promised, he offered her a job. The only condition was that she would have to move to New York to train.

Khan was torn. She wanted to break into Wall Street, but she knew if she accepted the offer it would probably mean the end of her marriage. Her husband, Sakhawat, was a traditional Asian Muslim man who liked to have his wife by his side, not burnishing her career three thousand miles away. She turned down the job, but Rajaratnam kept her in mind. From time to time, he would help her get interviews for analyst positions at brokerage firms such as Prudential Securities and Robertson Stephens. Unlike other analysts Khan knew, Rajaratnam was more of a friend than a business acquaintance. The two would have dinner together, sometimes with their spouses, when Rajaratnam visited California.

For Rajaratnam, it was part of doing business. His cultivation of Khan as a future source of inside information was perfect. Even before he ever asked her for anything, he made her feel that she owed him. He had gone out of his way to help her get a job on Wall Street, something she desperately wanted, making introductions to other companies and even offering her a job himself. So one day, when he would turn around and quiz her about the inner workings at her employer, Intel, she was happy to repay the favor. But answering one question made answering the next one easier. In December 1996, Khan called Rajaratnam and discovered he was leaving Needham to set up his own company. He suggested the two stay in touch.

Rajaratnam's first year at Galleon was heady. Four months after the hedge fund opened its doors, it was up 3 percent. Money started flooding in; investors were drawn by Galleon's impressive returns and the growing hype over tech. "Ask around the street about the market's hottest tech investor, and the name you keep hearing is Raj Rajaratnam," gushed *Barron's* in November 1997.

The glowing review masked a rocky patch that Galleon hit in the fall of 1997. Galleon was long—or had bullish bets—on technology stocks. After the Asian financial crisis triggered uncertainty, investors ran to less risky assets and shed their tech positions. In October alone, Galleon lost between 10 and 12 percent of its value. Rajaratnam needed to right his Galleon or the $800 million fund would sail away from him.

Rajaratnam picked up the phone and lobbed a call to his old friend from Intel, Khan. He flat out wanted to know how Intel was doing.

In all the years Khan had known him, Rajaratnam had never broached the topic of Intel with her. As he was not shy in his questioning with others, his behavior seemed to indicate that he saw Khan as a Hail Mary ask—the one favor to call in only if he absolutely had to. In her position, Khan had access to Intel's microprocessor bookings, which provide a snapshot of Intel's customers' expectations of their future demand: how many chips they would need in the coming months—not firm purchase orders, but estimates for Intel to keep a handle on its production. The reports list the top twenty personal computer customers and their upcoming demand for Intel processors. For a stock investor making a bet on a company's future performance, the reports were a gold mine. They could be used to figure out the anticipated revenue numbers for Intel (number of chips sold multiplied by the wholesale price equals revenue).

From then on, Rajaratnam brazenly called Khan every week at her Intel office to get the booking reports. He would ask Khan to verify rumors he was hearing in the market about Intel. Soon she was volunteering information. She passed along data she gleaned from colleagues. At first she was careful, communicating only over Intel's logged telephone line. It didn't raise eyebrows; her job as a market researcher involved talking to hedge fund managers and analysts. But later, strapped for time, she would fax documents to him. Khan never asked Rajaratnam what he did with the information, but given the business he was in, she naturally assumed he used it to trade stocks. Now when she complained about working at Intel, Rajaratnam would urge her to stay. He even offered to give her some extra money if she remained.

On March 6, 1998, Khan faxed a number of sheets of paper marked "Intel Confidential" to a fax number in New York. The papers laid out in great detail Intel's most sensitive and closely guarded customer order information. The "book to billing" reports not only listed the number of chip orders booked by several dozen major PC makers; they listed the actual number of chips shipped. With this information, any savvy analyst could divine Intel's future financial performance. More than two weeks later, on March 24, Khan faxed several pages of handwritten notes to a number Intel later learned belonged to Galleon. The notations on the faxed pages showed Intel's average selling price and the units sold for the first quarter of 1998. By doing some simple math and multiplying the two numbers, an analyst could arrive at Intel's revenue for the quarter. Comparing the confidential information about Intel's average selling price to similar reports for previous publicly announced quarterly information would give an ordinary analyst an extraordinary window into Intel's business. With a little work, an analyst could quickly figure out how well Intel's newer and more profitable computer chips were selling. Unbeknownst to Khan, each time she faxed anything, the hidden camera that Intel had fixed above the fax machine captured her every movement.

CHAPTER TWELVE

The Corner Office

After turning around Scandinavia, Rajat Gupta had the pick of his next McKinsey posting in the United States. Instead of returning to New York, he decided to try Chicago, a city he barely knew. A partner he was close to in the New York office had moved to the Chicago office some years earlier and suggested Gupta join him. As he did when he moved to Scandinavia, Gupta asked a colleague to buy him a house. This time, he didn't even go on a house-hunting trip. His colleague and his wife recommended a home for the Guptas and he bought it sight unseen. Happily for the colleague, the Guptas loved it.

At McKinsey during the late eighties, there were several avenues for advancement. Some rose by building tight client relationships and bringing in new assignments. Others moved ahead on the force of their intellect, creating studies that could help rethink entire industries. The least likely path to being a mover and a shaker was through managing. Gupta had built a reputation as a consummate manager, but he was at a company where managing was not revered.

McKinsey always accorded the highest respect to partners who served clients well. It was rare for a successful partner to aspire to a leadership role within the firm. But Gupta knew his selling point at McKinsey was as a leader. What made him successful in Scandinavia despite his outsider status was his ability to marshal the resources of the firm, connect colleagues from all over the McKinsey universe, and effectively help his team deliver for the clients they served. Not unlike his father, Ashwini Gupta, who could deliver eight tickets on a sold-out train to a needy group of young men, so could his son Rajat deliver the goods for a needy client.

And at a very young age, when most of his colleagues were sharp-elbowing each other in a bid to get ahead, Gupta mastered the art of enlightened management. He learned that he would succeed by making others successful. In his early years, when he struggled as an associate, he focused on pleasing his superiors rather than shining a light on his own work. As he matured, he fell back on lessons he'd picked up as a young boy following his father to Nehru's press conferences. Rajat observed that the Indian prime minister would make a point of working his way through a line and meeting everyone. Years later, he would do the same, making every person feel important, just as Nehru had, with great success.

Three years after Gupta got to Chicago, the office manager, Michael Murray, a friend and mentor, rotated off the job. Heading an office or being a member of one of McKinsey's personnel committees was always a highly coveted and powerful position. The personnel committees controlled promotion and in some instances compensation too. Office managers could make or break careers at McKinsey. Their power came from their control of staff assignments. They chose who got to work for which clients. Favorites got plum projects, while those not in the manager's inner circle got the rest. "Think of political patronage," says Skilling.

Gupta came to learn that Fred Gluck, then managing director, planned to name a new head of the Chicago office and that it was not going to be him. Gluck was of the view that after Scandinavia, Gupta did not need more management experience; moreover, he had someone else in mind for the Chicago job. It was a young director named Dick Ashley, a veteran of the Chicago office who knew the city well.

Gupta chewed over the prospect of the position going to someone else without having a chance to vie for it. *This is not right*, he thought to himself. *I do want to manage the Chicago office.* Even though he hadn't been in Chicago for long, he had earned the respect of his colleagues. The consultants in Chicago were a tight group; many, including Gupta, lived near each other in the affluent Chicago suburbs of Winnetka or Wilmette. On weekends, they socialized together with their new and growing families in tow.

Besides Geetanjali, the Guptas by now had two other daughters, Megha and Aditi. Despite the grueling travel regimen that accompanied a life in consulting, Gupta always found the time to change diapers, give baths, and soothe colicky babies. Often his wife, Anita, would find her jet-lagged, sleep-deprived husband lying on the family room couch with a baby resting on his chest.

As the Gupta girls grew older, their father played a hands-on role in their education. His specialty was mathematics. Every Saturday morning Gupta would wake up early, often after flying back late Friday evening, so he could tutor Geetanjali, the eldest, in math. It was important for their father to spend the little time he had "with us, not merely around us," recalled Aditi. In a family of voracious readers, Gupta would urge his daughters to put down their books so they could participate in joint activities such as family breakfasts and team cleaning. "Moral support" was one of his buzzwords. If one daughter was assigned a tedious task like cleaning her room, Gupta encouraged anyone hanging around to keep the other company. "If we resisted, it was pointed out that this was a breach of one's 'moral support' duty," recalled Megha.

As he had in his student days at Harvard, Gupta struck a balance between assimilating and retaining his Indian values and lifestyle. The Guptas decorated their home with Indian artifacts and paintings, and their daughters addressed their dad as "Baba." He in turn would call them by their Indian pet names.

When the Guptas first arrived in the United States, Christmas and Thanksgiving were just days off. But as the girls grew up, the family started celebrating the Western holidays as exuberantly as they did Diwali, the Hindu festival of lights. Extended family would descend from all corners of the country. Stragglers were welcomed too. The day before the holiday, the group, numbering thirty or so, would do the shopping and start preparing the feast. Gupta, the patriarch, who at home liked to slip into a long, loose, collarless shirt with matching pants known as a kurta pajama, pitched in.

During the feast, Gupta was one of the quietest members of the party. But after dinner he liked to draw his guests into playing cards or a board game like Scrabble or Pictionary. In the throes of competition, he came to life. Amid a game of Pictionary, the quiet Gupta could outshout anyone. Friends suspected that Gupta, a bridge fanatic, enjoyed the intellectual challenge as much as the thrill of winning. Scrabble to him was not just a sport of words; it was an exercise in gamesmanship. He always had an uncanny knack of knowing which tiles remained in the bag. And whatever the game, he approached it with the same focus that he applied to everything in life. Once a son's friend was obsessed with yo-yos and adept at performing all sorts of tricks with them. Gupta wanted to do the same, so he took directions from an eleven-year-old and practiced until he perfected the art of yo-yoing.

Like other Indian immigrants, the Guptas placed a high premium on education and family—not just the immediate Gupta clan but the extended family too. Gupta was "Baba" to his kids and "Big Baba" to a passel of nephews and nieces in India. They remembered his visits as Christmas come early. He and Anita would arrive with huge suitcases stuffed with gifts and chocolate and clothes. In the scarcity-filled India of the 1970s and 1980s, the Guptas knew their presents meant a lot. Over time, the Guptas lavished more expensive gifts on their families—a MacBook Pro, for example. In doing so, they were typical of an up-and-coming generation of Indian immigrants who were starting to prosper in the United States and wanted to share the fruits of their success with their families back in India.

In 1984, Gupta's father-in-law died unexpectedly, leaving the Mattoo family without a patriarch. Gupta assumed the mantle immediately, doing everything from making sure the Mattoo family could live one more year in government employee housing to taking on the role of baba to Anita's youngest brother, Arvind, who, like Gupta, was a teenager when he was orphaned. During the holidays, their home in the United States became his home. When Anita's younger sister came under pressure to marry after her father's death, Gupta suggested another path: come to America and go to business school. He helped her pick the schools, guided her through the treacherous application process, and then lent her the tuition.

Gupta knew he would have the support of the Chicago office if he was named its head. But to stick up his hand for the job ran counter to the culture of the firm. "It is your decision," Gupta told Gluck. But "I don't want to take myself out of the running. I won't make it easy for you. You really have to decide whether you want to have me" or someone else.

Gluck, who had grown up in a one-bedroom apartment with his parents, grandmother, and five siblings in Brooklyn, was not easily swayed. But as he mulled the Chicago position, a number of senior consultants in the office approached him and told him that they would prefer Gupta over his pick, Ashley. At one point, Gluck got a call from Mike Murray, the outgoing office manager, who said he was acting as a spokesperson for the Chicago office. His advice? Pick Gupta for the job.

In the end, Gupta believes Gluck asked him to lead the office "against his wishes—in the sense he wanted to make somebody else the office manager...not because he didn't like me or anything like that." However, "clearly I had the experience and I had the followership and he couldn't do anything else." The episode was instructive. Gupta easily could have let things lie, but he was happy that he was honest with himself and had spoken up to Gluck about his aspirations.

"Frankly, if I had not done that, I would have always regretted it," he said years later.

By the late 1980s, Gupta's career at McKinsey was picking up speed. Gone was the shy and slightly awkward HBS grad. As the head of the Chicago office, Gupta developed a reputation as a quietly effective manager. Even though McKinsey operated under the "one firm" policy, meaning that its partners were compensated based on the overall performance of the firm, people knew by the late eighties that Chicago—and Gupta's previous stomping ground Scandinavia—was highly profitable. If they weren't making money, McKinsey would not have staffed up.

The commercial success helped Gupta get noticed. In 1988, when Gluck was elected managing director, Gupta was actually one of the candidates on the nominating "slate of seven." At the time Gupta was placed on the ballot, he was in his late thirties; his rivals were a decade older than him.

"It was kind of a three-hundred-and-sixty-degree circle. I remember a time where I was late for everything in the firm," said Gupta several years later. "And this time, it seemed I was early for everything in the firm."

Though it was not apparent to the outside world, there was a generational shift going on at the firm during Gupta's years in Chicago that was an outgrowth of the economic pressures the firm faced during the early seventies. An older, client-focused generation was giving way to one that was more focused on revenue. And wherever Gupta went—be it Scandinavia or Chicago—revenue followed.

By the time Gluck was set to retire, McKinsey had grown significantly—its revenues doubled in his six years in the job to $1.2 billion. But in a harbinger of the future, 60 percent of that revenue came from overseas. The field was wide open for a new managing director to be a non-American—a first. John A. Byrne, writing in *BusinessWeek* magazine in September 1993, offered a rare peek into the succession dance. "Many insiders believe McKinsey may well elect the first non-American to head the firm. Among the front-runners: Christian Caspar in Scandinavia, Lukas Muehlemann in Switzerland, Norman Sanson in London and Henzler in Germany." Besides the four foreigners, there was an American candidate too, Don Waite, the head of the New York office. But the ultimate McKinsey insider had yet to commit to anyone.

It was well known that Caspar was a long shot. Even after Gupta's growth push, Scandinavia was still too small to matter. Sanson was seen as more of the same: another Anglo-Saxon candidate. And near the eleventh hour, Lukas Muehlemann, McKinsey's Swiss chief, bowed out of the race. Following a path taken by many before him, he left to take the CEO job at a client, Swiss Re.

As a member of the same generation, it was clear that Waite, the chairman of McKinsey's all-important Directors Review Committee, was Gluck's pick. And there was no doubt that he had the support of his troops in New York, one of the most powerful constituencies at McKinsey. Waite was considered and circumspect; since the mid-seventies he'd focused on building up McKinsey's banking practice, which at the time represented only 3 percent of the firm's client activities. By 1983, the financial institutions practice, which now included the insurance group, accounted for about a quarter of McKinsey's work in New York and London alone. It was the firm's largest practice. But if the conservative Waite was elected, there was no question he would put the brakes on growth. He let it be known that he felt the firm grew too fast in the eighties and that it "strained the fabric of the place."

Unlike Waite, Herbert Henzler was all about growth and being a star. He was larger-than-life—his nickname was "the colossus of Germany," a moniker that fit exceedingly well. His clients were old-line German giants including the industrial behemoth Siemens and carmaker Daimler—before it became DaimlerChrysler. Everything he did—even skiing—he accomplished with his outsized personality and drive. He was a contender by virtue of his enormous success in building up McKinsey's German practice. Apart from a brief downward blip following reunification in the early 1990s, Germany was viewed as the firm's most successful in terms of new recruits, client size, and penetration outside the United States.

But few actually thought Henzler would win the support of the partnership and be elected to the top spot. He was a maverick who spoke his mind. When asked to evaluate McKinsey's New York office, he rankled partners with his scathing critiques. From time to time, for instance, McKinsey would look at metrics like the number of Fortune 500 companies headquartered in big cities. New York was off the chart. Henzler would openly point to some of the large corporations in Manhattan that his colleagues in New York were not serving. The shot across the bow was on target but not a tactic that won friends.

Historically, the person picked to lead McKinsey was a reflection of the firm's aspirations. Before Gluck was elected, there was a broad desire among McKinsey's directors for the firm to step up its knowledge-building efforts—the rising competition from BCG and Bain made it a commercial imperative. In 1994, when Gluck was set to step down, there was a desire that McKinsey's new leader embody the varied complexion of the firm and be more client-centric.

"By the end of the 80s, there was a growing group within the firm that felt the pendulum swung too far towards practice development," says Skilling. "And that the practice development machine that Fred Gluck created outstripped the firm's ability to channel the thinking into specific clients. I think that at that point Rajat became the model of a different balance...There was a strong sense that what Fred built in the 80s was critical for the firm and Rajat would positively modify it for the future. This created a strong following among all the partners and directors, but particularly among the younger ones."

Gupta's election in March 1994 to the position of global managing director was a watershed in the history of sixty-eight-year-old McKinsey. By electing an Indian to its helm, McKinsey left no doubt that the firm was confidently embracing a diverse and global future and turning its back on a homogeneous past. Gupta always made it clear that he thought the criticism McKinsey received for being too patrician was overblown. "Did I ever find a glass ceiling?" he rhetorically asked years later. "I never found a glass ceiling partly because McKinsey is a truly meritocratic institution and partly because most glass ceilings are people in their minds, rather than true."

Despite the obvious symbolism of McKinsey having a non-American at its helm, Gupta's rise was important for another less-talked-about reason. At forty-five, Gupta was a member of McKinsey's up-and-coming new guard. Having received Marvin Bower's blessing in Scandinavia, he was the perfect person to bridge the chasm between the two generations. His quiet, measured manner was also exactly the kind of leadership style that McKinsey was prepared to accept from its first non-American chief. Someone like the German chief, Henzler, would have been too much for McKinsey to stomach. "He got the job because two stronger personalities were competing heavily," says Bala Balachandran, a friend of Gupta's from Chicago. "Rajat was the compromise candidate. He was sort of a consensus developer, not an antagonizer. They liked him because he was non-threatening."

Still, the old guard were blindsided by his elevation. Some of the elder statesmen who had squarely placed their chips on more traditional candidates tried to discount Gupta's victory. They claimed that there was a campaign to elect Gupta, an effort that involved heavy lobbying and phone calls between directors in various offices. McKinsey never formally educated its voting directors about the candidates. While it was not uncommon for there to be phone calls among various offices about potential candidates, some of the old guard felt that the lobbying before the 1994 election was unprecedented. Gupta's friends stumped hard for him.

When Gluck got wind of the grumblings, he wondered out loud whether the organized push had been orchestrated by Gupta himself. It was eerily similar to the events in 1990, when he was all but prepared to name Dick Ashley as the manager of the Chicago office and then he got the call from Murray telling him Gupta was the office's pick.

What Gluck may have underestimated was the voting power of the Skilling generation. Had Skilling not left McKinsey in 1990 to join a client, Enron, he would have been part of the firm's emerging new guard. And to his peer group, Gupta's rise was the culmination of the exciting and wrenching changes McKinsey had undergone and was set to capitalize upon. "The candidate for Managing Director has to reflect the aspirations of the firm. I don't think there was anyone in the running that met the test of 'aspiration' other than Rajat," declares Skilling. He "pioneered a new way of leveraging the firm's intellectual capital. I think Rajat was a shoo-in for election to Managing Director, and frankly, I don't think anyone had a chance against him. He was that good."

CHAPTER THIRTEEN

Raj's Edge

In late March 1998, Intel stopped filming Roomy Khan faxing confidential financial data to Raj Rajaratnam. The internal probe got tricky for the semiconductor giant. One employee noticed the sideways hidden camera and literally tried to yank it out. There was speculation in the department that Intel was spying on its own employees to see if they were stealing paper. The rumors were not good for morale.

Meanwhile, after receiving a poor performance review from a manager who was not briefed on the company's investigation, Khan decided to quit. Her departure threw a spanner into the probe. Without Khan making incriminating calls and sending improper faxes to Rajaratnam, it was hard to build a case against the Galleon chief or get Khan to make consensual calls. The investigation came to a standstill and Khan found a new job.

By 1999, the markets had recovered and the tech bubble reflated, and Rajaratnam again was flying. In 1999, his flagship technology fund posted a return of 96.3 percent. He started a new fund in June 1999, the Galleon New Media fund, to invest exclusively in Internet stocks. His assets under management swelled from $1 billion in 1998 to $5 billion on the back of spectacular returns, and on April 1, 2000, he closed Galleon to new investors. In a sign of his growing success, he threw a blowout Christmas party just before the turn of the millennium.

About three hundred brokers and clients packed a large ballroom in midtown Manhattan with an open bar brightly decorated with balloons and streamers and waited for the star attraction: legendary disco singer Donna Summer. Though the guests arrived early, the stage was empty for hours; Summer was more than an hour late. Despite his relaxed look, Rajaratnam was livid that he was kept waiting. He needn't have worried. When Summer appeared around 10 p.m., she electrified the crowd, belting out a mix of her old standbys, the sexy songs that made her popular—"Hot Stuff" and "She Works Hard for the Money," and her new repertoire, gospel-like religious songs. The party went on until the wee hours of the morning. On Wall Street, where it's the brokers who wine and dine commission-paying clients like Galleon to get them to divert more dollars their way, Rajaratnam's gesture of turning the tables and entertaining the brokers was noticed.

With his business thriving, Rajaratnam had opened an office in the heart of Silicon Valley, Santa Clara, California, in 1998. Not wanting to draw attention to his new beachhead in the epicenter of the tech world, Rajaratnam kept the phone number for the office unlisted. One of its new employees was Khan, whom Rajaratnam paid $120,000 plus a bonus to analyze stocks in the personal computer industry. Some of the technology world's biggest names fell under her purview—Dell, Compaq, Sun Microsystems, IBM, Altera, and others.

Rajaratnam told Khan that she should strive to find contacts inside companies so that they could give her "the edge." Khan quickly came to learn exactly what Rajaratnam meant when he talked about getting "the edge." He wanted her to ferret out confidential information about a company so Galleon could develop a view on a stock that diverged from the mainstream thinking on Wall Street. If Khan's inside sources proved correct, Galleon would make a killing when investors finally realized that Galleon's take on a stock was right and the market was wrong.

Unlike her job at Intel, Khan found Galleon to be a high-stress, pressure-cooker environment. In the spring of 1999, she quit after she ran afoul of a rule Rajaratnam had exempted her from at first. Khan traded in her personal account—something that Rajaratnam preferred employees avoid. Setting up a personal account and making trades while working at a hedge fund was an obvious red flag for regulators. It screamed insider trading. But for Khan it was lucrative. In the bubble of the late nineties, she like everyone else was making money on Internet stocks.

One day, months after she joined Galleon, Rajaratnam said to her, "Listen, you have to turn over your personal account to the fund. Everybody's rule has to apply here." Khan suspected a colleague in the small Santa Clara office whom she didn't like had put pressure on Rajaratnam to enforce the firm practice.

Khan talked it over with her husband and told Rajaratnam that she did not want to turn over her personal account to the fund.

Then you have to leave, Rajaratnam said.

The two parted ways amicably. Rajaratnam said that he respected Khan because she was very good at what she did.

A month after her departure from the Galleon Group, on April 15, 1999, two special agents for the FBI knocked on the door of Khan's modest home in Sunnyvale, California. The agents asked her about her dealings with Rajaratnam. She assumed they were referring to her conversations with him when she was still employed at Intel. She said that from time to time she would talk to him about coming to work for him. Once in a while, they would discuss a stock and how it was doing, but she insisted she never discussed her former employer, Intel, with him. She was adamant on the point. She never sent him any financial reports from Intel. She never disclosed any information to him and she never provided him with the company's profit margins or production numbers.

The agents then showed her printouts of photographs taken of her at a facsimile machine at Intel faxing reports to Galleon. They told Khan they had pictures of her faxing to Rajaratnam the kind of financial reports moments earlier she had attested to not having access to during her time working at Intel.

"Okay," Khan replied, unfazed by being caught in a lie. She told the agents she wanted to cooperate but she needed to make sure she did not have any "exposure." It was not as if she had "made a lot of money" on the information, she told them.

CHAPTER FOURTEEN

Building Offshore-istan

The new future that Rajat Gupta would forge for his country as the offshoring capital of the world had a curious start. One day in 1994 a request arrived out of the blue at the offices of McKinsey India. A German consultant wanted to set up a presentation slide production center in Kerala, a state in southern India, and was looking for some on-the-ground pointers. When Neeraj Bhargava, a McKinsey consultant in India, got on the phone with the German, he sensed his colleague was interested in Kerala because it was one of the lushest and greenest states in India, with beautiful, unspoiled beaches.

Since independence, Kerala had been governed on and off by India's Communist Party. The German was angling to set up the slide production center in Trivandrum, the state's capital, but Bhargava, having grown up in Kerala, knew its unions were fearless and suggested Chennai, the capital of Tamil Nadu, the state contiguous to Kerala. And so it happened that McKinsey took its first bold step into the brave new world of offshoring.

The story might have ended there had it not been for a young and hungry junior partner in McKinsey's New Delhi office. Anil Kumar had been tilling over the arcane area of remote business services—consultant-speak for supplying services regardless of a customer's geographic location. His vision was to take advantage of the declining price of global telecommunications in the 1990s and move offshore a myriad of business services—corporate research, financial analysis, legal transcription, any repeatable white-collar task—to the low-cost labor markets of the East. With a critical mass of idle but highly educated English-speaking Indians eager to work for cents on the dollar, Kumar was confident that his vision could become a reality with the right kind of backing. Fortuitously for Kumar, his mentor, Rajat Gupta, was now the head of the firm.

Despite his great intellect and obvious knack for problem solving, Kumar had made little impression on anyone since joining McKinsey's San Francisco office in 1986. He rarely smiled, and he hardly mixed with anyone in the office apart from a couple of South Asians there at the time or partners whose favor he tried to curry. "I do remember him coming into a conference room where we were meeting, and there was no one senior there, and he looked around the room and then walked out," said one person who worked with Kumar. Some attributed his lack of collegiality to being an outsider. He was not weaned in McKinsey's culture and values, having been hired into the firm out of Hewlett-Packard.

Kumar quickly realized that the only way he would make his mark at McKinsey was by contributing to its intellectual capital. In 1988, he was tapped to help start a fledgling Silicon Valley office in San Jose during an era when tech was not sexy. Without any clients, Kumar and a partner literally pounded the pavement. They drove up and down the valley in the partner's car as Kumar jotted down the names of companies whose signs they passed. Then he would cold-call the firms to pitch the business advisory services McKinsey could provide. His efforts paid off. Over five years, the office grew to about thirty-five people. In 1992, he was made a principal.

Kumar would have remained a faceless consultant had he not been enlisted to work in India by Tino Puri, McKinsey's first Indian hire and something of a legend at the firm. An intellectual tour de force, a giant among giants, Puri was fiercely respected by his colleagues, who even indulged his one weakness, chain-smoking.

In 1988, not long after Gluck took the helm of McKinsey, Puri traveled to India with him. There the two met with the heads of some of India's biggest business dynasties, industrial titans such as the Birlas and the Tatas. The aim of the trip was to explore the opportunities for McKinsey in India with the idea of opening an office in the near future. Gluck came away from the trip more convinced than ever that it was the right step. But he could not persuade Puri to move. In Puri's view, no one in India knew what a management consultant actually was, making the services of McKinsey a hard sell to clients. And the advice he got during the trip was that it was too early to start a McKinsey office.

As eager as Gluck was to plant the McKinsey flag in India, his hands were tied. Historically, McKinsey was willing to entertain opening an office almost anywhere as long as there was a partner who would relocate and set it up. But even as recently as 1987, India was too iffy a proposition for a consulting career. A plan to open an office was put on the back burner.

* * *

One day in August 1990, Paresh Vaish, a twenty-nine-year-old associate at McKinsey, was sitting in his apartment in Pasadena, California, packing his bags, when his phone rang. Vaish, the son of an Indian Railways executive in New Delhi, had come to the United States twelve years earlier on a scholarship to Dartmouth College. After graduating, he worked at Intel, earning enough money to pay his way through Harvard Business School.

For years, he had been angling to be sent to India by McKinsey. Homesick and longing for his rice and lentils rather than steak and potatoes, Vaish had finally decided to leave McKinsey and return to India on his own when Puri called.

As the number of South Asians at McKinsey had swelled, Puri had turned into a well-placed Sherpa to many of them, a father figure helping them navigate the sometimes treacherous inclines of the firm. It was well known that Puri was a mentor to Rajat Gupta, an up-and-coming McKinsey director whose star by 1990 shone brightest of all South Asians' at the firm, even more so than Puri's.

Vaish was excited to hear Puri on the other end of the phone. "When Tino calls, it is a bit like God calling," he remarked to friends. Puri had an interesting proposition for Vaish. McKinsey, he said, was just hired to work for Hindustan Motors, the flagship company of Indian conglomerate CK Birla Group, in Uttarpara, on the outskirts of Calcutta. The company was one of India's preeminent concerns, but its Hindustan Motors division was flailing, beset by a host of problems—low productivity, labor issues, and obsolete technology and fraying facilities.

In an era of rising oil prices and diminishing protections against foreign competition, its big, gas-guzzling Ambassador cars were an anachronism. With their recurring snafus, such as carburetor problems, they stood to lose out to a hot new arrival in the Indian market: the mass-produced and far cheaper Maruti Suzuki, which was being manufactured in India through a joint venture with Japan's Suzuki Motor Corp.

Knowing the country and its challenges, Puri did not sugarcoat the risks to Vaish. "We don't know what will happen," he said. The assignment was expected to last between three and six months. After that, no one could tell. It was an unsettling and promising opportunity at the same time. If Vaish was interested, he could be one of the engagement managers and lead a small McKinsey team in India. For a Delhi boy like Vaish, Calcutta was not home, but it was close enough.

Over the next six months, Vaish and a team from McKinsey's New York office decamped to a huge mosquito-ridden bungalow—a guesthouse of CK Birla's—that was on the premises of his sprawling and crumbling factory. During the course of its work, McKinsey made a slew of recommendations, some big and some small. To address the quality control issues, it proposed a questionnaire for dealer feedback so the company would have a systematic way of knowing about snafus. And to address some of its long-term strategic challenges, McKinsey recommended that Hindustan Motors revamp the Ambassador model and upgrade other vehicles, speed up delivery of cars, and boost productivity by reengineering the factory floor and reducing its workforce at the Uttarpara plant.

The McKinsey contingent was overwhelmed with work, its six-month project for Hindustan Motors turned into a three-year contract, and CK Birla became what McKinsey calls a radiating reference. Other assignments in India quickly followed. Big industrial conglomerates such as Larsen & Toubro, Mahindra & Mahindra, RPG Enterprises, and the Oberois, who run an eponymous chain of hotels, hired McKinsey. Many were less interested in McKinsey's services; indeed, some did not even know exactly what management consulting was. Rather, what they sought was the firm's cachet. They wanted to be able to broadcast to others—their customers and their friends—that they had the wherewithal to hire the US consulting giant. The McKinsey name had become a status symbol in one of the world's largest and fastest-growing markets. Yet the firm still did not have an office in India, and convincing Puri to move and set up one was turning into slow water torture. Herb Henzler, the McKinsey Germany head, asked Gupta with characteristic bluntness: "Can't you lean on Tino because Tino is too indecisive?"

"We are too good friends," Gupta demurred.

The last thing Gupta would have wanted to do was jeopardize his relationship with his mentor Puri. Years later, when Puri stepped down from managing the India office for McKinsey, Gupta traveled to Mumbai for his farewell party, which, like many events at McKinsey, was part social and part professional. Masquerading as a conference, the good-bye was held at a modest three-star hotel in Madh Island, a collection of fishing villages in northern Mumbai. As Gupta spoke of Puri and the role he'd played in his career, the phlegmatic Gupta choked up. Colleagues sensed his deep sense of debt to the man who had staked the path for him.

In 1992, Puri moved to Mumbai and opened the first McKinsey office in India out of two rooms in the Oberoi hotel. It was the only viable office space at the time for a prestigious Western company like McKinsey. Yet it came with a host of infrastructure and technological challenges common to doing business in India at the time. Power shortages meant that even some of the country's most established indigenous companies, such as Hindustan Motors, were deprived of electricity. At least the blackout was at a scheduled time every day for about an hour. When McKinsey set up its office in Delhi, one of its partners installed the switchboard because India was lacking in telephone engineers. Initially, because foreign equipment faced high import duties and was hard to come by, the firm had only one computer, which had to be shared between the Delhi and the Mumbai offices. The computer would be passed between the two locations regularly, with the handoff taking place at the airport.

And if the day-to-day logistical challenges of operating in India were not off-putting enough, McKinsey's Puri had to contend with the freewheeling style of Indian business. As eager as companies were to use McKinsey's services, they were less excited to pay for the work. By Indian standards, McKinsey's fees—though discounted for the Indian market—were astronomical. One week of a McKinsey engagement equaled the salary of some Indian companies' CEOs. In the early days, Puri used to joke that he was not sure if he was the strategic adviser of the companies McKinsey served or their banker. The reason: he had overdrafts from all of them.

It turned out that 1992 was the perfect time for McKinsey to hoist its flag in India. Just a year earlier, the country had teetered on the brink of bankruptcy after a spike in oil prices following the Gulf War sapped the country's foreign exchange reserves. In June 1991, at the peak of the panic, India's reserves plummeted to $1.2 billion, barely enough to pay for two weeks of imports. Industrial production was dropping and inflation was soaring. Instead of healing the problem with Band-Aid measures, a well-regarded Cambridge University economist who was then little known outside India overhauled the economy.

Manmohan Singh, India's new finance minister and a free marketeer, started hacking away at India's socialist undergrowth, getting rid of the License Raj, which had developed into a clunky cover for government intervention in industrial policy. Singh's reforms marked an important milestone for India, which had been muddling along since independence. They put the country on a trajectory of growth from which it would never look back.

Puri, rightly sensing that the Singh initiatives would unleash a flood of investment dollars into India and jump-start its anemic economy, wasted no time in staffing the new office in Mumbai. He got well-connected Indians in other McKinsey offices to return home to work in India. And he tapped Kumar, who had gone to

India's prestigious all-boys school, the Doon School, to move to New Delhi.

Doon was set up to serve a newly independent India just as Eton served England as a proving ground for future leaders in politics, media, and business. The model of the British "public school" was so fixed in the minds of Doon's creators that the first headmaster was Arthur Edward Foot, a science master at Eton. Foot's objective was that boys should "leave the Doon School as members of an aristocracy of service inspired by ideals of unselfishness, not of privilege, wealth or position."

Since its founding, sports and outdoor activities had played an outsized role at Doon, and it was certainly the case when Kumar arrived as a new boy in 1970. The school's position at the foothills of the Himalayas helped it attract some of the country's best mountaineers to its faculty. Doon's heroes, the masters who held boys in thrall, were towering, larger-than-life men like Gurdial Singh and R. L. Holdsworth, both magnificent mountaineers who took every advantage of the school's location. Every two years, the school would screen *Nine Atop Everest*, a film that chronicled the 1965 climb of the first Indian mountaineering team to scale Everest. Singh was part of that maiden ascent. Whenever the Singh character spoke in the film, the boys, in the ultimate form of hero worship, would chant his lines in unison. "To go mountain climbing with these men was an extraordinary thing," recalls Shomit Mitter, who was Kumar's junior. "These were the legends around which the school was built."

During his time at Doon, Mitter says that "your reflection among your peers was less about academic ability and more about sportsmanship." Indeed, achievement in sports was so important that for decades the school had been celebrating it by awarding standout sportsmen a navy-blue blazer known as the "games blazer." The blazers were rarely given. In every class, there were typically no more than a handful of games blazers awarded.

Kumar was not a gifted sportsman, and he wasn't much of an all-rounder either, the kind of boy who shone in drama and music as well as academics. As the years wore on, it was clear he lacked a natural charisma and the leadership qualities that would have more than made up for any other deficiencies. "If you were school captain or house captain you were a somebody," said Dhruv Khanna, serving as school captain counting among his achievements. "If you were a prefect, you were barely somebody."

The bookish and aloof Kumar was a monitor, a title below prefect that was as tedious and workaday as it sounded. Among the cognoscenti at Doon, it was a badge that inadvertently but very firmly sealed upon the beholder the official status of a "nobody." Kumar had a clique of friends, mostly from Kashmir House B, where he lived, or Bombay wallahs, slang for guys from Bombay, who came from the big city as he did. But "he was not in the 'in crowd,'" recalls Mitter. "He was academically very bright, but he wasn't one of the people in that year who would stand out."

Despite his quiet way, Kumar struck classmates as very ambitious. "He would go at it as if his life depended upon it," says a friend. Though not much of a natural athlete—unlike his classmates, who reveled in the flamboyant pageantry of team sports like cricket—Kumar focused on a more solitary activity, the long jump. By the end of his time at Doon he surprised everyone—even his closest friends—by his level of accomplishment. "He came first in the long-jump event during the interschool athletics competition, demonstrating an athletic finesse that no one knew he had," says Arjun Mahey, a classmate. Academics, not athletics, though, were where Kumar could truly shine.

Starting in 1971, after years of giving out games blazers, Doon began awarding black blazers to recognize academic excellence. In March 1974, a small headline in the *Doon Weekly* gave Kumar his first taste of fame. It declared that Kumar had won the scholars blazer. "For the next year, he walked around with a black jacket," recalls Dhruv Khanna, a former attorney who has built two cricket pitches in the midst of a California winery he acquired. "It was a very big deal because they were so scarce." But when the honors boards were hung up, Kumar's name was not on them. To be celebrated at Doon, one had to be an achiever in *both* academics and athletics. Kumar had entered Doon as a nobody, and despite a grueling amount of work, he would exit the school the same way. His family was proud, but inside, Kumar burned more deeply than ever with drive and ambition.

In 1975, Kumar sat for the IIT entrance exam along with a hundred thousand other students. He tested in the top 0.1 percent of applicants and was admitted to IIT Bombay. In 1980, he graduated third in his class with a degree in mechanical engineering. During his final year at IIT, he applied to Wharton and was accepted. At the same time, he found out that he had won a scholarship to study applied mechanics at the University of London's Imperial College. The scholarship was awarded by De Beers to one engineering student among two thousand graduating from the IITs nationwide. As torn as Kumar was by the opportunity to study at Imperial College, he had committed to Wharton so he declined the De Beers scholarship. When the dean of IIT Bombay learned of Kumar's decision, he prevailed upon him to seek a two-year deferral of his place at Wharton.The De Beers scholarship was prestigious, and it was important to the reputation of IIT Bombay that Kumar accept. In 1980, after Wharton granted Kumar only a one-year deferral, he headed to Imperial College to finish the two-year program in applied mechanics in a single year. He succeeded, completing it in ten months and graduating first in his class.

* * *

Ironically it was India—his place of birth, which he left to make his name in the United States—that breathed new life into Kumar's lackluster career. When he arrived in Delhi in 1993, India was only starting to emerge from the shackles of its tightly controlled economy. Against this backdrop, the blue-suited consultants from McKinsey stood out. They were often quoted in India's business bible, the *Economic Times*; and their stars, men like Puri and Gupta, were revered. Whenever they appeared at conferences, they were feted with garlands of flowers and treated like heads of state. It was hard not to respect the McKinsey men. Besides their intellectual prowess, it was well known that they were among the best-paid executives in the country. In the early nineties, their compensation was on par with that of chief executives of some of the country's biggest companies, and they lived like kings. Kumar rented a house in one of Delhi's finest neighborhoods, Vasant Vihar, and he employed an army of servants on his return.

Operating out of McKinsey's office in the Taj Mansingh hotel, Kumar worked his social network. He tapped his well-connected Doon School friends—the scions of India's biggest business families, such as the Oberois—to send projects his way. And he built lines into the country's oldest corporate dynasties, such as the sprawling Modi Group, with its interests in glass, rubber, and travel. No card in his Rolodex was left unflipped and no opportunity to network was squandered. He leaned on his father-in-law, Ratan Dayal, a longtime marketing executive at Burmah Shell, at one time regarded as the jewel in the crown of British companies in India.

Unlike the winner-take-all entrepreneurialism rampant today in Indian companies such as Reliance Industries, working at Burmah Shell was a genteel affair, an exercise in comfortable capitalism. Senior employees of Burmah Shell like Kumar's father-in-law basked in perks that were scarce in the India of the 1950s. When on business trips, they traveled in AC cars—shorthand in the Indian railway system for air-conditioned carriages. If traveling by car, they were allowed to take their bearers, or servants, with them. When they were posted to cities like Bangalore, the company arranged for its senior executives to have memberships at the top clubs in town and housed them in spacious company flats in the best neighborhoods. Anil Kumar met his wife, Malvika, Dayal's daughter, when the Dayals and Kumars lived in the same company quarters in Bombay. Kumar's father, Virendra Kumar, was also a Burmah Shell executive. The two began dating when Kumar was studying at IIT Bombay. Every weekend, he would make the trek by bus, train, and another bus to be with Malvika.

When Malvika and Anil returned to India in 1993, Anil was often seen accompanying his well-regarded father-in-law to the exclusive Delhi Golf Club, an oasis of green dating back to the 1930s, which sits smack in the center of the dusty metropolis. Standing next to him, Kumar developed an instant sheen and a respectability that otherwise would have taken decades to cultivate.

Kumar drew on purported links with prominent people in government like the respected Indian economist Montek Singh Ahluwalia, a behind-the-scenes architect of the economic reforms of the 1990s, to show he was connected. All the hobnobbing paid off. Within a few years of arriving in Delhi, Kumar achieved what he'd never managed to pull off in America: he became a member of the club. He was now in a position to effect change, and he had an important backer.

Even though Rajat Gupta, Kumar's new boss, left India in 1971, he was intimately familiar with India's problems and passionate about fixing them. Gupta knew tapping into India's English-speaking workforce to create a vibrant service industry would go a long way toward creating a viable future for India. He also knew Kumar was a controversial consultant. He had antagonized colleagues in New Delhi when he made a bid to poach a coworker's high-profile client. It was antithetical to McKinsey's storied culture to steal clients, but Kumar was Gupta's dark-haired boy wonder. Instead of reprimanding him, Gupta backed him over others in the office.

Sensing Gupta's fondness for him and receptivity to his ideas, Kumar approached Bhargava, who had worked on an important study that found that as global telecommunications rates dropped, work would migrate to low-cost locales such as India and the Philippines. Kumar suggested his colleague find other areas—corporate research, for example—where remote business services could be applied. "I'll get this thing approved by the shareholders committee," he told Bhargava, "but why don't you figure out how to roll it out."

Almost coincidentally, at the start of 1996, McKinsey hired Amit Bhatia, a former American Express executive in India. Bhatia's assignment was to fix McKinsey's Indian research department, then consisting of half a dozen people. Soon after arriving, he revamped the unit, hiring a bevy of MBAs. With the salaries McKinsey was offering—around $12,000 a year—"we could get tier-two and tier-three MBAs because we were McKinsey," says Bhatia.

In February 1997, as McKinsey was in the midst of a cost-cutting program, its Asia-Pacific research and information managers gathered in Kuala Lumpur, Malaysia, to brainstorm about resource sharing in the region. Bhatia proposed a research-and-information factory where all requests from consultants—anything from mobile telecom penetration in a given country to estimating market sizes and growth rates—were fielded. He met with immediate resistance; few of the local managers were willing to abdicate their fiefdoms for a centralized system. Indeed, the idea would have died had it not been for encouragement Bhatia received from Roger W. Ferguson Jr., McKinsey's global head of Research and Information.

"Let's work on this idea," he told Bhatia.

But before Ferguson could really run with it and sell it as a firmwide concept, it emerged that he would be nominated for one of two vacancies on the Federal Reserve Board. It was widely expected that he would be confirmed for the position. All of a sudden, Bhatia was on the hunt for a new champion.

Meanwhile, Kumar made a pitch to grow remote services. In 1997, a team from McKinsey India, coached by Kumar, presented their vision at an internal event known as the Practice Olympics. After taking over in 1994, Gupta had instituted the Practice Olympics globally as a way of encouraging McKinsey's practices to develop and showcase their most innovative ideas.

For its submission, the team from McKinsey India stripped the gross domestic product of two countries, the United States and Germany, analyzed every profession and every industry, and looked at what work could be moved offshore. If a job depended on local know-how or connections, it couldn't be transplanted, but if a job wasn't location-specific, it could be moved anywhere. The steep fall in telecommunications rates meant that it did not matter if a job was shipped from New York to Bangalore rather than from New York to Florida. From a cost perspective, there was little difference.

Extrapolating the results from the United States and Germany globally, the McKinsey India team estimated that $1 trillion worth of work could move to lower-cost high-skills locations such as India over the next two to three decades. The McKinsey India team did not win the first-place prize at the Asian regional meet of the Practice

Olympics in Bali, but it was given a special award for the most vivid imagination, meaning "great idea, but it will never happen."

By now, Bhatia had found a new backer, Jane Kirkland, a partner in McKinsey's Pittsburgh office, who was eager to run with the idea of a research hub. She enlisted Kumar, who took the proposition straight to his mentor, Gupta, and quickly sold him on it—not that it was a tough pitch. Bhatia was asking for only $250,000 at most in funding. (McKinsey says that to its knowledge, Kumar did not play such a role in the initiative.)

Thus the McKinsey Knowledge Center, or McKC to those in the know, was born. Just as blue-collar jobs moved outside the United States in the 1970s and 1980s, Kumar and Gupta advised McKinsey clients to export a host of high-end American business services—paralegal work, corporate research, financial analysis—to India. "Remote services became a big way to sell an engagement. They actually went to customers and said, 'We will help you outsource. We know how to do this,'" says Bhatia. "Had Anil not put in a word to Rajat, the Knowledge Center might not have seen the light of day."

As Kumar grew in stature at the firm, friends noticed a certain cockiness creep into him. Gone was the quiet, shy schoolboy who buried himself in his books. In his place was a man with a carefully groomed arrogance who wanted to impress—actually needed to impress—his friends with his newfound success. During his early years working in Delhi, he sought out old friends from his Doon School days. But by the mid-1990s, Kumar was established in town and his orbit of friends changed to match his growing power and influence. No longer was he willing to spend time idling with old school chums. Among his new circle were some of the leading lights of corporate India, men such as Sunil Mittal, the telecommunications magnate who would shoot into the global spotlight in 2008 when his company explored buying South Africa's MTN Group, and the Ambani brothers, Mukesh and Anil.

Mukesh Ambani was said to be fond of saying that Anil Kumar was "like God. He was everywhere." Certainly, wherever McKinsey's new managing partner Rajat Gupta was, Kumar made a point of appearing. Though he did not know Gupta well because they worked in different offices while they were in the United States, Kumar used his presence on the ground in India to deepen his relationship with Gupta. Colleagues in the New Delhi office would marvel at the way Kumar finagled getting booked on the same flight to Mumbai as Gupta when he visited India. In 1994, shortly after Gupta was elected managing director, he was invited into the offices of the *Times of India* for a meeting with its top editor, Gautam Adhikari. To everyone's surprise, Kumar showed up for the meeting too.

At McKinsey, a partner's power base derives from the strength of his client relationships. As a consequence, most partners are outwardly focused and view internal politics as a chore. Not Kumar. "Anil cultivated Rajat as sort of a corporate person would fawn over a CEO," says a partner. The two were a study in contrasts—Gupta was smooth and genial, while Kumar was abrasive and full of himself.

Vinit Khanna, an old friend from Doon, first noticed a change in Kumar in the mid-1990s. Khanna, fresh off a round-the-world trip that he completed in thirty days, marveled at being able to travel in business class and stay in luxury hotels on his own dime. Khanna had come to the United States in the early 1980s to attend Wharton; he was a year ahead of Kumar. Upon graduating from Wharton in 1982, Khanna struck out on his own and thrived importing Indian goods—such as the manhole covers ubiquitous in city streets—to America. When Khanna ran into Kumar, he recalled how it would have been unthinkable fifteen years earlier, when the two first arrived in America as somewhat impecunious college students, to even contemplate a trip like the one he'd just taken. Kumar quickly cut short his reverie and told Khanna he'd just returned from a round-the-world trip in seven days.

One-upmanship was a character trait of the new Kumar. In 2006, Khanna had tried to catch up with Kumar during a trip to London. Kumar told Khanna that he didn't have time to meet but perhaps Khanna would be willing to drop by Forty-Seven Park Street, a set of upscale time-share residences in tony Mayfair that Kumar was considering investing in. It houses the two-star Michelin restaurant Le

Gavroche, from which residents at Forty-Seven Park can order high-end takeaway served on bone china. Kumar said he was thinking of buying a membership in Forty-Seven Park but in the end didn't. He told Khanna that his good friend Sunil Mittal, the Indian telecommunications mogul, and other bigwigs lived close by so he could bunk with them during trips to London.

Khanna was impressed with Forty-Seven Park and wound up buying a number of associate memberships in the building. In 2012, Khanna ran into Kumar as attendants were escorting him to the first-class cabin on a British Airways flight to London. Sometime during the middle of the flight, Kumar walked over to Khanna's seat.

"How is Forty-Seven Park working out?" he asked. Khanna gushed about it, saying he was so grateful that Kumar had introduced him to it.

Midway in the conversation, Kumar let on to Khanna that he'd bought a place in the Savoy "after its refurbishment." Then he proceeded to regale his old friend with the superior amenities at the Savoy.

Rajat Gupta and his wife, Anita, heading into the White House for a state dinner in honor of Indian prime minister Dr. Manmohan Singh on November 24, 2009.

Danielle Chiesi, in a tank top (right); and her mother, in a floral-patterned dress; Galleon's Gary Rosenbach, in a T-shirt; and his wife, Susan (left), watch Kenny Rogers perform in the Rajaratnams' Greenwich, Connecticut, backyard. Raj is standing in the background wearing a cowboy hat.

Raj and his kid brother Rengan in Kenya for Raj's fiftieth-birthday bash. At the August 2007 event, guests wore black T-shirts that read "The Riotous, Rowdy, Rebellious Raj Tribe."

The campus of IIT Delhi, where Rajat Gupta graduated in 1971. The school has become an incubator for global leaders in technology and finance. (Courtesy of the *Hindu*.)

Kashmir House at the Doon School. The old boy network of Doscos, India's answer to Etonians, aided Anil Kumar as he helped launch McKinsey's business in India.

The aspiration of a Doon School boy as laid out by its first headmaster.

"Truly, we mean that the boys should leave the Doon School as members of an aristocracy, but it must be an aristocracy of service inspired by the ideals of unselfishness, not one of privilege, wealth or position."

Arthur Foot, Headmaster, at the official opening of the School on October 27, 1935

Sanjay Wadhwa, senior associate regional director of the New York office, came to the United States from India in 1986. Wadhwa paid for his undergraduate education by working fifty-hour weeks as a stockroom boy and cashier at a local drugstore.

US attorney for the Southern District of New York, Preet Bharara. Bharara, whose parents immigrated to New Jersey from India in 1970, would oversee the prosecution of his fellow South Asians Raj Rajaratnam and Rajat Gupta. (Courtesy of Rick Maiman.)

Special assistant US attorney, Andrew Michaelson, who started working on the Galleon case at the SEC and was later loaned out to the US attorney's office.

Rajat Gupta presents an award to Henry Kravis at the American India Foundation gala in 2009. After Gupta retired from McKinsey, he went to work for Kravis and his partners at Kohlberg Kravis Roberts & Co.

Rajat Gupta and Hillary Clinton at the American India Foundation gala awards dinner in April 2004.

Rajat Gupta and his lead attorney, Gary Naftalis. (Courtesy of Rick Maiman.)

Anil Kumar and his wife, Malvika, leave the Manhattan federal courthouse after his sentencing. (Courtesy of Rick Maiman.)

Raj Rajaratnam leaves the Manhattan federal courthouse after his conviction. His sentence of eleven years was the stiffest punishment doled out to date in an insider trading case. (Courtesy of Rick Maiman.)

CHAPTER FIFTEEN

Partying and Polycom

It was July 2, 2007, and Raj Rajaratnam was on his way to a much-needed vacation in Europe. Just three weeks earlier, he had given testimony to Wadhwa, Michaelson, and Markowitz at the SEC. Now he, his family, and a group of friends were headed to Château Grimaldi, a seventeenth-century castle in southern France with eleven bedrooms and nine baths set over twelve acres of beautiful gardens. Among the nearly two dozen taking the trip were Rajaratnam's good friends the Goels, Rajiv and his wife, Alka, and their kids.

Rajiv Goel and Raj had been friends since they were both MBA students at Wharton. The friendship was not always an equal one. Goel, a bumbling but good-natured sort, "was a follower [of Raj's]," says one Wharton classmate of the two men. "Whatever Raj asked him to do, he would do it."

In the weeks before the holiday, Rajiv Goel bombarded Rajaratnam with calls and emails. He was tireless in his excitement. The trip coincided with the annual art and music festival in the town of Aix-en-Provence, just four miles from the château. Goel thought it might be fun to attend and catch one of the cultural events. He and his family were already in France, but Rajaratnam still had a few matters to tie up at work. He planned to join them on July Fourth.

The trip was actually one of two vacations he was planning that summer. In August, he was going to charter a plane and take seventy of his friends to Kenya for a safari. The holidays were part of a summer-long birthday extravaganza. Two weeks earlier, on June 15, Rajaratnam had turned fifty years old, and to celebrate the milestone he rented a large boat and invited a couple hundred colleagues, friends, and family to a party he hosted on board. Dressed in jeans and a shirt that only Jimmy Buffett could love, Rajaratnam looked relaxed. In the spirit of the night, he wore a white captain's cap as he stood on the upper deck with a few close friends and engaged in a favorite pastime: smoking pot.

Rajaratnam enjoyed kicking back with a toke. In the early days of Galleon, he used to have rolled joints delivered to the office, which he would share with a few trusted lieutenants. But as Galleon got bigger it was harder to indulge the habit. In the middle of the passing, the boat's real captain appeared. As the sweet stench of pot hung strong in the air, the captain issued a stern warning: if the group did not stop smoking at once, he would dock the boat. Rajaratnam and his friends laughed loudly, oblivious to the no-nonsense look on the captain's face.

"I could buy this boat if I wanted," Rajaratnam boasted.

The captain was unimpressed and repeated the threat. Only when the group realized that he was preparing to steer the boat back to land did they put out their joints. (Rajaratnam denied that he smoked pot in an article in *Forbes* magazine in October 2010 and said he helped the boat's crew in getting some guests to stop smoking.) As the vessel with the rowdy revelers circled the island of Manhattan, it passed the southern tip of the city and Three World Financial Center. Inside, hard at work at the SEC's offices on the sixteenth floor, were Wadhwa and his team.

During the summer of 2007, the SEC lawyers combed through thousands and thousands of pages of Galleon emails, instant messages, chat room posts, and trading records. As part of the SEC subpoena it received, Galleon turned over more than 4 million documents: trade blotters recording Galleon's purchases and sales of securities, personal trading and investment information for Rajaratnam, calendar and scheduling information for him and others, trading data for a number of specific securities, and emails and IMs, among other things. Wadhwa and Michaelson suspected the avalanche of information was designed to confound them rather than cooperate with their investigation. For a while, Galleon succeeded.

When the SEC examiners were on-site at Galleon's offices earlier in the spring, they took two lists of investors in the company's funds. One list was organized on an electronically searchable, user-friendly Excel spreadsheet. The other list was a hard copy of investors that ran into the hundreds of pages. This list could be searched only manually. But for some reason when Michaelson, who was looking for investors in Galleon that were possible sources of inside information, punched in the name Anil Kumar, a contact in Rajaratnam's Rolodex, nothing came up in the electronic list. He eventually found Kumar's name, alongside that of an account holder, Manju Das, in the hard-copy list of investors. Next to Kumar's name was his address in California and his phone number. To Michaelson, Kumar and Das were nothing more than a couple of Indian-sounding needles in a haystack of data. Kumar, it appeared, was simply an investment adviser or stockbroker acting as a custodian for Das's account.

While Michaelson found the difference between the two lists curious—Kumar was on a printout but not the Excel sheet—there was no sign that Kumar was an informant of Rajaratnam's. When Michaelson asked Rajaratnam point-blank at the June deposition to identify "any investors in Galleon who are consultants" to publicly traded companies, Rajaratnam said he knew of none. He also could not think of any investors in Galleon who worked for Advanced Micro Devices, the company whose stock Rajaratnam so masterfully traded. Buried in a mountain of paper, Michaelson moved on, skipping over Kumar's name to the next investor on the list. Only in hindsight would he discover that pulling on the Kumar thread was a first step in unraveling a tapestry of information swapping that led all the way to the top of some of the nation's most respected firms, including McKinsey.

Jason Friedman almost went into journalism. As an undergraduate at Cornell University, Friedman, nearly six feet tall and well built, with an obvious sincerity, wrote for the *Cornell Daily Sun*. But after

a stint as a trial preparation assistant in the Manhattan district attorney's office, Friedman decided to become a lawyer. He was in the
same Harvard Law School class as Michaelson, but the two met for
the first time when Friedman joined the SEC from the New York law
firm of Simpson Thacher & Bartlett. On July 9, Friedman's first day
at the agency, Michaelson sat down with him in a spacious common
area in the SEC's offices—the space was originally supposed to have
a spiral staircase connecting the sixteenth floor with the seventeenth
floor. Surrounded by breathtaking views of the water, Michaelson
walked Friedman through the Sedna case, which had now morphed
into an investigation of Galleon. For three straight hours Michaelson
described the links between Rengan Rajaratnam and his big brother
Raj as well as the stocks in which they were suspected of trading on
inside information. Then Friedman started on a "deep dive" into the
phone records of Rajaratnam and some of his suspected informants.

Over the next several weeks, he dispatched subpoenas to the
phone companies. By August, thousands of pages of phone logs arrived, yielding about eight thousand "interesting" phone numbers.
Every one of them had to be examined. It was painstaking grunt
work—the kind of labor that would be done at a private law firm
by an associate. Law firms also owned sophisticated software programs that allowed a user to load phone logs and search them
electronically. Sanjay Wadhwa checked with his tech support team
and discovered that the SEC did not have the money to buy the software. So Friedman spent hours and hours scouring hard copies. With
a ruler in hand, he would match up phone calls between two parties
within a window of time around the suspicious trades Rajaratnam
had made.

As the SEC lawyers paged through Rajaratnam's phone records,
they came upon a trove of possible new informants. One frequent
caller that jumped out from the thousands of pages of phone logs
was Rajat Gupta. Unlike Wadhwa, Michaelson did not know who
Gupta was at first. A quick Google search told him all he needed
to know. He could not help but wonder what business a respected
figure in the corporate world like Gupta would have with a sketchy
trader like Rajaratnam. At the time, there was nothing besides the

existence of phone calls between the men to tie Gupta to Rajaratnam; there was no evidence to suggest the two had a deep financial relationship. But the SEC lawyers had some sense of Rajaratnam's circle now. If someone was in close communication with Rajaratnam, they were interested in learning more about him and his relationship with the Galleon manager. They put Gupta's name aside. It was thrown into a basket of other names that cropped up during the course of the agency's investigation.

As Wadhwa surveyed the names at the heart of the probe and the ones he and his team set aside to focus on later, he came to a sobering realization. Without setting out to do so, it appeared that the SEC was on the verge of untangling the biggest South Asian insider trading ring in the history of the US securities industry.

* * *

Shortly before 4 p.m. on July 2, Rajaratnam's phone rang. He was in his glass-walled corner office wrapping things up before setting off for France. On the other end of the line was Roomy Khan, the former Intel employee who had worked for him briefly in the 1990s before she left after trading for her own account. The two had fallen out of touch for a while, but several years later they reconnected. She had lobbed a call in to him because she needed a job, and she knew the best way to get one was to ply Rajaratnam with information. She started feeding him tips she'd received from sources in her wide circle of South Asian informants. Now she was calling Rajaratnam with a hot tidbit of information. He was eager to hear it.

After she stopped working for him in March 1999, Khan had set up her own financial consulting firm, Digital Age Capital, and focused on building it up. She spent most of the day holed up in her office on the telephone. Khan liked to be connected; she had five telephone lines in her house and an equal number of computers. In the five years that she had been out of touch with Rajaratnam, she had traded her own account. In 2000, she made about $40 million on high-flying Internet stocks—a huge amount for someone who just a year earlier was pulling in a base salary of $120,000 as a hedge fund trader. Khan was on fire. Her investment gains prompted friends to funnel money to her. One was Sunil Bhalla, general manager of the voice communications division at Polycom, the Pleasanton, California–based videoconferencing equipment maker. He lived near Khan in Silicon Valley.

Bhalla, an engineer by training, immigrated to the United States in 1980 after a two-year stint working for Union Carbide in Bhopal, India. Khan met Bhalla in 2002 when he started dating one of her best friends. Khan's friend wanted her to meet Bhalla so she could screen the new man in her life. She trusted Khan because Khan and her friend came from the same community. When they eventually wound up having dinner in Sunnyvale, California, at P.F. Chang's, a Chinese restaurant chain, Khan found she and Bhalla had a lot in common; they were both Punjabi and spoke the same Indian language. Outside India, links like these, though ever so tenuous, were ties that bound. Khan wasted no time in cultivating Bhalla on her own as a source.

She impressed him with her knowledge of investing. "Thanks for the tips on stocks," he emailed her in August 2002, soon after their first meeting. "I plan to act on your recommendations. Will be happy to split my profits." He signed off the email with a smiley face. In January 2003, over lunch at the Marriott in Santa Clara, Khan picked Bhalla's brain about semiconductor companies such as AMD and Intel. He was easy bait. He had just moved to California from Boston after a traumatic divorce and didn't have many friends in the area.

Khan was passionate about investing, putting in fourteen-hour days, and not long after they met, Bhalla decided that he wanted to avail himself of Khan's expertise. He had never traded stocks on his own and he had heard a lot about Khan's trading prowess from the woman he once dated, so he gave her authority over a $50,000 account that he held at Lehman Brothers. Khan had broad discretion to trade in the account; besides stocks, she could invest in options and other esoteric financial instruments. Rather than simply preserve his capital, Bhalla wanted to grow it, and he was willing to tolerate a high degree of risk. Khan traded derivatives in Bhalla's account, and at first she grew his portfolio, quickly doubling his money to

$100,000. Bhalla was very pleased, and in early November 2003 he sent her an email saying, "Thanks for doing so well on the stocks. I am proud of you!" Besides the stellar performance, Bhalla had another reason to be happy. Khan refused to charge him any fees for running his money.

"I manage for close friends and family, and it would be an insult to me if you offer to pay me any money," Khan told him when he first broached the idea. "You are Punjabi, you are part of the community. I would be happy to do it."

Khan came to look upon Bhalla and his new wife, Neelam, as friends and from time to time invited them to blowout parties or visited their house to pray. Like the Bhallas, Khan was a Hindu, and on occasions like Diwali, she would perform a *puja*, a ceremonial form of worship that involves lighting a lamp and making offerings of sweets and fruits to the gods. She often confided in the Bhallas about the problems she was having with her husband, Sakhawat. She had met Sakhawat in the mid-eighties when she was studying at Columbia University. Sakhawat was brilliant and Khan was irresistibly drawn to him, even though their relationship was fraught with problems from the start. Unlike Khan, Sakhawat was a Muslim. Khan ignored the difference, and a few years after meeting, the two were married even though her parents were dead set against the union.

In 2005, Khan's winning streak came to an abrupt end. She lost $5 million of her own money and all of Bhalla's. He was remarkably sanguine about the loss. "We are friends and will remain so no matter what happens with the account," he emailed her in March. The financial woes strained her marriage, though. Sakhawat, a traditional Asian husband, had never liked that his wife was as devoted to her work as she was to him. He blamed her for the losses. She in turn was upset with him because he had not worked in years.

"Do something," she implored. "Do something."

It was all the more frustrating because Sakhawat was one of the brightest men Khan knew. During the 1990s, Sakhawat Khan was granted thirty patents, and when Information Storage Devices Inc., a technology company he was working for, was sold, Sakhawat received a stash of cash and stock. By the time he was thirty-five, Sakhawat no longer needed to work for anyone. After the sale, Sakhawat moved to start his own company, Agate Semiconductor Inc., in a room attached to the bedroom of their first house, a modest ranch-style abode in Sunnyvale. When Agate Semiconductor was acquired in 2000 for $7 million, the Khans were enriched yet again, reaping a couple of million from the sale. At the same time, Roomy, emboldened by the $40 million she made trading Internet stocks, placed more bets on the market. Like many during the Internet boom, she was seduced by her own success.

The sudden wealth gave the Khans a foothold in a new and unfamiliar world of opulence. Roomy liked to spend money, and she spent it extravagantly. She bought a seventeen-carat diamond at Neiman Marcus. For running up a shopping tab of more than $1 million, the department store gave her a BMW.

In 2000, the couple splurged on their biggest purchase yet, a nine-thousand-square-foot mansion with six bedrooms and six and a half bathrooms and more than half a dozen marble fireplaces, in Atherton, California, the richest town in Silicon Valley, which locals call the "home of the bazillionaires." The price tag was $10.5 million. The Khans paid all cash. Their new house was on Isabella Avenue, several doors down from Oracle billionaire Larry Ellison's exquisitely simple but exorbitantly expensive Japanese-style abode. In their seven years living in Atherton, the Khans never got an invitation to visit Ellison's place or drop by the home of another neighbor, Carol Bartz, the former chief executive of Yahoo! Inc.

Set on one and a half acres of land, the Khans' new house had a pool, a tennis court, and a two-story guesthouse, which Roomy turned into an office. For the couple, who enjoyed throwing lavish parties, it was the perfect pad. After the acquisition of Agate Semiconductor, Sakhawat kicked back. He stopped working and went to business school and took up flight-training classes so he could learn to pilot a plane by himself. The Khans, who had been trying to have a child for some time, adopted a daughter, Priyanka, from Bangladesh, whom Sakhawat doted on. He went from being someone who was always focused on business to someone more devoted to family. In 2002, the Khans hired a housekeeper, a woman from El Salvador named Vilma Serralta. Every day, Serralta would start by waking the couple's daughter, who was three years old when Serralta joined the Khans, and feeding her breakfast. Then she would spend the day cleaning the huge main house, mopping, dusting, and vacuuming it before turning to the guesthouse that Roomy Khan used as an office. Khan insisted that the five bathrooms in the main house be cleaned every day and the ones in the guesthouse twice a week. When the Khans' daughter returned from school in the afternoon, Serralta would watch her, play with her, and keep her occupied while she prepared dinner. She adored the Khans' daughter, who was just as attached to Serralta, whom she called "Auntie Vilma." During her fourteen-hour days, the only respite Serralta got was occasional five- to ten-minute breaks. She dared not sit for longer because Sakhawat Khan was always keeping tabs on her, following her around the house to make sure she was never idle.

The Khans probably would have been able to weather the financial squall if they hadn't loaded up on debt to support their extravagant lifestyle. Even though the couple had paid cash for their Atherton house in 2000, the Khans took out a $5 million mortgage after the tech stock meltdown. To meet their monthly expenses—property taxes alone in Atherton were $200,000 a year—the Khans had to pull in $60,000 a month. At first, Roomy was printing enough money to generate the income the family needed, but the trading losses hit her hard.

To make matters worse, she was also reeling from the aftershocks of a real estate deal that went awry. In December 2002, an agent acting for the Khans cut a $26 million deal to sell two homes to an Englishman who said he was a Stanford University professor with a passing interest in real estate investing. Little did the Khans know that the man was on the lam after failing to pay more than £1,188,000 for six French masterpieces at auction. At the time he entered into the deal with the Khans, the UK authorities were seeking him as a con man. To the Khans' chagrin, he wound up pulling out of the real estate deal at the eleventh hour, leaving them with tens of thousands of dollars in lost fees that they were not able to recoup.

In 2005, Deutsche Bank sued Khan, alleging that she did not pay $600,000 in trading fees. Meanwhile, her domestic help, Serralta, was chafing at having to work eighty to ninety hours a week with only a day and a half off every other week; for all her duties, she said Khan paid her $250 a week.

Now strapped for cash, Roomy Khan tried to get a job, but this was easier said than done because of her earlier run-in with the FBI. After she had left Galleon, she pleaded guilty to wire fraud in April 2001 for her theft of corporate secrets from Intel—secrets she'd passed to Rajaratnam. It was a crime that carried a maximum prison sentence of five years and a fine of $250,000. But a year later, when Khan was sentenced, she was given probation. Her light sentence came at the behest of prosecutors, who disagreed with a presentencing report that called for a stiffer sanction. They said Khan deserved a lighter sentence because she "has provided the United States with substantial assistance in the investigation of another person." Neither the prosecutors nor Khan revealed the individual's name, but behind the scenes and unbeknownst to Rajaratnam, Khan had worked with the FBI to build a case against him.

After exhausting all avenues and not knowing where to turn, Khan in mid-2005 reached out to Rajaratnam. She'd stayed away from him for several years on the advice of her lawyer. But now that her legal troubles were behind her, she saw no harm in getting in touch. When she telephoned, he seemed happy to hear from her, even though it had been ages since the two had spoken. He always treated Khan as more than just a business acquaintance. She felt that he was more inclined to take her calls and listen to her ideas because she and his wife, Asha, came from the same part of India. When Khan told Rajaratnam that she was looking for a job, he seemed surprised.

"You are too wealthy to work for me," he said flatly.

At that point, Khan confided in him, telling him about the depth of the cash crunch that she and her husband, Sakhawat, faced. The interest rate on the mortgage of their Atherton house had doubled, driving her monthly expenses higher. She was having a hard time finding a job, though she failed to mention to Rajaratnam the real reason for her difficulty: her criminal record.

In the course of their conversation, Rajaratnam, who had no idea that Khan had snitched on him in the past, asked Khan what companies she had an "edge" on. Having worked for Rajaratnam before, Khan knew that he was asking her at which companies she had an insider. She said she had an "edge" on Polycom, the company where her friend Bhalla worked. Rajaratnam didn't hire Khan, but the two rekindled their relationship. When Rajaratnam came out to California in December 2005 for a Lehman conference at the St. Regis hotel in San Francisco, the two met. Khan, still hoping to parlay her tips into a job, invited Rajaratnam to her home. She wanted to show him her office space in her guesthouse so that Rajaratnam would know she was serious about working at Galleon. Rajaratnam told her he planned to fire his Internet analyst by year-end and hire her. A couple of months later, when Khan got wind that Rajaratnam had fired the analyst, she broached the topic of a job at Galleon again. This time, he said he wanted to wait until earnings season passed before having a discussion about it. She was starting to wonder if Rajaratnam was being sincere or stringing her along.

In an effort to ingratiate herself to Rajaratnam, Khan started to feed him a steady diet of tips on tech stocks and companies in other sectors. Her information on Polycom was uncannily on the money. In December 2005, she invited Bhalla and his new wife to her home for a holiday dinner. Khan liked to mix business with pleasure, and as Bhalla was leaving the party, she asked him how the quarter was going. He told her it was looking very good.

After the holidays, Khan followed up with him. Sometime early in January, around the tenth or eleventh of the month, she set up a meeting with him. To help focus the discussion, she arrived with an earnings model of Polycom and a snapshot of the company's profit estimates.

"So what's the expectation?" Bhalla asked. He wanted to know the revenue that Wall Street expected Polycom to generate that quarter. Khan threw out a number—$145 million or so.

"Oh, we can easily beat that," Bhalla replied.

Bhalla's information flew completely in the face of the prevailing view on Wall Street, where analysts were predicting that

Polycom would have a weak fourth quarter. As soon as Khan got the upbeat news, she started spreading the word, telling Rajaratnam and others in her circle that Polycom's fourth quarter was going to be good and the general outlook on future earnings was positive. On Thursday, January 12, at 10:30 a.m., Khan instant-messaged Rajaratnam: "hi u there?" There is no record of a phone conversation between Rajaratnam and Khan but three minutes later Rajaratnam messaged his favorite trader and said: "buy 60 PLCM," which is the ticker symbol for Polycom.

That morning in January 2006, just two days after Khan had bought 3,000 Polycom call options, making a calculation that Polycom's stock would rise, Rajaratnam's Technology fund started buying the stock. At 10:36 a.m., the fund acquired 60,000 shares. It was a nerve-racking position. Sometimes when a company is expected to unveil strong earnings, its stock starts to rise in anticipation, but in this case, Polycom's stock was not moving higher. Khan was worried and from time to time checked in with Bhalla, who reassured her that Polycom's earnings report would surpass expectations.

Over the next week, Galleon steadily acquired more shares of Polycom, and on Saturday, January 21, Rajaratnam called his brother Rengan from home; two days later, on Monday, when trading resumed, Rengan also began to acquire Polycom shares in his personal account and at his hedge fund Sedna.

After the market closed on Wednesday, January 25, Polycom released its fourth-quarter 2005 earnings, which showed revenue of $156.1 million, easily surpassing Wall Street estimates as Bhalla promised. Polycom's stock, which trades under the ticker symbol PLCM, rose 13 percent.

The next day, Rajaratnam instant-messaged Khan: "hey...tks for plcm idea." After the earnings were released, Bhalla also got in touch. Khan says he suggested she sell the Polycom stock in the midst of the rally and then, lapsing into Hindi, he asked her to put some of the winnings from the Polycom trade into his money-losing account at Lehman. But Khan, now worried that she might be forced to sell her sprawling Atherton estate, told Bhalla that she could not give him the money. She first had to attend to repairing her own finances.

Getting a job at a hedge fund like Galleon would be a start to fixing her problems.

A few weeks after the profitable Polycom trade, Khan met with Rajaratnam again while he was on a trip to San Francisco. Earnings season was over and Khan had helped Rajaratnam make money in the profit-reporting period that had just ended. Her tip on Polycom alone netted his Technology fund $482,960 in gains. There was no better time than now to bring up the subject of a job at Galleon. But when she raised the topic with Rajaratnam in San Francisco, he stalled. He said he would need to confer with his head trader before hiring her, and he now said that he thought she needed connections in New York before Galleon could bring her on board. Over the next couple of years, Khan and Rajaratnam stayed in touch; she continued to provide inside information on Polycom and stocks such as Google. Rajaratnam reciprocated, giving her his gleanings on stocks such as AMD and Intel. He never hired her. He didn't have to; she was already supplying him with insider tips.

A little before 4 p.m. on July 2, 2007, two days before Rajaratnam headed off for his family vacation in France, Khan called him to tell him about a hot tip she'd received from another source in her wide circle of South Asian informants. During the brief call, Khan told Rajaratnam she heard that Blackstone Group, the New York private equity firm, was planning to acquire Hilton Hotels Corp. The information was red-hot, meaning that the deal was going to be announced the next day.

An investor seeking to make money needed to act fast, buying shares before Blackstone unveiled the price it planned to pay for Hilton. Khan had already placed a trade in Hilton for her own account, buying 550 call options that would allow her to buy Hilton stock at a specified price at a future date. Over the next ten minutes, Rajaratnam and Khan spoke briefly two more times. It was too late for Galleon to place a trade that afternoon because the stock market was about to close. But the next morning, Tuesday, July 3, seven minutes after the market opened, one of Rajaratnam's lieutenants placed an order with J.P. Morgan to buy 500,000 shares of Hilton. Of that, 400,000 shares, or about $14 million of stock, were purchased for the Galleon Technology fund, the flagship fund at Galleon, which Rajaratnam ran—an odd trade for a tech fund considering that Hilton Hotels was as much a tech company as Intel was a hotelier. When Khan caught up with Rajaratnam later that day and asked if he had snapped up some Hilton stock, he said he missed it. The SEC probe had done little to curtail his bad behavior, but clearly it had made him more circumspect.

By the end of the trading day, purchases by Rajaratnam and scores of others who caught wind of the Hilton deal before it was announced pushed the company stock 6.4 percent higher, to $36.05. After the market closed, Blackstone said it would pay $47.50 a share in cash to buy Hilton for a total of $20 billion plus debt. The deal was a windfall for Rajaratnam, who netted a profit of almost $4.1 million, and for Khan and a host of others. When Rajaratnam eventually caught up with his friend Rajiv Goel in France, he mentioned making a boatload for him on Hilton. A purchase of 7,500 shares of Hilton stock was placed in Goel's Schwab account at 10:39 a.m. the day before Rajaratnam headed off to France, from an Internet protocol address at Galleon. The trade would ultimately become a costly one for Goel.

July 3 was only a half trading day because of the upcoming Independence Day holiday, but 7,470,686 shares of Hilton changed hands, more than twice as much as the average trading volume in the stock on a daily basis in the preceding fifty-two-week period. It was clear that someone knew Hilton was going to be acquired.

Israel Friedman, an SEC staff attorney, was struck by the hockey-stick-like rise in Hilton stock, and immediately after the Independence Day holiday he requested information on trading activity in Hilton from the NYSE. Friedman was a seasoned lawyer and a dogged digger. As a matter of practice, when he investigated cases, he not only subpoenaed phone records but also liked to obtain Internet protocol addresses, the unique numerical label identifying a certain computer in a network. It was an investigative tool that would prove important in unlocking the Galleon case.

As it happened, Israel Friedman sat in an office next to Michaelson. The two were friends and would often chat about their cases.

Reminded of the hours of meticulous phone logging Jason Friedman and Michaelson put in investigating Sedna, Galleon, and the Rajaratnam brothers, Israel Friedman drilled into the "blue sheets" (trading records) on Hilton stock. (In the analog days they were actually printed on blue paper.) Among the hundreds and hundreds of buyers and sellers of Hilton shares that day, there was Galleon. It placed an astonishingly large trade to buy Hilton stock just seven minutes into the trading cycle. It yielded a profit of $4 million, a huge gain on a single stock—not bad for half a day's work.

Rajaratnam either had contempt for the intelligence of Wadhwa and Michaelson, or he was so intoxicated by the prospect of a quick score that not only was he trading on inside information while he was the subject of an ongoing SEC investigation, but also he was now no longer limiting his trades to technology stocks, where he could arguably make the case that his investments were driven by his superior analysis of the industry. He was forging aggressively into sectors, for example, hospitality, where he had no special expertise and where a large trade by a technology fund would raise red flags.

Sanjay Wadhwa was taken aback by Rajaratnam's nerve— apparently, the higher the risk of breaking the law and getting away with it, the less the worry of being caught.

"Wow, he was just here a month ago," he remarked to colleagues.

CHAPTER SIXTEEN

Playing for Team USA

One day not long after the Blackstone takeover of Hilton in July 2007, Israel Friedman walked over to the desk of his SEC colleague Andrew Michaelson.

"Isn't this the woman you were talking about?" asked Friedman, pointing to a name, Roomy Khan, that was buried in a stack of trading records in Hilton stock.

Michaelson flipped through the sheaf of papers and noticed another name he'd come across months earlier. Rajiv Goel was one of the contacts in Rajaratnam's voluminous Rolodex. Now it looked like Goel was also someone who happened to trade in Hilton stock before the Blackstone takeover. Hoping that these eerily prescient trades could be the key to unlocking the investigation into Galleon, Michaelson decided to scour the Hilton blue sheets for other names that cropped up in Rajaratnam's electronic address book or emerged in the Galleon phone records that the SEC had subpoenaed. One individual with whom Rajaratnam seemed to be in frequent contact but to whom investigators could not tie any information about any stock was a McKinsey consultant named Anil Kumar.

If Kumar was indeed an informant of Rajaratnam's, he might well have traded in Hilton stock, Michaelson ventured. But when he ran Kumar's name through the blue-sheet data, he came up empty. It diminished his suspicions of Kumar's involvement in the ring. With no shady instant messages between Rajaratnam and Kumar and no incriminating trading activity, Michaelson moved on, not revisiting evidence that was sitting in a corner of his office.

Months before, Michaelson's colleagues in Texas were investigating the rally in ATI Technologies stock before its takeover by AMD in July 2006. In the course of that investigation, they forwarded Michaelson three boxes of documents, made up of deal histories listing bankers, lawyers, and consultants privy to the deals before they were announced. Buried in one of the boxes among some nine hundred names and hundreds of pages was Anil Kumar's name. He was listed as a consultant to AMD. Knowing that might have helped Michaelson make the link between Rajaratnam and Kumar.

Struck by the overlapping players in the Galleon and the Hilton cases, Sanjay Wadhwa and Markowitz pulled in Israel Friedman, who was working on the Hilton team, to join the Galleon effort. At first, the lawyers suspected that Blackstone, the New York private equity fund run by Stephen Schwarzman, might have been the source of the Hilton information. Blackstone invested $20 million in April 2007 in Galleon's Captain's fund, run by portfolio manager Todd Deutsch.

"Blackstone may have tipped Galleon," wrote B. J. Kang, the special agent for an FBI squad that focuses on economic crimes and securities fraud. The SEC lawyers chased down some inconclusive Blackstone leads, but Israel Friedman's discovery of Khan's trading in Hilton quickly sent them on a new, more promising trail.

Ever since Rajaratnam had given testimony in early June, Michaelson had been honing in on Khan, the former Intel employee who went by the instant-message handle "roomy81." Five days after Rajaratnam's visit, investigators uncovered an IM exchange dated January 9, 2006, between rajatgalleon and roomy81:

rajatgalleon: hey
rajatgalleon: u back
roomy81: I am here
roomy81: did not go any where
rajatgalleon: call me . . . just got back today
roomy81: please let me know on JNPR

roomy81: donot buy plcm till I het guidance
roomy81: want to make sure guidance OK

PLCM was the ticker symbol for Polycom, and JNPR was Juniper Networks, a Sunnyvale, California–based company that made switching routers. Amid the cryptic exchange, one line grabbed investigators: "till I [get] guidance...want to make sure guidance OK." Judging by the IMs, it looked like Khan had an informant at Polycom who was giving her the early read on its profit reports and its future earnings prospects. The exchange was too vague to build an insider trading case, but after more than a year and a half of investigating, the SEC was heartened. *Surely the IM must be the smoking gun,* thought the SEC lawyers. With evidence of both Khan and Rajaratnam making large purchases of Hilton shares on the same day, there was even more ammunition to support their suspicions that the two were more than casual friends. Indeed, it was increasingly looking like they were partners in crime.

The SEC lawyers poured their energies into learning more about Khan and her world of corporate insiders. Jason Friedman was assigned the task of diving deep into Khan's phone records to uncover her universe of contacts. It turned out to be far more time-consuming and painful than he first imagined. Khan was a phone junkie. She had nearly half a dozen landlines and at least three cell phones—all of which she used all the time. At one point, Friedman was so familiar with Khan's phone numbers that he could recite them all off the top of his head. For each of Khan's phone lines, Jason Friedman printed out the records for the relevant time period and tried to link Khan to a possible source of information. Trolling through the dense data in small print left him bleary-eyed.

One muggy day in August 2007, after weeks of combing through phone records, Jason Friedman came across a call between Khan and a number at Polycom's headquarters. A little later in the day, he found another call between one of Khan's other phones and the home number of a Polycom executive. Friedman identified the number, by simply Googling it, as belonging to a Sunil Bhalla. He did an Internet search and learned that Bhalla was a high-level Polycom executive. Excited, he ran across the hall into Wadhwa's office to report on his find.

After almost a year of investigating, the SEC for the first time had the circumstantial evidence to link Rajaratnam's trading in a stock to a source inside the company whose stock he was trading. The SEC had no evidence to suggest that Rajaratnam knew Bhalla, but it already had heaps of IMs between Khan and Rajaratnam and phone records that showed them speaking around the same time as the calls between Khan and Bhalla. Khan, it seemed, was the connective tissue between the Galleon chief and the Polycom executive.

It was an important breakthrough, and Wadhwa was eager to build on it quickly. When Friedman found Polycom dragging its feet in complying with his request for call logs, Wadhwa and his boss, Markowitz, a seasoned lawyer, lobbed calls to the company's outside lawyers, demanding they step up their efforts to produce the call histories. Worried that Polycom might alert Bhalla, a senior executive, to the SEC's inquiry, Friedman requested phone logs for several Polycom executives rather than asking for Bhalla's alone. Sandwiched among the list of names was Bhalla's.

As Friedman made progress on Polycom, Rajaratnam partied hard. In early August, he headed off to the Maasai Mara, one of Kenya's most acclaimed game reserves. Rajaratnam knew how to throw a fabulous party, and Kenya was a five-day extravaganza for the "Raj tribe," his seventy closest friends and family members. Before the bash even started, Rajaratnam, true to style, seduced the guests he flew out on a chartered plane with a hard-to-resist invitation. "Are you ready to leave the urban jungle and walk on the wild side?" the party invitation read. On August 5, after a brief stop in Nairobi, the group flew to the Mara. As they walked off the plane, they were greeted by a dozen Maasai natives dressed in bright red cloth and holding sharp spears; the natives were in the throes of a spell-binding dance.

To get his friends in the right mood, Rajaratnam supplied party favors: black T-shirts. One guest, a serious-looking individual with glasses, looked uncomfortable in his green pants, light blue windbreaker, and a black T-shirt, which read "The Riotous, Rowdy,

Rebellious Raj Tribe." Few knew it, but it was none other than Anil Kumar, a core member of the tribe. When the guests returned home, Rajaratnam sent them all a book with photos memorializing the trip. Inscribed at the front was his life motto: "Remember never grow up—and nothing is more serious than the pursuit of fun!!!"

* * *

By the end of the summer, it was clear to the SEC team working the Galleon case that nothing was more important than getting a Rajaratnam informant to flip. Two stocks, Polycom and Hilton, offered the most glaring examples of trading on inside information, but all the evidence that Michaelson and the two Friedmans—Jason and Israel—had developed was still circumstantial.

With an individual who is an occasional trader of stocks, that would not have mattered, but hedge funds like Galleon dive in and out of stocks all day, so it would be hard to tie the trades Galleon made to any one piece of information without the help of an insider. Wadhwa, Markowitz, and Michaelson felt that the criminal authorities needed to flip someone in Rajaratnam's inner circle, someone who could provide direct evidence of inside information being exchanged. Chances were that they would have only one shot at convincing a suspected member of the ring to cooperate with the government. If they failed, they risked blowing the entire investigation. The odds were high that the individual would inform Rajaratnam and he would stop his criminal activity.

Coincidentally, an unexpected discovery on another front helped convince the SEC lawyers that Khan was their best bet. Soon after the large trades in Hilton, the SEC turned over Khan's name to FBI special agent B. J. Kang. Agent Kang, known as B.J., looks like the archetypal FBI agent. He has a crew cut that he often wears slicked back, and a penetrating gaze. Kang did a quick background check and discovered that Khan had a criminal past. In fact, in 1999 she confessed to procuring inside information for none other than Raj Rajaratnam. Instead of paying her for the Intel information she purloined, Rajaratnam did favors for her, such as arranging job interviews. "Intel and the FBI agree that the primary culprit, and continuing threat is Rajaratnam," wrote Russell Atkinson, an FBI agent in the San Francisco bureau, in an April 29, 1998, email to agents in New York. "He is expected to continue his activity after Khan leaves, and is probably obtaining insider information from other companies currently." Atkinson suggested that someone in New York get in touch so the FBI could coordinate its efforts on both coasts. But after years of investigating, neither the SEC nor the FBI could show that any Galleon trade resulted from the information Khan stole for Rajaratnam from Intel. So in August 2002, the probe into Rajaratnam was closed. This time it would be different.

Khan had every incentive to cooperate. She had been in trouble with criminal authorities before. She got off easy the first time, but the courts were unlikely to be as lenient with a repeat offender. Encouraged by the knowledge of Khan's criminal past and equipped with evidence that she was back to breaking the law, the SEC lawyers started pushing prosecutors to get Khan on "Team USA"—a phrase Markowitz liked to use for flipping Khan and getting her to cooperate. In late September 2007, Wadhwa, Markowitz, Michaelson, and Jason Friedman met with Lauren Goldberg, the assistant US attorney in the Southern District working the case. Since telling prosecutors of the investigation in March, the SEC had been working hard to get lawyers in the Manhattan US attorney's office excited about the Galleon probe. (The US attorney's office has a crush of cases to handle, so it can take time before prosecutors focus on another agency's white-collar case.) Ahead of the meeting, Michaelson prepared an agenda. Near the top of it was Roomy Khan.

* * *

On November 28, 2007, Kang and another FBI agent appeared unannounced at Khan's lavish and heavily mortgaged California home. The imposing property at 168 Isabella Avenue was fittingly protected by high security gates, and the agents were let into the house by Khan's mother. There they found Khan, an overweight and voluble woman around fifty years old, in a state of panic.

Her marriage was in trouble and the Atherton house was on the market for $18 million. She had raised about $2 million by auctioning some diamonds through Sotheby's, disposing of pieces of art, and jettisoning a car. But she still had not made up the losses she had racked up in the account of her old friend Bhalla. For a while the two were out of touch. Khan stopped calling him because she was embarrassed by the trading mishap and overwhelmed by her own woes. She missed the friendship; a couple of times, when the situation on the home front had become unbearable, she and her mother had stopped by the Bhallas to unburden themselves and cry. But as much as she wanted to pay back Bhalla, she couldn't at first because her own finances were in a perilous state. "I personally have been going through very tough times," she emailed him in the spring, reaching out after a long hiatus. "I know I still need to recoup the deficit I created for you." He was remarkably sanguine—"Yes, personally losing all the money hurt a lot...however, I am not complaining and know that you are doing the best you can." Still she couldn't get it out of her mind. "I will make up your loss!!" she replied. "I do promise."

For an hour, the FBI agents asked questions and then let Khan talk, which she did freely but not always truthfully. Lying to the FBI agents who appeared on her doorstep in 1999 had not hurt her; she figured dissembling again wouldn't be a problem. She said that she got back in touch with Rajaratnam because she hoped he would hire her. When they asked about Bhalla, the Polycom executive, she admitted knowing him but denied speaking to him about the company.

She was insistent that she did not instant-message or email Rajaratnam about Polycom. In fact, she claimed that she no longer discussed companies with people. She'd learned her lesson after a little legal tangle she had with the FBI several years before. At that point, Kang confronted her with the Polycom instant messages and other incriminating material. Khan fled to the bathroom and returned a short while later, puffy-faced, evidently from crying. She adjusted quickly to her new reality and was ready to tell the truth—some of it, not all, for now. "If I don't cooperate this time," she told Kang, "I'll go to jail."

With Khan now ready to play for Team USA, investigators worked to tie up other loose ends. Israel Friedman, who had originally been sniffing around the suspicious trading in shares of Hilton before joining the Galleon probe, sent letters to Charles Schwab & Co. asking for account statements for Rajiv Goel and his wife, Alka (Goel was both a Wharton pal of Rajaratnam's and an Intel executive). As was his custom, Friedman also requested the IP addresses that would show who logged into the Goels' account to trade. When the documents arrived, the SEC lawyers discovered a guidebook to some of Galleon's more questionable trades. On the morning of July 3, 2007, before Blackstone unveiled its deal for Hilton, somebody at Galleon logged into Goel's account at Schwab and bought $264,284.95 of Hilton stock. He made about $78,000 on the trade. In twelve other instances that year, an individual at Galleon logged into the Goels' Schwab account and bought stocks. Some of the stocks were the same ones now under scrutiny by the SEC.

CHAPTER SEVENTEEN

The Wharton Mafia

Had Anil Kumar not gone to the University of Pennsylvania's Wharton School of business in 1981, he probably would have never met Raj Rajaratnam. Though both were from South Asia, the two were worlds apart in temperament, character, and looks. Rajaratnam was dark-skinned and heavyset, with a booming voice and an equally loud personality. His most attractive physical feature was his dazzlingly white gap-toothed grin, which he flashed whenever he was charming a woman or coaxing a friend into doing him a favor. He had a reputation for cutting corners, often skipping classes and bumming cigarettes off classmates so he wouldn't have to buy them himself. When challenged, his standard line was: "Go ahead and sue me."

His nickname among the South Asians at Wharton was "black bindass"—a Hinglish expression, part Hindi and part English, that conferred upon Rajaratnam the status of a cool cat: full of himself and caring little for others, but definitely cool. He gave off the impression that he was a rich kid. Unlike his South Asian cohorts, he was well traveled, having lived in Singapore, where his father was posted for some time, and England before coming to Wharton. Just one of a very small group of Sri Lankan aristocrats in the United States, he carried none of the arriviste baggage that students from India like Anil Kumar carried. Despite their social differences, though, the two men shared one similarity: neither could have better timed his arrival in America.

"You had this interesting demographic anomaly" with the Indian immigrants who came to America, explains Vijay Prashad, author of *Uncle Swami*. "You had people who missed two of the greatest social movements of the last century." One was the struggle for independence in India, and the other was the fight for civil rights in the United States. The Indian immigrants to the United States benefited from both movements even though they played no part in either. They were born or came of age in the wake of independence and were thrust into an India that was investing heavily in the middle class to give it a basic and technical education so it would have the know-how to help India catch up with the rest of the world. In effect, "the state was subsidizing the production of highly skilled labor," says Prashad. This push led to the creation of world-class institutions including the Indian Institutes of Technology, which sprang up in quick succession in the decade after independence. Upon reaching adulthood, these highly trained Indians rightly suspected that there would be a greater rate of return on their skills if they went abroad, so they left the country. In India, political leaders bemoaned "the brain drain," but the exodus couldn't have been more opportune for America—and for them.

Arriving in greater numbers at the start of the 1980s than before, South Asians like Anil Kumar and Raj Rajaratnam landed in the United States at a moment when professional opportunities that would have been closed to them a decade earlier were suddenly open. America, forced to reinvent itself amid the decline in manufacturing, was on the cusp of embarking on two new tracks, finance and technology, that coincidentally played to the strengths of the new Indian immigrants.

In Prashad's view, the end of the civil rights struggle and the opening up of opportunities for immigrants from South Asia undoubtedly shaped the mind-set of Indians in America and contributed to a sense of entitlement. "The attitude that underlies this community is that we are great because we are really talented, not because a special set of circumstances made us great." The risk, of course, is "if a person goes through life believing struggle is irrelevant, you don't have to work for anything, then why not take more than you are offered?

This is the twice-blessed generation, and my sense is some of them took this twice-blessedness literally, and this was their undoing."

When Rajat Gupta arrived in the United States in the early 1970s, there were only a smattering of South Asians at HBS and Wharton. There were so few that they invariably hung out together and became good friends. But when Raj Rajaratnam and Anil Kumar arrived at Wharton, Indian immigration into the United States had jumped to 22,600 in 1980, and with more than thirty South Asians in the class of 1983, there were enough to be cliques. A wide social chasm split the American-raised Indians from their across-the-world cousins. Americans of Indian descent were schooled in the United States and spoke English with an American twang. They sneered at the "OTBs" (off the boats) or "FOBs" (fresh off the boats) with their thick accents and their geeky ways. In their minds, they were cool and the new immigrants from India were definitely uncool.

For the most part, they felt more at ease with Americans than with Indians, and their only connection with their native land was eating Indian food at home and visiting in an annual pilgrimage that was as discomforting and awkward for them as it was for the cousins they met back in India. Rather than reaffirming their common identity, as their parents hoped, it only heightened the gulf between them.

The new wave of Indians, stepping off of Boeing 747s in the early 1980s, considered themselves superior to the assimilated. They had something the Indians who were bred in America would never have. They had a sense of belonging and an identity, born out of a vibrant five-thousand-year-old culture with a history rich in learning, music, and art. They looked upon the Indians who were raised in America with contempt and mocked them as ABCDs—or American-Born Confused Desis (think the Kelly Kapoor character on NBC's *The Office*). The combination of English and Hindi in the unflattering label underscored the cultural confusion they spotted in the Indians in America.

Despite hailing from the same country, it was as if the two sets of Indians, the ABCDs and the OTBs, grew up in parallel universes. Often the young Indians reared in America had to choose. They could be friends with Americans or with Indians, but they could not be friends with both. Though their ethnic origin should have been a unifying bond, US-raised Indians and immigrant Indians were almost as far apart as black Americans and white Americans.

Unlike the awkward Indian students at Wharton, Rajaratnam mingled easily with all crowds. He got along well with both Indians and Americans, straddling the different cultures effortlessly. His social grace was all the more remarkable because Rajaratnam did not truly belong to either community. He was a Tamil from Sri Lanka, a small pearl-drop-shaped island nation in the Indian Ocean, just to the southeast of India.

Rajaratnam's father, Jesuthasan, was emblematic of the success of the country's upper-middle-class Tamil community. He joined Singer Sewing Co. as a young man and eventually rose to be the head of its operations in South Asia. His success in business led to connections in politics; the two went hand in hand. In 1948, the British left Sri Lanka (then Ceylon) and the picture for Tamils, many of whom had migrated from India, changed. In the decades that followed, their position eroded as the government embarked on discriminatory policies that pushed Sinhalese nationals into ascendancy.

The turning point came in 1956, one year before Rajaratnam's birth. In what *New Yorker* writer Philip Gourevitch has called the "defining catastrophe of post-colonial Sri Lankan history," then prime minister S. W. R. D. Bandaranaike, the scion of a Sinhalese noble family, enacted a law that established Sinhalese as the sole official language of the country, replacing English. The "Sinhala-only" policy excluded Tamils, who were conversant in English, from careers in public service and access to other educational opportunities. It also marked the beginning of bloody ethnic violence between the Tamils and the Sinhalese, a perennial feature of the Sri Lankan landscape in the decades to follow.

Growing up as a young boy in the 1960s, the second oldest of five children, Rajaratnam enjoyed the privileged life common to Sri Lanka's Tamil elite at the time. The family lived in Cinnamon Gardens, an enclave of Colombo known for its stately whitewashed colonial-era homes kept cool by rows of swaying palm trees. Like most well-to-do Sri Lankan Tamils, the Rajaratnams firmly believed that the path to success in life lay in education, so they sent Raj and his siblings to the finest schools and, in later years, encouraged each of them to pursue a career rather than rely on the family's wealth.

Raj attended St. Thomas' Preparatory School, an institution patterned along the lines of an English public school, equivalent in manner to the Doon School in India from which Anil Kumar graduated. When he was seventeen years old, he was sent to study at Dulwich College, a boys' school in southeast London, better known for churning out writers like the Sri Lankan–born author Michael Ondaatje (*The English Patient*) than for minting hedge fund managers.

Decades after Rajaratnam left school, his time at Dulwich became part of a colorful fabric of tales he wove for himself. In an interview in 2011, he said he lived in the same room once occupied by P. G. Wodehouse, the writer of wonderfully witty books popular in Asia because of the humorous way they depict the British upper classes. Following a Dulwich tradition in which pupils write their names on the walls of their dorm rooms, he said, he affixed his name right under Wodehouse's. But by the time Rajaratnam arrived at Dulwich in September 1974, Wodehouse's old dormitory, Elm Lawn, had been converted into the headmaster's residence.

At Dulwich, Rajaratnam did not stand out either in the classroom or on the sports field. Rajaratnam rarely spoke about his time in England except when it suited his purpose—if he was trying to bond or curry favor with someone who was English. Colleagues sensed that his reticence came from being bullied at school or having a hard time assimilating into the England of the early seventies, which was a closed and some say racist society. He did speak publicly about his years in England in 2011, when he gave an interview to Suketu Mehta, an Indian writer and author of the acclaimed book *Maximum City*. Rajaratnam recalled that it was an era when the Far Right party the National Front was marching through the streets and beating up "Pakis." Rajaratnam remembers walking down a road in a rough London neighborhood with his uncle once when three white men rammed their shoulders into his uncle.

"We started pushing and shoving" but did not run. "Running has never been part of my M.O." Rajaratnam and his uncle got beaten up, but "I didn't get beaten up anymore than they did." The incident taught him an important lesson: "I was conscious of the fact that I could be attacked because of my ethnicity."

Rajaratnam stayed at Dulwich until December 1976, remaining an extra term to take exams that would determine if he would get a place at England's finest universities, Oxford and Cambridge. He did not, so in 1976 he headed to the University of Sussex, a middle-of-the-pack university on the outskirts of Brighton, a seaside resort town, where he got a bachelor of science in engineering before moving on to Wharton for his MBA.

Rajaratnam could not have cared less about the South Asian pecking order at Wharton. "He was so charismatic," says Anju Jessani, a former classmate of Rajaratnam's. "Everyone knew Raj." She says he "wasn't like all the other Indian students who were much more reserved and kept to themselves. He socialized with lots of people." His bawdy sense of humor and his single-minded focus on meeting beautiful women disarmed Americans, whose perception of South Asians was grounded more in caricature than in reality.

He appeared to skate through Wharton, working little but managing to pull off decent grades. Gregarious and outgoing, he was not clannish like his South Asian peers. For a time, he lived in the University of Pennsylvania's International House, a dormitory that drew students from all across the college, not just the Wharton School. His roommate was an American, Tom Fernandez.

Unlike many South Asians who buried their heads in their books, Rajaratnam often skipped class and relied on sycophants to lend him their notes, which they freely did. If friends wanted to borrow his notes, however, Rajaratnam would make the loan contingent on them agreeing to do him a favor, such as procuring marijuana or introducing him to a woman he was interested in. His galaxy of friends included classmates such as Krishen Sud, Tom Fernandez, and David Lau, who would join him years later as he rose in prominence on Wall Street.

* * *

When he arrived at Wharton, much as he had at Doon, Anil Kumar kept to a close circle of friends, mostly Indians. Rajaratnam wasn't part of the future McKinsey man's crowd. It isn't even clear that they liked one another.

Once, after a statistics exam, Rajaratnam remembers Kumar asking him, "How much did you get?" Rajaratnam replied: "Ninety-seven." Then he asked Kumar what he got.

"I don't want to tell you my grades," Kumar replied.

Kumar and Rajaratnam became acquainted less by choice than by accident. Kumar's roommate at Wharton was an Indian who happened to be friends with Rajaratnam too. He would often host curry dinners in their dormitory room at Penn's graduate towers, and Rajaratnam was a frequent guest.

"They were both incredibly smart but very different personalities," says Tushar Mody, who was in the same Wharton class and socialized with both from time to time. With Raj, "you knew what you were getting. Anil was quiet, observant and calculating."

One year when their classmate Anil Ambani (a member of the Ambani family of Reliance Industries fame) sent out Diwali cards to mark the Hindu festival of lights, Kumar made a mental note of the gesture.

"Boy, this guy is organized," Kumar told Mody. "He is keeping in touch with everyone." Over the years, Kumar mastered the networking skills he observed in Ambani as a young man, always making a point to follow up on a casual encounter with an important person. The one person in the Wharton class of 1983 that no one expected Kumar would keep in touch with was Rajaratnam.

CHAPTER EIGHTEEN

Reeling in Roomy

On January 3, 2008, Roomy Khan, accompanied by her attorney, arrived in New York to lay out the information she could provide the government as part of a proffer agreement. In a proffer, prosecutors promise they won't use an individual's statements against them, with some exceptions. Among the exceptions: if the individual lies. Initially, Khan was remarkably reticent. After the first day, Lauren Goldberg, the assistant US attorney who was working the Galleon case, read her the riot act. The next day, Khan came in ready to enlighten prosecutors on a new instance of insider trading of which they were not even aware.

She disclosed that in mid-2007 she passed along inside information to Rajaratnam on Google's poor second-quarter earnings. Khan claimed that she had received the tip from Shammara Hussain, a junior employee at Market Street Partners, an outside investor relations company that worked for Google. Khan met Hussain, then a pretty twenty-one-year-old, at a technology conference in San Francisco in late 2006. The two started talking and Khan discovered that Hussain was from Bangladesh, just like her husband. As it happened, Khan also knew Hussain's father, an engineer at none other than AMD. Hussain bragged that she knew a lot about stocks; she was even trading them during the conference. Eager to get closer to her, Khan started inviting her parents over for dinner. Soon Khan was playing the role of a South Asian "auntie" in Hussain's life, advising her on how to dress and telling her she was like a daughter.

Hussain was already on the SEC's radar. Months earlier, lawyers had spotted her number in Khan's phone records. When Jason Friedman, the junior member of the SEC's Galleon team, Googled the number, he found it on a website for a cricket club. It belonged to Hussain, an employee at the club. He also noticed that her number appeared on a BMW enthusiasts website under the name "shamz," where she posted a number of ads to sell BMWs. As Friedman surfed the website, he found countless posts by others groaning about her arrogance. He also discovered she was a blogger for stocks on a popular website called Seeking Alpha. And she had an account at Minekey.com, where she opined on a variety of subjects. "Saving money is boring…figuring out how to make a return is exciting," she wrote in one comment.

One day in mid-June 2007, Khan said that Hussain telephoned her and said, "Short Google."

"I am not going to short Google," Khan shot back. The company's stock was rising like a rocket; taking a bearish position was suicidal. A week to ten days later, Hussain called again to deliver the same message. This time she told Khan something that made her listen: "I'm on the IR team for Google…they are going to miss the numbers." IR was short for investor relations. Companies typically enlist their IR teams to help with announcing earnings and other corporate news.

Khan was apoplectic; she did not want Hussain telephoning her with inside information because of her previous run-in with the law.

"I do not want you to ever call me again from that number," Khan told Hussain. "Let's meet up in person."

Over the next couple of weeks, Khan met up with Hussain in Palo Alto a few times. At their first meeting, Hussain said she wanted a lot of money in return for her Google information—more than $100,000 or $200,000, Khan told prosecutors. (Khan never paid her any money.) During one meeting, Khan gave Hussain a cell phone with an account in the name of her cleaning lady so that any incoming calls from Hussain would appear to be coming to Khan from her cleaner and not from someone at an investor relations firm that worked for Google. As Hussain fed her details about Google's poor financial results, Khan passed the information on to Rajaratnam. After one call to him on July 13, Rajaratnam sold all his Google stock and took a $25 million short position. Later that month, when Google reported disappointing financial results as Hussain had predicted it would, Rajaratnam netted millions of dollars in profits. Khan made money too, locking in a profit of more than $500,000.

As forthcoming as Khan was about Hussain and Rajaratnam to government officials, she was lying about her trading in Hilton and would not divulge her source for the inside information. When prosecutors asked about the purchases of Hilton stock, Khan said she made the Hilton trades on the advice of her broker. He recommended three hotel companies and she picked Hilton, she said, because socialite Paris Hilton, an heir to the Hilton dynasty, had been arrested and was in jail. The news, she figured, would be good publicity for the hotel company and its stock would do well. Neither Michaelson nor the prosecutors from the US attorney's office bought Khan's story. But they could not tease the truth out of her.

By March 2008, after more than a year and a half of digging, Michaelson felt like he and his team at the SEC had hit a wall, and they were spinning their wheels. Of the twenty-eight stocks in which he suspected Rajaratnam made trades based on inside information, there were only two stocks, Polycom and Google, for which the authorities had direct evidence from Khan of corporate secrets being passed from employees inside the company to Galleon. With Hilton, where it was clear that both Rajaratnam and Khan traded before the Blackstone takeover, Michaelson did not know for sure who the tipper was—Rajaratnam or Khan. On countless other stocks, there was circumstantial evidence—phone calls between the two or incriminating instant messages that were quickly followed by corresponding trades.

Circumstantial evidence is generally enough to build an airtight insider trading case when the target of the investigation does not trade much, but Rajaratnam alone traded as many as 12 million shares a day. Even if the evidence was strong enough, Rajaratnam could always fall back on the hundreds of research reports he received each week from Wall Street brokerage firms, which usually contained a nugget that could be used to justify a trade. Or he could count on his army of in-house analysts (his "window dressing") to gin up research to support a trade.

Over the years, Rajaratnam developed clever ways of concealing Galleon's trading strategy. Typical was the way he indoctrinated Adam Smith, his clean-cut protégé, in the dark arts. Smith, who came to Galleon from Morgan Stanley in 2002, thrived at the New York hedge fund, and in 2006 he was promoted to portfolio manager. Early in his tenure investing money, he and Rajaratnam had several discussions about trading around a position, which meant buying *and* selling stock. For instance, if Galleon was expecting a positive event to buoy a stock, Rajaratnam told Smith to make purchases and sales of the stock. That way, if the government started investigating, Galleon could point to the sales and argue that they were inconsistent with a hedge fund being dead certain a positive event was imminent. The sale provided cover: Rajaratnam's trading patterns and the sheer amount of trading he did each day made it difficult to draw a direct link between an instant message, for example, about positive earnings and a bid to buy stock.

Even though months had gone by since he first began investigating, by the spring of 2008 Michaelson was no closer to finding Rajaratnam's source in several stocks than when he'd first started. AMD was the most nettlesome because it was the one instance when Michaelson was sure Rajaratnam had an insider feeding him information. He had reviewed Rajaratnam's IMs and emails and taken testimony from several people, yet he still had not come up with a real, credible source.

On March 3, 2008, before a meeting with the US attorney's office for the Southern District, Michaelson drafted a list of stocks in which the SEC believed that Galleon made trades using inside information. In the top right-hand corner, in small print, were the words "Privileged & Confidential." Beside each of the twenty-eight stocks on the list, Michaelson typed the suspected source, the insider at each of the publicly traded companies. For nearly half the companies listed,

Michaelson had not identified *any* possible inside source. For companies where he was not sure of the source, he identified the name in brackets. The first stock on the list was AMD. It had consumed much of the SEC's firepower. Next to the company Michaelson put in brackets the name Bharath Rangarajan.

While trolling through phone records over the summer, the SEC lawyers noticed that a number of calls were made from an AMD conference room outside its executive office. One of the contacts in Rajaratnam's electronic address book was Rangarajan. He was a vice president at AMD and was in the perfect place to know the strategic moves the semiconductor company was making in the fall of 2005. He and AMD chief executive Hector Ruiz were the architects of AMD's aggressive strategy in the market. But the only thing making him a person of interest was the presence of his name in Rajaratnam's Rolodex and the fact that he had access to inside information about AMD. There were no instant messages or emails before public announcements pointing to him being a source. It was a tenuous link, but for now, it was all that Michaelson had to go on.

As part of her discussions in January with the government, Khan agreed to tape some telephone conversations with Rajaratnam. Unbeknownst to her, prosecutors had been mulling making a request for surveillance of Rajaratnam's cellular phone for some time. Phone intercepts historically have been used in organized crime, drug, and terrorism cases but had not been applied in the investigation of an insider trading ring, even though in 1984 Congress expanded the list of crimes in the Federal Wiretap Act, often known as Title III, to include wire fraud. Among other things, insider trading violates the wire fraud statute.

The first hint the SEC's Sanjay Wadhwa had that wiretaps were being contemplated was a call he got in early 2008 from Lauren Goldberg, a Manhattan US attorney who was also working on the Galleon probe. "Have you looked at your accessibility to Title III wiretaps?" Goldberg asked Wadhwa. Under Title III, there are limitations on who can have access to wiretaps, generally only criminal authorities, not civil agencies like the SEC. In the Rajaratnam case, Goldberg was planning to seek a wiretap on the grounds that Rajaratnam might be committing wire or mail fraud. Wadhwa and Jason Friedman did some research on the topic and felt that the SEC could have access to wiretaps, but in the end the US attorney's office in Manhattan decided it was wiser to play it safe and not share any information their wiretaps uncovered with the SEC. The SEC was even kept in the dark about the decision because the statute places a number of restrictions on the government's disclosure of wiretaps. As far as Wadhwa and Friedman were concerned, the prospect of wiretapping Rajaratnam died a quiet death. They could only speculate on the reason why.

Before any US attorney's office in the country seeks a wiretap from the court, it requires approval from the Justice Department, which traditionally requires two things: probable cause and necessity. To satisfy probable cause, prosecutors need evidence of a telephone call related to the criminal conduct under investigation. Commonly described as a "dirty call," it has to take place on the very phone on which a wiretap is being sought. In addition, prosecutors have to show necessity, which means either that they have exhausted other investigative techniques—physical surveillance, use of confidential informants, review of trading records, among other things—before seeking a wiretap or that other methods that they have not tried are unlikely to work or could undermine the investigation.

As a veteran prosecutor, Goldberg knew the bar was high for a wiretap in a white-collar case like this. In 2008, US judges approved 1,891 phone intercepts; nearly 1,600 were for drug cases. Just 12 were for conspiracy, one of the most common charges filed against white-collar defendants. "We need a dirty call," Goldberg told Michaelson. It wasn't long before the US attorney's office had what it wanted.

On January 14, 2008, Khan, sitting in her home office in Atherton, California, with FBI agent Kang and a colleague looking on, picked up the phone and called Rajaratnam. To prepare, the one bit of advice Kang gave her was to act as normal as possible. When Khan phoned Rajaratnam, she found he was in a meeting and would have to call her back. A little while later, he did return her call from his work phone.

"What's going on with the earnings this season? Are you hearing anything on Intel?" Khan asked on the recorded call. Intel's revenue would be up 9 to 10 percent, Rajaratnam told her, and it would guide its earnings down by 8 percent. The next day, Intel reported revenue up 10.5 percent and, as part of its "guidance," said that next quarter's earnings would be down by 10 percent.

When Khan asked Rajaratnam about Xilinx, a company in which he always had "an edge," he confided, "Xilinx this quarter I think turned out well...I haven't made the call I've gotta make...I've gotta call Chris." Khan told investigators that she understood "Chris" to be Kris Chellam, a former executive of Xilinx and part of the Southeast Asian network that Raj had built up in Silicon Valley during his days at Needham & Co. Rajaratnam told Khan that he would check on Xilinx and she should call him back in a few days.

Three days later, on January 17, 2008, Khan telephoned Rajaratnam—this time on his cell phone.

"Hey, so, did you hear anything on Xilinx?" asked Khan.

"I think this quarter is okay," replied Rajaratnam. "Next quarter not so good."

Khan tried to probe a little more to unearth Rajaratnam's source.

"And you got it from somebody at the company or...?" she asked.

"Yeah, I mean, somebody who knows his stuff," Rajaratnam replied.

Later that day, Xilinx unveiled its fiscal third-quarter 2008 earnings and revenue, which turned out to be fine, as Rajaratnam had predicted.

Armed with the incriminating calls, Goldberg drew up a wiretap application in February 2008. In the application, the federal prosecutor sought permission from the court to intercept Rajaratnam's cell phone calls on the grounds that there was probable cause to believe that Rajaratnam was committing crimes over his phone. Like all wiretap requests, the application was reviewed by a lawyer at the Justice Department in Washington, DC, who wanted to know if physical surveillance of Rajaratnam had been tried. "It should have at least been attempted," the attorney at the Justice Department noted.

There was no physical surveillance of Rajaratnam, but on March 4, 2008, the day after the Justice Department attorney's email was received, FBI special agent Kang tried physical surveillance of Rajaratnam at his office in midtown Manhattan, at his Round Hill Road mansion in Greenwich, Connecticut, and at his Sutton Place apartment in New York City. He didn't find Rajaratnam. Only in the evening did Kang figure out why: Rajaratnam was in California. Before submitting the wiretap application, the attorney at the Justice Department in DC suggested that Goldberg explain the reason surveillance had not been tried on Rajaratnam. "It's a fairly apparent omission...My guess is that this wire will likely be litigated more aggressively than the average drug wire, so the necessity section is particularly important," the Justice Department official observed presciently.

PART THREE

Falling

CHAPTER NINETEEN

Moonlighting at McKinsey

As Anil Kumar looked around, he was pleased to see that so many luminaries from the corporate world had turned up for cocktails after the Manhattan conference for the Indian School of Business. Since Kumar's mentor at McKinsey, Rajat Gupta, had first hatched the idea in 1995 for a business program in India, his vision had grown, morphing from an early plan to start a management department at his alma mater, IIT Delhi, to what he had built now: a world-class business school with links to prestigious international institutions such as the Wharton School and the London Business School. No longer was it just Indians who were intrigued by its success.

At the drinks and dinner after the conference that cool evening in September 2003, Kumar was happy to see the computer magnate Michael Dell, a newly named board member of ISB, in the crowd. The Sri Lankan hedge fund manager Raj Rajaratnam was mingling too. Kumar had approached his old Wharton classmate Rajaratnam when he and Gupta raised the initial funding for the school. Though Rajaratnam was not Indian, he gave $1 million "anonymously" to the school in 2001. Kumar had never expected Rajaratnam's generosity to extend into seven figures.

When Kumar moved to India, he had lost touch with Rajaratnam but had heard through the grapevine that his classmate from Wharton profited spectacularly well during the dot-com boom. News of success traveled fast among South Asians. By 2001, the assets at Rajaratnam's Galleon fund made it one of the ten biggest hedge funds in the world.

When Kumar learned that Rajaratnam had decided to donate money to the fledgling business school, he told Gupta about the sizable donation. Lest Gupta forget, Kumar had friends with money too. He could tap them just as well as his boss. It was no secret that without Gupta, the Indian School of Business would not have gotten off the ground. Gupta marshaled his vast Rolodex of contacts to get the elites of corporate India to open up their wallets and contribute.

But Rajaratnam's $1 million donation was among the more sizable gifts, and Kumar had every reason to believe that the school could count on the thriving hedge fund manager to contribute more. He only wished he could bank on him hiring McKinsey to provide advisory work for the Galleon Group. Then he'd be making it rain on both fronts—business as well as philanthropy.

The truth was that in the fall of 2003 Anil Kumar was in deep trouble at McKinsey. It was the second big career setback for Kumar at the firm. Even though he had prospered with clients in India and was of the view that he would be named successor to Puri as office manager, he was passed over for the position. He felt betrayed and misled by his bosses. As shocked as Kumar was, his colleagues in India were not surprised. His work was brilliant; the problem was his personality. The first time he had been nominated to be a director he was rejected. Puri, then the managing director in India, suggested that Kumar meet with each of the principals in India and ask if they thought he could win partnership support or if he should quit. Kumar made the rounds, asking each what he could do to be a better partner and what their view of him was. The effort paid off. In 1997 he was promoted to director.

After he was passed over to run McKinsey India, Kumar picked himself up and headed back to California. When he arrived, he didn't have a practice group to join, so he decided to start an e-commerce practice for McKinsey with four e-business accelerators—centers with McKinsey project teams that could assist dot-com companies in getting off the ground. It was a prescient move. McKinsey was flooded with work from large technology companies looking for ways to provide Internet services for their customers. At the same time, there were scores of small tech companies who needed advice about whether they should merge with the behemoths or go it alone. The challenge Kumar faced was rewiring old-fashioned McKinsey so it could take advantage of the opportunities in the newfangled world.

Unlike the blue-chip companies that McKinsey traditionally served, many of the technology start-ups had only one currency to offer as payment: equity. If a hot new start-up boomed, colossal riches would accrue to McKinsey. The firm's intellectual muscle would be acting like venture capital.

McKinsey had long been averse to taking equity stakes in companies in lieu of cash payments. In the early eighties Bob Waterman recalls accepting stock for his services from Genentech, at the time a tiny San Francisco biotechnology firm with little in profits but a lot in promise. Waterman felt that the company had enormous potential and believed that the only way for McKinsey to get a foot in the emerging world of biotech was to do something unusual. There was no other way for Genentech to pay McKinsey. Waterman wasn't prepared, however, for the firestorm he sparked.

The move to take stock "elicited cries of horror from my partners," says Waterman. In the end, McKinsey sold the stock, forgoing a huge windfall a decade later when Swiss drug giant Roche acquired a majority stake in Genentech, a first step before ultimately buying the entire company for nearly $47 billion in 2009.

Even by the late eighties, the sentiment toward stock was little changed. Jeffrey Skilling, the former chief executive of Enron, remembers sitting on a committee to look at the appropriateness of nontraditional fee structures—equity interests or contingency fees and earn-outs that were tied to a company's performance. There was a lot of pressure from the consultants in New York to accept stock equity as payment. They were enthralled with the ability to act like investment bankers, and a critical number of clients were interested in the alternative payment plan, Skilling says. But as the committee mulled the idea, it was clear the nontraditional fee arrangements posed outright conflicts of interest in some cases and in others were totally at odds with the culture of the firm.

The case against contingency fees or earn-outs was clear: they posed an "insurmountable conflict of interest between the client and firm," says Skilling. For instance, if McKinsey is hired to help a client to reduce expenses and gets 20 percent of the first two years' expense reductions, "at that point the firm has an incentive to reduce expenses even if expense reduction, or some component of expense reduction is not in the client interest," says Skilling. It is "a direct conflict. We looked at a number of ways to structure such arrangements, but none eliminated the conflict."

Accepting equity instead of cash had a potentially more damaging consequence: "It seemed to us that there was a danger in almost any outcome: whether the concept was a failure or even if it was successful," says Skilling. "Say you take equity that is ultimately worth less than the normal fee level, the recriminations would fly."

But the problems of success could be more thorny. If the firm made a huge gain, how would the rewards be parceled out? Would the people on the specific client service team get a disproportionate payout? Ultimately, Skilling says, the committee decided "it was impossible to manage the conflicts and the internal 'shears' that it would cause, and concluded that it was not a good idea."

In 1998 McKinsey, now with Rajat Gupta as managing director, reluctantly moved to accept small-equity stakes in start-up companies that could not otherwise afford its fees. A committee was formed to vet any equity investment proposals. Only 50 percent of fees could be taken in equity, and the committee would consider investments under $1 million. The plan solved one vexing problem. It offered McKinsey a creative way to work for cash-strapped Internet companies that might someday be as big as IBM or Apple.

But it did nothing to solve another, perhaps more pressing, challenge: McKinsey, like many old-economy companies, was losing talented young associates to the brave new tech world. To help stanch the exodus, Kumar pushed for McKinsey to give junior consultants the opportunity to buy into its Internet start-up investments. Among the options mulled over was to allow associates to buy stakes in a pool of McKinsey clients that paid the firm equity instead of cash. It was an elegant way of giving junior consultants a reason to stay at the firm. Kumar's idea met with immediate resistance: it was mind-boggling to think that the firm had to cater to the whims of an aggressive group of twentysomethings.

But in the heady climate of the time, it was hard to argue with Kumar, and the tech consulting practice would grow to represent 25 to 30 percent of the firm's revenue. Even though he'd spent a good part of the decade in India, Kumar seemed to understand the Internet space better than most, and he had an impressive network around Silicon Valley with lines into the growing number of Indians becoming titans of technology. He claimed to be close to the Indian-born venture capitalist Vinod Khosla, who had cofounded Sun Microsystems in 1982. Khosla later became a renowned venture capitalist at Kleiner Perkins Caufield & Byers, which, in the thick of the Internet boom, invested in some of the era's biggest home runs, companies like Amazon, Google, and Netscape. Kumar dropped Khosla's name frequently in conversation and let it be known that he had gone with Khosla to visit with S. M. Krishna, then chief minister of Karnataka, the state in which the high-tech hub Bangalore is based.

During that trip he stunned family and friends when he professed to have little time for socializing. His excuse, or at least the one he gave them, was lame. "I have come in Vinod's aircraft," he told them. "I have no time to see anyone." (It does not appear that Kumar traveled with Khosla and it is not even clear if he met Krishna.)

On October 22, 1999, McKinsey executives woke up to a story in the *New York Times* carrying the headline "Big Consultants Woo Employees by Offering a Piece of the Action." Written by David Leonhardt, the story detailed Kumar's buy-in plan for associates. Everything about the article was distasteful to McKinsey's top executives, including Rajat Gupta. The headline, with its focus on giving employees "a piece of the action," ran counter to what McKinsey represented.

Even though it had been years since the principled Marvin Bower stalked the corridors of 55 East Fifty-Second Street, McKinsey's New York headquarters, clients still left the building with the impression that consulting at McKinsey was a profession, not a business. The last thing it wanted was for clients to think that its consultants hoped to profit alongside the companies it served. But it was exactly this kind of commercialism that veterans of the firm noticed creeping into the culture. The article revealed various options that McKinsey partners had been mulling for months, even though the firm was still in the throes of fine-tuning the details.

Don Waite, one of Gupta's rivals for the managing director's job and now a lieutenant, strode into a meeting waving the *New York Times* and said, "Have you seen this?"

The revelations in the article were bad enough, but what angered Waite and others was that one of their own, Anil Kumar, was widely quoted in the piece. McKinsey took extraordinary care cultivating its image. Whenever it embarked on a step that was a departure from traditional practice, McKinsey would ponder for months the reception its new initiative would get. By and large, McKinsey eschewed floating trial balloons in the press, but with his comments to the *New York Times*, that was exactly what Kumar had done. "We don't want the best talent to feel they don't have a vehicle to join in this wealth creation," Kumar told the *Times*. His remark with its obvious reference to personal profit went against the grain for McKinsey.

Top executives were so appalled that Gupta convened a meeting with his kitchen cabinet to decide what to do. Some thought Kumar should be fired for overstepping the boundaries. To send a message to the broader partners, one idea floated was to announce his dismissal at the directors' meeting. In the end, though, it was decided that Gupta would speak to Kumar and rebuke him sternly. He would receive a "slap on the wrist."

But by 2003, the implosion of the tech bubble hit Kumar and McKinsey hard. Kumar's gambit to have McKinsey plunge headlong into the tech space had profound and sobering implications for the firm and for his own career. From the beginning of 2001 to the end of 2002, McKinsey's gross revenues declined by some 12 percent, according to *A History of the Firm*, a book McKinsey privately published. Rumors spread through the ranks that the firm had to make a capital call to its partners, who were already reeling from the dramatic drop in revenue. Though unfounded, the rumors served to destabilize the firm. Meanwhile, the additional awards that directors received in December plummeted by 87 percent.

McKinsey's aggressive drive to recruit junior consultants in the late nineties compounded its problems when the bubble burst. During the buoyant times, Gupta's McKinsey was hiring young associates at a furious rate to keep pace with its burgeoning book of clients. Historically, new arrivals as a percentage of McKinsey's total consulting staff were 20 percent a year, but in the late nineties, the new blood soared to the mid-to-high 30 percent range. The jump had a profound impact on the partnership and its profitability.

Compensation per partner is hardwired to two economic statistics—hourly billing rates and the ratio of deployable associates to partners. "You want LOTS of associates per partner," explains Skilling. Between the mid-nineties and 2000, the ratio of directors to consulting staff, which includes associates, increased to 1:17 from 1:12. Even as revenues grew by more than three and a half times, the partnership grew more slowly, by about two and a half times, the McKinsey-sponsored company history declared. The effect of the discrepancy was to enrich the existing partners.

These numbers "suggest a HUGE increase in Director compensation," says Skilling. "It also suggests a selfishness of the directors since the ratio was not held constant." In effect, the firm wasn't naming new partners as fast as it was hiring associates. Growth profited the few. More money was spread over the same number of partners. It was the opposite environment from 1973, when Gupta joined McKinsey.

When the bubble burst in 2001, it aggravated McKinsey's pain.

McKinsey typically hired two thousand people a year, including business analysts. To get two thousand new recruits, it made roughly three thousand offers, giving it a 66 percent acceptance rate, one of the highest among large employers. But in 2001 McKinsey found that between twenty-seven and twenty-eight hundred applicants accepted its offers, a 95 percent acceptance rate. The high rate came at a time when the firm was already saddled with lots of consultants who in McKinsey parlance were "on the beach," or had nothing to do.

To address the mismatch between supply and demand, McKinsey decided it was not going to lay off people or renege on the offers it had made to business school graduates. Gupta was proud that the firm was able to keep its commitments to its new hires, but within the firm the policy that McKinsey embarked on to deal with the bust was arguably more controversial. The firm began culling its ranks through more rigorous performance reviews.

Between 2001 and 2004, its consulting staff fell from a little over seventy-five hundred to a little over fifty-five hundred. It was a stark change from the way McKinsey typically handled the departure of associates, who were given time to find another position or "counseled out," an elegant term that did not carry the obviously pejorative implication of being fired. Many at the firm openly blamed Kumar and his ilk in Silicon Valley for McKinsey's indiscriminate bloodletting. Rajat Gupta did not escape the criticism either. Everyone knew that without the backing of his mentor, Gupta, Kumar would have never succeeded in building up McKinsey's e-commerce practice.

Besides the implosion of his business, Kumar had another reason to worry about his future at McKinsey. His longtime mentor, Gupta, was retiring as managing director of McKinsey, and it was widely known that Gupta's successor, Ian Davis, planned to chart a different course. Davis, an upright Englishman with a degree in PPE—philosophy, politics, and economics—from Balliol College, Oxford, was keen for a return to the "values-based" McKinsey, not a growth-at-all-costs McKinsey. He was viewed as being disenchanted with McKinsey's growing and obvious commercialism and was not a big fan of Kumar, whom some colleagues felt embodied the business-driven culture that had seeped into the firm over the previous decade.

At one time, Kumar had given his friends in India the impression that he might someday be in a position to succeed Gupta. But now he was singing a different tune. "I have to find something beyond McKinsey," he told a friend. Kumar was too private and tight-lipped to divulge anything about his changed circumstances at McKinsey, but old friends sensed that Kumar's star at the firm had faded.

Upon ascending to the top job, McKinsey's new managing director, Davis, made it clear to Kumar that he had no plans to elevate him to a leadership role. Other senior partners at McKinsey advised Kumar that it might be time to seek employment elsewhere. Stung and disappointed, Kumar turned to Rajaratnam and confided in him, telling him all about his woes at work.

At the Indian School of Business cocktail party in September 2003, Kumar recalled that at one time Rajaratnam had shown interest in engaging McKinsey. In the summer of 2002, he came to Kumar with an intriguing business proposal. Rajaratnam said he received about $100 million a year in so-called soft dollars, which could be channeled to pay for stock research or consulting services. Soft dollars were controversial but legal. Regulators saw them as essentially kickbacks for diverting trading commissions to certain brokerage firms. Many big mutual funds like Fidelity Investments in Boston stopped accepting them, but Galleon, like many hedge funds, took a kinder view of soft dollars, regarding them as rebates on the fat brokerage commissions paid out each year to Wall Street.

Rajaratnam had suggested to Kumar that there might be a way for Galleon to put its soft dollars to work by hiring McKinsey. Kumar quickly mobilized a team to draft a proposal on the kind of industry research McKinsey could offer a technology fund such as Galleon. On September 26, 2002, before a call with Rajaratnam that day, McKinsey consultant Tom Stephenson sent Rajaratnam an eighteen-page PowerPoint presentation laying out the ways McKinsey could assist Galleon.

The document, marked "Confidential," boasted of McKinsey's strengths. It represented more than half the world's five hundred largest companies and was retained on thirty-five hundred engagements a year. In the high-tech sphere, McKinsey counted as clients eight of the ten largest semiconductor companies and nine of the top ten software companies. It was also a powerhouse in health care, another area of interest to Galleon. Its clients included seventeen US-based biotechnology companies, mainly on the West Coast. It could offer expertise in a variety of disciplines, among them the hot area of stem cell therapies. Tellingly, the presentation made no claim about McKinsey's knowledge and experience in serving hedge funds.

Rajaratnam was singularly unimpressed, but he did not let on. Instead, he politely listened to Stephenson's pitch and then asked some penetrating questions. After the meeting, he felt there was nothing the McKinsey consultant could tell him that he didn't already know. And he thought McKinsey's rates were far too high.

Stephenson, however, came away upbeat. "Good meeting with Raj," he said in an email he fired off to Kumar and the rest of the pitch team. "It seems like Raj's approach to investing matches well with our perspective on serving buy-side firms." Stephenson's read turned out to be off. Months lapsed after the McKinsey call with Rajaratnam. In early 2003, Kumar confronted Rajaratnam. He told him that he was disappointed that the Galleon hedge fund manager hadn't even bothered to respond to the McKinsey proposal after all the work his people had put into developing it.

"Just send it to me again," said Rajaratnam, raising Kumar's hopes once more.

Kumar dutifully followed up, getting his lieutenant to send another proposal that detailed McKinsey's areas of strength. With its army of experts and doctors as consultants, the firm could help a hedge fund like Galleon divine the winning drug therapies in the race to cure cancer or determine the speed with which consumers would adopt broadband at different price points. Again the pitch met with silence from Rajaratnam.

That fall evening in 2003, as the two men were leaving the Indian School of Business cocktail and dinner, Rajaratnam pulled Kumar aside.

"You know you sent that document," Rajaratnam said, referring to the proposal Kumar had sent about the ways McKinsey could advise Galleon. "You do realize that that's not really what I want. I would much rather have *you* as a consultant than McKinsey."

Kumar very matter-of-factly told Rajaratnam that he was not allowed by McKinsey to accept outside consulting work. But Rajaratnam persisted, preying on Kumar's ego and obvious envy of Rajaratnam's wealth.

"You work very, very hard, you travel a lot, you are underpaid," he told Kumar. "People have made fortunes while you were away in

India and you deserve more." Rajaratnam said he was willing to pay Kumar $500,000 to be a consultant to Galleon. All Kumar had to do was speak to him every four to six weeks and share his insights about the tech industry. "You have such good knowledge—it is worth a lot of money," he told Kumar. McKinsey wouldn't have to know anything about their arrangement. If Kumar could find someone outside the United States who would act as a go-between and accept the consulting work, then there was no reason McKinsey should find out about Kumar's moonlighting.

It was a tantalizing opportunity coming at a time when Kumar was feeling vulnerable.

Raj Rajaratnam always knew more than he let on. When he made his overture after the cocktail party in 2003, he knew that Kumar had spent time in India in the 1990s. As he brainstormed about setting up a consulting arrangement with Kumar, he suggested finding someone in India who could accept the payments for the consulting services. Then that person could have that money reinvested in one of Galleon's stable of funds.

"I don't think Indian regulations allow that," Kumar countered, again very matter-of-factly. Undeterred, Rajaratnam proposed creating an offshore company to receive payments from Galleon. "I can even tell you how to do that," he offered. But Kumar didn't want to deal with the messiness of an offshore entity.

Rajaratnam persisted with his pitch. He knew that the Kumars had an Indian housekeeper living with them in California. They had brought Manju Das over from Delhi to help take care of their son, Aman, who had a variety of health issues.

Rajaratnam asked Kumar if his housekeeper still carried an Indian passport. When he said she did, Rajaratnam offered up the perfect solution, a way of having Kumar consult for him without McKinsey ever knowing. Rajaratnam suggested that Kumar set up an account offshore in his housekeeper's name so the arrangement was kept well away from McKinsey. Kumar found the idea appealing because it would avoid awkward structures such as an offshore company. But he had a worry in the back of his head. If his housekeeper was going to be the recipient of the consulting payments Rajaratnam planned to make, then how could he be assured that he would get his money back? That's easy, Rajaratnam told him.

There was a standard way of dealing with this situation, Rajaratnam explained. Kumar would simply write a nominating letter that would be signed by his housekeeper, giving Kumar authorization to act on her behalf. Not long after their meeting at the ISB reception, Rajaratnam dictated the letter and Kumar typed it.

CHAPTER TWENTY

A Vanaprastha on the Hudson

By the late 1990s, as McKinsey was humming amid one of the greatest economic booms in modern-day history, Rajat Gupta began contemplating a life transition. In the Hindu religion, whose spiritual tenets Rajat soaked up during his coming of age in India, a man's life is divided into four stages. The first, known as brahmacharya, represents the early part of a man's life and is a time of learning during which a young man leaves home to spend time with a guru. The second stage is when a man becomes a householder, or grihastha. He marries, builds a home, and accumulates wealth for himself and society. Midway through life, a man starts becoming a vanaprastha, or hermit, characterized by a growing renunciation of physical, material, and sexual pleasures. At this point, a man is supposed to retreat into the forest, where he spends his days in prayer. It is all preparation for the final stage, sanyaasa, which is marked by a total devotion to God and no attachment to worldly pleasures.

At the height of the dot-com boom, McKinsey flew fifty-odd hand-picked members of the Harvard Business School class of 2000 to Château Élan, a sprawling thirty-five-hundred-acre luxury resort just outside Atlanta. Few if any of the HBS students descending on Atlanta that weekend had come for recreation or entertainment. They had traveled south to make one of the most important decisions of their lives: whether to join McKinsey after getting an MBA from Harvard Business School or dip their toes in the brave new economy.

The group was a cosmopolitan crew, and the big draw was the man whose very appointment to the top job changed the face of McKinsey, quite literally transforming it from a white-shoe consultancy into a multicultural meritocracy.

Rajat Gupta had a reputation for applying Indian philosophy to the Western business milieu. He liked to recite passages from the Hindu scriptures or draw parallels to Hinduism to explain his approach to business or elaborate on his vision of how a firm like McKinsey worked. Often he invoked verses to offer valuable life lessons. A Gupta principle that he drew from the Bhagavad Gita holds that man has a right to work but not to the fruits that arise from his labor.

When coworkers were confronted with a challenging situation, he would impress upon them "to do what you think is the right thing" and not to "really get attached to the fruits thereof" or worry about the results. Often his goal-driven American colleagues would challenge him, asking, "If something doesn't go right, 'Aren't you unhappy about it?'" Gupta would offer a philosopher king–like reply entirely uncharacteristic of the operating style of a corporate executive. It was as if he was more new age than new economy.

"I think if we judge ourselves by results too much, we're always out of balance...Either we are far happier than we should be or far sadder."

Gupta again turned to the subject of Hinduism in his speech to the young HBS students. Rightly suspecting that many in the audience did not have a clue about the topic, he laid out the four stages of a man's life. Then he surprised the group of mostly alpha males by declaring, "I think I am in my third stage," or becoming a vanaprastha, which is marked by a gradual retreat of a man into the woods.

The assertion did not go down well.

"It really struck me: here is the CEO of a major company and he is talking about retreating into the forest," said one student in the audience.

What the HBS students didn't know was that Gupta by the turn of the millennium was ready to channel his energies elsewhere. His first two terms at the helm of McKinsey were extraordinary and explosive, both aggressively expansionist and intently customer-satisfaction driven. He pushed a firm initiative called "100 percent cubed" that promised to make McKinsey more client-centric by delivering 100 percent of the firm, 100 percent of the time, to 100 percent of its clients.

He expanded the firm's footprint to eighty-four worldwide locations from fifty-eight, more than doubled the consulting staff to seventy-seven hundred from twenty-nine hundred, and nearly tripled its revenues to $3.4 billion from $1.2 billion in 1993. He pounded away at making McKinsey more global in outlook. During the February 1996 partners' meeting, held at Disney World, in Orlando, Florida, over which he presided, the global message was subliminally driven home.

Partners from each of McKinsey's offices were asked to march in an Olympic-like torch-carrying procession, singing "We Are the World," with each office displaying its homeland's distinctive cultural touchstone. As the London office walked in, looking regal with top hats on their heads, the Scandinavians sparked a furor by showing up with beautiful blondes on their arms. The display didn't sit well with the few women partners at the firm. Gupta's message of going global was on the nose and not exactly in the stuffed-shirt McKinsey tradition.

As he met with greater success, Gupta shed his simple ways. When Gupta was first elected managing director in 1994, he made a conscious—and surprising—choice to run the global consulting powerhouse from Chicago. Personally, it made sense. The Gupta girls were still in school. Uprooting them would have been wrenching for his family. Professionally, Gupta running McKinsey from Chicago implicitly signaled that New York's decades-old dominance over the rest of the firm was over.

As McKinsey's reach around the world grew, though, it was harder and harder for Gupta to remain in the Windy City. Most of McKinsey's overseas clients passed through New York when they came to the United States; rarely did they stop off in Chicago. In the late nineties, with his eldest daughter now in college and two others approaching university, Gupta relocated from the Chicago to the New York office. The move was very different from his previous two. This time, he did not buy a modest house sight unseen. He splurged, paying $6.125 million to buy the waterfront estate once owned by James Cash Penney Jr., a cofounder of the retailing empire J.C. Penney Corporation. As managing director of McKinsey, he could afford it; he was earning about $5 million a year.

The gracious cream-colored mansion in Westport, Connecticut, was built in the 1920s and had eight bedrooms and eight baths. It sat on more than two acres of land. When the Guptas bought the house, it was somewhat tired, but they poured money into it, lifting its image to fit with the public persona of its owner, who by the late 1990s was growing immeasurably in stature. The householder had reached his pinnacle.

The first three decades of Gupta's life in the United States had been marked by nonstop striving—making the top grade at HBS, getting a job at McKinsey and climbing its ranks, and then running a worldwide consulting juggernaut so it was operating at peak performance. But by 2000, Gupta appeared exhausted.

As exhilarating as growth was, it was also wearing. During the last few years of his second term, he was under tremendous pressure from partners to take the firm public, just like Goldman Sachs had done, or to seed a venture capital fund like rival Bain had done. "If I look back on my time as MD and where I made the most impact, I would pick the time when the bubble was going on and it was fascinating because lots and lots of people were getting instantly rich," he said years later. There was an "enormous amount of pressure to start new ventures, take equity ownership, to do a whole bunch of things to become more instantly rich where I had to take a strong personal stand. The most important contribution I made during my tenure as managing director is to make sure we didn't go public, we didn't start a venture fund, we didn't go into starting businesses."

Yet to McKinsey veterans the growth spurt that Gupta championed had frayed the firm, and his focus on growing the additional awards—or bonuses—ran against the company's values. Robert Waterman remembers attending a meeting of former directors like himself around the turn of the millennium. "I got a sense that the

firm had grown way too fast and we had lost a sense of profession-
alism in the process," says Waterman.

As Gupta approached a potential third term, colleagues sensed he
yearned to burnish his legacy outside the notoriously discreet firm.
He was a regular fixture at the World Economic Forum meetings in
Davos, and, closer to home, he plunged into a diverse array of outside activities. One was the American India Foundation.

In early February 2001, just six months after Gupta was invited to
the White House for a dinner in honor of India's prime minister, Bill
Clinton, now out of office, reached out to Gupta and Victor Menezes,
a Citibank executive, to brainstorm ways to help the earthquake-hit
Indian state of Gujarat. Menezes hosted a working lunch for members of the South Asian diaspora at Citibank's headquarters in New
York and after the meeting he and Gupta took up the mantle and ran
with it. They set up the American India Foundation, a charity to raise
money for victims of the earthquake. With its pedigreed founding fathers, Gupta and Menezes, AIF quickly became an A-list charity for
the Indian-American community in the United States.

At its 2008 spring gala, nine hundred corporate titans, philan-
thropists, and community leaders packed the Waldorf Astoria hotel
in New York to hear from one of independent India's own success
stories: Mukesh Ambani. Looking out onto a sea of women in
brightly colored silk saris and men in Nehru suits, Ambani, one of
the richest men in the world, declared, "There cannot be an island of
riches in an ocean of poverty." It was a glittering display of the enormous wealth of the South Asian diaspora in the United States. In one
night, AIF raised $3 million.

Gupta's forays into philanthropy thrust him into a new
league—far bigger than the ones he had played in in Chicago and
Scandinavia. In April 2001, when he traveled with Clinton to India
on a fact-finding mission, the two men forged a friendship. After
Gupta returned to America, he invited a photographer who traveled
with them to his home. "I heard you take good pictures and have
taken a lot of Bill Clinton's photos in the White House," he remarked
to the man during their trip. The photographer was soon hired to
take photos at the Gupta estate.

As managing director, Gupta had always devoted a significant chunk of time—as much as 25 percent—to ventures that had nothing to do with the firm. He never regretted it. His outside activities—and there were many—almost always redounded to McKinsey's benefit. His push into public health, he asserted years later, made him intimately acquainted with the heads of the major drug companies, many of whom were McKinsey clients or belonged to companies McKinsey hoped to enlist as clients. The interest in public health also helped him build ties with heads of state. It was his vision to start a quasi-public private health foundation in India that drew him deeper into the orbit of India's new prime minister, Dr. Manmohan Singh, and helped him earn Dr. Singh's respect.

But during his last term as managing director, Gupta's lack of focus was felt acutely among the partnership. He barely got elected to managing director when he stood for election the third time, and a number of McKinsey clients—Swissair, Kmart, and Global Crossing—filed for bankruptcy court protection during his final term.

The biggest black eye was Enron Corp. Because of its ties to the company's chief executive, Jeffrey Skilling, McKinsey had long held a big presence at Enron. At one point, the firm's annual billings to Enron exceeded $10 million. The public Gupta took the setbacks in stride. "In these turbulent times, with our serving more than half the Fortune 500 companies, there are bound to be some clients who get into trouble," he told *BusinessWeek* magazine in July 2002.

He started spending more time in Stamford, Connecticut, where he had an office, and he distracted himself with outside interests—the World Economic Forum at Davos, AIF—and in 2002, he joined the board of the Global Fund to Fight AIDS, Tuberculosis and Malaria, one of his most important philanthropic achievements. Gupta helped conceive the "one-stop shop" organization, believing that a unified effort was the best way to combat the three killer diseases. He had been motivated in part because his Harvard friend David Manly had died of AIDS. It was a death he felt could have been prevented.

His activities outside McKinsey drew him into the company of an ever-widening group of influential businessmen. Many were South

Asian luminaries like Raj Rajaratnam who could write out big checks, not just collect them from rich donors. Gupta first learned about Rajaratnam from Kumar, who told him that Rajaratnam had given $1 million anonymously to ISB in 2001. When Gupta was raising money on behalf of AIF for earthquake relief in Gujarat, in step with his new friend Bill Clinton, he approached Rajaratnam directly. Again, the Galleon hedge fund manager gave generously.

The charitable gift stuck in Gupta's mind. He had had a rough time raising money for the earthquake relief effort. When Rajaratnam opened his checkbook so effortlessly, Gupta was impressed. Someone so generous was surely a good man. He and Rajaratnam formed a casual friendship, though in the early years, certainly while Gupta was still at the helm of McKinsey, they weren't close. They traveled in different circles.

Ironically, during the peak of the dot-com boom, Gupta could have easily joined Rajaratnam's big-money crowd. Offers were flooding in from private equity firms and technology start-ups looking for a seasoned manager, but Gupta resisted. His wife, Anita, would tell his colleagues at McKinsey that Gupta enjoyed the stature that came with being global managing director. He could always trade places with Rajaratnam, but the Galleon chief could never trade places with him.

But after the tech hemorrhage and the criticism that came with it, Gupta stepped down as managing director amid a period of darkness. No longer the can't-miss global genius, he was now being portrayed as the man who grew McKinsey too far too fast, leaving his successor with a laundry list of problems.

In 2003, shortly after Ian Davis was elected to the position of worldwide managing director, John Byrne, a writer for *Business Week*, got a call from Davis's handlers. Would Byrne agree to be interviewed for a videotaped piece that would be shown to McKinsey's partners at their next meeting? The topic of the interview was the subject of Byrne's story a year earlier, "Inside McKinsey," which focused on whether the firm had overreached.

"The new leadership was basically saying things got out of control under Rajat and we are moving back to the basics of Marvin Bower," says Byrne today. "To some degree, that was a repudiation of his leadership of the firm."

Longtime friends sensed that Gupta felt lost.

"He was feeling literally crazy" after he stepped down as managing director, says Bala Balachandran, a neighbor of his in Winnetka and the dean of the Great Lakes Institute of Management in Chennai, India, one of a handful of new business schools that have sprung up in India since the founding of Gupta's Indian School of Business. Balachandran remembers visiting Gupta after he relinquished his position as global managing director. In previous years, the two sat and talked in his generous and beautifully decorated office on McKinsey's executive floor. But now Gupta was relegated to a much smaller office on a different floor, and he was obviously embarrassed by the new digs.

He said, "Bala, I am sorry I couldn't take you to the big office," Balachandran recalls. His sense of having lost sway and influence was palpable. As Balachandran looks back on his friendship with Gupta, he sees a man who was always "tossed between two forces." On one side, Gupta was "very humble, accessible, and open," and on the other side, he was enamored with prestige, power, and the finer aspects of life. He liked to name-drop. "He was very proud of saying 'I hired Chelsea Clinton—I hired Hillary Clinton's daughter,'" says Balachandran.

Another case in point: at the turn of the millennium, Gupta and Anil Ambani wanted to expand the campus of the Indian School of Business. Ratan Tata, one of the wealthiest men in India, known for his very modest lifestyle, and an ISB board member, asked the two: "Are you trying to build a five-star luxury hotel for a business school?" Saying that he did not want to build a "Taj Mahal or a mausoleum" for ISB, Tata scaled back his involvement in ISB. Balachandran said Gupta approached him and asked him to talk to Tata. "I said to Rajat, 'You can't have your cake and eat it too,'" says Balachandran.

Gupta's retirement as managing director at McKinsey was a pivotal turning point in his life. "Up to his McKinsey days, he was guided by the McKinsey guidelines and values. He was governed by

McKinsey and not Rajat. He was on the right side," says Balachandran. "After McKinsey, he put his eggs in the basket of money rather than reputation. He stepped up his quest for money because his professional superiority had climaxed."

In April 2004, Gupta traveled to Columbia University to speak to Srikumar Rao's Creativity and Personal Mastery class. Much of his talk was devoted to trotting out his usual philosophies, but at one point a student asked him about his attitude toward money and wealth creation. Gupta offered a remarkably honest response.

"When I look at myself, yeah, I am driven by money," he said. "I like many creature comforts. I want to make sure I take care of my kids well and so on and so forth. And when I live in this society you do get fairly materialistic, so I look at that. I am disappointed. I am probably more materialistic today than I was before and I think money is very seductive...you have to watch out for it because the more you have it, you get used to comforts, and you get used to, you know, big houses and vacation homes, and going and doing whatever you want, and so it is very seductive. However much you say that you will not fall into the trap of it, you do fall into the trap of it."

CHAPTER TWENTY-ONE

The Dishonorable Dosco

That is "very useful information," said Rajaratnam as he listened intently to Kumar.

Starting in late 2003, just a few months after their discussion at the Indian School of Business reception, Kumar was already delivering: two giant computer companies, Hewlett-Packard and Dell, who were loyal Intel customers historically, were in advanced talks to move some of their business to Kumar's client Advanced Micro Devices. Over the next couple of months, Kumar kept Rajaratnam abreast of the twists and turns of the negotiations, giving him a heads-up when discussions with Dell fell apart and alerting him when talks with Hewlett-Packard heated up.

On occasion, Rajaratnam would ask Kumar if he would buy AMD stock. Knowing if Kumar would invest his own hard-earned cash in the company would be a good guide for Rajaratnam of whether he should buy the stock. Kumar reiterated that he was not allowed to buy AMD stock under McKinsey's rules, but he was so excited about the deal, he told Rajaratnam he would buy stock if he could.

Kumar had long reveled in his role as consigliere to some of America's biggest technology companies, and one of his most cherished clients was Advanced Micro Devices, Inc., a Sunnyvale, California, company that supplied chips to personal computer companies. AMD was founded in 1969 by the colorful tech entrepreneur Jerry Sanders, who received as much notoriety for his parties, fancy cars, and Beverly Hills mansions as he did for taking on semiconductor giant Intel Corp. When AMD prospered, Sanders built a shrine to himself: an opulent headquarters building in Sunnyvale that came to be known as "Jerry's White House."

In the world of semiconductors, the rivalry between AMD and Intel is legendary. AMD was the David to the Goliath Intel. Together, they control the chip market. During most of their historic rivalry, AMD was the long-suffering laggard, but in 2003, AMD executives champed at the bit, excited because the company had devised a new computer chip, Opteron. It was their lethal weapon in the fight to win market share away from Intel. Within AMD, secrecy naturally surrounded the new product. Thanks to Opteron, AMD was on the cusp of winning a big order from one of Intel's most long-term and loyal customers, Hewlett-Packard Co.

After overtures from AMD's most senior executives, HP was coming to the view that AMD's new chip was the best for some of its server systems. But the deal was not sealed yet. So as not to run the risk of a leak that would let Intel retaliate and sabotage its plans, AMD gave its efforts to grow market share the code name MAID, an acronym for Microsoft, AMD, IBM, and Dell. The companies represented the firms that were integral to the efforts to gain market share. From the beginning, only a few people knew about the MAID initiative. One happened to be Kumar.

Unlike rival consultants, Kumar enjoyed a privileged perch at AMD. He was a confidant of the company's chief executive, Dr. Hector Ruiz. Kumar and McKinsey did work for Ruiz when he was the president of Motorola's semiconductor unit. Though the two came from different socioeconomic backgrounds, they were alike in one important way: they were nerds. Ruiz, the engineer, had a PhD in quantum electronics. Kumar, the consultant, had a master's degree in applied mechanics.

At AMD, Ruiz treated Kumar as a strategic sounding board and often called him, sometimes at home, to bounce ideas off him. Among the coterie of obsequious advisers who tried to pitch their services to AMD, Kumar was by far the most knowledgeable, a bold and big thinker whom Ruiz trusted implicitly. Like Ruiz, who, after he was widowed, met his second wife at a daycare center where they both took their children, Kumar was a family man. Both men were immigrants to the United States, though Ruiz had a far more inspiring tale of hope and triumph, which lent a soft edge to an otherwise imperious facade. Ruiz was born into a poor Mexican family. As a young man, he would walk across the border every day from his home in Piedras Negras to attend high school in the South Texas town of Eagle Pass. He didn't start learning English until he was sixteen, but he graduated as valedictorian.

Not long after Ruiz assumed the reins in 2002, Kumar appeared at AMD. When he was at Motorola, Ruiz was known as "Hector the Dissector" for his large-scale job cuts. At AMD, he also embarked on a program to slash costs and enlisted McKinsey's help. Longtime AMD employees marveled at the access Kumar and McKinsey were given. They were shown product road maps and future financial projections, even though some of the advice they served up bordered on the absurd. During one of its first projects for AMD, McKinsey briefly considered an idea to cut costs by unscrewing every other lightbulb in AMD's offices.

In a sign of their elevated importance, the men from McKinsey were installed in a conference room just outside Mahogany Row, the wood-paneled executive floor at AMD's Sunnyvale headquarters. Sanders personally recruited Ruiz to be his successor at AMD, but before Ruiz arrived, the company for the most part avoided consultants, which made Kumar all the more obvious. Without notice, he would appear at executive events like the once-a-year gathering AMD held for its 250 employees who were at the level of vice president and above. Kumar milled around, not participating in the formal presentations, but he was unnervingly visible to employees, who sensed that the McKinsey man's presence could mean only one thing: cost cutting. Their fears were quickly borne out. In November 2002, Ruiz announced that the company would lay off two thousand staffers, or 15 percent of its worldwide workforce.

At Ruiz's behest, Kumar was invited to attend meetings of AMD's strategic council, which gathered every four to six weeks, sometimes overseas, to hash out the company's most pressing strategic challenges. He was part of a coveted inner circle, the only non-AMD executive present among the cabal of top executives. "I was at the heart, inside almost the body of the company," Kumar would gush. Over the years, Kumar came to identify personally with his client's long battle with Intel. He fervently believed that AMD's new chip was better than Intel's microprocessor, and he liked Ruiz personally and was rooting for him to succeed. In title, Kumar was a consultant to AMD. But in his heart he was an insider. All his life, Kumar had struggled to be appreciated and recognized. Finally, at AMD he was.

"I am being treated like a confidant by the CEO," he bragged to Rajaratnam. "I am part of his senior-most four, five, six people thinking through how AMD is going to win in the marketplace." Like everyone who knew Kumar, Rajaratnam had grown accustomed to indulging his friend's sense of self-importance, though at times it was tiring.

Stroking Kumar's bruised ego would eventually allow Raj Rajaratnam to lure Kumar into his web of tipsters. Ever since Kumar had returned to Silicon Valley from India, Kumar and Rajaratnam had casually swapped insights about the technology space. From time to time—about three or four times a year—Rajaratnam would pick Kumar's brain and ask him questions with unknowable answers, such as: are the lofty prices in the technology sector a sign of a bubble, and if so, will the bubble burst?

For his part, Kumar shared his thoughts on the Internet and explained the way it would transform companies. Kumar appreciated the give-and-take; Rajaratnam was very knowledgeable about technology, and the idea that he would be interested in Kumar's perspective inflated Kumar's sense of importance. Naturally, Rajaratnam was delighted to hear that Kumar was in the inner sanctum of AMD. By early 2004, the details of the "consulting" arrangement between Rajaratnam and Kumar were finalized. When Rajaratnam first floated the idea that Kumar moonlight for him and get paid for it, the issue that made Kumar lose sleep was that McKinsey might come to know. Rajaratnam helped ease his worry. All Kumar had to do was to find someone else who would be willing to enter into a consulting arrangement with Rajaratnam.

Since Rajaratnam planned to pay for Kumar's services with soft dollars—rebates from trading firms—the money could not be funneled directly to Kumar's housekeeper, Manju Das. There had to be a conduit, an entity that appeared to provide consulting services to Galleon, through which the money passed. After some effort, Kumar found someone in Europe willing to enter into a consulting agreement with Galleon. The firm, Pecos Trading, would bill Galleon for its services and transfer the money it received to an account in Kumar's housekeeper's name, at Galleon. As part of the setup, Kumar would be the custodian of his housekeeper Manju Das's account at Galleon. The beauty of it all was that there would be no paper trail leading back to him at McKinsey.

On January 16, 2004, Pecos Trading received its first payment of $125,000. Soon, just as Kumar had predicted, Hewlett-Packard unveiled a $400 million trial order to use AMD's Opteron chip in some of its existing servers. It was a huge order. Hewlett-Packard was a behemoth, so any shift of orders, even a small one, by the Palo Alto–based company would buoy AMD's business and dramatically reshape the semiconductor landscape.

But the honeymoon between Rajaratnam, the handler, and Kumar, the mole, was fading fast. Now that Kumar was a paid consultant, Rajaratnam wanted to speak to him more than a few times a year. And he was no longer content with hearing Kumar's eggheaded musings on the big-picture trends in the technology industry. When they chatted, Rajaratnam came to the conversations armed with a battery of questions about AMD. How was the quarter going? What were their strategic plans? Did they have any thoughts of buying another company? He was particularly interested in what AMD was going to tell Wall Street about its future prospects.

In the investment world, a company's statement about its future business is known as "guidance." Often, even if a company reports blockbuster earnings, negative "guidance" can bury a stock because investors in stocks are making a bet on a company's future performance. Rajaratnam told Kumar that "guidance" was a key fact and he wanted him to get it as often as possible.

At first, Kumar felt at sea. He was a consultant at heart, preoccupied with weighty subjects like a company's strategic direction.

He had little interest in picayune day-to-day matters like a company's quarterly profits. He knew that "guidance"—the company's forecast of its future, the nugget that Rajaratnam singled out as important—was difficult to come by because it was typically set by companies late in the earnings reporting process. But Kumar felt like he owed Rajaratnam something now that he was being paid and he had to try as hard as he could to get the information Rajaratnam wanted. Ironically, his old Doon School values kicked in. If he was being paid to do a job, he had to perform to the best of his ability.

When Rajaratnam first offered to compensate Kumar to keep a list of investment ideas and call him once a month, he told Kumar that he knew Kumar would keep his promise only if he was paid. "You will not remember to keep a list if you don't get money from me," Rajaratnam said. Rajaratnam knew that the only currency sealing the bond between him and Kumar was cold cash. Kumar always looked upon Rajaratnam with a certain disdain. He didn't think Rajaratnam was his intellectual equal. Few people rose to that level. "I have all the brains and you have all the billions," he liked to tell Rajaratnam, repeating a variation of a line he often used with his Wharton friends who had made it big on Wall Street.

If there was one thing the two men could agree on, it was that they couldn't have been more different. Rajaratnam's billions had made him loud and boorish. He rarely censored himself now—even with clients whose business he was seeking to win. One evening in 2005, he met with two former executives of the London hedge fund company Man Group PLC for cocktails at Opia, an upscale French restaurant in Manhattan that Rajaratnam was invested in. At some point, the conversation invariably digressed to women. Rajaratnam regaled his guests with his sexual joking. An attendee recalled him saying his idea of a good time was to get a few girls on his lap and spank them. He made a motion with his hand to show the executives exactly how.

Had he been there that evening, Kumar would have been appalled. In all the years Rajaratnam knew him, he never saw Kumar laugh and be really happy. He was so stiff that one former colleague of Kumar's described him as trapped in the "prison of his personality." He fancied himself a Renaissance man who could speak eloquently about art and drama. He was formal to the point of awkwardness. When his high school class at Doon was putting together a directory for their thirty-fifth reunion in 2009, Kumar supplied his secretary's contact details and his address at McKinsey in New York. Almost everyone else in Kumar's class provided their personal contact information.

Though there was little in the way of shared interests, Kumar was now inextricably tied to Rajaratnam's largesse, so he scraped around for morsels of tradable information. From time to time, when he attended meetings with AMD's senior executives, he would overhear snippets—"We are doing quite well" or "Intel is fighting us and hurting profits, so this quarter will look bad." He slipped the tidbits to Rajaratnam.

At times, Rajaratnam tried to reciprocate. He treated the informants in his financial underworld much like a mafia capo controls his foot soldiers. He made sure that he always had something on them, and he liked to tie them as closely to him as he was to them. Sometimes lending a hand—helping them with their work—was a way to draw his informants deeper into his web. On two occasions, Rajaratnam FedExed packages of slides running fifty pages long detailing new product plans for AMD's archrival, Intel, to Kumar. He didn't tell him beforehand he was sending the slides.

When Kumar opened the package, he was terrified. There was an open-door policy in his office at McKinsey in Silicon Valley. What if one of his colleagues walked in and saw the confidential Intel documents lying around? What would he say if he was asked where they came from? Kumar quickly asked his secretary to shred the slides. He couldn't admit to himself just how dirty his business was with Rajaratnam. He had to keep up the charade that he was only providing big-picture pontifications to Galleon, not inside information, but the lies he told himself were getting harder to believe every day.

Even though Rajaratnam was making good money on AMD, he told Kumar in 2005 that his advice was not as valuable as he'd expected it would be. Kumar failed to get the detailed quarterly financial results that Rajaratnam was looking for from AMD or other McKinsey clients. Rajaratnam knew it was time to tie Kumar's compensation to his information. Kumar would get paid now only if his information paid.

Rajaratnam proposed that they change the relationship. Instead of giving Kumar cash, he would buy based on Kumar's information and split any trading profits. The plan left Kumar queasy. He thought a consulting-like arrangement more appropriate and less risky. If Rajaratnam bought shares, how would he let Kumar know that he had bought the shares or tell him what price he had paid? Rajaratnam would probably have to email him or post some documents to him. It was a scheme that seemed too prone to discovery.

It was also a setup that would force Kumar to come face-to-face with what he was doing. Somehow, Kumar felt a little sheltered by the cash-for-information deal he had cooked up with Rajaratnam; he could rationalize the whole arrangement. After all, he didn't know exactly what Rajaratnam was doing with the information he supplied. But if Rajaratnam started buying shares based on the tips he provided, there would be a direct link between the information he gave and the money he made. This tit for tat struck him as a much bigger crime. Emotionally, he thought, it would stare him in the face and make him feel uncomfortable. At the very least, it would be hard to ignore his role in the seamy affair.

For a while, the two debated an alternative payment plan. As they thought about a new arrangement, for three months Rajaratnam did not pay Kumar. Finally Kumar suggested something even better than the stock-trading scheme; it was a payment plan akin to an arrangement McKinsey had with some of its clients. He told Rajaratnam he would be happy if at the end of each year Rajaratnam decided how much to pay him based on his judgment of Kumar's contribution for the year. He would be like a nonsalaried investment banker. All of his pay would be in the form of a bonus, decided by his boss, Rajaratnam.

Anil Kumar had always done well for himself when he was trying to perform for a higher-up, be it his masters at Doon or his mentor, Rajat Gupta, at McKinsey. He felt comfortable in the employee/boss dynamic. Rajaratnam was more than comfortable. He had Kumar right where he wanted him.

CHAPTER TWENTY-TWO

On the New Silk Route

Galleon employees first started noticing Rajat Gupta visiting their offices in the spring of 2005. Their boss, Raj Rajaratnam, was a consummate networker, always meeting new people, many of them South Asians. Some came to talk to him about Galleon—either a job at the hedge fund or an investment with it. But many more came to chat with Rajaratnam about new ventures. If there was one thing Galleon employees knew about their boss, it was that he had his fingers in an array of businesses. He owned a share in Manhattan restaurant Rosa Mexicano; he had a 5 percent stake in a large Sri Lankan conglomerate; and he even was an early investor in Marquis Jet, a private plane leasing company. (One of the perks of the investment was that Rajaratnam received free flying time. When Galleon was still small, he flew the firm down to New Orleans for a company trip in a Gulfstream IV private jet.)

But Gupta was distinctive, different from many of the other callers. He was impressive in an understated way. Whereas Rajaratnam was garrulous, his new friend was quiet but always polite. Since stepping down from the helm of McKinsey, Rajat Gupta, by now fifty-seven years old, had been casting about trying to determine his next move in life.

Gupta had always been intrigued by the investment business. He was a prodigious investor, soaking money into everything from private equity to friends' start-up ventures. When the daughter of new age physician Deepak Chopra was trying to launch an Internet company, Gupta, who believed in lending a hand to enterprising youngsters, readily agreed to invest $250,000. The business never took off and Gupta was not able to recoup his investment, but he never once mentioned the loss to Chopra. It was not the only time he had lost money on the Internet. During the dot-com bust of 2001, Gupta had suffered searing losses in technology stocks, but he made a killing on an investment in Scandent Solutions, a company started by a friend of his, Ramesh Vangal. Now that he was gradually phasing out of McKinsey, he was thinking about getting into the investment business himself. As he did with everything in his life, he approached it with lofty aspirations.

Gupta and a friend, Ravi Trehan, whom Gupta met one summer when Trehan rented a guesthouse in Connecticut from Gupta, had come to sound out Rajaratnam on the idea of buying an investment management company. The firm—which Trehan had found in Florida—was a so-called fund of funds, which raises money from institutional and high-net-worth investors and then allocates money to different kinds of hedge funds. Gupta and Trehan, a seasoned investor with an enviable track record of structuring deals, told Rajaratnam that they thought they could buy the company for 2 percent of assets. At the time, investment managers were trading at about 10 percent of assets. Gupta and Trehan were looking for $100 million from Rajaratnam as equity capital to buy the company. Rajaratnam was skeptical and the plan went nowhere, but another idea caught his imagination.

It was an investment vehicle called Voyager Capital Partners. Voyager, essentially a creation of Trehan's, would invest in a smattering of funds and strategies—some run by Galleon and some by Trehan's investment firm BroadStreet Group.

The beauty of Voyager was that it would be highly leveraged, which amplified its investment firepower. Essentially the fund would borrow money, invest it, and then seek to pay back the debt after its investors made an acceptable profit. Under the structure, Rajaratnam put in $40 million, giving him an 80 percent stake in the entity, Trehan invested $5 million for 10 percent of the equity, and Gupta

$5 million for 10 percent. On the back of the $50 million in equity, Voyager borrowed $350 million, pumping up the vehicle's investment capacity—and the potential returns—to its three partners.

Most of the loan—$300 million—came from Lehman Brothers, which bore the least risk in the event there were losses in Voyager. The three equity partners—Gupta, Trehan, and Rajaratnam—carried the greatest risk. If there were losses in Voyager, they would shoulder them first.

From the start, Voyager was highly lucrative for its partners and even more so for BroadStreet, which was Voyager's investment manager, doing the paperwork, allocating the money to different funds, and receiving fees for its role. On January 11, 2006, just three months after Voyager was set up, the equity of the shareholders stood at $58,382,958, a return of nearly 17 percent. But while the profits were piling up, the goodwill between the two key partners, Trehan and Rajaratnam, frayed.

One day in early 2006, Rajaratnam, Gupta, and Trehan were meeting at Galleon's offices when Rajaratnam started laying into Trehan. Instead of BroadStreet serving as the investment manager of Voyager, Rajaratnam was angling for Galleon to be making the asset allocation decisions at Voyager (and getting a bit of the lucrative management fees). At one point, Rajaratnam became so abusive that Trehan, a seasoned investor with a successful track record, got fed up and said, "I don't want to do business with you if that is the way you are going to act." Then Trehan walked out of Rajaratnam's office. Gupta stayed. He did not follow his friend.

People noticed that Rajaratnam always addressed Gupta with great deference, unlike the way he treated others. He liked to refer to Gupta as a South Asian "rock star" and explained to friends that Gupta was a half generation older than him and, in Asia, it was the custom to treat elders with respect. Shortly after the falling out, Trehan sold his investment in Voyager to Rajaratnam and for a while, Rajaratnam owned 90 percent of the equity of the vehicle and Gupta held 10 percent.

In 2006, Gupta was starting to focus on his life after McKinsey; even though he had stepped down as managing director in 2003, he remained a partner and had signaled to colleagues that he wanted to stay on at the firm until 2008, when he turned sixty. His outside activities, though, were making it increasingly difficult for him to continue. One of the most nettlesome was a new money management company that Gupta was in the throes of setting up even as he was still on McKinsey's payroll as a partner.

In early 2006, Gupta confided in Kumar that he wanted to start a large, world-class asset management company, focused not just on hedge funds but on private equity too, that would be targeted at investing in South Asia—mainly India but also China and, to a lesser extent, the Islamic world, Pakistan and the Middle East. His plan was to enlist well-regarded money managers of South Asian origin to run the assets. Gupta said he had already teamed up with three other partners, Parag Saxena, who had expertise in private equity; Rajaratnam, who was a hedge fund pro; and Mark Schwartz, a former Goldman Sachs executive who had worked for many years in Asia. The foursome had an ambitious goal: they wanted to raise $2 billion for the new fund. They were deeply committed to the project, proposing to match the total amount raised—ultimately $1.25 billion—by putting in 10 percent of their own money. The seed money of $130 million was to be divided equally, but Gupta told his partners to count him in for less: $22.5 million.

The new venture, which was called Taj Capital and later renamed New Silk Route (NSR), at first operated out of space adjacent to Galleon's offices on the thirty-fourth floor at 590 Madison Avenue. To facilitate his movements in and out of Galleon's offices, Gupta also received a key card allowing him to come and go as he pleased. Sometimes, his free access caused problems for Rajaratnam. One time, Gupta arrived at the office without an appointment. Rajaratnam told his secretary, Caryn Eisenberg, to lie and tell Gupta he wasn't there. But Gupta was determined to find him. He got into the office using his key card and eventually tracked Rajaratnam down.

Gupta poured his energies into raising money for the new fund, tapping into his impressive array of contacts. In mid-2006, when the four partners settled on their plans, the group put together a priority list of investors to target. Gupta was responsible for reaching out to some of the biggest names on the list. He and Schwartz were to go after the investment officers of the endowments for preeminent institutions such as Harvard University, where Gupta's daughter worked, and Yale. They were also to reach out to Bill Gates and the Walton Family Foundation. (Harvard did not invest, citing as a factor a conflict of interest because Gupta's daughter worked there; Goldman also passed on the opportunity, raising similar concerns, in this case because Gupta was a board member.) Gupta alone would approach Edgar Bronfman Jr., whose family built a fortune through the spirits company Seagram, even though his McKinsey colleague Anil Kumar, who had been considering joining the fund, had already spoken to Bronfman's older brother, Sam.

The lifeboat out of McKinsey now awaited Kumar, but it was the last thing he wanted to pursue. His dissatisfaction with his lot had prompted him to toy with outside ventures, but he knew in his heart that he was most comfortable as a salaryman at a big firm. He desperately hoped that in three years when a new managing director ascended to the helm of McKinsey, his career would be back on track.

For now, though, he figured that it didn't hurt to be deeply involved in the planning of NSR. Operating against company practices, Kumar often fired off emails about the new fund from his account at McKinsey. Sometimes his efforts landed him in near scrapes with his employer. In early October 2006, Kumar sent an email with the subject line "URGENT" in all capitals to the founding partners of NSR. Two of them, Rajaratnam and Saxena, planned to have a meeting with a potential investor, Dr. Hosein Khajeh-Hosseiny, at Northgate, a "fund of funds" that allocated money to various private equity firms. Many of Northgate's principals had worked at McKinsey. "I spoke with Dr. Hosselnys [*sic*] asst yesterday. Given Northgate's special relationship with McKinsey she was puzzled as to why I was joining this meeting today," Kumar wrote to them. The best positioning for these meetings is that "I am a 'founding investor' and an old school friend of Raj and Parag."

McKinsey failed to spot Kumar's work for NSR and that Kumar was angling to be paid hundreds of thousands of dollars by NSR for his efforts even as he was on McKinsey's payroll. Kumar's second attempt to moonlight never came to anything because one of the principals of NSR, Parag Saxena, was vehemently opposed to the idea. As a compromise, it was agreed that Kumar would receive a stake, albeit smaller than that of the founding principals, if he decided to join NSR in three years.

Meanwhile, Gupta's outside activities, while he was still affiliated with McKinsey, did not go unnoticed. Ironically, though, it was not his fund-raising for NSR that came to McKinsey's attention but rather his desire to join the board of Goldman Sachs. In 2005, Lloyd Blankfein's predecessor and former secretary of the Treasury Henry M. "Hank" Paulson Jr. had approached Gupta about joining the Goldman board of directors. Paulson had first met Gupta when the two were working on an assignment for Sara Lee. Many years later, in 1996, John Bryan, Sara Lee's chief executive, reintroduced the two at his sixtieth-birthday party at his home in Chicago. When Gupta moved to New York, the two became better acquainted. They both served on a Harvard Business School alumni advisory committee, and one year Gupta invited Paulson, a nature lover, on a trip to Indonesia to see the Komodo dragons, a large species of lizard.

The first time Paulson approached Gupta about joining the Goldman board, he appeared eager but then demurred. McKinsey would not waive the restriction it had prohibiting partners from joining corporate boards. But in November 2006, Gupta retired as a partner and became a consultant to the firm. Almost immediately he stepped onto the Goldman board, taking up the first of many board seats. In 2007, he was named a director on the board of consumer products giant Procter & Gamble. Two years earlier, Gupta helped P&G's then chairman and CEO A. G. Lafley sketch the company's $57 billion takeover bid to buy Gillette. And when the talks hit a roadblock, Gupta, who was close to Gillette's then chief executive James Kilts, helped bring the two back to the negotiating table. He sat for hours with the men in a room hashing out their differences until a deal was struck. Kilts remembers Gupta's role to this day. At a thorny point in the talks, there was only one person Lafley and he trusted to call: "That person was Rajat."

As a former managing director of McKinsey and a consultant to the firm now, Gupta still retained many of his old perks, including his Stamford office, his countless McKinsey phones and BlackBerry, and his access to the company's email, which he would rely on to solicit investors for NSR.

Tireless in his fund-raising, Gupta turned to his vast database of contacts to find people to pitch. He fired off dozens and dozens of impersonal, form-like letters to McKinsey partners he had worked with at the firm as well as to corporate chieftains he had come to know over the years and even to neighbors. "I hope you remember me," he started one letter he emailed to Robert Devlin, the former chief executive of insurer American General. A letter he sent to former Citigroup chief Sandy Weill, whom he knew from being on the board of Weill Cornell Medical College, was emblematic of the marketing push: "Dear Sandy, I am the chairman of a new 1.5 billion dollar private equity fund called New Silk Route (NSR) and I would very much like you to consider investing in it." Gupta went on to lay out brief profiles of his investment partners, noting that they had put in $125 million of their own money. "We are now in the process of offering the final $200 million to a few friends and family in the range of $1–5 million each and hope to have a final close in the next 30 days."

As part of the NSR fund-raising drive, Gupta sent similar letters to Ajit Jain of Berkshire Hathaway, a top lieutenant of Buffett's and a contender to succeed him; Herb Allison of TIAA-CREF; Goldman board members John Bryan and Bill George; Marcus Wallenberg, a member of the prominent Swedish family; PepsiCo chief executive Indra Nooyi; and dozens of others. The efforts paid off, and NSR succeeded in raising $1.3 billion for its private equity arm; its capital drive for the hedge fund side failed, though, and that business was never launched.

It was around this time that Gupta's relationship with Rajaratnam deepened too. He and Kumar started advising Rajaratnam on ways that he could boost his assets at Galleon, and in late 2006, Gupta moved to exercise his option to lift his stake in Voyager, which had racked up strong returns. He borrowed $5 million from Rajaratnam to buy out Trehan's stake in the investment vehicle, giving him a 20 percent stake in the heavily leveraged entity. He also helped facilitate a high-interest bridge loan from Rajaratnam to his friend Ramesh Vangal, now of Katra Holdings, whose company, Scandent, Gupta had invested in many years ago and had made a lot of money on. Gupta and Vangal were working to buy a bank in South India called Tamilnad Mercantile Bank, which they ultimately succeeded in purchasing with other investors in May 2007. For a while in December 2006, as Vangal dragged his feet on repaying the loan, Gupta's relationship with Rajaratnam turned thorny.

On Thursday, December 21, 2006, after not hearing a peep from Vangal, Rajaratnam fired off an angry email to Gupta: "We still have not received total payment for Katra Finance, nor has Mr. Vangal contacted me as he indicated to our CFO yesterday. Under the circumstances I am not able to meet you for lunch today and I am cancelling all further meetings for TAJ Capital." The email was signed formally, "Regards, Raj Rajaratnam," and not "Raj," as he normally signed missives to Gupta.

The chasing of the money came down to the wire. On December 28, George Lau, a Galleon executive, sent an email to Gupta from his BlackBerry saying, "Our team has been chasing Ramesh's team on a daily basis and we still have not received a 100% signal that the wire has been sent out. Tomorrow is the last day of the month and the funds have to be in our account. Please advise what else I can do??"

Gupta replied, "Rest assured please tell Raj that he should also believe I have been working nonstop the past 7 days to make this happen." When Vangal repaid the loan not long after, Gupta and Rajaratnam got back to lunching together. But the balance of power in the relationship had changed.

CHAPTER TWENTY-THREE

The Million-Dollar Man

"Anil, this can wait until you return from London. We trust you!" emailed Peg O'Malley, the executive assistant to AMD's chief administrative officer and top lawyer, Tom McCoy, on September 28, 2005. O'Malley had just sent Kumar a confidentiality agreement for a top secret assignment called Project Super Nova that AMD was in the early stages of hatching. The company was looking to hire McKinsey as an adviser. As was often the case, Kumar was traveling overseas and was not in a position to sign the nondisclosure agreement immediately, but O'Malley was not worried. Kumar was one of the most trusted and discreet advisers AMD retained, and no one had any reason to doubt his loyalty to the company.

The explosive growth of video games and other graphics-driven computer applications laid bare a gaping hole in AMD's panoply of products. Both AMD and its archrival, Intel, were in the business of making the "brains," or the microprocessor, of a computer. Both specialized in chips that did the computational functions of a personal computer, the "left brain," if you will. Neither owned the market in graphics chips, or the so-called right brain functions, which had exploded with the growing use of computers as game consoles.

Intel had a slight edge over AMD. It already sold integrated chip sets with built-in graphics, allowing it to offer hardware companies a package of chips that worked well together instead of having its customers buy one chip from one company and another chip from a different firm. AMD, by contrast, relied on graphics chips from the two biggest manufacturers, Nvidia, a Santa Clara, California–based company, and ATI Technologies, an Ontario, Canada–based company. Besides developing graphics chips for personal computers, ATI designed the chips used in Nintendo's GameCube and Microsoft's popular Xbox.

A looming strategic challenge for AMD if it was to close the gap between it and Intel was to enlarge its graphic chips footprint by buying or partnering with either Nvidia or ATI Technologies.

Few people within AMD knew about Project Supernova, the code name for a possible merger of AMD with either Nvidia or ATI Technologies. The plan was so closely guarded that Kumar, who had already signed a general agreement with AMD not to disclose confidential information about the company, was required to enter into another nondisclosure agreement that would cover his work on Project Supernova. Even the confidentiality agreement was confidential. Sharing it or copying it was not permitted without the prior permission of Bharath Rangarajan, the AMD strategy czar.

The reason for the high level of paranoia was simple. In any merger deal, secrecy is paramount. Companies abhor leaks because they can kill a deal. When word spreads that one firm is looking to buy another, the stock price of the target company will jump, making the acquisition more expensive, possibly prohibitively so. At AMD, executives were so nervous that they even changed the code name from Project Supernova to Go Big.

It was not long after Kumar signed the confidentiality agreement that he started divulging details of AMD's supersecret plan to buy a graphics chip maker to Rajaratnam. On some days, he did not even wait to return to his office at McKinsey before calling Rajaratnam. Instead, he would slip into a conference room where the McKinsey team decamped. There, away from his colleagues, he picked up the phone and called Rajaratnam.

AMD had been a favorite company of Rajaratnam's for years. He'd tracked AMD when he started covering semiconductor firms twenty years before at Needham & Co. Rajaratnam used to keep a poster board in the office with a list of companies. Next to the companies were Galleon employees' names. Rajaratnam expected these inner-circle Galleon analysts to cultivate corporate insiders to get revenue, guidance, and margin information for the companies they covered. If a trusted analyst didn't call a company or his information was wrong, he was fired. Next to Rajaratnam's name on the poster board was AMD. He made no secret of the fact that he was wired into AMD. In Galleon's lexicon, he was "the axe," or the authority on the stock. Often when speaking to Ali Far, who worked for Galleon in Santa Clara, California, Rajaratnam would refer to a source at the company, saying, "my guy from AMD."

Few at Galleon would have ever imagined his "guy" was a strait-laced McKinsey consultant as plugged into AMD as any high-level company insider. Kumar's gleanings on AMD gave Rajaratnam a unique window into the company at a pivotal time in its history. He learned of AMD's game-changing strategic steps and new products long before most investors were aware of the shifts, giving him an edge on how to reevaluate the stock. Most investors knew Opteron, AMD's new chip, was getting positive feedback in the market, but few knew the impact it would have on AMD's profitability. Thanks to Kumar, Rajaratnam kept tabs on Opteron every step of the way.

"Are you absolutely sure?" Rajaratnam asked.

He was rarely surprised by anything in the technology space. He was too familiar with the ever-changing dynamics of the industry and its various players to be caught flatfooted. But the potential merger Kumar told him about in the spring of 2006, a tie-up between giant semiconductor company Advanced Micro Devices and graphics maker ATI Technologies, appeared like a bolt out of the blue. In his mind, it defied logic. If AMD was going to buy a graphics company, it should be the stronger of the two, Nvidia.

Yet Kumar was convinced the company AMD was lusting after was none other than ATI, the Canadian tech firm founded in the early eighties by a tourist who happened to be visiting from Hong Kong.

"C'mon...I'm in the inner circle over here," Kumar boasted. "I know everything about this company. And they're very very keen to do ATI."

Over the years, the relationship between Rajaratnam and Kumar had turned rather sadomasochistic. In a savvy move, Rajaratnam taunted Kumar from time to time, chiding him that he, a hedge fund trader, knew more about AMD than Kumar did. Undercutting Kumar's confidence in his indispensable role at AMD made him want to perform for Rajaratnam—not just for a monetary payoff, but almost for a paternalistic pat on the back.

Now, for the first time, Kumar could show Rajaratnam just how key a player he was. Kumar was in the loop about an important development at AMD that no one was expecting—not even Rajaratnam. If AMD pulled it off, it could be a winning strategy for the company. Kumar was excited.

He told Rajaratnam that AMD was looking at both ATI and Nvidia. If it was impossible to strike a deal with Nvidia because it was too expensive, AMD would consider buying ATI. Rajaratnam was very intrigued because the information was counter to the prevailing market view. At Galleon, Rajaratnam honed the strategy of "arbitraging consensus," or developing a view on a stock that varied from the mainstream thinking on Wall Street. Galleon's aim was to profit when the company's stock price rose or fell as investors moved away from Wall Street's herd mentality and came closer to Galleon's way of thinking. In efficient markets, the easiest way to "arbitrage consensus" is to have inside information—a tip, for instance, that a large semiconductor company is poised to make an unexpected acquisition or that a firm is expected to report an earnings shortfall.

For a couple of months, AMD considered both Nvidia and ATI, but by mid-December 2005, it was clear that ATI was the target. Nvidia was simply too expensive. To keep the talks tightly under wraps, the companies were assigned code names. AMD was Los Angeles and ATI was San Antonio. Sometimes code names in deals refer to the companies' headquarters cities. But AMD and ATI were so intent on keeping the talks confidential that they picked code names designed to throw people off the trail. ATI was actually based in Markham, Canada, and the only link AMD had to Los Angeles was that its founder, Sanders, had an office in Beverly Hills.

In anticipation of a deal early in 2006, McKinsey proposed

putting together a team that would help AMD prepare for the acquisition and would give it the behind-the-scenes support it needed in its
negotiations with ATI. For a full team—a partner, devoting 50 percent of his time to the AMD assignment, a full-time engagement
manager, an associate, and one of the firm's valuation experts providing support—McKinsey said it would charge $400,000 a month,
prorated. AMD would also be required to cover 18 percent of the
billed amount in expenses.

On December 20, 2005, McKinsey's Paul Roche sent Kumar an
email with an update on the early talks between AMD and ATI.
"Their mtg with San Antonio went well," he wrote. Roche said the
companies agreed on a timeline, proposing to reach terms by early
February and unveiling the deal by the end of the first quarter. Rangarajan, the AMD vice president in charge of strategy, was eager to
get McKinsey signed on to work on the project immediately. But Bob
Rivet—the company's chief financial officer, who had a reputation
for never seeing a cost he liked—balked. "Think we should play it
out but if he's still squishy should talk to Bob," wrote Roche.

Soon after, Kumar called Rajaratnam and told him that AMD's
conversations with Nvidia were not going anywhere. However, early
discussions had already started with its rival, ATI Technologies.

This information is "red-hot," Kumar told Rajaratnam. "Please
do keep this to yourself. Don't let anyone else know."

"No one is going to know about this," Rajaratnam reassured him.

After more than two years of feeding him information, Kumar
seemed to have little sense of exactly how Rajaratnam made his
money. He looked at Rajaratnam's profession as a consultant would,
thinking he was obsessed with big-picture machinations, and, much
like Warren Buffett, bought and held stocks for years. If the company
that Kumar tipped him on did well, Rajaratnam would make some
money. For someone so smart, Kumar had little understanding of
how event-driven hedge funds like Galleon really worked.

As the talks progressed, Kumar briefed Rajaratnam regularly, telephoning him about once a month to keep him posted. At times he
was almost breathless in his excitement. "ATI looks like the candidate," Kumar gushed. "This is going to shock the industry." From

the work the McKinsey team was doing, Kumar knew that Advanced Micro Devices would be required to pay a big premium on ATI's current share price if it was to consummate the marriage. At the time, ATI's stock was trading at $16 to $17; it had not risen above $21 a share in the previous five years, but ATI felt the market undervalued it. To get ATI to take a bid seriously but still give AMD some maneuvering room so it could sweeten its offer if needed, the company proposed an initial offer price of $20 a share.

When Kumar told Rajaratnam the bid, he was stunned.

"This is completely ridiculous. It makes no sense whatsoever. I can't believe AMD is going to do it," he said. Rajaratnam was amazed that AMD would pay such a huge price for a graphics company that was not even the industry leader.

Again he asked Kumar, "Are you absolutely sure AMD management is going to do it?"

Ever knowledgeable on such matters, Kumar explained that ATI was a strategic must-have for AMD and the company was willing to open up its wallet to acquire it.

"Wow, this is very useful," said Rajaratnam. Then he went to work feeding his network of informers. Soon after Kumar briefed him on the serious nature of the talks between AMD and ATI, Rajaratnam started spreading the word to his inner circle, ignoring Kumar's explicit request to keep the information to himself.

"Buy some atyt," rajatgalleon instant-messaged quintussf on April 19, 2006. "I will tell u why on fon."

"Quintussf" was the instant-message handle for Frank "Quint" Slattery, who ran an unregistered hedge fund in Connecticut called Symmetry Peak in which Rajaratnam invested some money. Slattery was a fervid instant messager who had been in trouble five years earlier for an IM he sent. In 2001, the software firm PeopleSoft publicly blamed Slattery, then twenty-eight years old, for suggesting that the SEC was probing PeopleSoft for accounting irregularities. Even a whiff of a regulatory investigation into accounting missteps can pummel a stock, which is exactly what happened with PeopleSoft. The company's shares plunged 27 percent even though Slattery retracted the rumor in a subsequent instant message.

The public dress-down did not diminish his appetite for swapping information. Several times a day, Rajaratnam and Slattery kibitzed about investment ideas—many flowing out of insider tips that either Rajaratnam or Slattery picked up from their vast array of contacts. They chatted about stocks like Google, quizzing each other on who had a "good read" on the company. Rajaratnam was the undisputed king on AMD. "U are the best on it," Slattery acknowledged once.

Over the years, Rajaratnam learned that one of the easiest ways to build a network of loyal informants was to invest in fledgling hedge funds set up by young and hungry investment managers—and then make them dependent on you to beat the market. Whenever they could, they paid you back in the best currency around, information. It was exactly the course Rajaratnam took with his own brother Rengan when he invested $1 million in Rengan's family and friends fund at Sedna Capital. It was Rengan's trades in AMD that had launched the SEC investigation in 2006.

Rajaratnam had seeded more than forty hedge funds, typically giving their founders $1 million to get rolling. A handful of funds got $5 million. Most of the funds—Slattery's Symmetry Peak or Peter Wright's Paw Partners—flew below the radar; they were too small to draw any attention. But for Rajaratnam they were a gold mine. The funds he seeded "became an informal information network because the people who started the hedge funds were beholden to him" says one former Galleon employee. (The nature of the information Slattery and Wright provided was not known and neither man was ever charged with wrongdoing.)

When Rajaratnam first began on Wall Street, before 2000, information flowed more freely and frequently from companies to money managers and stock analysts. Before the millennium, when the SEC put in place Regulation FD—short for "fair disclosure"—chief executives regularly gave previews of their companies' profit picture or lifted the veil on new, groundbreaking products at private meetings with institutional investors and research analysts. It was such a common practice that some hedge fund managers freely touted their strategy of "information arbitrage"—a way of making money by having confidential information that is at variance with the prevailing market view—in their pitch books to new investors.

The advent of "Reg FD" changed all that. It transformed the discourse between corporate America and Wall Street by requiring companies to disclose corporate news to everyone or to no one at all. In leveling the playing field between small investors and big institutions, the new SEC rule aimed to diminish the "edge" that investment managers and the Wall Street analysts that provided research to them had long enjoyed. What it effectively meant was that investment managers like Rajaratnam had to work harder than ever to beat the market, even if it meant trafficking in "hot" information.

One of the ways for funds like Galleon around Reg FD was to develop deep nonofficial sources at companies who could pass information on the sly. In the technology space, no one was more skilled at ferreting out corporate moles than Rajaratnam. The only difference between his days at Needham and his days at Galleon was that he and his employees at Galleon had to be more vigilant about the way information was received and passed. Rajaratnam was generally careful about not saying too much in emails and instant messages. Whenever an IM chat drifted in the direction of the passing of sensitive information, he would suggest speaking "on fon" or offer to "call u?" He urged all his traders and analysts to exercise the same caution.

Soon after former Morgan Stanley employee Adam Smith joined Galleon as an analyst in 2002, he had a conversation with Rajaratnam about putting confidential, nonpublic information in emails. Rajaratnam told Smith to avoid it and if, for whatever reason, news had to be conveyed via email, he suggested Smith be vague. Galleon did not want any record of the passing of nonpublic information in its computer system. It was all the more important since in January 2006 Galleon had registered with the SEC. A fund registered with the SEC is required to deliver books and records such as emails and IMs to the agency upon demand.

Smith quickly mastered the art of communicating nonpublic information in a cryptic way. He had a unique style, a form of Wall Street Morse code that he developed in his early years as an investment banker at Morgan Stanley. As at most banks, one of the tasks assigned to young bankers at Morgan Stanley is dreaming up clever code names for companies involved in an impending merger so that if deal documents are accidentally left on a copy or fax machine, others within the firm have no way of divining the deal.

In 2005, while at Galleon, Smith learned from a former Morgan Stanley colleague, that Integrated Circuit Systems, a public company that sold electronic components, was being acquired by Integrated Device Technology. In the spring of 2005, Smith sent a flurry of emails in which he referred to the "Two Eyes" or sometimes simply "Eyes." It was code for the tie-up between Integrated Circuit and Integrated Device, two companies whose names began with the letter *I.* On April 21, 2005, Smith sent Rajaratnam an email entitled "Eyes": "the date is set for May 16," he wrote in the body of the message.

Smith had learned from his former colleague that the merger was set to be unveiled on that date, but he sent the email only to Rajaratnam. He was nervous that others at Galleon would come to know that he had confidential information. In the past, when he passed on nonpublic information to traders at Galleon, they had circulated it among their friends on Wall Street, but in this instance, because it was highly sensitive information, he wanted to make sure it didn't come back to haunt him.

Smith turned out to be off by a month in his timing, but he was correct about the most important fact: a tie-up between the two "eyes," Integrated Circuit and Integrated Device. On June 15, the companies unveiled a $1.7 billion merger deal; Galleon's technology fund wound up making nearly $2.7 million on the Integrated Circuit stock it held. After the deal was announced, Rajaratnam told Smith that his old Morgan Stanley pal was a good contact and he should stay in touch with him. It left Smith with a sinking feeling in his stomach. Knowing that it was his inside information that led Galleon to buy the stock made him feel queasy.

* * *

As word of AMD's interest in acquiring ATI Technologies spread around town, it inevitably triggered public speculation. "Need to move quick," McKinsey consultant Paul Roche tapped out in an email. It was May 31, 2006, and Apjit Walia, a well-connected analyst at Royal Bank of Canada Capital Markets, had just published a report saying that a rumored tie-up between AMD and ATI Technologies "may be likely." It was a gutsy call; almost as soon as Walia published his piece, other analysts mocked the idea. "This rumor surfaces occasionally, and has been making the rounds within Taiwan in the past several weeks," wrote David Hodgson at Genuity Capital Markets. "We heard from ATI's CEO this morning and he...had also heard the ATYT/AMD [rumors] in Taiwan in the past few weeks but he didn't have a clue where the information came from." Hodgson added that another ATI source "laughed at the suggestion of the link-up" and Hodgson rated the probability as "very low."

Walia's reasons for a merger—expected synergies from a deal that were consistent with AMD's strategy—were not particularly compelling. But at Galleon, traders paid attention to Walia's report. It was well known he was a friend of Rajaratnam's. He was often seen visiting the Galleon offices, and Rajaratnam told colleagues that he wanted to be a mentor to the young, up-and-coming analyst. They suspected Walia had learned of the proposed acquisition from none other than Rajaratnam.

By late May, Kumar knew the AMD-ATI deal was going to happen—it was just a matter of when and at what price. AMD's board gave Ruiz, the company's chief executive, the green light to offer as much as $24 a share for ATI, which was trading at around $16.51 at the time. Kumar briefed Rajaratnam, telling him management was very keen to do the deal and had a lot of leeway from the board to craft a transaction.

Not surprisingly, now that the deal had moved from rumor to reality, the Walia report was discomforting. At McKinsey and AMD, it sparked consternation. AMD was hoping to get the deal consummated in secret. How had word leaked? After all its meticulous planning and code names to keep its deal with ATI supersecret, AMD's worst fears—of a leak—were coming true. Between the start of May and the end of the month, ATI Technologies' stock jumped 6.4 percent. More worrisome, a number of large investors like the powerful mutual fund group Janus voiced their opposition to the deal. The talks were still supposed to be confidential, however, so AMD's spin doctors found their hands tied. There was little they could do to sell the merits of the merger to some of the company's largest shareholders.

On the morning of Thursday, June 29, before the market opened, Rajaratnam dropped by the office of Adam Smith, who'd made a bundle of money a year earlier on the merger of two technology companies, the "eyes" deal. He and Rajaratnam had talked recently about another technology deal possibly in the offing. In early May, Smith lunched with his former colleague, the Morgan Stanley banker. For months, Smith had been hearing rumors about a possible acquisition of ATI by AMD. He knew his boss, Rajaratnam, was accumulating ATI stock. But Smith didn't think the speculation was credible. When Smith asked his Morgan Stanley friend about ATI, he was surprised by his response.

"They are not just rumors," the former colleague of Smith's said. "A deal is under way." After his lunch, Smith called Rajaratnam. When he reached him, he told him that he had met with a banker at Morgan Stanley, who said a deal between AMD and ATI Technologies was happening. Smith was one of the more promising hires Rajaratnam made for Galleon. Even though he was a banker by background, Smith quickly caught on to the business of managing money. It was comforting for Rajaratnam to have some extra reassurance that the huge bet Galleon was making on ATI stock was a smart gamble. Not only had many of Galleon's funds been accumulating ATI stock, but even the hedge fund's risk book, which was supposed to take positions to offset the holdings in Galleon's individual portfolios, was loading up on ATI stock. Galleon was betting its franchise on the deal.

That morning in late June, ATI reported its fiscal third-quarter earnings and said its outlook for the rest of the year was bleak. Rajaratnam wanted to capitalize on the expected dip in ATI stock and add to Galleon's position when the market opened. After the morning meeting, he stopped by Smith's office with a specific purpose in mind. He wanted Smith to write an email outlining the reasons to buy ATI stock.

Smith needed no explanation. He had worked long enough at Galleon and understood the reason Rajaratnam was making the request. He simply wanted to have a written record of the "legitimate" reasons that had prompted Galleon to buy ATI stock on a day when most investors were dumping it indiscriminately in the face of a torrent of unexpected negative news. He wanted to make sure that Galleon had a credible cover story, an email it could point to outlining every possible reason to buy ATI stock except for the real reason, a possible acquisition, so that in the event regulators starting looking into Galleon's purchase of stock, they would be convinced that it was rooted in sound investment analysis and not in inside information.

Shortly after Rajaratnam left his office, Smith crafted an email entitled "ATYT—what to do." Even though "the guidance" ATI Technologies had provided was worse than expected, Smith said he was "FIRMLY" convinced it was a conservative number. He told Rajaratnam that he strongly advised buying the stock and he listed a number of reasons to own it—the company had a great product cycle, its margins were increasing, and it had market share to gain. He omitted the imminent acquisition by AMD.

At 9:10 a.m., Smith sent the email to Rajaratnam. Shortly thereafter, when the market opened for trading, Galleon began loading up on ATI stock.

June was a busy month for AMD. Ruiz and his bankers were busy negotiating the terms of the company's acquisition of ATI, which entered its final stretch with a deal set to be unveiled on July 10. At the same time, the company held separate discussions with the big computer maker Dell. AMD was seeking to extend the relationship between the two companies and get Dell to use AMD chips in its desktops and laptops. If it was successful, it would be a coup for AMD, allowing the semiconductor company to make new inroads into Intel's turf and pave the way for it to gain market share. On June 26, Dell's chief executive officer, Kevin Rollins, hosted a dinner for AMD's CEO, Ruiz, and some other executives. At the dinner, Rollins told Ruiz that they should target August 12 as the day to launch their tie-up. As a member of AMD's inner circle, Kumar naturally was briefed on the plan.

Investigators suspect but did not prove that Kumar told Rajaratnam about the pending announcement with Dell. It was exciting news. A month after its ATI acquisition, AMD was poised to unveil another strategic breakthrough to help close the gap with longtime rival Intel. It was the kind of news that got Kumar, the consultant, jazzed. And it likely was the reason Rajaratnam decided to hold AMD stock until at least August 13, a day after the expected public disclosure that Dell and AMD would be doing more business.

It was this news and the suspicious instant messaging about August 13 that first piqued SEC lawyer Andrew Michaelson's investigative instincts.

On July 5, a week before AMD was set to unveil its ATI deal, Bharath Rangarajan, AMD's strategy czar, sent an email to the merger team. "Due to a variety of circumstances, we will need to push out the Go Big announcement by two weeks." Unbeknownst to players in the market, AMD and ATI Technologies were still a dollar apart on the share price that AMD would pay to acquire ATI. Rangarajan, naturally worried about an eleventh-hour leak, cautioned, "I would appreciate it if all of you would please let those already involved know and not pull in any more people."

When Kumar got the news, he was excited. "So july 24 is action week!" he emailed from his BlackBerry. But others on the McKinsey team were on edge. The longer it takes to negotiate a merger deal, the higher the risk that details of the deal will leak out, forcing up the price of the target company and making the acquisition more expensive. Vanessa Colella, a member of the McKinsey team, suggested a discussion the next day "about whether or not there should be a communication to people in the know about the critical importance of NDA" or the nondisclosure agreement that McKinsey signed as part of its engagement by AMD.

On July 24, a little over six months after they started talking, AMD and ATI announced a $5.4 billion merger that would create a "processing powerhouse." As part of the deal, AMD would pay $4.2 billion in cash to ATI shareholders and 57 million shares of AMD common stock, or a total of $20.47 a share. It was a big payday for Rajaratnam, who had accumulated $89.4 million worth of ATI shares, snapping up the stock whenever it slipped. He booked a profit of nearly $23 million on the deal.

He was so elated that he hosted an impromptu celebration in his office. As his traders toasted the huge win with champagne, Rajaratnam placed a call to Kumar at home to thank him.

"That was fantastic," he said. "We are all cheering you right now."

Kumar got a sinking feeling in his stomach. The last thing he wanted was to have a crowd of people gathered in Rajaratnam's office celebrating him with champagne. His anxiety would soon dissipate. In early 2007, as SEC lawyers were rooting around Sedna Capital's trades in AMD and starting to focus on Galleon, Raj Rajaratnam paid Kumar a $1 million bonus for the AMD information. It was a huge sum. Instead of sending the money through circuitous channels, Rajaratnam simply transferred the $1 million from Galleon's HSBC account in New York to Kumar's in India. Affixed at the bottom of a fax effecting the transfer was Rajaratnam's signature.

CHAPTER TWENTY-FOUR

"You've Gotta Be a Hustler"

Whenever Rajaratnam flew out to California, he made it a point to stop by the Goels' house. Rajiv Goel had been Rajaratnam's buddy since the two were at Wharton in the early eighties, getting their MBAs together. Over *chaat*—an Indian savory snack that Goel's wife, Alka, was particularly good at making—Goel and Rajaratnam would kibitz about their kids and their jobs. Unlike so many of the relationships in Rajaratnam's life, which were all business, his relationship with Goel was purely social. But that was about to change. Goel was now working as an executive at Intel Treasury, which supported the venture capital arm of Intel Corp., the semiconductor giant that went head-to-head with AMD. Rajaratnam boasted to Goel that he was astonishingly accurate when it came to predicting Intel's financial results. He said he knew two women who were privy to Intel's book of orders—a tally that would give a savvy investor a window into Intel's future revenue. The women would routinely fill him in on the information. As a thank-you, Rajaratnam said he gave each a BMW. Goel was in awe.

What he didn't know was that Rajaratnam's boast was more bravado than anything else. By 2001, Rajaratnam was in the market for a new source on Intel. Since Roomy Khan had left the company, he found himself at a loose end. He no longer had an insider in one of the biggest companies in the technology universe that he covered. He'd tried to find replacements for Khan to no avail.

234

Born in Bombay, now Mumbai, Goel, with his tidy mustache, looked more like an efficient bookkeeper than an executive at a technology company. Awkward and inept to the point of being comical, Goel was always stuck in one kind of jam or another. He bounced around from job to job after graduating from Wharton in 1983. For a time, he left America and returned to India, but then he came back. He was forever unhappy with his work and pay and saw Rajaratnam as a lifeline. Unlike Kumar, whose speech was clipped and who rarely engaged in pointless small talk, Goel enjoyed an easy camaraderie with Rajaratnam. Their conversations were freewheeling and they kidded each other like brothers. While Rajaratnam and Goel had stayed in touch intermittently during the eighties and nineties, their friendship blossomed after Goel started working at Intel's Treasury department in January 2000.

In 2003, reeling from the aftershocks of the collapse in the technology bubble, Galleon closed its California office. Rajaratnam asked Goel to do him a favor: could he keep an eye out for the happenings in Silicon Valley? He told Goel he was interested in learning about the ups and downs of the real estate market and getting a sense of people's moods. The questions seemed innocuous enough. Goel was happy to oblige an old friend he admired. He promised to keep his eyes peeled.

Rajaratnam knew that Goel had not prospered in the way he had since leaving Wharton. Like Kumar, Goel returned to work in India at the wrong time (when the lumbering Indian economy was still muddling along) and came back to the United States as Silicon Valley started to crest. He missed out on the Indian boom and all the riches that fell to entrepreneurs who staked their futures on it, and he came back to a California that was so effervescent it would take years before he and his wife could even afford to buy a house.

Sensing that Goel felt left behind, Rajaratnam tried to help whenever he could. In 2005, Goel asked Rajaratnam if he would trade stocks on his behalf in his brokerage account.

"You're a star trader," Goel declared. "I don't know how to trade stocks...Can you help me make some money?" Rajaratnam readily agreed. To make it easier, Goel gave him the log-in details and the password to his account at Charles Schwab. It never would have occurred to him not to trust Rajaratnam with his personal financial details. If there was a friend he trusted, it was Rajaratnam.

It was around this time that Goel was feeling more settled at Intel. After being promoted to director a year earlier, he planned on buying his first house in California. The property he and his wife, Alka, liked was in Los Altos, an elegant suburban village outside San Francisco known for its stellar schools. Goel was nervous about the investment and worried it was way above his budget. At the time he was making around $400,000 a year. When Rajaratnam saw that Goel dithered, he stepped in.

"Hey, I can help you," Rajaratnam said. He lent Goel $100,000 for the down payment on a four-bedroom house with a landscaped garden and pool. Even with the outlay from Rajaratnam, Goel struggled to buy the $2.1 million property. He borrowed $1.68 million from the bank to finance his new house. Though he promised to pay back the personal loan to Rajaratnam, he never did.

The relationship between the two deepened a year later when an unexpected calamity hit Goel. His father, who was in his late eighties, was hospitalized and put in intensive care. Goel flew to India several times and even took to sleeping on the hospital floor to keep an eye on his dad. At one point, he confided in Rajaratnam that something had been preying on his mind: if his father died and the family property had to be divided, would he and his brother be able to keep their dad's apartment, which was valued at as much as $1 million? Without giving it a second thought, Rajaratnam wired $500,000 from a bank account that he and his wife had at Chase Manhattan Bank. Goel had never seen so much money in his life. While he was growing up in India, there had always been a mystique surrounding wealthy people and their Swiss bank accounts, so Goel set up an account at Credit Suisse and had the money, ultimately meant for India, sent to Switzerland. Before the money could reach its final destination, though, another disaster hit the Goels. The house they'd bought a year earlier, the one Rajaratnam lent them the money to buy, had become infested with rats, which had eaten through the ground floor. Goel had to fork out a few hundred thousand dollars to get rid of the infestation.

When Goel was at Wharton, he'd looked up to Rajaratnam, and in the years since, his respect for him had only grown. Rajaratnam had succeeded beyond anyone's wildest imagination, and he had done so on his terms. Unlike Goel, he worked for no one; he was his own boss. It was a position Goel sometimes wished for himself. In his role at Intel Treasury, Goel was a salaryman, but he knew from working closely with colleagues at Intel Capital, who were paid bonuses and compensated more lavishly, that there were great riches to be reaped in the investing world. In 2008, just as he was coming off a career coup, his disaffection hit a peak.

Goel had spent the previous year structuring a recapitalization of a company in Intel Capital's portfolio called SMART Technologies. Goel was charged with helping Intel monetize its $1 million investment in the Calgary company, which developed and made interactive whiteboards. At first, the husband-and-wife team that owned a majority stake in SMART Technologies saw Goel's efforts as a distraction to their plans to grow the company. But Goel's persistence paid off. He introduced the company to Apax Partners, a London private equity firm, which made an offer for a minority stake in the company. At Goel's prodding, Apax even boosted its original offer price by more than 10 percent to $925 million. And then, at the eleventh hour, Goel saved the deal by devising "a brilliant structure" that allowed Intel's ownership stake in SMART Technologies to remain little changed and kept Apax from having control.

"Rajiv's deal instincts were right all along," gushed his boss in a letter nominating him for an internal Intel award. "Apax was too invested in the deal to walk away." The deal turned out to be very lucrative for Intel; it led to $120 million of capital gains. Goel won an award and was invited to a black-tie banquet. But for all his work, he received only a small bonus. The security of a guaranteed $400,000 annual salary paled in comparison to the easy street where his friend Rajaratnam lived.

Goel was feeling underappreciated when one day in late March 2008, he picked up the phone and called Rajaratnam to vent.

"Get me a job with one of your powerful friends, man," he began. "I'm tired of this company."

Despite his elevated status in the South Asian community, Rajaratnam never balked at introducing Goel to his powerful friends. In November 2006, when Goel was planning a trip to New York City, he reached out to Rajaratnam. Perhaps "we could meet...I am itching to buy an expensive bottle of wine! (SMILEY FACE)," he emailed. Goel knew that Rajaratnam was close to Parag Saxena, one of Gupta's partners in his private equity venture. Goel had some expertise investing in companies at Intel and thought he might parlay his experience into a job at the fund.

When Goel came to New York, he met with Rajaratnam's partners in New Silk Route over drinks in the lobby of the Four Seasons Hotel on Fifty-Seventh Street. Nothing came of the meeting, but Rajaratnam's gesture was one of the reasons Goel so valued their friendship. Not everyone in Rajaratnam's place would have made the introduction. Rajaratnam was a real friend; he always put his neck on the line for Goel, even when there didn't seem to be anything in it for him in return.

When Goel, pleading for help in finding a job, told Rajaratnam of the Intel award he was getting, Rajaratnam cut to the crux of the matter.

"Did you get an award or did you get cash?" asked Rajaratnam. He knew how to press all the right buttons and move people around like pawns on his personal chessboard.

"No, no, they don't give cash, no," replied Goel, a little taken aback. "They hold a special banquet for this."

"Are you gonna speak?" Rajaratnam then asked.

"It's a formal thing," Goel said, dodging the question. "You gotta wear a tux and everything. It's like a big affair."

When Rajaratnam pressed Goel on what he had done to win the award, Goel portrayed himself as an iconoclast. "You gotta be a hustler and you gotta be a maverick. You gotta say 'To hell with it' uh...you know, when your superiors or when your management tells you to do it one way, screw it, I'll do it the way I want...Basically I'm taking a dig at the management, no?" Goel said, seeking Rajaratnam's approval. "And I'm saying maverick. I mean, everybody and their mother was opposing the deal...so they're [sic] thinking is 'Yeah, this guy will never be able to do it.'"

Rajaratnam sensed the depth of Goel's dissatisfaction. At Galleon he was the boss, not the underpaid and overworked employee, but for a moment he traded places and pretended to put himself in Goel's shoes.

"You should not have any expectations of financial rewards but a lot of psychic rewards," Rajaratnam suggested Goel point out in his write-up.

"Yeah," Goel chuckled, "lot of back-patting."

After the call, like a child running home with a good report card, Goel sent Rajaratnam the nominating letter his manager wrote for the Intel award. In his forwarding message to Rajaratnam, he remarked, "The deal complexity is much higher than depicted but nonetheless makes good reading."

Over the years, as the friendship between the two deepened, their families vacationed together and their daughters bonded. After one holiday the families took to Italy in 2008, the Goels left early to visit London. The Rajaratnams stayed behind, but their daughters missed the Goel girls. "Dad has nobody to pick on so he's picking on us," the Rajaratnam girls wrote. "Thanks for inviting and planning a great vacation. We will remember you as we eat another pasta tonight. Have fun in London and see you soon." As a postscript, the Rajaratnam girls added, "New York rocks and California sucks." Goel wasn't sure if he agreed with the assessment, but he was happy that his friendship with Raj had grown to encompass his family.

CHAPTER TWENTY-FIVE

The Richest Maid in Silicon Valley

It was shortly before 8 a.m. on Tuesday, March 25, 2008, and an irritable Anil Kumar was stuck in a taxi in the middle of Tokyo on his way to work. It had been four years since Kumar had begun leading his double life, McKinsey consultant by day and Rajaratnam informant by night. Neither was easy. He treaded water at McKinsey but was planning a move to New York in the summer for a new job—a sideways step—to boost his career prospects when Ian Davis, McKinsey's managing director, stepped down in 2009.

After stopping in Tokyo, Kumar was headed to Singapore and then planned to go to India. As exhausting as his schedule was, there was a more pressing reason for his irritation.

"This taxi driver doesn't know where he is going," he bristled.

Rajaratnam, hanging on the other end of the phone, some seven thousand miles away and in a different time zone, laughed.

It was hard to fathom the confusion. McKinsey's Tokyo office was well known in Japan. It stood tall in a commercial block of the Roppongi section. For the longest time, the office was run by Kenichi Ohmae, a legendary Japanese businessman and aspiring politician. It was a sign of Ohmae's importance that for a time when he reigned, there was a security guard planted outside his office with a gun sitting on his desk in full view. (McKinsey says that to its knowledge, this is not accurate.) Word was that Ohmae had so many friends—and enemies—in Japan that he required protection even at the office.

With its buzzing discos and throbbing clubs, Roppongi was a continent away from Kumar's world. As a senior partner, he spent his life on planes, logging as many as forty thousand miles a month to visit clients. He shuttled so often between New York and Silicon Valley that McKinsey assigned him an office in each place. In addition, he had two home offices, one in Saratoga, California, and the other in his apartment in the Time Warner Center in New York so he could field calls from clients on weekends or catch up on emails after hours.

Some of his colleagues griped about the grueling travel regimen that accompanied a career in consulting, but Kumar seemed to relish his peripatetic life. He liked to inject the names of cities he was passing through into emails or phone conversations, much like practiced name-droppers slip in mentions of their rich and famous friends. Kumar had a fetish for both. "Cambodia and Angkor Wat were amazing!!" or "I'm here with... Sunil Mittal and Sunil Munjal," two Indian business tycoons. All it took was a standard query about his well-being, a simple "how are you?" to elicit a reflex-like reply about the city he happened to be in or the company he was keeping. It was as if he thought all the jet-setting conferred upon him a certain gravitas and imbued him with an importance that otherwise was not apparent.

He had three cell phones, one for each of the continents he worked in, Asia, Europe, and America. Ostensibly the trove of phones was to keep McKinsey's costs down, but it also served another purpose: it affirmed Kumar's position in the caste system of the business world. He was no nine-to-fiver, consigned to short-haul trips within the borders of one country. No, Anil Kumar liked to think of himself as a *macher*, a Yiddish term meaning a "maker," the kind of person who made things happen. He was a pivotal player in the new global economy, so in demand that his old colleagues in New Delhi would joke that he spent most of his life on a plane or on the phone.

In recent years, regardless of where he was—Mumbai, Dublin, Tokyo—Kumar had fallen into a predictable pattern. He made it a point to call his new best friend, Rajaratnam. Fortunately for him, Kumar occupied a privileged place in Rajaratnam's ever-expanding universe of contacts. He was on a list of about ten people whose calls were so important that Rajaratnam told his secretary, Caryn Eisenberg, to disturb him if he was in a meeting or find him if he was not in his office. It was an "honor" bestowed on very few—and it was coming from someone who was an acknowledged master of the universe, not a wannabe.

By 2008, Raj Rajaratnam was so successful that he made it to the Forbes 400 "Richest People in America" list for the first time. He hung out with hedge fund rock stars like himself, playing in a fantasy football league whose members included Stanley Druckenmiller and Paul Tudor Jones. The price of admission said it all: members had to pony up $100,000 each to play. And the celebrations for winning were over-the-top.

In February, to mark the victory by Michael Daffy, a Goldman Sachs executive in the league, Rajaratnam, Druckenmiller, and a handful of others took off from the West 30th Street Heliport in helicopters and headed down to Atlantic City for an overnight trip to the Borgata hotel and casino. When they arrived, they were met by limousines that took them to the hotel. There they were joined by Paul Tudor Jones, one of the oldest members of the league. They started the evening with drinks and dinner and ended it with a night of gambling. The next morning, at 6:30, the hard-charging traders left the Borgata for the Atlantic City airport.

Rajaratnam's success made him a business celebrity in the South Asian community. He was one of six Asians on the Forbes list. Whenever he dined out, young South Asians gravitated to his table to pay homage and sound him out on a business proposition or hit him up for a job. Rajaratnam was always open and welcoming. He enjoyed the adulation, the verbal stroking that inevitably ensued. Many times, he would hand fawning visitors his business card. Little did they know that Rajaratnam's world was neatly divided between the people he wanted to know and the people who wanted to know him. He cleverly devised a system to keep the two groups separate. His business card did not list his direct line; only a select group of people had that number. All others were given his secretary Eisenberg's line. Invariably, the next day when an admirer telephoned, mistaking

Rajaratnam's warmth for something more, Rajaratnam avoided the call. It was his secretary's job to keep callers like this at bay.

Kumar sounded excited when he called Rajaratnam that Tuesday morning from Tokyo. In the normal course of business, senior partners at McKinsey are called upon to oversee the work of other consultants. It is part of the rigorous evaluation process that is integral to the fabric of McKinsey. In the midst of supervising a colleague who was doing some confidential work for Fujitsu, Kumar got some information that he was sure Rajaratnam would find as scintillating as he did. China's biggest computer maker, Lenovo Group, which four years earlier had sent shock waves through the computer industry when it bought IBM's PC business, was in serious talks with Fujitsu to buy its personal computer business.

"It's not a dead certainty yet," Kumar said. Then, stating what must have seemed like the obvious to a veteran investor like Rajaratnam, he explained why. Getting a Japanese company to sell a business is "like an act of God."

"Right," snapped Rajaratnam. Whenever he was excited about a piece of information, he peppered Kumar with penetrating follow-up questions, but when he was bored with an idea he responded with monosyllabic answers. Even though the two had been conversing for years, Kumar did not always pick up on Rajaratnam's subtle signals. Sometimes, as was the case that day, Rajaratnam would have to change the subject to get Kumar off the topic and onto a new one. Even then, Kumar was like a dog with a bone. He would stubbornly cling to his tantalizing tip. Minutes later, seemingly out of the blue, he would return to it. Despite the home run on the AMD and ATI deal, Kumar was deeply insecure about his place in Rajaratnam's world.

"I don't know how to play" the Fujitsu-Lenovo deal, said Rajaratnam. Not sensing Rajaratnam's disinterest, Kumar had brought up the transaction a second time.

"So I'll tell you how to play, it's very straightforward," said Kumar, taking an irritatingly didactic tone. He was clearly oblivious to the mounting investing pressures his friend was facing in the spring of 2008. Rajaratnam had just come off one of the most stressful weeks of trading in his life. A week before, Bear Stearns & Co., the fifth-largest investment bank in the United States, had all but collapsed under the weight of a bad bet that two of its hedge funds made on shoddy subprime loans. Bear had stumped up $3 billion the previous summer to rescue the funds, but by March, investors pummeled its stock, betting the company was effectively insolvent. They were right.

At times like these, it was best to stick to safe, surefire ideas like the tip Kumar had given him about an Indian energy company called Hindustan Oil Exploration Corp. Kumar had learned from a corporate lawyer and friend in India that its shares were set to be bought up in an open tender offer.

"So that's a certainty, right?" Rajaratnam asked.

"Yeah," replied Kumar.

"So every day I'll accumulate a little bit whatever I can, in the market," Rajaratnam ventured.

Trading Hindustan Oil was very different from playing Fujitsu, a conglomerate jettisoning a part of its business. With Fujitsu, it was not clear who would come out on top: the Chinese or the Japanese.

But to the know-it-all Kumar, playing the Fujitsu-Lenovo deal was an obvious trade. Personal computer buyers were tightening their belts on information technology spending amid the slowing economy and were looking for the best deals.

"Lenovo will be the winner" because Dell and HP will have a tough time matching the lower costs that Lenovo, which makes more of its computers in China, enjoys, Kumar explained. McKinsey was a great example of the trend. In a recent overhaul, it decided to buy all its laptops from low-cost Lenovo. Then, suddenly awakening to a complexity that Rajaratnam spotted straightaway, Kumar conceded: "Now, you know, you're right, somehow markets may also say 'God, they've got this big bear of a cost structure now, because they've got this big fat high cost Japanese company.'"

"Right," said Rajaratnam. It was exactly the kind of wishy-washy investment idea from the talking-head types at McKinsey that he could not afford right now.

Wall Street had been closed for the Good Friday holiday. In most years, traders welcomed the break, but now there was so much uncertainty swirling that even a day away from the markets unnerved them. Rajaratnam had originally planned to join Kumar in Singapore later in the week, and then the two were set to fly to India together to look at possible investments. But with the stock markets seesawing in the wake of Bear's collapse, Rajaratnam felt he had better stay strapped to his desk.

"I am not sure whether I'm going to Asia right now...you know, it's just crazy and I just need to be here, right?" he said.

"I didn't check on what happened today. Was it down again?" asked the clueless Kumar. Rajaratnam, by contrast, was so driven by the markets that his moods hinged on their performance. "Sometimes, my wife is the most beautiful woman in the world," he would say, referring to days when the markets went his way. "And sometimes she is a midget."

By 2008, the rocky state of the stock market was hurting Kumar's cherished client, AMD, too. Its acquisition of ATI Technologies in 2006 had saddled it with a mountain of debt. Although the company dreamed up wonderful new computer chip designs, investors fretted that it did not have the stash of cash it needed to build the factories to manufacture them. What most investors didn't know was that behind closed doors the company was quietly hatching an innovative plan that would enable it to build the chip factories without a big cash outlay. Instead of footing the bill all on its own, AMD looked to find a deep-pocketed investor—perhaps a cash-rich sovereign wealth fund—that could bankroll the plants. The supersecret initiative was code-named Asset-Lite. The moniker reflected the notion that once the deal was done, AMD would own fewer factories, or assets, because the facilities would be spun off.

Kumar began briefing Rajaratnam regularly on the Asset-Lite strategy. In the winter of 2007, they spoke once every three weeks because Kumar was planning to move to New York to lead the McKinsey Asia Center, which advised US companies about business opportunities in Asia, and Asian companies about the United States. Kumar wanted to give McKinsey one last chance to elevate him, but if he wasn't going up at McKinsey, this time around he'd get out.

During their conversations, Kumar told Rajaratnam that if AMD spun off its manufacturing facilities, it would lift a huge financial burden off the company: "It will be fantastic."

"Oh, this is going to be just like ATYT," replied Rajaratnam. It was hard to forget AMD's 2006 acquisition of ATI Technologies, a deal that made Rajaratnam tens of millions of dollars.

Yes, Kumar agreed, it would be just like ATI.

As the months progressed, it became clear that it would be nothing like ATI. Rajaratnam was under the impression that the investment in the chip-making facility was imminent, but when Kumar called from Tokyo, he got a rude shock.

"It could take two more months," said Kumar. "It's not like weeks."

"Oh my God," said Rajaratnam, remaining remarkably cool in the face of news that he clearly was not expecting. Always flexible, Rajaratnam suggested he salvage the situation by lightening his position in AMD the next time the markets rallied.

Despite his winning tip on AMD-ATI, by 2008 Kumar was on shaky ground, eclipsed by a rival who enjoyed nowhere near the stature in the corporate world that he did but had much more to offer to Rajaratnam. Rajaratnam had told Kumar that there was a woman on Wall Street named Danielle Chiesi who he said was having an intimate relationship with Ruiz, the AMD chief executive and Kumar's client. (Ruiz denies that he was ever involved with Danielle Chiesi and the relationship is otherwise unsubstantiated.) Kumar did not know it, but Chiesi was Rajaratnam's newest acolyte. After she asked a Galleon analyst for an introduction, they met for lunch. The two hit it off, and soon Chiesi was getting invitations to Rajaratnam's parties. Guests noticed her at Rajaratnam's birthday bash on the boat in June when she took to the dance floor alone and kept changing from one low-cut slinky outfit into another. In September, she and her mother were invited to the clambake at Rajaratnam's Greenwich estate, where Kenny Rogers sang his hit "The Gambler" ("You got to know when to hold 'em, know when to fold 'em, know when to walk away and know when to run"). It was a favorite of Rajaratnam's and he had Rogers sing it over and over again.

Rajaratnam believed that through Ruiz, Chiesi came to learn of AMD's bid to spin off its facility to make computer chips and create a joint venture that would be 50 percent owned by a Middle Eastern sovereign wealth fund.

"Your value to me is a little bit diminished," he told Kumar.

Then he pressed Kumar to see Ruiz and tell him to stop the purported pillow talk. Lest Kumar be confused into thinking that Raj was trying to save Ruiz's marriage, he made it clear to Kumar that his issue was that Chiesi was freely sprinkling Ruiz's secrets to everyone who would listen on Wall Street. What irritated him was that the loose-lipped Chiesi robbed him of the "edge" he had at AMD. She was muddying the waters in a stream of insider information that was his alone to fish.

"Raj, you've got to be kidding me," said Kumar, flabbergasted by the request. "Dr. Ruiz—he is my client. He is older than me." Rajaratnam wanted Kumar's morally challenged job description expanded to include verbal subterfuge. Kumar was comfortable transgressing the law, but he was far less at ease with the idea of crossing social norms.

His pushback came at a trying time in his relationship with Rajaratnam. Ever since his big tip in 2006 on the AMD–ATI Technologies talks, Kumar's hot streak had gone stone cold. In 2007, he told Rajaratnam that the industry of business intelligence, in which companies use software to mine mountains of information stored in widely available databases, was ripe for consolidation. The tip piqued Rajaratnam's curiosity. "How do you know?" he asked.

Kumar explained that he was providing consulting services to a company called Business Objects, a French-American firm that made intelligence software. Naively, or perhaps simply because it was easier this way for him to rationalize his behavior, Kumar believed that Rajaratnam would buy stocks in three or four companies in the sector and hopefully in a year they would rise and Rajaratnam would make a profit.

In July 2007, at a time when Business Objects was getting hammered by Microsoft and Oracle, Kumar attended an offsite meeting the company was holding in Napa Valley, California. Kumar passed on the bleak prospects that Business Objects was facing to Rajaratnam.

Sometime after, he got a call from Rajaratnam.

"Anil, are you absolutely sure they are doing badly?" Rajaratnam quizzed him. What was puzzling Rajaratnam was the performance of Business Objects stock in the market. If the company was indeed struggling, then why was its stock inching up? It was as if all the players in the market were in on a big secret and somewhat surprisingly had left the master of divining secrets out of the loop.

It wouldn't have mattered to Rajaratnam except that he'd traded on Kumar's tip, accumulating a sizable short position in Business Objects stock, by essentially borrowing shares on the belief that he would be able to buy them back at a cheaper price as the market appreciated the company's challenges. Every dollar rise in the stock cost Rajaratnam money on his bearish bet on Business Objects. Uneasy with the rally, Rajaratnam told Kumar that he was halving his short position.

A few months later, in October 2007, Business Objects announced that German technology giant SAP was acquiring it for $6.78 billion, a move that sent its shares soaring and saddled Galleon with more losses—around $5 million on a realized and unrealized basis. Rajaratnam told Kumar he was very upset about the money-losing trade and in 2007 he did not pay him. A few months had passed since the Business Objects fiasco but Kumar still smarted from the rebuke. At the same time, managing the elaborate consulting arrangement with Galleon was getting harder.

In 2008, Morgan Stanley, which handled administration details for Galleon, pushed for verification that Manju Das (Kumar's housekeeper, who received the consulting payments made by Rajaratnam to Kumar) was an offshore investor living in India and not required to pay US taxes. Among other items, it sought a notarized passport, certified copies of two forms of address such as utility bills, and a bank assurance letter for Manju Das.

"Let me look into this and see what can be done," Kumar emailed an investor relations employee at Galleon. "May be tricky."

The reason it was "tricky" was simple. Even though Das, his

housekeeper, lived with him and his wife and son in California, Kumar had given his in-laws' address in New Delhi as Das's home. In doing so, he established falsely that she was an offshore investor in Galleon and thus not liable for US taxes.

He set up the account because Kumar's principal concern was to avoid having his consulting arrangement with Rajaratnam traced back to him or McKinsey. If he indicated that Das lived in the United States at his address, it wouldn't take much time to connect him with her.

Under the original arrangement he put in place, account statements for Das were sent to his in-laws' house in the Delhi suburb of Vasant Vihar but naturally addressed to Das, the account holder. The setup raised logistical problems from the start. "My concern is with Manju's mail—there is always the possibility of it being handed over to one of her relatives by mistake/returned/handed over to others. They do ask and come here occasionally to get news of her," wrote Kumar's mother-in-law, Reva Dayal, in 2005. Perhaps her son-in-law could find another solution.

In 2006, soon after Galleon registered with the SEC, Rajaratnam started pressing Kumar to move his money out of the Manju Das account and into an offshore vehicle. He told Kumar that it was a wise move since the SEC was starting to scrutinize matters like this more closely. He didn't mention that his brother Rengan's hedge fund, Sedna Capital, was being examined. If the probe moved to focus on Galleon and Rajaratnam, investigators might be able to connect Das with Kumar.

It was important now more than ever for Raj Rajaratnam to give the impression that Galleon was complying with SEC regulations. Kumar said he knew someone in Switzerland who worked with Asian investors on affairs like this but generally did not like having US investors as clients because of the stiffer regulatory environment in the States. After some arm-twisting, the Swiss gentleman agreed to buy the holdings in Galleon from Manju Das and transfer them into a financial institution called Ambit. Kumar thought it was the perfect way to deal with all the inquiries he was getting on the account. Ambit was an institutional investor and unlikely to raise the same kind of red flags as an individual.

"From a Morgan Stanley Fund Services perspective, they should not care if an LP has sold their stake to another party, for whatever consideration. All they may ask for is a transfer form," Kumar emailed Galleon's investor relations' staffer Shireen Gianchandani on May 26, 2008. "It is the most elegant solution to the predicament. And hopefully one which will not require too many documents." Kumar asked Gianchandani not to proceed yet or to copy anyone on their correspondence.

"Bottom line is to avoid redemption of the funds from Manju's Galleon account into a bank account in her name for immediate reinvestment back into Galleon," he wrote. "That would be a painful exercise."

The transfer wasn't as simple as Kumar thought. To move assets from the Das account into Ambit, Morgan Stanley required two proofs of address for Das. When Gianchandani raised the issue with Kumar, she met with obvious irritation.

"Manju Das comes from a village in the remote areas of Bengal," he wrote in a July 17 email to Gianchandani. "It is not customary to have utility or water bills in these areas. The permanent address, as noted in her passport, is in that district and this is used by all authorities as proof of address." Apparently annoyed that his arguments so far had not succeeded in swatting away the issue, Kumar concluded by saying, "In India, a notarized copy of the passport with current and permanent address is considered as adequate proof of residence since passports are only issued upon physical verification of residence by a local administrator."

But Kumar kept bumping up against Morgan Stanley, which was still not satisfied. Frustrated that he was not getting anywhere close to resolving the situation, he devised a way to get the necessary documents. He turned to someone he had known for years: Dr. Alok Mathur, a physician who had been his in-laws' doctor for twenty-five years.

At Kumar's behest, Mathur wrote a letter certifying that Das was in his care for ten years and confirming Das's address in Delhi. For the second proof of identity, Kumar reached out to an assistant at McKinsey in Delhi to obtain a notarized copy of his housekeeper's passport.

"Dear Mr. Mahindroo, do you know of a notary who will easily and conveniently sign letters/copies/affidavit et cetera?" Kumar emailed on August 1.

"There is no need to know anybody," replied Mahindroo. "They are businessmen and just shop keepers. They have to charge and sign."

It seemed as if Kumar had solved the problem until the documents were delivered to Morgan Stanley. The investment bank rejected them as proofs of address again. "We will require 2 original or certified (notarized) utility bills," Morgan Stanley's Sinead Hayes replied to Kumar on Monday, September 8, 2008. The words "2 original or certified (notarized) utility bills" were highlighted in bold. Hayes told Kumar that if he could not supply the required information, "please provide an explanation and I will escalate to our compliance department."

It was the last thing Kumar needed. He tried to deflect the issue again with an argument he'd tried unsuccessfully earlier. "In India, there are not utility or fuel bills in all individual's names, since the infrastructure is so weak," he emailed Hayes a couple of days later. "The same holds true for the financial/banking infrastructure, and many people have historically held money in other forms, or in joint accounts with other people in other cities from where they live. It has been a country where money matters are dealt with on faith (for example, you can buy jewelry in one city and pay in another, months later, based on good faith). Each country has its own custom, and you can do the same in Japan."

But Morgan Stanley was not buying Kumar's explanation. It kept up its demand for the proof of Manju Das's address. As stock markets imploded all around him and the financial system teetered on the verge of a great meltdown, Kumar accelerated his efforts to get the documents Morgan Stanley wanted. On October 25, 2008, he emailed an employee at HSBC in Bangalore, India, asking for a letter simply stating that Manju Das, a resident of New Delhi, had an account with the bank. "If you can email a pdf copy immediately, that would help a lot," Kumar wrote to HSBC.

However, when the bank sent Kumar a draft of the letter, the true state of affairs intruded into the virtual reality that Kumar was desperately seeking to craft for Manju Das. In a letter dated October 25, 2008, HSBC said that Das had been an account holder at the bank since October 20, 2008—for only five days. Kumar knew the letter would sound alarms at Morgan Stanley. What had started out as a simple transfer of assets from one account to another had turned into a clerical nightmare that took up far more time than Kumar had first imagined it would. He did not want any more hassles, so he emailed HSBC in Bangalore and said, "Please resend a new letter with the words 'from 20 October 2008' deleted.

"Need this asap please."

CHAPTER TWENTY-SIX

The Wire

Anil Kumar sounded preoccupied.

"Are you in the middle of something else?" Rajaratnam asked.

It was a little before 2 p.m. on Friday, May 2, 2008, and Rajaratnam was in Washington for an investor conference, catching up on calls before boarding a plane to Toronto.

"May be leaving in two minutes, but uh...tell me quickly," said Kumar. It was hard to tell if Kumar was in a real rush or he simply wanted to give the impression he was frightfully busy. In the circles he trafficked in, there were two traits that made someone important, being connected and being so in demand that one never had enough time. Rajaratnam had heard from an associate that Kumar was close to Mukesh Ambani, the head of formidable Reliance Industries. Kumar and Rajaratnam were in the same Wharton class as Mukesh's kid brother, Anil.

Like many Indian families, the Ambani brothers for the longest time lived under the same roof—Sea Wind, a tower at Cuffe Parade, an enclave of the wealthy in south Mumbai. The two had one of the fiercest sibling rivalries around, and while they were living together—Mukesh moved out in 2010 to a soaring skyscraper—they were locked in a battle over the price Anil Ambani should pay for natural gas from Mukesh's field, the largest in the country.

Rajaratnam told Kumar that there was some interesting chatter in the market about Reliance and its interest in semiconductors. He had heard from an investment banker that Reliance was searching for a way to enter the semiconductor space.

Kumar had caught up recently with Mukesh Ambani, who had been in New York for the American India Foundation fifth annual spring gala at the Waldorf. He had formed his own impressions of Ambani's ambitions in the semiconductor space. They were not nearly as grandiose as what Rajaratnam envisioned.

"Are you going to do AMD?" Kumar asked Ambani. "It's gonna be a big deal."

"Anil, for that size deal I'm not ready yet, I need to understand the industry," said Ambani flatly.

Kumar told Rajaratnam that Ambani was more likely to pursue a far smaller acquisition—the purchase of the Far Eastern assets of a company called Spansion. In fact, Reliance was set to submit an offer for the Spansion assets the next day.

"Do you think we should buy some Spansion for other funds?" Rajaratnam asked.

"Uhm...let me see what offer comes in as of tomorrow," Kumar replied.

Minutes after hanging up with Kumar, Rajaratnam telephoned Kris Chellam and another colleague. Rajaratnam had known Chellam almost from the time he got started in the business, following him around Silicon Valley as he bounced from Atmel to Xilinx before coming to work for Rajaratnam at Galleon. Chellam was a regular at Rajaratnam's infamous wild and sexually charged Super Bowl parties in Miami.

"Somebody is gonna put a term sheet for Spansion," Rajaratnam told the two. "May third is the deadline, which is I think tomorrow, right?"

Rajaratnam said he asked Kumar whether he should buy some Spansion for Galleon but Kumar had told him to wait.

"This is the one that we also have to make sure that we keep our conversations just privileged to the three of us," said Rajaratnam. "You know, you just have to be careful, right?"

One of the best ways to protect themselves, Rajaratnam suggested, was to create an email trail. He would start the chain by sending an email to the two of them saying: "You know, have you guys thought of Spansion? The stock looks cheap, right?"

Then they could offer to get the Galleon analyst who covered Spansion to do some work on the stock. Alternatively, Rajaratnam could send a more general email. "Something like, you know, 'there's a basket of semiconductor companies like Lattice, Spansion and Atmel...see what you think,'" Rajaratnam said. "And you should say, 'Atmel and Spansion look good.' You know, so that we just protect ourselves."

"Have a corporate record," replied Chellam.

"Yeah, we just have a email trail, right, that uh...I brought it up," said Rajaratnam.

* * *

Sixty blocks south of Galleon's midtown office, an FBI agent was sitting in a secure room with about ten other agents, each with a headset, tuned in real time to a call between Rajaratnam and his associates.

Roomy Khan's calls to Rajaratnam had suggested that there was indeed criminal activity taking place on his cell phone, so on March 7, 2008, Lauren Goldberg, the prosecutor who had given Khan a lecture when she first sat down with the government, presented a wiretap affidavit to the court seeking permission for the feds to eavesdrop on Rajaratnam's conversations. Federal judge Gerard E. Lynch approved a wiretap on Rajaratnam's cell phone for thirty days. His work phone and his home phone were not tapped. Now, for the first time, the FBI was in a position to get an insider's glimpse into Rajaratnam's relationship with Kumar, Gupta, and a host of others. Three days after Lynch's authorization, the FBI intercepted calls over Rajaratnam's cell phone, monitoring both outgoing and incoming calls. Each time a call came into Rajaratnam's cell phone, a number would pop up on a computer screen in front of the agent manning the wire. Typically the agent would listen to the call on a headset and write on lined sheets the initials of the callers.

Under Title III, the statute governing wiretaps, "non-pertinent phone calls" such as a target speaking to his mother must be "minimized," which means not listening to and not recording the call. If the call appears to be "non-pertinent," the agent manning the wire has to turn down the volume, which also stops the recording, wait a few minutes, and then turn up the volume to see if it has turned to a "pertinent" subject. If the call is with someone who always seems to be "non-pertinent," they generally have to "minimize" the entire call.

Some agents are more adept than others at manning the wire, a job that within the FBI is known for its drudgery. A few times during the investigation a call that could have yielded important evidence got "minimized," meaning it isn't recorded at all. It is hard to fault the FBI agents, though. Before a wiretap goes up, prosecutors are required to read the agents manning the wire a speech that lasts about twenty minutes. Prosecutors impress upon agents that one way a wiretap can be suppressed or thrown out later is if an agent fails to minimize a call properly. Judges are all over the map on their views of calls that aren't minimized properly; some exclude the specific call, whereas others disallow the whole wire, potentially jeopardizing an entire investigation and killing a case.

In mid-April, Andrew Michaelson—the SEC line attorney who had built up the investigation from suspected cherry picking of investments at tiny Sedna Capital to insider trading at giant Galleon—was lent to the US attorney's office in Manhattan to work on the Galleon case. Before he left the SEC, there had been a small breakthrough in the investigation. On April 2, Roomy Khan, after months of obfuscation and ridiculous stories, admitted that she had made trades in Hilton stock based on inside information. As part of an agreement with prosecutors, Khan had been cooperating, but she had been holding out on revealing the Hilton informant because she had met the source through her cousin, whom she was trying to protect. Her source was Deep Shah, a young analyst at Moody's, the credit-rating agency, whom SEC lawyer Jason Friedman had identified the previous summer when he drilled down into Khan's world. At the time, Friedman knew only that Shah was one of the hundreds of contacts in Khan's Rolodex. He had no way of knowing that as a

Moody's analyst Shah had been briefed on the Hilton deal before it was announced.

As Khan told the story, one day in late 2006 her cousin telephoned her and said that his roommate worked at Moody's and was privy to a lot of buyout information before it was unveiled. Moody's, which provides widely watched ratings on corporate credit, is often briefed on deals before they are announced, as they were in the Hilton case, so they can develop a new rating when a takeover is unveiled.

"You know you can make a lot of money," said her cousin. Then he put his roommate, Shah, on the phone. In their very first conversation, Shah served up a takeover tip—the trouble was it was Friday evening and the deal was going to be unveiled on Monday before the market opened. There was no window for Khan to trade in; however, when the deal was announced on Monday exactly as Shah had predicted, Khan knew she had a new surefire source. For the Hilton insider tip, she told prosecutors she paid Shah $10,000. The tip was red-hot; Shah called her on July 2 soon after learning about it from a colleague who had been briefed by Hilton. (Shah has denied being the source of the Hilton tips.)

"Didi," he said, using the Hindi word for "older sister" when he got in touch with her. "This is happening tomorrow so better get on it right away."

Khan shielded Shah for as long as she could, risking her own cooperation with the government to protect her cousin, who had introduced them. Soon after she agreed to help the feds and record calls on phones she was given by the FBI, she got a new cell phone, which she had registered in the name of her gardener. She used the cell phone to make calls to a few in her circle, including Shah, whom investigators believe did not return to the United States from India after she casually mentioned that she had gotten some inquiries on Hilton from the SEC. Prosecutors discovered her scam when they noticed the new caller reaching out to people in Khan's circle. When prosecutors finally discovered that the phone number was in the name of Khan's gardener, they summoned Khan to New York and ordered her to quit playing games.

By the spring of 2008, it had been one and a half years since

Michaelson and Wadhwa had first started sifting through the trading records, emails, and instant messages at Sedna and noticed the curious exchanges between Sedna's cofounder Rengan Rajaratnam and his brother Raj at Galleon on stocks like AMD. They had taken testimony from both brothers and reviewed thousands of pages of documents, yet the only stocks on which they had direct evidence of insider trading by Rajaratnam were Polycom, Google, and now Hilton.

Upon arriving at One St. Andrew's Plaza, where the prosecutors in the US attorney's office sit, Michaelson received a thick folder of material from B. J. Kang, the FBI agent working the Galleon case. It contained a slug of recordings that soon came to be known as the "Clearwire" calls.

After nearly two years of Sisyphean frustration, particularly with AMD, Michaelson started to feel optimistic. At the SEC, investigating was like a game of connect the dots—linking a phone call, for instance, to a trade soon after. But sitting in the US attorney's office with his headphones on, listening to the wiretaps, he was riveted. Not only were the dots connected, but he was inside the room. It was the early days and already the wiretaps were yielding heaps of direct evidence that Rajaratnam received confidential nonpublic information from a wide circle of informants. For the first time, there was a sense at the US attorney's office that the case prosecutors were developing was going to be huge—in terms of not just the number of people but also their prominence.

As Michaelson delved into the file of Clearwire calls that Kang gave him, he found for the first time direct evidence of the passing of confidential corporate secrets between Goel and Rajaratnam, the two friends from Wharton.

Starting in late March 2008, Goel, who worked at Intel Treasury, began briefing Rajaratnam on Intel's plans to invest $1 billion in a new wireless venture with an all-star cast of technology companies—Clearwire, Sprint Nextel, Time Warner, and Comcast, among others. The move was part of a bid by Intel to spur the rapid adoption of a longer-range wireless technology called WiMAX. In 2006, Intel Capital invested $600 million in Clearwire, a company led by cellular pioneer Craig McCaw, which was a large holder of frequencies suitable for WiMAX.

Now Intel Capital was in the midst of talks to take the assets of Sprint and Clearwire and create a nationwide geographical footprint of cellular broadcasting licenses. While Goel worked on the initial 2006 investment by Intel into Clearwire, he was not involved in the latest deal. However, he came to know of it because of the size of Intel's investment.

On March 19, Goel was feeling a little tired and came home early. He was supposed to meet with an Intel vice president to get an update on Intel's investment in the new venture. At about 5 p.m. West Coast time, he called Rajaratnam, ostensibly to engage in some of their usual freewheeling banter.

"I just called to say you're a good man," Goel started.

"Why?" Rajaratnam asked.

"I just called to say that you're a good man, that's all," Goel repeated.

"Why am I a good man?" Rajaratnam asked again.

"I just thought that you are one of the better guys that I know," Goel said.

"That's highly suspicious," said Rajaratnam.

The two traded compliments back and forth until Rajaratnam concurred that Goel was a "good guy too. When I see you I'll give you a kiss on the cheek."

"No, no, no," insisted Goel.

Before he hung up, Goel told Rajaratnam: "*Aacha*, listen," using a Hindi word for "okay." He had not had a chance to meet with the Intel vice president, but he knew that the Intel board was not going to consider the Clearwire deal that day.

Rajaratnam thanked him for the information, and with that, the two said good-bye. When they hung up, so did the agent at the FBI, which was now monitoring Rajaratnam's cell phone in real time.

Over the next few days, as the FBI listened in, Goel called regularly, filling Rajaratnam in on the details of the Intel investment so that he could figure out how to assign a value to the new entity. He generally called Rajaratnam from home, but it was hard to talk at times. Goel's kids made fun of the hushed tones that their father used when he spoke to Rajaratnam.

"What do you have?" Rajaratnam asked. "Bunch of hyenas there?"

"No, no, no. No, they are laughing at the way I talk to you," Goel explained.

Between March 24 and 25, Galleon bought 385,000 shares of Clearwire stock, the majority of which was allocated to the technology fund Rajaratnam ran. But before he could accumulate a bigger position, he got scooped.

"Oh dude, we're fucked," said Rengan, who called his brother Raj on the evening of March 25 to tell him word of the deal was public. "It's all over the *Wall Street Journal.*"

"What price does it say?" asked Rajaratnam.

Rengan said the *Journal* story was short on details but did reveal that the company was looking to raise as much as $3 billion.

"Shit," said Rajaratnam.

As they listened in on the conversations between Raj and Rengan Rajaratnam, the investigators began to form a picture of the family and the role each of the brothers played in it. They took to comparing the Rajaratnam brothers to members of the Corleone family depicted in Mario Puzo's novel *The Godfather.* In their minds, Raj Rajaratnam was Michael Corleone, the youngest and wiliest son of Don Vito Corleone, who was chosen by his father to succeed him as the head of the crime family. Like Michael Corleone, Rajaratnam was smooth and effective. He devised ways to get potential sources like Goel indebted to him and then he started asking for information.

Rengan most resembled Michael Corleone's older brother Sonny, who was portrayed as a hothead and a ruthless killer. Rengan's bombastic answers during his deposition reminded them of Sonny. R. K. Rajaratnam, the former ConAgra executive who came to work for his brother Raj, was in their minds Fredrico "Fredo" Corleone. He had a twisted face like Fredo and was widely considered inept, the weakest link among the trio of brothers.

By May 2008, the investigation was nearly two years old and there was growing concern that as witnesses were approached, word of the investigation could trickle out. It was important for the government to be in a position to bring a case on a hair trigger. The decision posed more issues for the SEC than for the US attorney's office, which needs only to get a magistrate to sign off on a warrant before an arrest can be made (or immediately after one takes place).

By contrast, the SEC's enforcement division needs to get authorization to file a complaint from a majority of its commissioners. To get the green light, Sanjay Wadhwa, who by this time had been promoted to assistant director, had to put together an action memorandum, which essentially lays out the enforcement division's recommendations to charge a potential defendant.

On the weekend of May 11, 2008, Jason Friedman was set to accompany his fiancée and his future mother-in-law to Carlyle on the Green, an event venue on the grounds of Bethpage State Park in Long Island. There they would plan the menu for their wedding in two months. One of the important decisions Friedman and his fiancée were going to make that day was choosing a design for their wedding cake. But before he could even get out the door, he got a call from Wadhwa.

Criminal authorities were planning to approach Ephraim Karpel, a well-liked figure among Wall Street's clubby traders. Karpel had worked for eighteen years at Mutual Shares, an investment company run by the famed stock picker Michael Price. The government believed Karpel was a participant in an overlapping insider trading ring involving Zvi Goffer, a trader who had worked briefly at Galleon. The FBI was wiretapping Goffer's phone and decided to approach Karpel after they listened in on a call between him and Goffer on December 31, 2007. In the call, Karpel told Goffer that drugstore chain Walgreens had made an offer to acquire Matria Healthcare.

"I've got the trade for the month of January for you," Karpel told Goffer. "It's coming from a banker."

Whenever law enforcement officers move to approach a witness in the hopes of flipping the individual and getting him or her to cooperate, they have to balance two competing dynamics. On one hand, if a witness cooperates, it can be a tremendous boost to an investigation, opening up new avenues of inquiry or cementing ongoing cases against potential defendants. But if a witness cannot be flipped, the approached may go to the target and warn the person, shutting down chances of getting additional evidence and even destroying potentially incriminating material. The authorities would then be forced to make arrests and the cover would be blown off a probe.

As the government prepared for the approach to Karpel, they hatched a backup plan in the event that things did not go according to plan. The last person anyone wanted to lose at this late stage was Rajaratnam, whom investigators singled out as the conspiracy's ringleader. Rajaratnam, they believed, had a jet parked at New Jersey's Teterboro Airport and could flee at a moment's notice. If the planned approach failed, the government decided it would move to arrest Rajaratnam.

Sanjay Wadhwa and Judy, his girlfriend at the time, were planning on spending the entire weekend at his parents' house in Edison, New Jersey, to celebrate Mother's Day. But when Wadhwa learned that the criminal authorities were planning an approach of Karpel, he cut short his weekend plans and came into the office on Saturday. Working all weekend, he and Friedman put together an action memorandum recommending civil charges against Rajaratnam, Khan, Shammara Hussain (the young woman who provided Khan with the Google tip), Bhalla (the Polycom executive), and Goel. Without the wiretaps, they did not know about Kumar's role in the Galleon web.

In June, as planned, two FBI agents approached Karpel outside the Applejack Diner on the corner of Fifty-Fifth Street and Broadway. The agents escorted him into the restaurant and, seated at the back, told him that they had evidence of him passing inside information to his friend Goffer. Karpel quickly decided to cooperate but the effort ultimately took a toll on him. In May 2011, two days after federal prosecutors played for a jury a conversation Karpel had secretly recorded with another trader, he hanged himself in his Fifth Avenue office.

When it appeared that the approach to Karpel had gone off as the FBI hoped, Wadhwa, who lost a weekend to drafting charge recommendations, got a call from his former colleague Michaelson to hold off.

"All is good," said Michaelson. "Let us continue building the investigation."

In July, he and Wadhwa headed to Jason Friedman's wedding in Long Island. As he cut into his wedding cake, Friedman for the first time noticed the design on it. On top of the four-tier chocolate with cannoli cream cake were fresh white and cream flowers surrounded by a ring of beading on each row.

CHAPTER TWENTY-SEVEN

"I Played Him Like a Finely Tuned Piano"

In the summer of 2008, as Manhattan emptied out and New Yorkers left the city for their vacation homes in the Hamptons, Andrew Michaelson, the SEC lawyer on loan to the US attorney's office, stayed tethered to his desk in a drab office overlooking the Metropolitan Correctional Center. His docket was full, and the FBI wiretap of Rajaratnam's phone was producing new pieces of information.

Since May, the FBI agents manning the wiretap, who listened in to Rajaratnam's cell phone from as early as 6 a.m. to as late as midnight, seven days a week, had noticed a new caller crackling across the telephone wires. Most of the calls the agents monitored were between men. Their conversations were typically all business with some predictable locker-room banter interspersed.

The new caller was a woman named Danielle Chiesi. Her conversations with Rajaratnam on his cell phone titillated, touching on everything from sex to sport. Trading corporate news, Chiesi once said, was "like an orgasm." It soon became clear to the agents and Michaelson that she inhabited a world of powerful men whom she played off one another to make her living. Her galaxy of sources was so impressive that Rajaratnam could not ignore her.

On Thursday, July 24, Chiesi telephoned Rajaratnam at 9:18 p.m., shortly after she got off the phone with a family friend who worked as a senior executive in marketing at Akamai Technologies.

Chiesi had learned that Akamai, which manages Internet traffic for companies, planned to give pessimistic guidance to Wall Street analysts when it unveiled its profits the following week.

On reaching Rajaratnam, Chiesi didn't waste a moment in getting to the point.

"Please don't fuck me on this," she told Rajaratnam. "[Akamai] they're gonna guide down."

Chiesi was pleased with the way she had handled the call with her Akamai source. Instead of asking him directly about the company, she acted as if she didn't care and started talking to him about their mutual family members.

"I played him like a finely tuned piano," she declared.

It was then that the Akamai executive dropped the bombshell.

He said, "You know, oh by the way, we're gonna guide down on Wednesday."

By the summer of 2008, the headwinds buffeting the financial markets were getting stronger by the day. Trading stocks was treacherous, and surefire investments that months earlier would have worked out the way traders imagined were suddenly going askew. The markets were so unpredictable that fundamental forces that normally drove individual stocks were no longer a factor, superseded by the market's seemingly capricious moves—down one day, up another.

Chiesi worked for New Castle Partners, and only four months earlier, she'd seen the unforgiving nature of Wall Street up close. Bear Stearns, which owned New Castle, nearly imploded. Many of Chiesi's friends found themselves out of work after JPMorgan Chase took over Bear. The lucky ones, the ones who had managed to hang on to their jobs, saw a lifetime's worth of savings vanish in weeks. Bear was the sort of firm where many employees didn't diversify and had the lion's share of their retirement savings in company stock—a stock that plummeted from nearly $93 in February 2008 to less than $5 a share in March. Chiesi was fortunate to still have her job, but her life savings was decimated. Trading on business news was no longer just for excitement; increasingly it was for survival.

Within Akamai, the betting was that the profit outlook was so bad that the company's stock would drop to $25 from its then price of $32. "You know what baby, I don't know about you, but I need it," Chiesi told Rajaratnam.

"Please just give me a chance to short it a little bit," she pleaded with him. The Akamai tip, she confided, was the "best thing" she'd heard all day.

Chiesi worried that Rajaratnam, eager to make money, would scramble to borrow as much Akamai stock as he could find to sell short, making it harder for Chiesi to accumulate enough shares for herself. When a number of players in the market are trying to short a stock, selling borrowed shares in the hope the shares drop in value and can be bought back at a cheaper price, it's sometimes difficult to find shares to borrow or it can be very expensive to borrow them.

"I'm not going to say anything," he reassured her. "You short it as much as you want."

"But just between the two of us, and just between us, that's it...Fuck your whole desk. I don't want anybody to know," Chiesi reiterated.

Rajaratnam promised to be "radio silent."

Chiesi had a soft spot for Rajaratnam. There was no need to tell him about the Akamai tip—she really needed a home-run trade all to herself—and Rajaratnam would never know if she held back the information. But she would not dream of keeping a hot tip from Rajaratnam. Chiesi thought the two of them a team; they shared everything. It was not clear that Rajaratnam felt the same way.

* * *

The summer of 2008 was also a busy one for Rajaratnam. He was in the thick of growing Galleon, with $7.2 billion in assets under management. A few months earlier, ahead of the onset of turbulent times, Rajaratnam had raised money. Galleon was coming off a great run. In 2006 its diversified fund returned 25.69 percent, and in 2007 it posted a respectable 12.2 percent return. But it was already clear that 2008 was not going to be as robust. As of the end of March, the diversified fund was down 2.96 percent for the year, making it all the more important for Galleon to shore up its investment coffers. There was always a risk that as markets turned south, skittish investors would start to pull money out of Galleon and move it into safer investments.

In February, Rajaratnam hired Ayad Alhadi, a seasoned marketer whom he hoped would help Galleon unlock the millions of dollars sitting in the Middle East among the sovereign wealth funds of the region's oil-rich countries. He was also in talks with Rajat Gupta to head Galleon International, a Pan-Asian emerging markets hedge fund, and help Galleon tap into new investors.

Gupta was one of the few players in the corporate world who could be described as truly global. He was connected in India in a way that Rajaratnam, an outsider, a Sri Lankan Tamil, could never be, despite all the billions to his name. He counted men like Mukesh Ambani as friends; he had known Ambani for more than twenty years. Besides sitting on the boards of American companies, Gupta also served on the boards of foreign companies. His best-paying directorship was as a board member for the Russian bank Sberbank, which paid him $525,000 in 2008. And he also participated in gilded charities, the kind that burnished his philanthropic résumé. He had been an adviser to the Bill and Melinda Gates Foundation since 2004, and as head of the board of its Indian AIDS initiative Avahan, which in Sanskrit means "call to action," Gupta was credited with persuading the foundation to give $47 million for AIDS programs in India. If Rajaratnam was looking for someone to give Galleon global cachet, there was no one better than Gupta.

Even though Gupta was approaching his sixtieth birthday, he was still very much in the game, ever eager to stay a player. He was a tireless traveler, always whizzing around the globe. On the way to India that April, he stopped in the Middle East and joined Galleon's new man Alhadi for a day in some meetings with prominent institutional investors—the Abu Dhabi Investment Council, First Gulf Bank, and Emirates Bank International. Gupta did not say much at the meetings, restricting his remarks to basic facts about Galleon—its size and its funds. But his presence at the meetings and his years atop McKinsey impressed investors.

In late April, the Abu Dhabi Investment Council signaled that it wanted to invest $50 million in the Galleon Diversified Offshore fund. In another instance, Larry Currie, a representative of a potential investor, National Commercial Bank, specifically asked if he could meet with Gupta when he visited New York. The Saudi Arabian bank considered investing as much as $100 million in Galleon's funds. Goldman Sachs owned 10 percent of National Commercial Bank Capital, the bank's investment entity, and Alhadi had a hunch that Gupta's Goldman link would help National Commercial Bank gain more comfort with Galleon.

He turned out to be right. A week after meeting with Gupta, Currie called Alhadi and said that National Commercial Bank wanted to start with an investment of between $25 and $30 million in Galleon funds. As Rajaratnam had suspected all along, Gupta's reputation was unmatched. He only wished his friend leveraged his connections to benefit Galleon more.

For Rajaratnam, the problem with Gupta was that like so many high-achieving executives, he was overcommitted. By the summer of 2008, he had his fingers in a myriad of ventures. New Silk Route, the private equity fund he helped found with Rajaratnam, was sucking more time from Gupta than it should have. His countless board positions, corporate and philanthropic, ate into his schedule. And if that were not enough, he was contemplating raising $600 million for a telecommunications fund.

"It's now reached a point where it's physically and humanly impossible to do the things he's doing right," said Kumar in a May 28, 2008, conversation with Rajaratnam.

Though nothing was settled, Gupta was talking with private equity titan Henry Kravis about a possible role at Kohlberg Kravis Roberts & Co. The two were tossing around the idea of Gupta being a senior adviser and, with his experience at McKinsey, helping KKR build state-of-the-art infrastructure for a professional services firm. The trouble was that Goldman, on whose board Gupta sat, was not keen about having Gupta take on the role. Goldman and KKR were both major players in the same business, private equity, and the firms had a relationship with each other across several lines. Gupta could not understand Goldman's position. Several members of the bank's board had links to private equity firms.

The issue between Goldman and Gupta came to a head in one of the most unlikely places: Beijing. Both Gupta and Blankfein were in China in early August 2008, catching the Summer Olympics and attending the Tsinghua University board meeting. In full view of others, including Gupta's wife, Goldman's chief executive, Blankfein, gave Gupta an ultimatum: he had to choose between Goldman and KKR.

In mid-August, after the Blankfeins and Guptas returned from China, Blankfein met again with Gupta in his office. Sitting in his customary place, a straight-backed chair, opposite Gupta, who was seated on the tan couch in his office, Blankfein reiterated that it would be difficult for Gupta to remain at Goldman if he were to pursue the KKR role. Kohlberg Kravis Roberts was just too big a player in the private equity space for Goldman to have a sitting board member that also worked for a rival like KKR. Forced to choose, Gupta said he planned to take the KKR job. A press release announcing his retirement was drafted.

As prestigious as sitting on the Goldman board was, working for KKR would vault Gupta to a whole new level, catapulting him into a rarefied world of high rollers. Some of the richest men on the island of Manhattan—Henry Kravis and Stephen Schwarzman—had made their fortunes in private equity. Rajaratnam suspected it was Gupta's desire to be in "the billionaire [*sic*] circle" of Kravis and Schwarzman and not the "hundreds of millionaires circle" that was associated with Goldman Sachs directors that had prompted Gupta to explore the KKR opportunity. Though Gupta's starting take would be modest by industry standards—about $5 million—over time, a position at KKR would pull him into a galaxy of untold riches and influence like Kravis and his rival Schwarzman. The Blackstone chief's wealth had enriched the New York Public Library—not to mention given it a new name.

Gupta seemed intrigued by the possibilities, but Rajaratnam lamented that the KKR job would mean less time for him. A month earlier, when Gupta had told him about the KKR opportunity, he said to him that he would take it in a "heartbeat." But he knew

Gupta's going to KKR would mean less time to raise funds for Galleon. "He'll divide his week into a hundred different parts. And he will tell KKR I'm gonna give you two days a week right. And he'll tell me that then he'll tell everybody that you know," he told Kumar.

Rajaratnam was mulling giving Gupta a 10 percent stake in Galleon International in exchange for his role as chairman of the entity. But he said Gupta was angling for more. "See with me he's not giving me the luxury of saying why don't you come up with a package," Rajaratnam told Kumar. "He's telling me I want so much."

Rajaratnam, a pro at prying money out of investors' fists, knew that if he racked up great returns, money would flood into the fund.

What Gupta does is "he gives a little bit of a cachet in South Asia and globally you know," Rajaratnam told Kumar. As they spoke, he was coming to the view that a 10 percent stake in Galleon International, vested over five years at 2 percent, was the best he could do for Gupta.

"The worst he's gonna do is he's gonna say well I don't think that's enough and I'll say okay, you know," said Rajaratnam.

He had called Kumar for a "sanity check" and he had got one.

* * *

At the US attorney's office in Lower Manhattan, the Akamai call was a huge breakthrough. The wiretapped call from Chiesi to Rajaratnam on July 24 involved the passing of material, nonpublic information. It was not speculation or rumor. When investigators followed up by subpoenaing Chiesi's phone records, they found out that just as she told Rajaratnam, Chiesi had spoken to an Akamai executive before calling him that Thursday night. There was no doubt about the veracity of the tip: it was coming from a company insider. And only a week passed between the tip and the trade.

After a number of promising but false starts, Michaelson finally had a call he could build into a compelling case. As he listened to the cell phone calls, Michaelson kept a checklist of the elements he needed to build the case. He required evidence that Rajaratnam was receiving information that was material and not in the public domain. Then he had to find out if Rajaratnam traded on that information consistent with the information he received. Did the information come to pass? That is, did the company make an' announcement along the lines of the information Rajaratnam received? Did the stock move as predicted? Last, did Rajaratnam place trades in accordance with the information and make a substantial profit from the trades?

Unlike the information conveyed in other wiretapped calls between Rajaratnam and his moles, the information Chiesi provided Rajaratnam about Akamai lowering its guidance actually came to pass and resulted in a monster trade. On Wednesday, July 30, Akamai Technologies unveiled a pessimistic outlook for the rest of 2008. Its stock fell 7.91, or 25 percent, to $23.34. Soon after Chiesi phoned him with the tip, Rajaratnam shorted 200,000 shares of Akamai; most of the position was allocated to the technology fund he personally ran. Even as Galleon grew and Rajaratnam's management responsibilities swelled exponentially, he never relinquished running Galleon's core technology fund. Over the next several days, Rajaratnam placed more bearish bets on Akamai, selling short an additional 375,000 shares. He also ramped up his negative position in the stock by buying put options—another security that allows an investor to make a bearish bet. Despite promising Chiesi that he would not tell anyone else about her tip, Rajaratnam spread the word.

"hope u shorted some akam," rajatgalleon, the IM handle for Rajaratnam, instant-messaged Joe Liu, a trader working for him, on July 30.

"thank you, Raj. Indeed, I did some," joeliu2003 instant-messaged back. (Liu has never been charged in connection with the Galleon case.)

In the technology fund he ran, Rajaratnam made $5,139,851 in profit from the Akamai purchases. Chiesi's New Castle funds made $2,437,976 on Akamai. And the best part of it all for Michaelson and the Southern District was that after they both booked winnings on Akamai, Rajaratnam telephoned Chiesi to congratulate her.

"I just wanted to say, thank you," he phoned to tell Chiesi on July 30. "You know what, I think you did it in such a classy way. In the sense you didn't call him, you know, and that way you maintain the relationship. You don't have to tell him that you played it hard."

When the stock fell to $28.50, Rajaratnam confessed to Chiesi that he "banged it," selling another 150,000 shares short.

Chiesi was on a high. "It's a conquest," she said. "It's mentally, mentally fabulous for me."

That evening, she headed to the Chinese consulate on the western edge of midtown Manhattan for a reception, which the ambassador would be attending. Like many in the financial world, Chiesi was hyped up about China—"I wanna own China as you know, I need to own them," she told Rajaratnam. With the Akamai trade at her back, she felt more optimistic than ever about her meeting with the Chinese. "You know the coolest part?" she asked rhetorically. "I am going in there with so much confidence right now. This is big for me."

For investigators, the coolest part was that the entire conversation was on tape. Not long after prosecutors heard the Chiesi calls, they made a new wiretap application—this time they asked a federal judge for permission to eavesdrop on her.

CHAPTER TWENTY-EIGHT

A Friend on the Board

"Raj?" said the cheerful voice on the other end of the phone. "Hi. It's Renee."

Renee (pronounced "Ree-nee") Gomes was tall, thin, and always upbeat. She was Rajat Gupta's secretary, one of the perks that came with the position of global managing director. Even after Gupta retired from the helm of McKinsey, the firm still provided him with a secretary and an office. In Stamford, Connecticut, where Gomes was based, there was even an ample anteroom for her to sit in and attend to Gupta's affairs. She loved working for him. She raved to others that Gupta was a true gentleman, always respectful of her and mindful of her time off.

Gomes was an "old school" secretary. Gupta rarely placed his own calls, so Gomes took care of the dialing. At times, she got to follow her peripatetic boss around the globe, accompanying him to McKinsey meetings or sometimes joining him on his trips to India. Gupta trusted her implicitly. She had full access to his correspondence and often responded to emails on his behalf.

It was early in the evening of Tuesday, July 29, 2008, and Gomes had her boss, Gupta, on the line for Rajaratnam. When Gupta traveled abroad, as he frequently did, he would call Gomes and ask her to patch him through to people he was trying to reach. Rajaratnam, who was working from Connecticut, was particularly eager to speak to Gupta. That coming Thursday at noon, he was going to be lunching with Gary Cohn, one of the top executives at Goldman Sachs. Rick Schutte, Galleon's chief operating officer who had worked at Goldman, rising to managing director before coming to Galleon, was to join the lunch, as were a number of Goldman executives.

As one of the biggest payers of stock commissions to Goldman—in 2008 Galleon shelled out $35 million in commissions to Goldman—Rajaratnam regularly received audiences with the New York investment bank's top executives. It was one of the privileges that came from being so big and throwing so much business to the firm. Goldman was Galleon's largest trading partner, and the hedge fund funneled the biggest volume of its transactions through Goldman.

One of the reasons Cohn was going to Galleon that day was to address the growing concern among Galleon executives about the safety of their assets during the 2008 financial crisis. Galleon, like many hedge funds, held assets at securities firms. Goldman had about $600 million of Galleon assets in custody. The near collapse of Bear Stearns a few months before had focused investors on a growing risk: the failure of a securities firm would likely result in investor assets being frozen. Galleon had about $200 million of investor assets at Bear, and had the firm been forced to file for bankruptcy protection, a surety if J.P. Morgan and the US government didn't back up the bank, Galleon would have been one company in a long line of creditors.

Rajaratnam had heard that Goldman might be shopping for a commercial bank, and he was looking for intel.

"There's a rumor that Goldman might look to buy a commercial bank," Rajaratnam said to Gupta. "Have you heard anything along that line?"

Just a month earlier, Goldman's twelve-person board of directors was in St. Petersburg, Russia, for the investment bank's full board meeting. Almost all the Goldman board was present—even its newest director, the steel magnate Lakshmi Mittal, who was the only other Indian on Goldman's board besides Gupta.

By the middle of 2008, Gupta was also on the boards of Procter & Gamble, AMR Corp., the parent of American Airlines, and outsourcing firm Genpact. He also held a seat on the board of the Qatar

Financial Centre, and in 2009, his corporate board seats paid him more than $3.2 million, according to *Fortune* magazine.

Most of the board meetings were routine affairs that Gupta attended alone or dialed into from his office, but some involved international travel. When she could, Gupta's wife, Anita, tried to join him for the board gatherings overseas. It was one way to catch up with her busy husband. With the Guptas' youngest daughter, Deepali, headed to Brown University in the fall and their eldest daughter, Geetanjali, married, Anita and Rajat were empty nesters. (The Gupta girls had actually been away from home from the time they were teenagers; they chose to go to boarding school. Two attended Phillips Exeter Academy, saving them and their parents from the invariable adolescent-age fights about important issues like dating.) After years of dedicating themselves to nurturing their family, Anita and Rajat for the first time were soon going to be spending more hours with each other than they had in a long while.

On Friday, June 27, at about 4 p.m., Anita arrived in St. Petersburg on a British Airways flight from New York, changing planes in London. Her husband, who was coming in from Moscow, met her at the airport, and the two headed to the Hotel Astoria, as popular under Russia's new capitalists as it was under its old Communist overlords. Nearly a century earlier, while in power, Lenin addressed the crowds from the balcony of the hotel's suite 211, now ironically renamed the Royal Suite. As Gupta sat all Saturday in Goldman board meetings, which were held in a conference room on the ground floor of the hotel, Anita joined the other spouses taking in the city sights—Yusupov Palace, where the mystic Rasputin was assassinated, and the famous bronze horseman statue of Peter the Great.

Gupta told Rajaratnam that there had been a big discussion at the June board meeting in Russia about the possibility of Goldman acquiring a commercial bank. "It was a, uh, divided discussion in the board," Gupta divulged. "I think more people saying why, because in essence it's a low return business," even though it could be "interesting to develop a deposit base which is a low cost source of funding."

Goldman wasn't having trouble funding itself or anything, Gupta assured Rajaratnam.

It's just that "you know we should explore more global sources of funding," said Gupta. The idea that Goldman should look at insurance or other similar businesses was broached.

"They're an opportunistic group so if Wachovia was a good deal and they, you know, it's quite conceivable they'd come and say let's go buy Wachovia," Gupta told Rajaratnam.

"Or even AIG right," replied Rajaratnam.

"Or even AIG," concurred Gupta.

CHAPTER TWENTY-NINE

A Tragic Call

It was Thursday, September 11, 2008, and Raj Rajaratnam was starting to feel like a boxer fighting the legend Muhammad Ali. "I know he's stronger and he's faster, but you're in the ring with him," declared Rajaratnam, weary after getting beaten up day after day in the markets. "You know, you try to survive and hope that he gets tired."

It was 7:30 in the evening, and to say it had been a hellish week was an understatement. Rumors of impending financial doom had roiled the stock market, taking investors like Rajaratnam on a scary roller-coaster ride. Rajaratnam, an eternal optimist, had spent the summer buying stock whenever the market dipped. Now he was getting killed. His flagship Galleon Technology fund was being pounded, whipped by the temperamental market. The stock of Lehman Brothers, which had opened on Monday at $18 a share, was hovering somewhere between $3 and $4 by Thursday, its swift fall an ominous portent of events to come. He needed a win.

"You know, look, it's very stressful," Rajaratnam confided, trading in his usual bravado for a rare display of vulnerability. Investing in stocks was starting to seem like gambling, no different from placing chips on the roulette wheel in Las Vegas. "You know, you go to the casino," said Rajaratnam, "you say okay, you know Schlumberger, which is a great company, was at 100, it's 82, right?...And you just don't know whether it's gonna go to 70."

"Exactly," replied Anil Kumar. He may have said the word, but there was no sign the consultant had any sense of the pain that the trader was feeling in September 2008. Kumar was actually calling from Dublin, where he was huddled in a retreat with members of the Young Presidents' Organization, a collection of up-and-comers who liked to gather every once in a while to gab. He was too preoccupied with his own hobnobbing to be distracted by a financial market pileup.

"Anand Mahindra's got 50 people meeting in Montauk in New York" in October. "I guess it's some suburb or something of New York," Kumar told Rajaratnam. (Actually, the event was in a far less glitzy part of New York—Mohonk.) Mahindra was one of the most respected figures in Indian business, having studied at Harvard College and Harvard Business School before returning to India to oversee his family's industrial conglomerate. Mahindra has invited some of India's biggest business tycoons to "talk about the future of India kind of thing," said Kumar.

"He's invited me to it," he added.

Rajaratnam knew Kumar too well to take the bait. He'd once remarked to their mutual friend Gupta that Kumar was constantly "scheming is not the right word, but constantly trying to figure out what other people's angles are." It was astonishing, but "he seems to know what everybody else is worth, you know he leads with, 'Oh Sunil Mittal is worth $20 billion.'" Presciently, Rajaratnam pointed out that there were pitfalls to viewing the world through Kumar's prism.

"You know, when he starts thinking like that," said Rajaratnam, not finishing his sentence. He didn't have to complete it; it was obvious to Gupta or anyone else what he meant, and if there was any doubt, he added: "You build the business and the money will come, you know?"

Unlike Kumar, the salaried consultant who got paid simply for showing up, Rajaratnam was an entrepreneur who built an investment empire with his very own blood, sweat, and tears. The ebullient markets in recent years made people forget about the hard work, long hours, and risks he had taken to create Galleon. But September 2008 was a vivid reminder that there was a reason he was a billionaire. Every day that he ventured into the treacherous waters of investing, he stood the chance of getting wiped out. Three years earlier, after the tsunami devastated his native country, Sri Lanka, Rajaratnam, who had been vacationing there at the time and had witnessed the havoc firsthand, hosted a fund-raiser at the Stone Rose Lounge on the fourth floor of the plush Time Warner Center with its spectacular views of Central Park. As beautiful women in slinky dresses gathered by the sleek rosewood bar and sipped cocktails, Rajaratnam delivered a powerful and moving speech. He likened Sri Lanka's fishermen to hedge fund managers. "Every morning they go out to sea and try and catch as many fish as they can," he told the thousand who had gathered. "And every night, just like hedge fund managers, they come back to port and eat what they catch." Yes, and every once in a while, just like the Sri Lankan fishermen, hedge fund managers faced financial tsunamis that were as violent and humbling as the natural ones. Kumar, the consultant, just didn't get it.

Sitting in Dublin, Kumar was completely out of touch with Rajaratnam's world, clueless to the minute-by-minute pressures traders like him were facing. He wasn't even up on the news. KDB, the Korea Development Bank, had pulled the plug on its talks to buy a stake in Lehman Brothers earlier that week. In Manhattan, it was the only thing players in the financial markets were buzzing about.

"I asked my guy there if KDB is gonna buy and he sort of gave this slightly, he said, don't believe everything you read in the press kind of reply," said Kumar.

"When did you ask him?" asked Rajaratnam.

"A week ago," replied Kumar, not realizing that by September 11 the markets were moving so quickly that even news that was minutes old was stale.

"You know, the thing is, a week ago they were negotiating very hard," said Rajaratnam. "Right?"

"Hm," said Kumar.

"On Tuesday they announced that they were not interested," continued Rajaratnam. "They couldn't come to terms, right?"

"Hm," said Kumar again. It was all he could say. As always, Rajaratnam had the last word.

* * *

A month earlier, shortly after 11 a.m. on August 15, Kumar had telephoned Rajaratnam to tell him that after months of negotiations, AMD and a Middle Eastern sovereign wealth fund called Mubadala had finally reached an agreement for the fund to invest between $6 and $8 billion in a manufacturing facility to make computer chips.

"So yesterday they agreed on, at least they've shaken hands, and said they're going ahead with the deal," Kumar told Rajaratnam. A transaction was set to be announced the week after Labor Day.

Minutes after Rajaratnam hung up with Kumar, he started spreading the good news. He first called Danielle Chiesi, who he knew had an "edge" on AMD because of her close ties to the company's chief executive, Hector Ruiz.

"Have you spoken to Hector?" Rajaratnam asked.

Chiesi said she had had a brief conversation with Ruiz and he was expecting a deal to be inked in "mid September or something like that." With markets as volatile as these, it was always safe to have a second source.

Rajaratnam passed along what he had heard minutes earlier: "Right so yesterday we had ummm shake hands," he told Chiesi using the very same phrase Kumar had used to signal that an agreement was in place.

A few hours later, Rajaratnam called his brother Rengan to tell him that he had heard that AMD had a tentative agreement with the Arabs. He had already bought some shares of AMD for himself and was snapping up some for his brother.

"Alright, thanks a lot, man, I appreciate it," Rengan replied. Swapping tips from insiders was a family business in the Rajaratnam clan. Three and a half hours later, Rengan called his brother back. He had just spoken to an old classmate of his from Stanford Business School, another McKinsey consultant named David Palecek, who headed McKinsey's semiconductor group and worked for Kumar.

Rengan said he asked Palecek, "What do you think of AMD?"

"He's like buy it, buy as much as you can as soon as you can," reported Rengan. "He finally spilled his beans" and said the Arabs were putting some money in. "He thinks the stock's gonna rip."

Always looking for new recruits to their network of insiders, Rengan told his brother that his old business school pal was someone worth enlisting.

"You know, he's a little dirty," said Rengan. "I'll tell you why, 'cause because he...kind of volunteered 'cause when I said AMD, kind of volunteered the information on the investments." When Palecek said that all of his best ideas were inside information, Rengan assured him that was a workable problem. Galleon could hire Palecek's wife, Melissa, as a consultant. (This characterization did not sit well with Palecek's wife or her attorney, Catherine L. Redlich. Palecek died in 2010 at the age of thirty-seven of complications from a staph infection, and Redlich says, "Mrs. Palecek has authorized me to state on her behalf that she was never offered a consultant position at Galleon and never discussed such a possibility with her husband. Rengan may have hoped that his old Stanford classmate would prove to be 'a little dirty,' or more likely he was simply promoting himself to his brother, but he was incorrect." McKinsey agrees and adds that it has seen "no convincing evidence" indicating Palecek actually shared or agreed to share any confidential client information.)

By the end of that day in August, Galleon's technology funds had quadrupled their position in AMD stock to 4 million shares. Rajaratnam was making a big bet that AMD's tie-up with the Arabs was going to yield a huge payday, much like the deal between AMD and ATI Technologies two years earlier. But as the dog days of summer wore on, AMD's stock kept trending lower. Even though the tie-up with Mubadala was positive news, spelling an end to rumors of AMD having to file for bankruptcy court protection, the company's stock slid in the weeks preceding the expected deal. Rajaratnam and Chiesi were flummoxed; whenever they talked they griped that the stock was behaving badly. They were not the only ones disappointed.

Sitting at his desk at the US attorney's office at One St. Andrew's Plaza, Michaelson too was waiting patiently for the AMD deal. When he first heard Kumar tell Rajaratnam that the two parties had shaken hands, he was excited, as eager for the deal as Rajaratnam but for different reasons. For Michaelson, here was another tip—a potential deal on which to build an insider trading case. But by the second week of September, the prospects of a profitable inside trade appeared to be dimming. The announcement that Kumar pegged for after Labor Day was being pushed back. Now sitting with his headphones listening to Kumar and Rajaratnam speak, and watching the financial markets convulsing, Michaelson was pessimistic that AMD would turn out to be a winning trade for either Rajaratnam or him.

"It's not September 15th," Kumar told Rajaratnam. "It's gonna be October first week, but it's all on track."

Kumar tried to sound reassuring. "I think all the approvals and all have kind of happened, it's now most of, most of the details."

"Right," replied Rajaratnam, sounding skeptical.

The deal eventually was announced on October 7, but it wasn't the home run either Rajaratnam or Michaelson were seeking. Galleon lost money on its investment in AMD. Technology stocks, like much of the market, got clobbered in the wake of Lehman Brothers' move to file for bankruptcy on September 15.

* * *

Geetanjali Gupta vividly remembers the weekend after the collapse of Lehman Brothers. She was coming home from Boston to celebrate her thirtieth birthday. The Guptas were actually preparing to celebrate two birthdays that weekend. Her mother's was on September 21, a day after hers. On Saturday, September 20, Geetanjali was in the library, lined on two walls with books and overlooking a swimming pool, at her parents' home in Westport talking to her father.

Earlier that year, in June, Gupta had shared one of the most important moments between a father and a daughter: he'd given his daughter away in marriage. In most Indian families, Geetanjali's nuptials to a Nigerian would have caused a stir. Indeed, Geetanjali's own cousin watched in awe when she first introduced her then boyfriend to the family at one boisterous Thanksgiving. "Many Indian parents (mine included) forbade dating and, and would never sanction relationships with non-Indians... That my 'perfect' cousin

Sonu, Rajat's oldest child, was not only allowed to date a Nigerian, but to do so out in the open with her parents' blessing, was literally unheard of in the Indian community," says Geetanjali's cousin. "I was so, so proud that it was my uncle who made it clear (not by any explicit words, or drawing undue attention, but by his gentle, obvious inclusiveness) that he supported" the union.

For the wedding, which was held at the Gupta estate in Westport, Gupta wanted everything to be perfect. He spent hours planning and refining the landscaping arrangements for the outdoor affair. He even got involved in the minutiae like the placement of flowers. On the day, as his daughter stood in a red saree under the canopy of a wedding pavilion bedecked with flowers, the normally stoic Gupta could not hide his emotions. In his speech giving Geetanjali away, Gupta spoke of his respect for his daughter's integrity. Before each of his actions, he would ask himself, What would Geetanjali think? Then, for the first time, guests noticed something they had never seen in Gupta before: tears in his eyes.

Three months later, on the weekend of Geetanjali's birthday, Gupta was very upset and stressed. It was unlike him to be visibly agitated. Both at work and at home, he was normally calm and collected. He rarely got angry, mainly because he felt there was almost nothing that important to get angry about. Sometimes his family would say that his apparent detachment was too extreme. It seemed like he didn't care at times—he didn't get angry enough or worked up about an issue. He was never good at deep psychoanalysis, but he wondered whether it was because he'd lost his parents at a young age. "At that point, nothing seemed to matter that much," he said years later.

Gupta told his daughter that he was upset about the performance of an investment called Voyager that he had partnered with Rajaratnam on and was having difficulty getting information about it. Geetanjali did not know Rajaratnam; she had met him only once, when Rajaratnam went with her father to Harvard to pitch New Silk Route, the fund they were starting. Geetanjali is an investment analyst at Harvard Management Company, which oversees the university's endowment, a potential investor in the fund. Gupta told his daughter he was angry because he had reason to believe that Rajaratnam had pulled money out of the fund without telling him. If he had, he wanted to know why he was not allowed to withdraw his money too.

And after the collapse of Lehman Brothers, Gupta had come to learn that the $10 million he had invested in the Voyager fund, a vehicle that was managed by Rajaratnam, had evaporated to nothing. He felt that it was Rajaratnam's responsibility to make him whole; after all, Gupta was only a passive investor in the fund. The unflappable Gupta was so angry that he later contemplated suing Rajaratnam. Ultimately, he never took legal action. It would turn out to be a costly mistake.

CHAPTER THIRTY

"Buy Goldman Sachs, Buy Goldman Sachs"

It was around 10 a.m. on September 23, 2008, and Byron David Trott, a tall, silver-haired banker, sat in his New York office on the seventeenth floor of Goldman Sachs's headquarters building, preparing for a call. As he glanced at the television screen hanging in his office, he saw his former mentor and boss, Hank Paulson, giving testimony before a congressional committee. Ever since the collapse of Lehman Brothers a week earlier, Paulson, who had become Treasury secretary in 2006, was ubiquitous, hitting the airwaves and Capitol Hill in a bid to impress upon Americans the magnitude of the financial crisis facing the country.

Trott turned away from the television and gave some thought to the call he was about to place. A few days earlier, at the behest of Goldman's chief executive, Lloyd Blankfein, Trott had approached Warren Buffett, the most famed investor in America, and proposed he invest in Goldman Sachs. Blankfein, Goldman's chief executive, personally asked Trott to sound out Buffett on the idea. Blankfein knew that Trott was the one person at Goldman who had a special line into Buffett, who made investments in a vast swath of companies across a wide array of industries through his investment vehicle, Berkshire Hathaway Inc. Trott had officially covered Buffett on behalf of Goldman's investment banking division since 2002. He had done a number of deals for him since that time, and 2008 was shaping up to be a particularly busy year.

Trott knew that the original deal Blankfein wanted him to show Buffett would fall on deaf ears. There was not enough of a potential gain to tempt the "Oracle of Omaha" into taking the risk. As it turned out, Trott was right. The pitch to Buffett amounted to a fifteen-second conversation. Trott only hoped that today's conversation would last longer.

It was a week and a day after the collapse of Lehman Brothers, and fear and chaos still ruled the stock markets. Financial stocks were in deep distress. Washington Mutual, the nation's biggest savings and loan, was teetering on the brink, and lots of banks were staring into the abyss. By the end of the week, the Federal Deposit Insurance Corp. would step in and seize WaMu, making it the largest bank failure in US history.

Less than twenty-four hours earlier, Trott was wrapping up a client meeting in a Chicago suburb when his cell phone rang. It was Jon Winkelried, a friend and one of Goldman's two copresidents. Winkelried told Trott that Goldman was preparing to launch a common stock offering of between $5 and $10 billion to raise capital.

Trott asked Winkelried if Goldman had lined up a cornerstone investor, a marquee name that would commit a significant amount of capital—about $2 to $3 billion in this case—to the offering. Often, in a public stock sale, if a company can persuade a well-regarded investor to commit a significant amount of money, then the stock is more likely to fly off the shelf because potential buyers, drawn by the presence of a savvy investor, are likely to follow.

Winkelried said Goldman had not lined up a cornerstone investor.

That's a big mistake, Trott told his friend. Trott suggested he fly to New York at once and meet with Goldman executives to brainstorm about finding an investor. That evening, Trott caught a flight out of Chicago for New York.

At 9 the next morning, he met with Winkelried and Goldman chief financial officer David Viniar in the executive offices on the thirtieth floor of the bank's headquarters building at 85 Broad Street. Blankfein, who was en route to LaGuardia Airport, where he was set to fly out to Washington, DC, for meetings, was patched in via telephone. Trott outlined for Blankfein, Winkelried, and Viniar the type of deal he thought Warren Buffett would be interested in. He still thought enticing Buffett to invest in a securities firm was a long shot. After all, Buffett had all but sworn off investment banks after his horrific experience with Salomon Brothers in the early 1990s. But Trott thought if there was a possibility of getting Buffett to invest in Goldman, the deal would have to be one that paid him a fat dividend.

Goldman's top executives agreed to let Trott feel out Buffett and gave him the leeway to negotiate any deal. When Trott reached Buffett in Omaha, he was settling into a typical day. He had attended to some Berkshire Hathaway affairs in the morning, and soon he would be headed to Dairy Queen—a company Berkshire owned in its portfolio of companies—with his grandkids.

"Forget what we discussed in the past," Trott told Buffett. "You and I both know you were not going to do that." Goldman had a new deal in mind, Trott told Buffett, one that would involve the firm raising a large amount of money. Goldman wanted Buffett to be a cornerstone investor of significant size in the capital-raising move.

"I am listening," Buffett said.

Trott said Goldman was prepared to offer Buffett an esoteric security—perpetual preferred shares with warrants—that paid Buffett a juicy dividend on a $5 billion investment and gave him the opportunity to buy additional shares of Goldman stock at a set price.

"I am still listening," Buffett said. For Goldman, getting Buffett to buy a perpetual preferred security was important. It was considered Tier 1 capital, a measure used by regulators of a bank's strength based on the ratio of core equity to assets. At a time when investors in financial services companies were obsessed with the amount of debt investment banks were shouldering, the raising of Tier 1 money would send a strong signal to the markets: Goldman was shedding its debt load.

For the privilege of getting Buffett to invest, and essentially bestowing upon the bank the security industry equivalent of the Good Housekeeping Seal of Approval, Goldman was prepared to offer Buffett a security paying a 10 percent dividend.

Buffett said he was prepared to accept the proposal on one condition. He insisted that the four senior executives of Goldman—Blankfein, Winkelried, Gary Cohn, and David Viniar—not sell any of their stock before his security was called or redeemed. It was vintage Buffett: he wasn't going to put his money on the line if Goldman's senior executives were not prepared to risk theirs. Buffett told Trott that he was headed to Dairy Queen and wasn't to be disturbed until 2:30.

After hanging up, Trott reached Winkelried, who was on his way to the United Nations.

"I think Warren will do this," he said.

The two agreed that they and Goldman's other top executives—Viniar, its razor-sharp chief financial officer; Greg Palm, its powerful top lawyer; and John F. W. Rogers, a seasoned Washington insider and Blankfein's consigliere—would meet on the thirtieth floor at 85 Broad Street at 12:30 to discuss the terms. The wisecracking Blankfein, who grew up in a federal housing project in East New York, would be patched in again, as he had been during the morning meeting. Then Trott, a veteran of Goldman who had started at the firm in 1982 and climbed its ranks, went off to teach a class on negotiating skills to the firm's new managing directors and vice presidents.

It was shortly after 1 p.m. on Tuesday, September 23, when Lissette Jorgensen, a Goldman vice president who aspired to be a concert pianist before starting on Wall Street, got her marching orders. Her full-time position was to support Goldman's powerful twelve-person board of directors. Jorgensen and her staff compiled materials for board meetings, looked after scheduling matters, and even scouted for locations where Goldman could hold its board meetings.

All morning the thirtieth floor, the executive floor at Goldman where Jorgensen sat, buzzed with activity. Trott, the banker from Chicago, was seen on the floor. He was holed up in a meeting with a couple of Goldman executives. Typically, when meetings were deemed top secret, they took place on the executive floor so fewer rank-and-file employees could see the comings and goings of important people. But to everyone on the floor it was clear something was up. What, exactly, no one knew.

A half hour earlier, at 12:30, Goldman's top brass met and Trott outlined the terms of the deal he and Buffett had sketched out. "We all agreed it was a good deal to take," said Trott years later. As soon as the meeting broke up, Jorgensen was told to reach out to all of Goldman's board members and inform them that the bank planned to hold an emergency meeting of the board that afternoon. Goldman wanted to schedule the call before the market closed.

Jorgensen quickly hit the phones, reaching out to the executive assistants of Goldman's board members. At first, when Jorgensen got in touch with Rajat Gupta's secretary, Renee Gomes, Gomes said that Gupta had a conflict. He had an important governmental meeting that he couldn't reschedule. It had been a back-to-back day for Gupta that had started practically at dawn. But about half an hour before the 3:15 p.m. board meeting was set to begin, Gomes got back in touch with Jorgensen. Her boss would be able to attend the board meeting via telephone.

Caryn Eisenberg, Raj Rajaratnam's executive assistant, who sat just outside his glass-walled corner office, knew that one of her boss's cardinal rules was that he was not to be disturbed during the first thirty minutes of the trading day, from 9:30 to 10 a.m., and during the last half hour of the trading day, from 3:30 to 4 p.m. Rajaratnam gave her instructions on how to handle calls that came in during those times. They were not to be put through unless the callers were on a list of about ten people that Eisenberg had inherited from his previous secretary, Anita Teglasi. Rajaratnam was ruthless about pruning the list and limiting it to people he wanted to hear from during the crucial opening and closing minutes of the market. From time to time, he would take people off the list and put new people on it.

Like many secretaries, Eisenberg scribbled some of the names in a notebook she kept. It wasn't a complete tally and not all the names were correctly spelled. But the list helped her remember which callers she was supposed to put through. If Rajaratnam was on the phone or in a meeting, she was to pass him a note when they called. If he was not in his own office but somewhere in the Galleon offices that day, she was to find him and tell him of the call.

One of the names on the list was Rajat Gupta. Eisenberg had seen

Gupta many times in the Galleon offices since she started working at the firm in January 2008. Gupta sometimes came to Galleon because he had appointments with Rajaratnam; at other times, he showed up unannounced. When he arrived without warning, Rajaratnam would sometimes instruct Eisenberg to lie and tell Gupta that he was not around. When the two men met, they generally got together behind closed doors in Rajaratnam's corner office, not far from Galleon's noisy trading desk. Rajaratnam sat close to his dozen or so most trusted traders. His office, with floor-to-ceiling glass walls, had a sliding panel that was typically kept open. Through the panel, Rajaratnam could bark buy and sell orders to his traders, who would then execute them at the best price available.

For some time, Galleon had been bearish on financial stocks. Even before the near collapse of Bear Stearns in March, Galleon had been taking negative bets on finance companies such as AIG and the mortgage brokers. The one bank that Galleon was favorably disposed toward was Goldman Sachs—a view that was confirmed when Goldman's president, Gary Cohn, came in for a sandwich lunch in late July. Unlike with the other Wall Street investment banks, Galleon's biggest concern with Goldman was not its exposure to bad mortgages but rather its risk to poor counterparties. At the lunch, attended by Rajaratnam and two of his colleagues, Cohn alleviated any concerns.

"None of our peers have the technology and risk management systems that we do," Cohn boldly declared. "At the end of the day, the CEO of UBS has no idea how its risk assets have done. We know exactly what our risk assets have done and what our balance sheet looks like." When asked what Goldman could do if its risk assets overwhelmed the bank's capital base, Cohn replied that Goldman could buy an entity with steady capital like an insurance company or it could raise equity.

By September, though, Cohn's bold predictions were starting to ring hollow. As the capital markets seized up, in the wake of Lehman's collapse, and insurance companies were looking as troubled as banks, Galleon turned negative on Goldman. On September 16, Will Keaten, Galleon's Goldman analyst, fired off an email laying out his thoughts on Goldman. The first sentence summed up his view. "I'd rather be short in this environment," Keaten wrote. Internally, Galleon portfolios that once had used Goldman's stock to hedge bearish positions in other financial services stocks now took negative bets on Goldman too.

Shortly after 3:54 p.m. on Tuesday, September 23, a minute after Gupta hung up from the Goldman board call, Gomes, Gupta's secretary, dialed Rajaratnam's direct line and a minute later patched in her boss, Gupta. He and Rajaratnam were going through a rough patch; for weeks Gupta had been trying to get information about his Voyager investment, but he was making no headway. He wanted to catch Rajaratnam before heading into his next meeting. As it happened, his was the only call to come into Rajaratnam's direct line since 2:27 p.m. that day.

Eisenberg picked up the phone when it rang. The man on the other end of the line said he needed to speak to Rajaratnam urgently. Eisenberg could not identify the caller, except she knew that he was on the list of VIP callers jotted down in her red notebook. Rajaratnam was not in his office, but Eisenberg could hear his voice, so she put the call on hold and went to get him.

When Eisenberg told Rajaratnam that someone, one of the important callers, was on the phone and wanted to speak to him at once, Rajaratnam rushed back to his office and picked up the phone. The two had a fleeting conversation; it lasted thirty-five seconds at most. But as soon as Rajaratnam got off the phone, he summoned his lieutenant, Gary Rosenbach, into his office. More than a decade earlier it was Rosenbach who had helped Rajaratnam start Galleon.

Rosenbach walked into Rajaratnam's office and closed the door. When he reappeared less than a minute later, he went to the trading desk, got on the phone, and shouted, "Buy Goldman Sachs. Buy Goldman Sachs." He uttered the words not just once but a few times.

It was critical that Rosenbach move fast. The New York Stock Exchange, where Goldman's stock is listed, closes at 4 p.m. At 3:56:44 p.m., less than four minutes before trading finished for the day, Rosenbach managed to buy a total of nearly $25 million of Goldman stock, most of it for Rajaratnam's portfolio. Originally, he had sought to buy 250,000 shares, or about $31 million of stock, but even a pro like him could get only part of his order filled so late in the day. (Rosenbach has not been charged with any wrongdoing.)

Around the same time, Ananth Muniyappa, a junior trader, sat at the trading desk about ten feet away from Rajaratnam's office. At Galleon, portfolio managers like Rajaratnam decide what stocks to buy and sell, and traders like Muniyappa are in charge of moving stocks in and out of portfolios. Muniyappa and about a dozen Galleon traders were clustered in a T formation outside Rajaratnam's office; three or four feet separated one from the next, and there were no partitions dividing them. Ian Horowitz, the trader who executed Rajaratnam's trades, sat closest to the boss's office. Muniyappa, who would pinch-hit and place trades for Rajaratnam when Horowitz was sick or out of the office, was next to him.

With just three and a half minutes left in the trading day and Horowitz absent, Rajaratnam turned to Muniyappa and ordered him to buy 100,000 shares of Goldman Sachs stock. Purchasing a large quantity of stock—roughly $12.5 million—is hard ordinarily, but it was doubly difficult now because it was so late in the trading day. Since about 3:30 that Tuesday afternoon, Goldman's stock had risen appreciably, suggesting that someone in the market had a strong suspicion or even knew that positive news about Goldman was imminent. Unlike Horowitz, who had accrued many tight relationships with Wall Street brokers from his years as a trader, Muniyappa was a novice. He could not strong-arm or sweet-talk brokers into filling a huge order on such a tight deadline.

Muniyappa speed-dialed Ted Backer, a broker at Morgan Stanley, and told him that he wanted to buy 100,000 shares of Goldman stock. At first, Backer told Muniyappa that all he could get was 40,000 shares of Goldman. But at 4:01 p.m., a minute after trading ended for the day, Backer instant-messaged Muniyappa:

"bgt 67,200 GS @ 124.0343, fyi," using the abbreviation "bgt" for "bought" and "GS" for "Goldman." "I had to beat the sh.t out of the trader to get that 40K at that price." Muniyappa allocated 217,200 shares of Goldman stock to Rajaratnam's portfolio—150,000 of the shares Rosenbach bought and the 67,200 shares he purchased. Rosenbach kept 50,000 shares for his portfolio.

But shortly after 5:45 p.m., when headlines started streaming across Bloomberg News about Buffett's company, Berkshire Hathaway, purchasing $5 billion worth of Goldman preferred stock, all hell broke loose at Galleon. Leon Shaulov, a portfolio manager whom Muniyappa sat next to, was livid. His face was red, his hair was flying all over the place, and his eyes were popping out. Shaulov, who together with Rosenbach ran the trading-oriented Buccaneers fund and was not in Rajaratnam's inner circle, had a big bearish bet on financial stocks and appeared to be seething because no one at Galleon had tipped him off to the Buffett news.

At 6:16 p.m., he fired off an angry email to Rosenbach.

"Thx for the heads up btw. I'm short 170mm fins," he said, noting that he had a bearish bet of $170 million on financial stocks. "Not one word from anyone. Thnku very much… What I give vs what I get back is disgusting. But at least all my deferred (compensation) is in bucc." He was referring to the practice at Galleon where some portfolio managers had the opportunity to defer substantial portions of their income by investing in the funds they or others managed. He then added in what sounds like sarcasm, "That'll help me. Fucking bull shit."

Rosenbach replied: "Number." He was not going to discuss the Buffett tip on the company email.

The next morning, when Rajaratnam telephoned the office to check on the amount of Goldman stock Galleon would get in the offering that was planned on the back of the Berkshire investment, Ian Horowitz, his longtime trader, picked up the telephone. Rajaratnam was angling for Galleon to get 2.5 million shares. Rumor had it that Gary Cohn, Goldman's copresident, was deciding how much stock would be allocated to the long roster of Goldman clients hungering for it. Rajaratnam wanted to make sure he and others knew that Galleon "didn't pull a single dollar out" or yank its assets amid the market mayhem. It was a time in the markets when loyalty mattered, and Galleon had been deeply loyal to Goldman.

Rajaratnam didn't waste time in updating Horowitz on the panicked few minutes of trading late in the day before.

"So, big drama yesterday," Rajaratnam told Horowitz. "I got a call at 3:58, right?...Saying something good might happen to Goldman. Right?"

Rajaratnam said he instructed Muniyappa to buy him some Goldman stock but he "was fucking around" so he asked Rosenbach to place the order.

"Mm hmm," said Horowitz, and nothing more.

An hour later, Rajaratnam telephoned Horowitz again to check on the amount of Goldman stock Galleon would receive in the upcoming offering. He was irritated, stuck in bumper-to-bumper traffic because of the United Nations General Assembly meeting.

"I stressed enough the importance," Horowitz told Rajaratnam. "We've been, we've been doing a majority of our business and Adam's business with them. Even last week with all the bullshit going on we continue to go to them for trading. I don't think that went unnoticed."

After agreeing that the matter was out of both their hands, Rajaratnam turned to the late flurry of trading the previous day. Even though Rosenbach had defused Shaulov's tantrum, it was still preying on Rajaratnam's mind. Mentioning again that he had gotten a call that "something good" was going to happen to Goldman, Rajaratnam said, "Yeah, at 3:58 I can't...yell out in the fucking hall," Rajaratnam said.

"No, you did nothing wrong," Horowitz assured Rajaratnam.

Then he wisely advised: "We'll talk about it when you come in."

CHAPTER THIRTY-ONE

Trading at the Setai

Ever since taking the reins of Goldman Sachs in May 2006, Lloyd Blankfein had a simple rule when it came to dealing with the investment bank's board of directors. He preferred to call them before they called him. From time to time, he would telephone board members one by one, checking each off a list after updating every member on Goldman's financial performance. Sometimes his interaction with Goldman board members was more informal. He often ran into directors like Rajat Gupta in Davos, Switzerland, or on New York's Upper West Side. (Gupta was a neighbor of his. He had a pied-à-terre in the Century Building, next door to Blankfein's more palatial pad at 15 Central Park West.)

Whenever Blankfein encountered board members he would give them an update on the state of the world at Goldman Sachs. He saw it as his job as chief executive to keep his board abreast of developments at the firm. In his mind, it was good corporate governance 101. And it was all the more important in the fall of 2008, when the financial markets were so tempestuous that Goldman could be making money one day and losing it the next. In September alone, an unusually trying period, Blankfein spoke with his board as a group half a dozen times.

On October 23, 2008, about eight or nine weeks into Goldman's fourth quarter, Blankfein decided he needed to update Goldman's board of directors on the investment bank's financial performance.

Securities analysts were calling for Goldman to earn $2.76 a share, but Blankfein knew from the daily and weekly profit-and-loss reports he was privy to that Wall Street was way off the mark in its forecast for Goldman's earnings. The investment bank was actually going to lose money in the fourth quarter, something that had never happened since the firm went public in 1999. Blankfein had known about the losses for weeks, but they had finally risen to a level at which he felt he had no choice but to inform the board.

Just that day, in the morning's newspapers, there was a hint that things were going badly; the *Wall Street Journal* reported that Goldman was planning to lay off 10 percent of its workforce, or about 3,250 people. But in the wake of the Lehman collapse, the Goldman news was unremarkable; everyone knew 2008 was going to be an awful year for the securities industry, and even Goldman, the biggest money machine on Wall Street, was likely to be scathed.

Shortly before 9 a.m., Lissette Jorgensen called the various assistants of Goldman's twelve directors to schedule a board meeting at 4:15 p.m. that afternoon. Of Goldman's nine external board members, only one, Stephen Friedman, said he would definitely not be able to make the call. Ironically, Friedman was the firm's senior partner in 1994, the most perilous time in Goldman's history before the present. Of all the directors, he had the best sense of what Blankfein was facing.

As usual, Rajat Gupta had a packed day ahead that wasn't made any easier by the fact that he was crossing time zones. When Jorgensen called Gomes, his assistant, she said she expected her boss would be able to join the board call. He was flying in from Barcelona, Spain, on American Airlines Flight 151, which was set to land at JFK Airport at 1:45 p.m. His usual driver, Tahir, would pick him up and take him to his home in Westport, Connecticut. Before the Goldman meeting, Gupta had a couple of other calls to make—one to discuss an upcoming leaders conference in Dubai and another to prepare for a November board meeting. Though he had started his day in Europe, he planned to work a full US day. After the Goldman board meeting, there were a couple of other calls on his calendar.

On Friday, he and his wife were headed to Providence for the Brown University parents' day weekend, where they would visit their youngest daughter, Deepali, who was in her freshman year. The Guptas were friends of Brown's president, Dr. Ruth Simmons, who, as it happened, also sat on the Goldman board. Simmons invited the Guptas to be her personal guests at the keynote address that broadcaster Jane Pauley was set to deliver. After the speech, the Guptas were to join Simmons at her home for dinner.

At 4:16 p.m., Gomes dialed into the Goldman call and patched her boss in. Sitting in the boardroom on the thirtieth floor, Blankfein told directors that Goldman was going to post a loss in the fourth quarter—contrary to what analysts were expecting. Any trading revenue Goldman booked in the quarter was being offset by losses in its portfolio of assets. Blankfein's disclosure sparked a debate: after posting profits all these years, why was Goldman suddenly going to lose money? No director could point to anything more than the environment. At 4:49 p.m. the board call ended.

Twenty-three seconds later, Gupta's secretary telephoned Rajaratnam's direct work line and patched in the home office number of Gupta. The two were going through a rocky patch in their relations. Only a year and a half earlier, when Marshall Lux, a McKinsey partner, passed along a hello from Rajaratnam, Gupta gushed, "Raj is one of the most outstanding hedge fund managers and a very close friend." During his capital-raising trips to the Middle East earlier that year, Gupta spoke highly of Rajaratnam's investing prowess.

But by mid-October Gupta's concerns about Rajaratnam's handling of Voyager were growing. He confided in his protégé Kumar that the $10 million he invested in Voyager had evaporated after Lehman's collapse on September 15. Raj "dropped the ball," Gupta told Kumar. He felt Rajaratnam had a "moral and ethical responsibility" to make him whole because he was only a passive investor in Voyager and Rajaratnam was the one running the fund. He wanted Kumar to speak to Rajaratnam. Kumar was reluctant. Getting between the two titans in his life was not appealing. He didn't know the background of the Voyager investment and figured Gupta and Rajaratnam would find a way to talk through it.

Despite his unhappiness with Rajaratnam's handling of Voyager, Gupta kept his lines open to him. On October 5, just as he was about to fly out to Europe, Gupta lobbed a call to Rajaratnam on his cell phone. Again, upon his return, on October 10, he telephoned to see how Rajaratnam was doing.

"I know it must be an awful and busy week," said Gupta on a voice mail he left. "I hope you are holding up well. Uh, and I'll, uh, try to give you a call over the weekend to just catch up. Uh all the best to you, talk to you soon. Buh-bye."

After the Goldman board meeting on October 23, Gomes patched Gupta through to Rajaratnam's office line. While Rajaratnam's cell phone was being wiretapped during this period, neither his office nor home phones were. For twelve minutes and thirty seconds, from 4:50 p.m. to 5:03 p.m., the two were connected.

The next morning, as soon as the markets opened, Rajaratnam, who had purchased 150,000 shares of Goldman stock for his technology portfolio three days earlier, started dumping the stock. He sold 50,000 shares at 9:31 a.m. and another 100,000 shares in a little more than an hour. The sales saved Galleon $3.8 million in potential losses; over the next few weeks, as word filtered out that Goldman was going to lose money in the fourth quarter, the investment bank's stock slid to $52 from $108.58.

Later that same morning, Rajaratnam was catching up with David Lau, the new head of his Singapore office and an old friend from Wharton. Risky assets and currencies were plunging overseas on fears of a global economic slowdown. Lau called Rajaratnam to see what he was seeing in the US markets. In the middle of their conversation, Rajaratnam told Lau, "I heard yesterday from somebody who's on the Board of Goldman Sachs, that they are gonna lose $2 per share. The Street has them making $2.50...They have zero revenues because their trading revenues are offset by asset losses..."

Not one to miss an opportunity to make a quick buck, Rajaratnam said, "I don't think that's built into the Goldman Sachs stock price...I'm gonna whack it you know."

* * *

Soon after Lev Dassin became acting US attorney for the Southern District of New York, he put up a yellow Post-it note on his computer. On it were scribbled the words "Takedowns in Spring"—a pointed reminder that the criminal investigation into Galleon had been percolating for more than one and a half years. Arrests were imminent. As the US attorney, one of Dassin's jobs is to help decide when to bring cases. If a case is brought too early, prosecutors run the risk that they could miss chasing leads that would allow them to bring a far bigger action or uncover separate but related illegal activity. At the same time, when an investigation drags on for years, evidence grows stale and memories fade.

The financial meltdown in September 2008 and the shocking revelations two months later that respected securities industry executive Bernard Madoff was running a Ponzi scheme that went undetected for decades shone a harsh spotlight on the SEC. Then presidential candidate John McCain, reflecting the mood of the time, called for the firing of SEC chairman Christopher Cox. Morale at the agency plummeted. One former SEC lawyer was asked at his mother's birthday party, "How does it make you feel that your agency is absolutely incompetent?"

Pressure for a blockbuster case was mounting, and there was no case more obvious than Galleon. The SEC had already gotten authorization for a civil action to be filed, and yet some six months later, no complaint had been brought. During a meeting in April 2009 with lawyers from the SEC's Division of Enforcement, Mary L. Schapiro, who by then had replaced Cox at the agency's helm, was blunt about the stakes: "If we don't get serious about this process, we may cease to exist," she said.

Dassin, the new acting US attorney in Manhattan, was not the kind of man to be swayed by political pressure. But as the months wore on and the Bush administration prepared to hand over the reins of government to President Barack Obama and his team, Dassin needled his lieutenant Raymond Lohier about Galleon.

"Did I miss the takedowns?" Dassin would ask Lohier. It was his low-key but effective way of holding his lieutenant's feet to the fire.

As it happened, in December 2008, just around the time Dassin became acting US attorney in Manhattan, the court-authorized wiretaps on Rajaratnam's phone ended. They were in place for nine months and yielded mountains of direct evidence of Rajaratnam trading on inside information on a broad swath of stocks— Goldman, AMD, Akamai, and PeopleSoft, among others. There was ample material from which prosecutors could draw to build an airtight case against the Galleon hedge fund manager. But, more important, by wiretapping his cell phone, criminal authorities were now in a perfect position to bring cases against key members of his ring—Chiesi, Kumar, and Goel—and even widen the probe to ensnare others.

One of the most intriguing new suspects was Rajat Gupta, the former McKinsey managing director. The October 24 call between Rajaratnam and Lau confirmed Michaelson's early suspicions that Gupta was tipping Rajaratnam to inside information he gleaned from his positions on corporate boards. But Michaelson had learned from experience that a promising call didn't necessarily translate into a bulletproof case. What if Rajaratnam never traded on the information Gupta gave him or if the tip never came to pass? By keeping the wiretap active on Rajaratnam's cell phone for an extra month, Michaelson hoped to gather more material and perhaps find calls between Gupta and Rajaratnam that would give prosecutors the direct evidence to make a case against someone as prominent in business as Gupta. After all, the recordings had already helped prosecutors widen their net.

In the course of wiretapping the cell phone of Rajaratnam's former associate Ali Far, investigators stumbled upon calls between him and Rajaratnam. When he worked at Galleon, Far was nicknamed Rajaratnam's "butler" because he always did his boss's bidding. In early January 2009 in one wiretapped conversation with his former boss, Far divulged that Atheros Communications Inc. would surpass Wall Street's expectations and "do 98, 99 million" in quarterly revenue, a tidbit he gleaned from Ali Hariri, an Atheros executive.

Armed with intercepts of calls between Rajaratnam and Far, FBI agent B. J. Kang approached Far at his California home on April 1,

2009. The move very nearly blew the cover on the entire investigation—and not because of any fault of Kang's. Far didn't know it, but he was on investigators' radar early in the probe. In the summer of 2007, Apjit Walia, the RBC Capital Markets analyst and friend of Rajaratnam's who speculated about the AMD-ATI acquisition, told the SEC that he had met Far a year earlier at a dinner at a restaurant called Le Souk, which Rajaratnam and his brother Rengan also attended.

Soon after Agent Kang approached Far at his home, Far told his business partner Richard Choo-Beng Lee of the unexpected visit from the FBI. Since quitting Galleon, Far had started a hedge fund with Lee, a native of Malaysia, called Spherix Capital LLC, and the two were enjoying a decent year. Their fund was up 10 percent already. Upon discovering that Far told Lee of their overture to him, the criminal authorities had only one choice: they had to approach Lee in the event that he informed someone else and the entire investigation, which was covert, was exposed.

Not long after the visit to Far, Kang knocked on Lee's door in San Jose, California. When Lee answered, he refused to respond to Kang's questions, but soon after, Lee got himself a lawyer and the two traveled to New York to meet with Michaelson and Joshua Klein, a prosecutor in the Manhattan US attorney's office. Since joining the criminal authorities a year earlier, Michaelson had been busy, sifting through hundreds and hundreds of hours of wiretaps, deciding which offered the most promising material on which to build a criminal case against Rajaratnam. The probe was ripe enough that at any point a decision could be made to pull the trigger.

The showdown between Lee and the prosecutors was important. If prosecutors did not succeed in convincing Lee to cooperate, they risked the possibility of their investigation going public and jeopardizing all the hard work they had poured into it over the years. There was another complexity—a logistical one. As it happened, Lee was visiting the US attorney's office in Manhattan on the same day as his business partner, Far. Prosecutors had to make sure the two didn't run into each other; they didn't want to give them the opportunity to match up their stories.

On meeting the New York prosecutors, Jeffrey Bornstein, Lee's lawyer, didn't mince words. He wanted to know the evidence prosecutors had against his client. Klein and Michaelson played him recordings of some of the most incriminating calls featuring Lee. Without a cooperating witness offering context, tapes—even powerful ones like the recordings the government had involving Lee—can seem unimpressive. To a layperson listening—a potential juror, for instance—it would be hard to figure out what was going on.

At first, Bornstein, the lawyer from California, appeared unfazed.

"Are these even coming in?" he asked the New York prosecutors. It was unclear if Bornstein knew that the recordings had been obtained through court-authorized wiretaps—the prosecutors certainly didn't tell him the origin of the tapes—so it was difficult to tell if he was querying whether the wiretaps would be deemed admissible or he was simply asking if the prosecutors planned to use them.

"They're going to come in," Klein answered firmly.

Then he played more tapes; with each one, Bornstein grew more apprehensive. He was in a tricky spot. He had little information to go on but had to advise Lee, his client, on the most important decision he probably had faced in his life: should he sign up with the government or roll the dice and decide to fight?

"This is your one chance to cooperate," said Klein, the prosecutor, looking Lee squarely in the eyes. "If you don't cooperate, we will prosecute you, we will convict you and you will go to jail."

Klein's manner left no doubt that the New York prosecutors meant business. Within weeks, Lee agreed to cooperate with the government. He started making consensual recorded telephone calls to one of his former bosses, the granddaddy of the hedge fund world, SAC's Steven Cohen. On the pretext of seeking to get a job again at SAC, Lee telephoned Cohen a number of times. In the course of conversation, he rattled off about twenty stocks, many technology company shares, in which he could obtain confidential, nonpublic information. Cohen did not respond to Lee's overture; he remained silent. On one call, he suggested he and Lee meet. It was a tantalizing overture, but it would ultimately not lead to charges. By the summer of 2009, Wall Street was rife with rumors of an insider trading probe and the word was that Lee and Far were cooperating. All of a sudden, Cohen stopped taking Lee's calls.

At the time, though, by managing to "flip" both Far and Lee without the world knowing, prosecutors had forestalled having to take public their covert operation. Little did they know that the cover was coming off the government's probe. Shortly after they met with prosecutors in the US attorney's office in Manhattan, Far and Lee suddenly shut down their hedge fund. They had no choice. Once they were approached by the FBI, they would have had a fiduciary obligation to their investors to disclose that they were targets of criminal investigations if they kept managing money. To keep their cooperation with the government under wraps, the only option they had was to close down Spherix. Naturally, shuttering their fund triggered questions. Nobody throws in the towel on Wall Street when they are making money.

During the first week of October 2009, Rajaratnam and Kumar and their wives, Asha and Malvika, headed to Trinidad to attend the wedding of a woman who had once worked for both men. On their return, they stopped in Miami to chill out at Rajaratnam's luxury condominium in the Setai hotel, an oceanfront resort in the heart of South Beach.

On the afternoon of October 7, as the two were lounging in deck chairs, reading books and chatting, Rajaratnam got a call. He looked at his phone and then excused himself, walking down the beach to have a private conversation. When he returned, he seemed excited. He told Kumar that he had gotten a call from a Cisco Systems executive who said Cisco was buying a company called Starent.

Then Rajaratnam confided that something was bothering him. "You know Anil, I am really disappointed," he said. "There is another gentleman who used to work for me and I'm told is now wearing a wiretap. I have to be really careful...I can't believe he is betraying me." Rajaratnam said he suspected the former employee who was wearing a wire was someone called Ali Far. He suggested that Kumar buy prepaid phones to call him in the future so that no one could trace the calls.

Later that afternoon, when Kumar returned to his room, he flipped open his laptop and logged into his Charles Schwab account. Then he bought 300 shares of Starent stock at about $27.97 a share, or over $8,300. "I thought let me just buy a few shares of Starent to see if this thing ever happens."

It did. The following week, on October 13, Cisco unveiled an agreement to buy Starent Networks for $2.9 billion, or $35 a share. Kumar made a quick buck, netting a profit of a little more than $2,000 in six days.

CHAPTER THIRTY-TWO

Handcuffs for Breakfast

On Thursday, October 15, 2009, Raj Rajaratnam was sitting at his curved desk in his glass-walled corner office on the thirty-fourth floor of the IBM Building, basking in his own success. By 2009, Galleon Group, the hedge fund company he had built from scratch, managed about $6 billion in assets and employed nearly 130 investment professionals—among them analysts and portfolio managers. Rajaratnam had every reason to feel pleased; his sprawling investment empire now stretched from Menlo Park to Mumbai and he was pouring money into markets as far afield as Sri Lanka. He had only to look outside his office to feel satisfied. There sat rows and rows of traders and analysts, all jockeying to make money for him and, along the way, themselves. Whenever he had a hot tip, all he had to do was slide one of the glass panels and shout to the traders on the desk. Invariably, they jumped; they knew a tip from their boss was as good as gold.

It was hard to believe, but friends of his—icons like Art Samberg of Pequot Capital—were no longer in the investing game. They had been felled by regulatory probes or the recession. Somehow—most probably because of Rajaratnam's tenaciousness and drive—Galleon had survived. It had weathered the most brutal financial crisis since the Great Depression, coming out on top even as some of the brokerage firms it did business with, such as Lehman Brothers and Merrill Lynch, had failed or disappeared as independent, stand-alone firms. Of the three largest technology funds at the start of the decade, Rajaratnam's Galleon was the only one still in business. The other two, the Bowman Technology fund, run by former Fidelity manager Lawrence A. Bowman, and Andor Capital Management, spearheaded by former Goldman Sachs technology analyst Daniel Benton, had shuttered. Bowman was a casualty of the 2001 tech bust, and Benton had thrown in the towel in 2008, one of nearly fifteen hundred to close its doors amid the market meltdown.

Rajaratnam escaped by the skin of his teeth, even though his funds suffered blistering losses and large outflows too. Amid it all, he had never violated the one shibboleth held sacred in the hedge fund world: he was proud that he had not imposed "gates" on investors, prohibiting them from withdrawing their money from Galleon. "It is our investors' money and they have the right to do whatever they want with it even if it means withdrawing all the funds from Galleon and destroying our firm," Rajaratnam had told employees the previous year.

For stock investors like him, 2008 had been a roller-coaster ride, but in the end, he was happy he had hung on. By 2009, the markets had snapped back and his Galleon group of funds was on track to earn 20 percent in performance fees, the lucrative payments that had propelled him to the billionaires' club in the first place. Some big investors—so-called funds of funds—which allocate money to hedge funds, were close to pouring their money back in after pulling their cash in 2008. Galleon was on a list of about ten different funds that large asset allocators were considering funnelling cash to, Rajaratnam had learned. After a horrific 2008, it looked like 2009 was going to be just fine.

Rajaratnam was finally feeling relaxed and good about the world. He and his wife, Asha, were set to leave for London the next day for the premiere of *Today's Special*, an independent film he helped finance. It was a comedy about a New York chef and it had a cast of South Asian luminaries that featured Aasif Mandvi, a correspondent on Jon Stewart's *The Daily Show*, and cookbook writer Madhur Jaffrey.

Rajaratnam was excited about the trip. In the last few years, he had been forging into areas beyond investing. Filmmaking was one new passion. Another was philanthropy. He wanted to build a legacy that outlasted his investment empire. His efforts to help Sri Lankans rebuild destroyed homes and livelihoods after the tsunami in December 2004 had been noticed. When the Sri Lankan leader Chandrika Bandaranaike Kumaratunga spoke at the Asia Society in 2005, Rajaratnam posed a question.

"Is this *the* Raj Rajaratnam?" Kumaratunga asked when she heard his name. She then singled him out as someone who had been a special friend to Sri Lanka.

That Thursday afternoon in October, when an old associate stopped by to see him, Rajaratnam was upbeat. He was in the midst of hatching a grand plan to expand Galleon, making it one of the biggest hedge fund companies around.

"I am the last man standing," he told the visitor, gently stroking his belly as he reclined comfortably in his leather chair. "I want to raise $5 billion. I want to double in size over the next five years." He had no clue how much evidence the government had amassed on him during the financial meltdown of 2008.

* * *

On that very same October 15, in the wee hours of the morning, B. J. Kang, the FBI special agent working the Galleon case, was talking with a member of the Office of Customs and Border Protection. FBI agents like Kang stay in close touch with the border police because they are in a position to alert the FBI if the target of an arrest is preparing to flee. Kang learned something interesting. Rajaratnam had bought a plane ticket on Wednesday, October 14, to fly to London, Heathrow. He was set to leave two days later. Kang also found out that Rajaratnam had made a call to his daughter around 3 a.m. Thursday. The wiretaps were no longer in place, but in anticipation of imminent arrests, the FBI had sought authorization from the court some time back for what is known as "pen register data"—essentially a running ticker of calls in and out of a potential defendant's phone in an effort to keep tabs on his comings and goings. The pen register data had picked up Rajaratnam's call to his daughter. Its odd timing, coming in the dead of night, only raised alarms.

Originally, the arrests of Rajaratnam and his ring had been planned for the end of the month. Among law enforcement officers, the anticipated takedowns came to be known as the Halloween Day arrests. Typically the FBI likes to arrest people on Tuesdays, Wednesdays, and Thursdays. It tries to avoid Mondays because it is harder to rejigger plans over a weekend, and it also eschews Fridays because if bail issues aren't resolved, a defendant stands the risk of spending the weekend in jail.

Jonathan R. Streeter, a nine-year veteran of the US attorney's office in Manhattan, had been juggling the Galleon case all year along with a few others. When Streeter secured a guilty plea in May from Marc Dreier, a once prominent New York lawyer who bilked hedge funds and other investors out of $700 million, colleagues expected Streeter to parlay the victory into a lucrative private sector job—one that involved defending deep-pocketed white-collar criminals. He had actually stayed in public sector service longer than most. Few knew it, but he had an important legacy to protect. His uncle, Michael Armstrong, had been the chief of the securities fraud division at the US attorney's office in Manhattan between 1965 and 1967 and was the chief counsel to the Knapp Commission, created to investigate public allegations of corruption in the New York Police Department made by officer Frank Serpico. When Streeter was in eighth grade, he was reading *Serpico* for a book report, and he saw his uncle's name mentioned all over the last hundred pages. Inspired, he ultimately decided to become a lawyer.

Late in the morning of October 15, the boyish-looking Streeter was coming out of a job interview when he glanced at his BlackBerry. There was an email from the office informing him that the Galleon takedowns were set for the next day. All year, Streeter had been through several false alarms for arrests in the Galleon case, but there was no way of knowing if this was another fire drill or the real thing. He rushed back to the office. When he returned, his colleagues, Klein and Michaelson, were deep in discussions about the nitty-gritty:

Would the FBI arrest half a dozen people or many more? Would all the arrests take place simultaneously or be staggered? What was the office's position on bail? Streeter jumped into the fray; there were less than eighteen hours to go before the arrests and a ton of logistical details to finalize.

At 11:27 a.m., Sanjay Wadhwa at the SEC sent an email to David Rosenfeld, the SEC's associate regional director of the New York area. "Breaking News," Wadhwa wrote. "The FBI just learned that Raj may be leaving the country so there is a chance they may arrest Raj tomorrow morning with Goel and Kumar." He was referring to Rajiv Goel, the Intel executive, and Anil Kumar, the McKinsey partner, whom Wadhwa suspected were part of Rajaratnam's insider trading ring. A few minutes earlier, Wadhwa had gotten a call from FBI agent Kang briefing him on developments overnight. Lacking access to the wiretaps, Wadhwa and his team at the SEC had been building their case with old-fashioned circumstantial evidence. For months, they had been itching to bring a civil action against Rajaratnam and some of his moles. They had developed solid circumstantial insider trading cases against Rajaratnam and key members of his ring in a handful of stocks such as Google, Polycom, Intel, and Hilton. But the authorities at the US attorney's office in Manhattan were not ready to pull the trigger on a criminal complaint.

"Trust me, we are developing good evidence," Klein told Wadhwa. Knowing that the only two things the US attorney's office could not share with the SEC were Title III wiretaps and grand jury material, Wadhwa suspected it was the wiretaps that had been yielding important evidence for prosecutors. In less than twenty-four hours, he would learn for the first time exactly what some of that evidence was.

Under the plan finalized by the US attorney's office in Manhattan Thursday afternoon, three teams of FBI agents would fan out across Manhattan early Friday morning. One team would head to Sutton Place, where Rajaratnam lived, another to an address nearby where Chiesi lived; a third would head to the Time Warner Center, where Kumar lived. Two other teams were on standby to make additional arrests depending on the outcomes of the Chiesi takedown, and when the West Coast woke up, a sixth FBI arrest team would take Goel into custody.

The day before, the Manhattan US attorney's office filed two complaints under seal. One complaint named only Raj Rajaratnam, Rajiv Goel, and Anil Kumar, and in it there was a reference to a "CC-1," which stood for "coconspirator 1." In the other complaint, there was no reference to a CC-1. She was named as Danielle Chiesi along with two other defendants, Bob Moffat and Mark Kurland. These two new names were curious: Moffat was a longtime senior vice president at IBM; Kurland was the cofounder of a billion-dollar hedge fund. Prosecutors had drafted two complaints in the event that if Chiesi cooperated when FBI agents came to arrest her, the US attorney's office would unseal only one complaint, where she was referred to as "CC-1." It would hold off on the arrests of the IBM executive, Moffat, with whom Chiesi was having an affair and who was supplying her with inside tips, and Kurland, her longtime lover and boss, who traded on the tips she got from Moffat. Law enforcers knew Chiesi would have only a short window in which she could be helpful to the government.

Investigators wanted her to make a recorded call to one of the prominent executives she was heard talking with on the wiretap and to place calls to various hedge fund managers she knew whom investigators suspected were trading on inside information. It wouldn't be long after Rajaratnam's arrest before Chiesi became toxic. In the hedge fund community, where news travels fast, traders would soon figure out the identity of CC-1.

At about 6 a.m. on Friday, October 16, 2009, FBI agent Kathleen Queally, dressed in a business suit but armed with a gun, and four other agents went to 418 East Fifty-Ninth Street, a modern high-rise building overlooking the Queensboro Bridge. They approached the doorman and told him they were there to see Chiesi but asked him not to call up to her as he normally would to alert her to a visitor. One of the FBI agents stayed with the doorman to make sure he didn't phone Chiesi. When they arrived at her apartment on the thirty-fifth floor, Queally and another agent stationed themselves on either side of her door as Agent Diane Wehner knocked.

She rapped on the door several times, repeatedly announcing "FBI" and "Police," but there was no response, so she phoned the apartment, hoping to rouse Chiesi. She failed to stir her, and one of the other FBI agents phoned her colleague downstairs to get the doorman to call up.

When Chiesi first heard people outside her apartment yelling "FBI, FBI," she thought it was a joke. Halloween was just around the corner. Perhaps the early morning visitors were pranksters. When she finally realized it was the police, she opened the door. She looked like she had just rolled out of bed. Her blond hair, usually perfectly coiffed, was uncombed. Without makeup, she looked nothing like the seductress who made a living teasing inside information out of some of America's most powerful executives.

"Is my mom okay?" she asked when she saw the agents. "Is my family fine?"

The officers told her that they had a warrant for her arrest. She asked if they could speak in the hallway because her apartment was a mess. She was actually worried that there could be a joint lying around from a party the night before. The agents insisted on entering the apartment; they swept the rooms, checking to see that there were no weapons and that no one else was in it. All they found was Chiesi's pet cat, Amadea, and her fish. Meanwhile, Agents Queally and Wehner sat down with Chiesi in her den. They said they were there to discuss an insider trading matter and told her that she had a special opportunity to help herself. If she took them up on their offer and cooperated, she might not be arrested that day, though she would be taken into custody at some point. When Chiesi asked if she would be able to work in the business ever again, the agents told her that she would probably have to find something else to do.

At about the same time as Chiesi was approached, another FBI team headed to Rajaratnam's building in nearby Sutton Place, where he lived in a duplex with his wife and kids and his parents. Police blocked off a strip of the street; cruisers and unmarked sedans parked in front of his building. Following the same procedure, another team of FBI agents, led by Kang, went up to Rajaratnam's apartment unannounced and rang his doorbell. Rajaratnam was on his exercise bike looking out onto the East River and thinking about the number of shirts he would have to pack for his trip to London later that day. Unlike with Chiesi, there was no doubt that the FBI was going to arrest Rajaratnam, the man they considered the mastermind of the insider trading ring, that morning. With his wife and kids watching, the agents quickly searched the apartment and then whisked Rajaratnam out. They led him into a car waiting outside to take him to Twenty-Six Federal Plaza, where the FBI has its headquarters, for processing. A diabetic, Rajaratnam didn't get a chance to grab breakfast before leaving.

When they arrived in Lower Manhattan, Rajaratnam was fingerprinted and then handcuffed to a rail that runs along the wall in an interrogation room. Two FBI agents, one playing good cop and the other bad cop, pushed him to make a confession. Kang, the lead FBI agent on the case, started off playing him recordings of the evidence the government had amassed after wiretapping his phone for nine months. The message was clear: the government had Rajaratnam over a barrel. It had no interest in a deal. He was the big fish. The government was not going to let him get away so easily. However, Kang wanted Rajaratnam to make calls to some prominent hedge fund managers the FBI suspected of trafficking in inside information. He declined. When Kang brought up the name Gupta, Rajaratnam refused to offer up any information.

Meanwhile, a few blocks from Rajaratnam's apartment, Chiesi was sitting in the den with the FBI agents, toying with whether to cooperate or not. The agents then presented Chiesi with the evidence the government had developed against her. They told her that the feds had been wiretapping her phone and that her friend Raj Rajaratnam already had been arrested.

The FBI agents sitting in Chiesi's den asked her to write a telephone number on a piece of paper. It was the phone number of Hector Ruiz, the AMD chief executive. The agents wanted Chiesi to make a consensual recorded call to him: in the course of wiretapping Chiesi's phone, they had heard calls between Ruiz and her, but there was insufficient evidence to build a case against the AMD chief. At worst, Ruiz's behavior was reckless, but there was not enough to suggest that it was criminal. (Ruiz has not been charged with wrong-doing in the Galleon case, and there has been no evidence that he had a relationship with Chiesi.) Chiesi appeared reluctant to make the call, and in any event, it was too early in the morning to call Ruiz, who was out on the West Coast.

At about 7:30 a.m., the FBI agents, unimpressed with Chiesi's level of cooperation, told her they were putting her under arrest and taking her downtown for processing. They found a white sweater for her to wear; they told her she could not go in her hooded sweatshirt or wear sneakers with laces. As they were leaving, Chiesi confessed to Agent Wehner that she wasn't wearing a bra.

"Should I have one on?" she asked.

"Well your sweater's big enough and bulky enough, you probably don't need one," Chiesi remembers Wehner replying. Then, about an hour later, Wehner and the other agents headed down to Twenty-Six Federal Plaza with Chiesi.

She did not know it at the time, but the agents had set a 7:30 a.m. deadline for putting her under arrest. The FBI had two other arrest teams in place that were in a position to take Moffat and Kurland into custody if Chiesi was unwilling to cooperate. The agents gave the Moffat and Kurland teams the green light to move against the two men; by the time the Moffat squad arrived at his house, he was long gone—to work. He later surrendered.

After pulling an all-nighter at the SEC finalizing the civil complaints against Rajaratnam and his ring, Wadhwa got a call at about 7 a.m. from his colleague Jason Friedman. "They are charging this guy Mark Kurland," Friedman told Wadhwa, referring to the criminal complaint he had just seen. The SEC had been emailed a copy of the US attorney's complaint.

"Who the hell is Kurland?" asked an exhausted Wadhwa.

Without the wiretaps, the SEC had succeeded in building civil cases on their own against Rajaratnam, Chiesi, Goel, Kumar, and Moffat. But they had missed Kurland. Now they scrambled to get the authorization to file civil charges against him.

* * *

On that very same October morning, albeit an ocean away, Dominic Barton was in the honeymoon period of his inaugural three-year term as managing director of McKinsey. He was in Madrid meeting with clients but looking forward to his allotted once-a-month weekend reunion with his family. Before his election, Barton had headed McKinsey in Asia. But as the new managing director he now had to spend more time in London, the home to the company's worldwide headquarters. His wife remained at their residence in Shanghai while his two teenage children attended boarding school in Singapore.

McKinsey was a notoriously competitive environment, and Barton had personal experience with the company's "up or out" employment philosophy. The first time Barton was put up for partner—each consultant has three opportunities to be nominated—word came back from the global personnel committee that he didn't stand a chance. There were company-wide concerns about Barton's problem-solving skills and his tendency to tell clients about his moments of indecision. The second time he was turned down, a McKinsey higher-up called him and "he started quoting these Biblical verses to me." He finally made partner on his third and last try. "I'm sure there were splinters on my back going across the bar, because that was *close*...I said to myself then, 'My bar will be higher than McKinsey's.'"

Barton had just stepped into his car when his phone rang. He was alerted that one of McKinsey's senior partners, Anil Kumar, had collapsed at his New York pied-à-terre in the tony Time Warner Center and had been rushed to a hospital. Barton and Kumar weren't close, but they knew each other from their time working in Asia. He was startled to learn exactly why fifty-one-year-old Kumar had been rushed to the hospital. Kumar had fainted and hit his head on the marble floor inside his home just as federal agents came in to arrest him for selling McKinsey client secrets. Kumar's perp walk—the first time a McKinsey consultant had been arrested on the job—was at that moment split-screening on every Bloomberg terminal in the world alongside the arrest of the buyer of McKinsey's secrets, Raj Rajaratnam.

PART FOUR

Trials

CHAPTER THIRTY-THREE

"Why Is It So Quiet Around Here?"

On any other day, the trading floor at Galleon would be buzzing in the early morning, tense in anticipation of the 8:30 a.m. meeting. But on the morning of Friday, October 16, the trading floor at Galleon was eerily quiet, shrouded in a funereal silence, its mood taut, not so much in eager expectation as in deep dread. Portfolio manager Adam Smith sat in his office overlooking Fifty-Seventh Street, just a few doors down the hall from Rajaratnam's, trying to digest the news he had just learned when a colleague strode in.

"Why is it so quiet around here?" asked the colleague.

Smith shut his door and walked back to his desk.

"Haven't you heard?" he asked in a hushed tone. "Raj has been arrested."

"What? For terrorism?"

As outrageous as it sounded, the question wasn't a joke. Among Rajaratnam's close associates there was speculation about their boss's ties to the Liberation Tigers of Tamil Eelam (LTTE), or Tamil Tigers, as the insurgent group was known. In his early years at Galleon, Rajaratnam had fielded a fantasy football team called the Tamil Tigers, whose name he later changed to the Yankee Slayers. At the office, Rajaratnam liked to boast that he was close to Velupillai Prabhakaran, theTamil insurgent leader killed in battle, and in November 2002, he delivered a rousing appeal for Prabhakaran's cause at an event at the DoubleTree hotel in Somerset, New Jersey.

Nearly four years later, when the government filed a complaint in federal court in the Eastern District of New York and charged ten people with providing material support to the LTTE, Rajaratnam was referenced in the matter—not directly but as "individual B," a person who gave $2 million in donations to a US charity called the Tamil Rehabilitation Organization. TRO USA, the group to which Rajaratnam contributed money, was involved in raising funds for relief activities in early 2005 after the tsunami pummeled Sri Lanka. The group later came under scrutiny for its ties to the Tamil Tigers. Rajaratnam's lawyer Jim Walden told the *Wall Street Journal* that his client made charitable donations to "rebuild homes destroyed by the tsunami" and asserted that he was not involved with the Tamil Tigers. There is no suggestion in the complaint that Rajaratnam and other donors knew their money was being routed to the LTTE. Rajaratnam was never charged in connection with the terrorism probe, though several of the indicted defendants entered guilty pleas.

Galleon's Adam Smith disabused his colleague about the nature of Rajaratnam's arrest and told him of the insider trading charges. A little earlier, Rajaratnam's chauffeur, a stocky man with light brown hair, had telephoned with the grim news. For a long time, lawyers at the SEC had fixed their investigative lens on the chauffeur. While digging into the Galleon case, they discovered a number of calls made from Rajaratnam's phone to a phone registered in the chauffeur's name. At the same time, they noticed that calls were made from the driver's phone to many of the same numbers called from Rajaratnam's phone. After months of chasing what seemed like a promising lead, the SEC lawyers found that the phone registered to the chauffeur was in a limo, one Rajaratnam used while shuttling around town.

At 8:30 a.m., Galleon's portfolio managers and analysts gathered in the big conference room in the middle of the office for their daily ritual: the morning meeting. Richard Schutte, who became president of Galleon's domestic business sixteen days earlier, presided. Before heading into the meeting, he'd gotten wind from Galleon trader Ian Horowitz that Raj had been arrested, but Horowitz was sketchy on details.

Schutte ran the meeting as if it were any other morning, quizzing analysts on the companies they covered and getting a rundown of the day's market-moving news. No mention was made of Rajaratnam. He was often on the road so there was nothing unusual about his absence. In the middle of the meeting, Schutte was pulled out by a colleague who had received a call from Rajaratnam. He didn't return to the conference room.

Shortly after 10 a.m., stories started streaming across the newswires of Rajaratnam's arrest. At 10:18 a.m., David Faber went on CNBC with the news. Galleon employees looked away from their trading screens and turned to the 50-inch flat-screen TV hanging above the T-shaped trading desk. Instead of market-moving news, shots of their boss, Rajaratnam, in a blue jacket, green cardigan, and white shirt, being led away in handcuffs by two FBI agents, filled the screen.

Schutte returned to the trading floor and said lawyers would brief anxious employees in the coming days on the next steps. Then he met with a smaller group of portfolio managers, Leon Shaulov, Adam Smith, and others, to give them their marching orders.

"We need to liquidate the portfolios," Schutte said. Rajaratnam's arrest was sure to prompt nervous investors to pull cash out of Galleon. It was still early in the day, but already Galleon was being bombarded with phone calls. One investor who lived in Rajaratnam's building had actually telephoned the office early in the morning after seeing the Galleon chief being led out of the high-rise in handcuffs. There were other issues to consider. Rajaratnam was the "key" man at the hedge fund—the star trader who was so critical that investors had to be told if for whatever reason he was no longer calling the shots. If the surviving managers kept running money, they stood the risk of exposure to legal liability.

Every man in the room knew that Wall Street rivals would rush to exploit the news of Rajaratnam's arrest even as they feigned sympathy on the phone. Competitors would make a calculated bet that Galleon would have to dump stocks at fire-sale prices; then, as they did in 1998 when high-flying hedge fund Long-Term Capital Management got in trouble, they would hammer stocks they suspected

319

were in Galleon's portfolio, making money as the stocks tumbled amid Galleon's indiscriminate selling and creating a death spiral that fed upon itself. Galleon had not capsized amid the financial tsunami of 2008, but the arrest of its founder was sure to torpedo it.

As the portfolio managers scrambled to reduce the risk in their trading books, they got their own taste of Wall Street's gallows humor. It was the kind of adolescent ribbing they normally found funny. Not long after the arrests hit their Bloomberg screens, traders started emailing a song that had a chorus set to the 1934 Shirley Temple hit, "On the Good Ship Lollipop":

> *It's the good ship Galleon.*
> *When Wall Street has a rally on,*
> *When traders trade,*
> *Everyone in the place gets paid.*
> *Make money, money.*
> *Make money, money.*

The catchy ditty was uncannily on the money. It even touched on companies like Intel—"our first trade was 100,000 warrants of Intel"—that were now at the center of the government's allegations against Rajaratnam.

Not long after the perp walk footage hit airwaves, the Southern District's two criminal complaints (one against Rajaratnam, Kumar, and Goel; and the other against Chiesi, Moffat, and Kurland) were unsealed, and the SEC's civil action was filed. Though the SEC and the US attorney's office carry out parallel investigations, their complaints—civil by the SEC and criminal by the US attorney's office—are generally unveiled simultaneously.

Rajaratnam was charged with trading on inside information in a raft of stocks—Akamai, AMD, Clearwire (the company in which Intel Capital was invested), Google, and others. Two of his tippers were identified. They were Goel, the Intel Treasury executive; and Kumar, the McKinsey consultant.

But the complaint also referred to a CC-1, or coconspirator 1, and a CW, or cooperating witness, as providing information to and receiving information from Rajaratnam. It was not immediately obvious that CC-1 was Danielle Chiesi, named in the separate complaint.

The legal actions raised as many questions among Galleon employees as they answered. It was clear the government's case was built on recorded telephone calls made by the CW, the cooperating witness, also known as Tipper A in the SEC action. Though the complaints offered some details about the person—the individual had worked for Galleon in the late nineties, said the SEC filing—no one was exactly sure who it was. Paranoia set in.

As Galleon traders and analysts read the criminal complaint, they were shaken to see that it was filled with unedited excerpts of conversations between Rajaratnam and his alleged coconspirators. The feds said in the criminal filing that the government had intercepted calls on Rajaratnam's cell phone and the landlines and cell phone of CC-1. It also noted that the CW made consensual recorded calls for the government. With nerves fraying and everyone on edge, traders began to speculate that their friends were spying on them, recording conversations for the government.

"We would say, 'Is the person in the next room an informant?'" recalls a Galleon trader who was at the office that day. It was smart to be wary. The weekend after Rajaratnam's arrest, FBI agents began knocking on the doors of his associates to see if they could persuade them to cooperate. They visited Michael Cardillo, a Galleon portfolio manager, in the lobby of his building in November 2009. Not long after, in an effort to save his skin, Cardillo, who burst into tears when he heard of Rajaratnam's arrest, began to cooperate. In January 2010, just ten days before he was set to attend the wedding of Galleon analyst Michael Fisherman, Cardillo wore a wire and secretly recorded a conversation with Fisherman in an unsuccessful effort to get him to admit to trading on inside information. On another occasion, the FBI instructed Cardillo to lie to his friend Fisherman, who has not been charged.

At the time of the arrests, though, there were no moles in Galleon's New York office. The Galleon informant—the mysterious CW—was one thousand miles away. It was Roomy Khan, sitting in a house far smaller and shabbier-looking than the mansion she once owned in Atherton, California. During her two years cooperating with the FBI, she had not told her husband she was moonlighting for the feds. One day, not long after Rajaratnam's arrest, her husband was reading an article in a newspaper about the case, which mentioned the cooperating witness who helped crack it. He looked at his wife and declared, "This is you."

Amid the Friday morning frenzy, as Galleon's executives fielded calls from investors and dumped stocks, they noticed one Galleon employee on a singular mission. Raj's brother Rengan spent most of the morning running back and forth to Raj's office gathering up papers.

Shortly before noon, Adam Smith saw Rengan walk "dramatically" into his big brother's office and collect a bunch of notebooks. Even in his days at Needham, Raj Rajaratnam was a feverish note taker, capturing his conversations with companies like AMD and Atmel in great detail. Over the years, Smith himself saw Rajaratnam carry around notebooks with handwritten scrawls about stocks. They looked much the same as the notebooks he saw Rengan lift out of his brother's office that morning. In the afternoon, Rengan left carrying a big file, a Galleon employee noticed. Rajaratnam's lawyers would later argue that the papers Rengan retrieved were simply "documents reflecting Rajaratnam's charitable donations and real property holdings" for "assisting counsel" during Rajaratnam's first appearance in court and his bail hearing. The papers Rengan was seen taking have not been identified.

But the file grabbing stuck in Smith's mind. More than a year after Rajaratnam's arrest, Smith was confronted by criminal authorities after being caught receiving inside information on a wiretap. Smith did not know it, but at the time of Rajaratnam's arrest he was on the government's radar; he had been captured giving inside information to Rajaratnam during 2008 when the FBI was wiretapping Rajaratnam's phone. In the summer of 2010, the government obtained court authorization to wiretap a cell phone used by Smith, and on July 28, it picked him up receiving information from a source in Taiwan who said that Nvidia Corp.'s quarterly revenue would fall short of expectations. That same day, Smith sold 100,000 shares of Nvidia and, after the market closed, Nvidia, as Smith's source had told him, revised downward its revenue.

In December 2010, Smith told the criminal authorities of the file sweeping and a subsequent encounter he had with Rengan. Earlier that year, around springtime, Rengan telephoned Smith and asked to meet. The two were not close, so Rengan's overture was odd. When they got together at a Starbucks in Manhattan, the purpose of the meeting quickly became clear to Smith. Rengan wanted reassurance from Smith that he had not seen Rengan leaving Galleon's offices with Rajaratnam's notebooks on the day of his brother's arrest. Then Rengan sought to confirm that the reference during a May 2008 wiretapped call to someone with the same first name as Smith's Morgan Stanley source was not a reference to the banker who had tipped off Smith on the merger of two technology companies whose names started with the letter *I*. Rengan wanted to clarify that the person Smith had mentioned in the call was another person with a similar first name, an analyst who worked for a Wall Street brokerage firm and, unlike the Morgan Stanley banker, this person would not be considered a corporate insider. It was important because the wiretaps had picked up Smith referring to information that he received from his Morgan Stanley source. But if the source was an analyst rather than a banker, he could hardly be viewed as relaying inside information. It appeared that Rengan was trying to use the coincidence of names as a way to get Smith to cover Galleon's tracks if authorities ever asked him about some information he passed along from his Morgan Stanley source on a wiretapped call.

Before leaving, Rengan told Smith that Raj sent his regards and wanted Smith to know that he had nothing to worry about. Smith had always held the elder Rajaratnam in high esteem. During the morning meetings, like a teacher's pet, he made a point of sitting at the head of the table, near Rajaratnam. Like his boss, Smith took his own fastidious notes and learned to develop corporate insiders.

Naturally, he was more anxious than most in the wake of Rajaratnam's arrest. He kept a stack of small notepads in his office containing corporate information and his conversations with analysts. After he learned that Rajaratnam was in custody, he threw a full notebook in the trash. That evening when he left work, he brought home a personal laptop that he kept in the office. For years, colleagues had warned Smith that keeping a personal laptop at work was a recipe for disaster—a clear sign that he needed to keep some of his communications off the firm's servers. When he returned to his house in rural upstate New York, he threw away the laptop in the garbage. Sometime later, an IT worker at Galleon asked him for the laptop. Rather than confessing he had tossed it out, he said he'd lost it.

As quietly chaotic as life at the Galleon offices was, no one was in more distress than Raj Rajaratnam. When he was arrested, Rajaratnam was caught off guard with no emergency *if I'm ever arrested* plans in place. He didn't even have a criminal defense attorney to call. So he arranged for a call to be made to Dennis Friedman, cochair of Gibson, Dunn & Crutcher's mergers and acquisitions practice. Rajaratnam had worked with Friedman, who had advised on a number of technology deals over the years.

Friedman enlisted Jim Walden, the cochair of the firm's white-collar defense and investigations practice, to go to Twenty-Six Federal Plaza to represent Rajaratnam. By the time Walden arrived downtown around 9 a.m. Friday, a support group for Rajaratnam had already formed. His wife, Asha, naturally anxious, was there. So was his brother Rengan. Over the course of the day, others showed up: his lieutenant Rick Schutte; Galleon's chief operating officer, George Lau; his sister; Geoffrey Canada, the chief executive of the Harlem Children's Zone; and others. By the middle of the afternoon, when Rajaratnam was expected to be presented before a US magistrate judge and his bail terms set, there were more than twenty friends and family members milling around in Courtroom 5A, a small, low-ceilinged room on the fifth floor of the federal courthouse at 500 Pearl Street. US magistrate judge Douglas F. Eaton was presiding that afternoon.

Shortly after 3 p.m., amid loud sounds of metal clanging, a door in the wall of the courtroom opened. Two deputy US marshals emerged with Rajaratnam and Kumar in tow. Moments earlier, they had been released from the lockup cell just outside. They were held together in the minutes before their court appearance. It was the first time they'd seen each other since the week before when, returning from a wedding, they stopped off and relaxed at Rajaratnam's luxury condo in South Beach.

After recovering from that morning's fainting spell, Kumar looked devastated and was livid. It later emerged that he blamed Rajaratnam for getting him into the mess. Rajaratnam's wife admitted as much in a text she sent to Kumar's wife, Malvika, after the arrest. "I'm sorry," Asha wrote. Rajaratnam was also furious. He was angry at the way he had been treated by the FBI agents. When he was first arrested and brought downtown, he was not allowed to use the bathroom.

Neither Rajaratnam nor Kumar was handcuffed, but as they sat at the same defense table, flanked by their respective lawyers, there stood a deputy US marshal behind each of them in the event either had an urge to flee.

Jon Streeter, the assistant US attorney who was handling the bail proceedings for Kumar, kicked off for the government and divulged that it had already reached a bail package for Kumar—a $5 million personal recognizance bond signed by Kumar, his wife, and his son, Aman. The bond would be secured by his home, valued at $2.5 million, upon which there was only a $500,000 mortgage remaining. His passport was seized by agents upon his arrest.

"It would be a violation of your bail conditions if you were to attempt to acquire a new passport of any kind, or indeed, to buy a bus ticket, or a train ticket, or a plane ticket that would take you outside the forty-eight states. Just attempting to do that would subject you to re-arrest for violating your bail conditions," Judge Eaton warned Kumar before the defendant left the courtroom to do the paperwork.

Then Eaton turned to Rajaratnam.

"We have a grave concern in this case about flight risk," said Joshua Klein, the assistant US attorney for Manhattan who was handling the Rajaratnam bail proceedings. He recommended that bail be denied. Not only did Rajaratnam have the incentive to flee, Klein argued, but he had the means to escape. "This is someone who is a Sri

Lankan citizen, in addition to being a US citizen. He owns property in Sri Lanka. He holds a brokerage account in Sri Lanka. In effect, he's got a life in Sri Lanka that's waiting for him should he choose to flee."

Jim Walden, Rajaratnam's attorney, the first of several lawyers representing Rajaratnam, countered, painting a different picture of his client, a man who had been married to one woman all his life, who had given more than $20 million to charity over the last five years, and who cared for his two elderly parents, "aged eighty-one and seventy-seven, not in some far-away nursing home, but living under his roof...He is a respected member of this community. He is an intrinsic member of this community." Walden said that Geoffrey Canada, the Harlem Children's Zone head, looked him in the eye and said, "Mr. Walden, I don't have much, but what I have I can tell you I would bet on Mr. Rajaratnam coming back to court any day of the week."

In his arguments, Walden also took a swipe at the government case and resorted to the *they just don't get it* defense common among lawyers fighting insider trading charges. Prosecutors "misunderstand words like use your Rolodex, and be radio silent, and we need an edge, because they don't understand the business that Mr. Rajaratnam is legitimately employed in," Walden told the court.

Walden had proposed a $5 million bail package that would be secured by Rajaratnam's apartment. But Klein felt the bail was too low. Judge Eaton agreed with Klein. He set bail at $100 million and released Rajaratnam providing that he, his wife, and four others sign a personal recognizance bond, a promise that the defendant would return to court when required. He also limited Rajaratnam to traveling within a fifty-mile radius of New York City. Walden appealed to Judge Eaton to extend the mileage limit "a bit."

"Tell me why," said Judge Eaton.

"Mr. Rajaratnam's daughter is at Penn" and he would very much like to visit her, Walden explained.

"So if you could at least extend to the Philadelphia area," continued Walden.

"Yes, that's about a hundred and five miles. Yeah," Eaton agreed.

"We're grateful, Your Honor. Thank you," responded Walden.

Rajaratnam started his day looking forward to a trip to London to attend a movie premiere. He ended that same day trying to get permission to travel to Philadelphia.

The following week, Rajaratnam returned to the Galleon office a changed man. He hardly looked anyone in the eye, and instead of walking with the usual spring in his step, he trudged the corridors with shoulders slouched. Galleon employees were struck by his gait. Rajaratnam was not a trudger.

Speaking at the morning meeting, he was angry and defiant. He declared that he was innocent and his trades in stocks were rooted in the "mosaic" method, a style of investing that pieced together tiny bits of information to develop a larger investment thesis about a stock, and not on inside information. Oddly, he also spoke about the money he had given to Sri Lanka, prompting some to wonder if he believed the insider trading charges were linked to his financial support of the Tamil Rehabilitation Organization.

Back in the office, Rajaratnam also sought to take care of some important unfinished business. A week after his arrest, Rajaratnam brought a fax to Smith and said he hoped Smith could deal with it. The fax contained research notes from an analyst in Taiwan who generally transmitted his work, which at times contained confidential information, via fax rather than email so that there would be no electronic trail. Smith didn't know if this fax had inside information, but he understood his boss's instruction: he threw the fax in the trash.

Knowing that it would be impossible to resuscitate Galleon, Rajaratnam quickly reduced the firm's liabilities. He laid off employees and shifted the skeleton staff to a shabby building that housed its back-office operations. There, in a small, windowless room, he worked on building his defense. He talked to colleagues about digging up the tiny bits of "mosaic" that he was convinced supported his investment decisions. Sometimes his own colleagues found his efforts absurd. He tried to pin his last-minute purchases of Goldman stock on September 23, 2008, to optimism over the Troubled Asset Relief Program. He claimed to friends that he paid a consultant in

Washington, DC, who told him that day that TARP would fly. To the rest of the market, it was weeks later when TARP seemed like a viable proposition.

Meanwhile, with the bail hearings behind them, Jon Streeter, Joshua Klein, and the SEC lawyer who'd been working the investigation since 2006, Andrew Michaelson, poured their energies into building their legal cases. They got help from a committed new source, McKinsey.

Blindsided by the arrest of one of its most senior partners, McKinsey suspended Kumar indefinitely (he'd leave the company completely in one-and-a-half months) and immediately launched an internal investigation of Kumar's guilt. In November, less than a month after the arrests, McKinsey's lawyers at Cravath, Swaine & Moore went to the US attorney's office at One St. Andrew's Plaza to present their findings to Streeter, Klein, and Michaelson.

Though McKinsey was not charged in the complaint—only one of its senior employees was named—firms face the possibility of being criminally charged for the sins of their employees. The government considers several factors in weighing whether to charge a firm, including who at the company was aware of the wrongdoing and how pervasive it was. A decade before—in a case that McKinsey's lawyers were no doubt familiar with, given McKinsey's work for the same client, Enron—Arthur Andersen, Enron's auditor, was convicted of shredding documents related to the fallen energy giant. Though the Supreme Court later overturned the conviction, the damage was already done. Arthur Andersen went out of business. Since the Arthur Andersen case, savvy firms had learned that it was best to get on the good side of law enforcement early on, even though in McKinsey's case there was little risk of the firm being indicted. Invariably, whenever firms cooperated with the government, they wound up casting charged employees as "bad apples" among unsuspecting management. It was a tack McKinsey would take with prosecutors.

Armed with a thick binder of emails and other documents, the Cravath lawyers showed prosecutors what they had found. The revelations were startling. McKinsey's lawyers discovered that Manju Das—the name Michaelson had spotted a couple of years earlier on Galleon's investor list—was actually Kumar's housekeeper. Despite Kumar's assertions to Morgan Stanley that Das lived in India, McKinsey had evidence of the lie. McKinsey found Das's immigration card indicating she had come to the United States as the Kumars' housekeeper. Among the personal details listed on the card was that Das had buckteeth.

"You would think if she was getting $125,000 a quarter she would fix her buckteeth," joked one of the Cravath lawyers. For the first time since they'd started focusing on Kumar nearly two years before, prosecutors had a possible money trail from Kumar to Rajaratnam through Kumar's nanny. It was a great sledgehammer to hold over Kumar to flip him.

As careful as Kumar had been to conceal his scheme by sending emails from his Hotmail account, invariably some of the email responses landed in his McKinsey account. In other cases, Kumar had faxes instrumental in pulling off the subterfuge sent to McKinsey India.

With the McKinsey emails now in hand, prosecutors grew confident.

Anil Kumar, meanwhile, was growing increasingly nervous. When Kumar was first arrested he hired criminal defense attorney Charles Clayman to represent him. He actually had no need to worry about his legal bills. Rajaratnam offered him a joint defense, meaning that he would pick up Kumar's legal tab. When a friend asked Kumar why he didn't take up Rajaratnam on his offer, Kumar said cryptically, "You don't know what I know."

After getting advice from close friends, Kumar changed lawyers. He got himself the biggest gun in town, Robert Morvillo, the seventy-one-year-old dean of white-collar securities fraud defense. After he was released following his arrest, Rajaratnam had reached out to Morvillo to represent him, but at the time Morvillo had to decline. A partner at his firm, Larry Iason, had been retained already by Mark Kurland, the Bear Stearns executive turned hedge manager who was taken into custody that day. When Kurland got a new lawyer, Morvillo became available to represent Kumar.

Like a lot of criminal defense lawyers, Morvillo got his start at the US attorney's office in Manhattan under the legendary Robert Morgenthau. Under Morgenthau, Morvillo rose to head the securities fraud unit and later became chief of the Criminal Division. In 1973, Morvillo quit the government for the more profitable pastures of private practice. At a time when representing white-collar criminals was sneered at by white-shoe firms, Morvillo set about making a respectable and pioneering practice out of defending politicians and businessmen with legal woes—most prominent among them AIG chief Maurice Greenberg and Martha Stewart.

When Streeter learned that Kumar had hired Morvillo, he was dead certain Kumar was going to fight the charge. In his mind, nobody hired Bob Morvillo to flip. In mid-November, Morvillo, new to the case, came to his old stomping ground, the Manhattan US attorney's office, and met with Streeter, Klein, and Michaelson.

"I am playing catchup football here," Morvillo told the prosecutors. "You need to tell me what this is about."

Streeter and Klein laid out some of the evidence prosecutors had assembled—snippets of wiretaps and documents attesting to Manju Das being Kumar's housekeeper and an investor in Galleon. As powerful as the evidence was, it was not an open-and-shut case. The most important deal involving Kumar that investigators captured on the wiretap recordings was the Arab investment in AMD's semiconductor manufacturing facility. But the transaction was a difficult one on which to build a compelling case to present before a jury. Rajaratnam and Galleon had actually lost money playing the deal because AMD's stock dived in the fall 2008 stock market sell-off.

Morvillo believed he could fight the wiretaps. Without someone to piece it all together, a jury would have a hard time deciphering the recordings. And the money-losing tip on AMD wasn't exactly a brilliant example of insider trading. But the money trail—the offshore payments of cash and the evasion of taxes—would be harder to defend. The government would struggle to prove the payments to Kumar since all the individuals who could speak to the money trail were not likely to be available to testify. Many with knowledge of the arrangement lived in Switzerland. But there was still the huge risk that a jury would ask, If Kumar had nothing to hide, why was he getting paid in a Swiss account?

As he did with all clients, Morvillo and his second son, Greg, who was enlisted by his father to work on the case, explained to Kumar that if he wanted to cooperate and strike a deal with the government—promising to help with its case against Rajaratnam in the hope of future leniency—he would have to flip fully. Piecemeal measures of cooperation generally don't work with the US government and more often than not backfire. In Kumar's case, flipping fully would mean telling prosecutors about AMD's $5.4 billion acquisition of ATI Technologies in 2006, which produced a nearly $23 million windfall for Galleon and triggered Kumar's biggest payday ever from Rajaratnam.

Kumar was at a crossroads. He could be an asset to prosecutors: he had given Rajaratnam inside information two years before the court-ordered wiretap was placed on Rajaratnam's cell phone. Prosecutors suspected Rajaratnam had made money on AMD's acquisition of ATI using inside information, but they lacked the proof to charge him. Coming clean had a potential downside, though. He could face bigger financial penalties—he had not reported to the IRS the $1 million bonus he had received from Rajaratnam. But his disclosure could also save him from going to jail for a long time.

Kumar was not inclined to go through a protracted legal fight and face a trial. He was clever enough to know that if the case was litigated, he could be wiped out financially, and his reputation, already in shambles, would fray fast. He authorized Morvillo to open discussions about cooperating, and in early December 2009, Morvillo telephoned Klein to give him a short version of the story involving Manju Das.

Within a couple of weeks, Kumar himself was traipsing to the US attorney's office to tell prosecutors about his half-life of crime. It was a huge breakthrough for the prosecution, early on in the case. All of a sudden, the government had a credible, articulate insider who could walk members of a jury through the wiretaps and tell them about a tip—AMD's acquisition of ATI—on which Rajaratnam had made a boatload. In Kumar, they found an accomplice of

Rajaratnam's who could deconstruct the evidence and bring it to life in a courtroom.

The McKinsey consultant, they hoped, could also help them chase down promising leads. At the end of his first proffer session, the government lawyers, seeking to build a case against others caught on the wiretaps, asked Kumar about Rajat Gupta. "He would never be so stupid to do what I did," said Kumar, shaking his head as he spoke.

Getting Kumar's cooperation made it easier for the government to avoid calling Roomy Khan as a witness in any trial. Besides obfuscating about her Hilton source and getting a cell phone in the name of her gardener after she started assisting the government, prosecutors had recently learned that she and her husband, Sakhawat, had submitted a doctored work schedule in connection with a civil lawsuit that had been filed by their former nanny and housekeeper. If Rajaratnam took the government's case to trial, Khan's credibility could crumble amid a mountain of her own lies.

It took prosecutors only two in-person meetings with Kumar before they decided to sign him up as a cooperator. Unlike most cooperators, he told a cogent, linear story starting with Rajaratnam's overture to him in 2003 straight up to his own embrace of crime with his trading in Starent a week before his arrest. He did not play down or overembellish his criminal activities. He was the first cooperator in a case that until then had been greeted with great skepticism. And soon he would be regarded as the best cooperator. He was as effective a witness for the government as he was an informant for Rajaratnam.

CHAPTER THIRTY-FOUR

"He's a Bad Man"

Being Goldman's chief counsel came with its share of perks for Greg Palm. He had a spacious corner office with a panoramic view of New York Harbor and an eye to the Statue of Liberty. The job also had its tough moments. Earlier in the day on December 11, 2009, he had to break the news to Goldman's CEO, Lloyd Blankfein, that one of the firm's most revered board members—Rajat Gupta—was potentially going to be drawn into an ongoing insider trading investigation involving the Galleon hedge fund. After meeting with Blankfein, Palm briefed Goldman's president, Gary Cohn. Then he and Blankfein informed John Bryan, Goldman's outside presiding director and the former CEO of Sara Lee. Bryan was also the person on Goldman's board who knew Gupta the best.

Bryan had been a mentor to Gupta, helping him break into the upper echelons of the global business elite. It was Bryan who got Gupta on the board of trustees of the University of Chicago in 1995 and it was Bryan who introduced Gupta to the World Economic Forum in Davos, Switzerland. Bryan had been the US chairman of Davos three times during the 1990s and thought Gupta might benefit from the global exposure.

Palm told Bryan that the US attorney's office had evidence that might draw Gupta into the Galleon hedge fund scandal. Worse than that, Palm's source had reported that the inside information that

Gupta had trafficked in came from the Goldman board meeting in which the board had discussed whether or not to approve Warren Buffett's $5 billion investment in the firm. Bryan did not give the allegation a moment of serious thought. The Gupta he knew was a quiet individual, someone who was deeply steeped in the practice of confidentiality. Under no circumstance could Bryan imagine Gupta leaking information to Rajaratnam.

"It is unfortunate that they are going to try and link Rajat to this," he told Palm. As big a fish as Rajaratnam was, Gupta was an even bigger fish, the kind of global business celebrity prosecutors would be all too eager to catch in their net.

"Call Rajat and tell him," Bryan urged Palm. He suspected it was all a big misunderstanding that would get sorted out quickly. Palm was not so sure. Palm's gut told him that there was something there. His source and Goldman's outside lawyer Steve Peikin had pointed to a call being made from Gupta's McKinsey phone to Rajaratnam's line straight after a Goldman board meeting.

Palm caught up with Gupta as he was at the airport. Palm started off his call with Gupta on December 11, 2009, with two unusual disclosures—tip-offs that the conversation they were about to have would be uncomfortable and could potentially make Goldman and Gupta adversaries. Palm told Gupta that he had arranged to have a colleague on the line to listen in on their conversation. Typically, Palm liked to have one-on-one conversations, but he had decided that since the topic was very sensitive it was important that there be an extra set of ears and an extra pair of hands to record exactly what was said and to monitor Gupta's reaction.

If Gupta had still not registered that this call would be different from any other he had had with a Goldman official, Palm said something else that should have put him on notice.

"We are representing the corporation, and not you," Palm told him.

Palm wanted to make sure that there was no doubt in Gupta's mind that this was not a privileged conversation that would be protected by lawyer-client confidentiality. If the matter evolved into something much bigger, as Palm was expecting, the contents of his conversation with Gupta could be handed over to law enforcement officers investigating the matter.

"What can you tell me about Raj Rajaratnam, and have you ever provided him with information about what we do?" Palm asked, sticking to a script that he had worked out before the call.

Gupta was clearly taken aback by the question, not entirely sure what Palm was driving at.

"What are you talking about?" he asked.

Palm explained to Gupta that Goldman had come to learn that Gupta may have been in contact with Rajaratnam and provided him with information about the firm.

Gupta did not fly off the handle or turn evasive. He comported himself in exactly the way Palm and others at Goldman had grown accustomed to expect. Very calmly and cerebrally, he denied that he had ever provided Rajaratnam with confidential information about Goldman. Then he went on to explain why the charge was preposterous. He told Palm and the other Goldman lawyer who was listening in on the conversation that he and Rajaratnam at one time had been business partners on a venture called New Silk Route. But the two had had a falling-out and were no longer close. Their parting had stemmed from a soured investment that Gupta had entered into many years back.

Gupta said he had poured $10 million into an investment vehicle with Rajaratnam, who had invested more money in the entity. Rajaratnam, Gupta said he later learned, had taken his money out. Meanwhile, Gupta's $10 million investment had gone to zero. Gupta said he had hired accountants and lawyers and was planning to sue Rajaratnam but then the Galleon chief was arrested.

"Why would I help out someone with whom I had a dispute?" he asked rhetorically. Gupta said he took the issue seriously and was happy to discuss it more fully with Goldman but he had a flight to catch.

After the two hung up, Palm reviewed the call with his colleague. Gupta, they both agreed, sounded credible. During the fifteen-minute conversation, he had never wavered from his story that he had been swindled out of $10 million by Rajaratnam. Over the course of the day, Palm had more conversations with Gupta. In one, he recommended Gupta get his own lawyer. When Gupta asked if Palm had any suggestions, he offered a couple of names. Andy Levander, who turned out to be conflicted because he was representing another defendant in the Galleon case, and Gary Naftalis, a New York defense lawyer with an impressive résumé and a long history of representing clients in criminal cases.

* * *

Two weeks after the exchanges between Palm and Gupta, Sanjay Wadhwa was in his office on the sixteenth floor of Three World Financial Center tying up loose ends after a manic year. He still had a stack of calls to return, some of which had been received before the holidays. Near the top of the pile was a message to call Steve Peikin, Goldman Sachs's outside lawyer at Sullivan & Cromwell. The law firm had been busy lately, helping Goldman defend itself against a formal notice from the SEC that it was preparing to file civil fraud charges against the firm. The charges related to the bank's $1 billion Abacus deal that helped hedge fund manager John Paulson make a killing betting against mortgage securities.

On Christmas Day, Peikin finally managed to get away for a vacation in Patagonia with his family. Although he desperately needed a break, it wasn't working out that way. One day, as he stood on a glacier holding an ice axe, getting ready to climb a mountain, his BlackBerry rang. It was Palm, the Goldman lawyer. (After the episode, Peikin was always skeptical when anyone claimed to be unreachable because of poor cell phone reception.)

Unlike the Goldman lawyer Palm, Wadhwa and Friedman reached Peikin at a more convenient spot: his Patagonia hotel. Peikin said he needed to come in and talk to the SEC because his client, Goldman, had learned that there were wiretapped intercepts of conversations between Rajaratnam and his lieutenants suggesting that Rajaratnam had received information about Buffett's $5 billion investment in Goldman from a director. The news was a huge revelation to Wadhwa and Friedman. Unlike prosecutors at the Manhattan US attorney's office, the SEC lawyers were still operating in the dark without access to the wiretaps. Peikin said he had discussed the matter with the criminal authorities and told Wadhwa and Friedman that Goldman planned to conduct an inquiry of its own. But there was only so much Goldman could do. It did not have access to phone records or the subpoena power to get them. And it did not have a complete window into Galleon's trading in Goldman stock to ascertain if developments at its board meetings were followed up by trading by Galleon.

On January 4, 2010, Gary Naftalis, who by now had been retained by Gupta to represent him, headed to a meeting at Goldman Sachs with his partner Alan Friedman. The two were there to meet with Palm and Norm Feit, Goldman's head of litigation, as well as Goldman's outside lawyers from Sullivan & Cromwell, namely, Steve Peikin and Gandolfo V. "Vince" DiBlasi, a well-respected criminal defense attorney. At the meeting Naftalis insisted that Gupta was innocent and never gave Rajaratnam any information of any kind. It was ridiculous to think that Gupta would have tipped off Rajaratnam. Gupta believed the Galleon hedge fund manager had stolen $10 million from him. His story was consistent. Later on government investigators would learn of a conversation Goldman director Claes Dahlbäck had with Gupta not long after Rajaratnam was taken into custody. Dahlbäck was reading an article in a newspaper about Rajaratnam and looked up and asked Gupta, "Do you know him?"

"He's a bad man," Gupta replied.

After Naftalis laid out the reasons for his client's innocence, Palm, as an aside, obliquely raised an issue that was at the forefront of his mind. From the outset, Palm believed it was vital that if Gupta chose to stand for reelection to the board in the spring, the investment bank disclose to its shareholders that Gupta was being investigated in connection with the Galleon case.

"Our proxy is coming out in a few months," Palm told Naftalis. "Hopefully we can figure this stuff out [before then]." From time to time over the next several weeks, Palm continued to broach the issue about the proxy in conversations with Naftalis.

In February, Gupta himself sat down with Peikin, DiBlasi, and Adam Fee, another Sullivan & Cromwell lawyer, for an informal interview in the presence of his lawyers, Naftalis, Friedman, and Robin Wilcox. Gupta told the lawyers that he and Rajaratnam spoke all the time about investments, but he was steadfast in his assertion that he did not tip Rajaratnam to any news about Goldman. He fell back on the same argument he'd made to Palm on the very first phone call. Why would he tip off Rajaratnam when he believed the Galleon hedge fund manager had "stolen" money from him? Before the meeting adjourned, Peikin asked Gupta for the name of the lawyer he had contacted in connection with suing Rajaratnam. Peikin never received it.

By March 2010, there was still no resolution to the government's investigation into Gupta, and instead of dying down, it appeared to be heating up. The uncomfortable job of telling Gupta that Goldman was serious that the investigation be disclosed in the firm's proxy if Gupta stood for reelection fell to John Bryan, Goldman's lead director and Gupta's patron. If there was anyone who could persuade Gupta that it was not in his best interests to stand for reelection, it was Bryan.

On March 3, the day before Goldman's board meetings were to start, Bryan arranged to meet with Gupta at his hotel, the Four Seasons in New York. Normally if the two men were in the same city they tried to have dinner together. But Gupta had a previous engagement that evening, so he and Bryan met at 5 p.m. instead.

Bryan told Gupta of Goldman's intentions to disclose the investigation—if he stood for reelection. Gupta was upset. He was vehement about his innocence, and Goldman's proposed action only served to undermine it.

Gupta turned to Bryan and asked, "What would you do? My reputation is the most important thing I have."

"I wouldn't for a minute decide to stay on a board that is going to qualify my election," Bryan told Gupta. Gupta, in Bryan's view, could not afford to have the investigation come to light. Even if the claims were untrue, a whiff of alleged wrongdoing could smear Gupta's reputation and damage him irreparably. If Bryan was in Gupta's position, he would gracefully choose to bow out.

At first, Gupta was bothered by the suggestion. He had done nothing wrong, he told Bryan, and by choosing not to stand for reelection, he felt he would be acknowledging that he had crossed a line. For two hours, the two men talked. Gupta was adamant that he was the victim of Rajaratnam's chicanery. He was passionate about his innocence, and Bryan found him persuasive. Bryan believed nothing would come of the investigation, but Goldman's top lawyer, Palm, insisted it be disclosed. The fact remained that Gupta had to choose the lesser of two negatives. Then Bryan and Gupta worked out what they would say when the corporate governance and nominating committee of the Goldman board met in two days.

Shortly before 8 a.m. on Friday, March 5, Bryan, Gupta, and seven other members of the corporate governance committee filed into the investment bank's light-wood-paneled boardroom on the thirtieth floor of its 85 Broad Street headquarters building. Blankfein, as part of Goldman's management team, was not a member of the corporate governance committee, which comprises independent directors, but that morning Blankfein was present. Bryan, the panel's chairman, started by announcing that Gupta was not going to stand for reelection to the board and planned to retire, as he had thought of doing a year earlier when he was seeking to take up the KKR position. Gupta followed with a few words delivering the same message. "As some of you may have known, I thought of resigning my directorship before the financial crisis," he said. "The company wanted me to stay on as I did, but now is a good time for me to go." The news took the outside directors by surprise. Blankfein commended him for his four years of service and in an effort not to embarrass him in front of his peers offered no public reason for his unexpected resignation. After the meeting broke up, however, he and Palm privately briefed the remaining Goldman board members about the circumstances behind Gupta's move.

Several hours later, Blankfein's consigliere, John F. W. Rogers, was at the Delta shuttle, preparing to return home to Washington, DC (as he did every Friday), when he ran into Gupta. Rogers had worked closely with Gupta when he was joining the board in 2006 and enjoyed a good relationship with him. When Gupta saw Rogers, he assured him that the allegations were entirely untrue.

"I am the victim here," he told Rogers and then apologized for any inconvenience it caused Goldman. Gupta appeared frustrated. He didn't know what to do about the growing investigation, which was starting to spill over into his public life as a respected corporate statesman. Rogers was not the only one to notice the toll the brewing scandal was taking on Gupta.

The next day Gupta was the keynote speaker at an Investing in India event at Harvard Business School. Alok "Rodinhood" Kejriwal, a Mumbai-based digital entrepreneur, had high expectations for Gupta's HBS speech. But the only thing that impressed Kejriwal was Gupta's "killer" haircut. "In 2010 March, I saw a broken man on that dais," said Kejriwal. "He sounded defeated, he sounded tired...There was no strength, no authority in his voice."

Like most of the roughly two hundred attendees in the audience, Kejriwal had no way of knowing what was going on in Gupta's life at the time. The revelations that regulators were investigating him in connection with the Galleon hedge fund case had not yet surfaced publicly. All Kejriwal remembers thinking as he sat in the audience was, *What the hell is wrong with Rajat Gupta?*

"It seemed like he was a mannequin from Madame Tussauds."

In mid-April, as Gupta was preparing for the Procter & Gamble board meeting, the *Wall Street Journal* reported that prosecutors were examining whether he had shared confidential information about Goldman with Rajaratnam. The story left Gupta feeling helpless and frustrated. The only misstep he had made was to place an ill-timed phone call to Rajaratnam to inquire about his missing $10 million—and not to fill Rajaratnam in on confidential information from a Goldman board meeting. But that call now threatened to destroy him.

When his business partners pressed him about the accusation that had surfaced in the *Journal*, he brushed it off, saying, "It's nothing. It's nothing." Old friends from his days in India, his time in Europe, and his years in Chicago stuck by him, but Gupta noticed that his newer friends, the ones he had made since he moved to New

York, were distancing themselves from him. One day, soon after the *Journal* story, a shopper at a Costco near Westport noticed a visibly agitated Gupta speaking somewhat loudly into his cell phone.

"No one is even taking my calls anymore," he declared to the person on the other end. "At least you are taking my calls."

CHAPTER THIRTY-FIVE

The Gupta File

In early June 2010, Steve Peikin arrived at the New York offices of the SEC, armed with a thick binder, to make a presentation to Sanjay Wadhwa and two lieutenants. After leaving the US attorney's office, Peikin became Goldman's outside lawyer at Sullivan & Cromwell. He occupied an interesting position in the information flow in the case. Besides Goldman, he had another important client at the time: Hector Ruiz, the AMD chief executive, who was captured on wiretap recordings giving nonpublic information to Danielle Chiesi. She promised to keep the information confidential.

As part of an informal joint defense agreement, which provides for disclosure of information among lawyers in the pact, Peikin had learned through his representation of Ruiz that Gupta had been caught on a wiretap intercept. Each time the US attorney's office sought to "re-up" its wiretap—legal slang for getting a judge to allow the FBI to wiretap a defendant's phone for another month—the attorneys submitted a wiretap application that included the highlights from calls they had recorded. By December, these applications were in the hands of defense lawyers. Peikin called Palm after getting permission from his client Ruiz, among others, to share the materials with Goldman Sachs.

At the meeting with the SEC attorneys who were trying to piece together Rajat Gupta's role in the Galleon insider trader ring, Peikin laid out the facts about Gupta as Goldman knew them. He walked the SEC through Goldman's board meetings, and who was privy to what information and when. Most important, he enlightened the SEC lawyers on the wiretap intercepts. It was excerpts of these recordings that originally raised his antennae and triggered his call to Goldman's general counsel, Greg Palm. In one, Rajaratnam was boasting of hearing about Buffett's $5 billion investment from a Goldman director. In another Gupta was captured transmitting non-public information about discussions at a Goldman board meeting in St. Petersburg, Russia, to Rajaratnam.

The conversation between Gupta and Rajaratnam didn't rise to criminal behavior; however, it pointed to the free and easy flow of information between the two. Peikin's revelations were news to the SEC and confirmed Wadhwa's gut feeling that it was worth pouring resources into building a circumstantial insider trading case against Gupta. At the time, the agency was still struggling to get its hands on the fourteen thousand hours of recorded conversations in the Galleon case. Under the law, a civil body like the SEC is typically not allowed access to the wiretaps.

After Peikin left the SEC, Jason Friedman requested Gupta's phone records from McKinsey and subpoenaed phone companies. Trolling through Gupta's phone records reminded Friedman of his deep dive into Roomy Khan's call logs. Gupta had several phones—at least thirteen—and he used them all. As Friedman lined up the timeline of board meetings and the calls from Gupta to Rajaratnam, he was struck by a remarkable pattern. Time and time again, after the Goldman board met, there were calls from Gupta to Rajaratnam. The most obvious synchronicity was the call Gupta placed after the Buffett investment.

On August 2, 2010, the SEC sent a subpoena for documents to Gupta seeking information about his investments, any communication with Rajaratnam at certain relevant times, any transfers of money, and his Rolodex. Getting the Rolodex ultimately turned out to be far more complicated than the SEC lawyers had imagined. Before Gupta would relinquish his Rolodex, which included the numbers of famous figures including Bill Gates and Bill Clinton, his lawyers entered into a protracted back-and-forth over which numbers among his hundreds and hundreds of contacts would be protected.

A day after the SEC sent the document subpoena, Jason Friedman telephoned Gupta's defense attorney Gary Naftalis and told him that once the SEC lawyers reviewed the documents, he planned to seek testimony from Gupta. "Can you get us some dates that he is available?" Friedman asked. Not long after, he and John Henderson raised the issue with Naftalis's associate Robin Wilcox, the Kramer Levin lawyer charged with meeting the SEC's document request. They asked her if she knew Gupta's travel schedule. She said she didn't but told them she would check to see if anyone did.

In early November, after not receiving information on Gupta's availability, Friedman issued a subpoena for Gupta's testimony. It got the attention the SEC lawyers suspected it would. Wilcox immediately telephoned Henderson and asked, "Why did you issue a subpoena?"

Gupta, she asserted, wanted to testify. It was simply a matter of scheduling. The date that the SEC lawyers proposed, November 30, didn't work; Naftalis was tied up with an appearance for another case involving another big-name client, Muriel Siebert.

Then the SEC lawyers heard from Naftalis.

On Tuesday, November 16, the Kramer Levin lawyer traipsed to the SEC to meet with Friedman and Henderson. Naftalis said Gupta was willing to provide testimony to the SEC but "we don't want to be dragged into the Rajaratnam trial." Naftalis told the lawyers his chief concern was that if Gupta gave testimony to the SEC, it would be given to the US attorney's office, which would be required to share it with Rajaratnam's lawyers, who might seek to call Gupta as a defense witness in the upcoming trial. Why would anyone representing Rajat Gupta want that?

There was another issue too. With the testimony passing through so many hands, the risk of a leak was high. The first leak—the April 2010 story in the *Journal*—had dented Gupta's reputation, but he had survived it. After doing their due diligence, Procter & Gamble and AMR, the parent of American Airlines, ultimately decided to keep Gupta on their boards. They weren't likely to look so kindly on his presence there if there was a second leak—a newspaper reporting that Gupta was giving testimony at the SEC in connection with the Galleon case. Just a month before, *Fortune* magazine had run a devastating piece entitled "Rajat Gupta: Touched by Scandal," which had shone a harsh light on Gupta's board seats. Naftalis knew that the last thing corporate boards want is controversy over their directors.

Naftalis told the SEC lawyers that his client Gupta was "an honorable, good guy. He is not going anywhere. There are no offshore funds. There is no statute of limitations. You want to hear his story. We want you to hear his story. What is the harm in waiting?"

"Our investigation is ripe," countered Friedman. He said the SEC was happy to consider another day but it was not prepared to postpone Gupta's testimony indefinitely. The SEC lawyers' concern was that Gupta was still sitting on a number of boards. In its role as corporate watchdog, the SEC could not stand by if it had reason to believe that Gupta was breaching his duties as a director.

Naftalis asked the two lawyers if there was an "access order," meaning that if Gupta testified, his testimony would be shared with the Manhattan US attorney's office. The lawyers didn't answer. Then Naftalis said that if the SEC was not willing to hold off until after the Rajaratnam trial, he wanted assurances such as a protective order ensuring that Gupta's testimony did not go to anyone else—at least until after the Rajaratnam trial. The SEC lawyers were not amenable. Before leaving, Naftalis told them that if he hadn't been persuasive enough, then he wanted to speak to their superiors.

"Fine," said Friedman. Naftalis should know, though, that he and his colleague were acting with the backing of their bosses, Wadhwa and George Canellos, who had joined the SEC the summer before from the New York law firm Milbank, Tweed, Hadley & McCloy. Naftalis ultimately did not appeal to Canellos—he decided to reserve that option for later—and a date for testimony was set for December 22.

Three days before Christmas 2010, and nearly five months after Friedman first made the request, Gupta and his lawyers went to the SEC to give testimony. Predictably, Gupta invoked his Fifth Amendment privilege against self-incrimination and the deposition ended in forty-two minutes.

Wadhwa knew that if the SEC were to build its case against Gupta, it required witnesses who could testify to the fact that Gupta was in possession of nonpublic information such as the news of Goldman's fourth-quarter 2008 earnings and the Buffett investment in Goldman. One day late in the fall of 2010, George Canellos, director of the SEC's New York Regional Office; Wadhwa; and the staff attorneys on the Gupta case called Peikin with their Goldman wish list. Among the executives they wanted to interview were Byron Trott, the banker who crafted the Buffett investment; John F. W. Rogers, the secretary of the board, who could speak to the duties of board members; and most important, Lloyd Blankfein, Goldman's chief executive. Blankfein was key because he could tell them what had been communicated to Gupta before Buffett's investment of September 2008 and then a month later, during a Goldman board posting call, in which directors were updated on Goldman's financial results.

"The reason I am calling is that sooner would be better than later," said Canellos.

"Sure," replied Peikin.

The Goldman lawyer's biggest concern about any interview of Blankfein was rooted in optics. "If anybody gets a load of Lloyd Blankfein in the lobby of the SEC, Goldman is going to lose 10 percent of its market cap in an afternoon," Peikin told the SEC lawyers. He floated a number of proposals. Perhaps the SEC could come to Goldman to interview Blankfein? No way, said Wadhwa. He didn't spell it out, but the message was clear. The government does not travel to interview anybody. Then Peikin suggested that Blankfein could be whisked through security or, even better, avoid it altogether. Again, Wadhwa was adamant that there be no special privileges for Blankfein. He would be subject to the same security checks as any other visitor to the SEC. After toying with interviewing Blankfein late one evening, the SEC and Goldman ultimately agreed that he would answer questions on Friday, January 7, 2011, at 10:30 a.m.

* * *

Before the US attorney's case against Raj Rajaratnam could begin, Jon Streeter, the lead prosecutor, needed one major pretrial victory: he needed the wiretaps to be admissible in court. Soon after Rajaratnam's arrest, his lawyers gave prosecutors a hint of his battle plan. "The government's unprecedented use of electronic surveillance in this case" violated Rajaratnam's constitutional rights, wrote John Dowd, his new lawyer.

After Rajaratnam was rebuffed by Martha Stewart's former lawyer, the late Robert Morvillo, he spoke to Dowd, a feisty attorney at Akin Gump Strauss Hauer & Feld in Washington, DC. Dowd told Rajaratnam exactly what he wanted to hear: losing was not an option. He was hired quickly and went to work trying to neuter the government's case.

On May 7, 2010, Rajaratnam's lawyers filed a motion to suppress the recordings, arguing among other things that the statute does not authorize the use of wiretaps to investigate insider trading and that in seeking to establish probable cause the wiretap application made false statements and contained important omissions. The most notable: Roomy Khan's prior felony conviction. In addition, Rajaratnam's lawyers said the affidavit misstated or omitted material facts regarding "necessity," which requires prosecutors to show, before seeking a wiretap, that other investigative techniques had been tried and failed or were unlikely to work. Here Rajaratnam's lawyers pointed to the SEC inquiry for which Galleon had produced millions of pages of documents.

Most seasoned trial lawyers handicapping the fight between the United States of America and Raj Rajaratnam believed the case would be won or lost on the wiretaps. If the wiretaps were allowed in, the betting was the government would win. If they weren't, the defense had a shot.

On August 12, 2010, after listening to arguments from both sides, the judge presiding over the Rajaratnam case, Judge Richard J. Holwell, decided that he would accede to the defense's request and hold a hearing to help him rule on the matter. The proceeding, known as a Franks hearing—its name is derived from the case *Franks v. Delaware*—is held to determine if an affidavit to obtain a search warrant, or in this case a wiretap, relied on false statements.

For prosecutors like Streeter who were accustomed to putting on a case and having the burden of proof rest on their shoulders, the Franks hearing turned the tables. Unlike at trial, in a Franks hearing, the onus lay on the defense to prove that investigators did not pursue other techniques before filing for the wiretaps. One of the witnesses the defense planned to call was none other than Andrew Michaelson, the SEC lawyer who was lent to the US attorney's office to help build the case against Rajaratnam. It was unusual to have someone on a government trial team testify in a hearing before the trial. It put Michaelson in the awkward seat of a witness and Streeter in the even more uncomfortable position of preparing him. In the weeks before the hearing, the nervous Michaelson would needle Streeter, "When is my prep session?"

On October 4, federal judge Holwell began hearing testimony from four witnesses called by Rajaratnam's lawyers. Before President George W. Bush appointed Holwell to the bench, he was a litigation partner at the New York law firm White & Case and was known for defending securities fraud cases much like the one playing out in his courtroom. With his lean frame and tidy mustache, Judge Holwell looks like a colonial-era British military officer. He has an army-like efficiency about him; he listens intently to opposing lawyers' arguments but is careful to keep them brief and to the point.

The first witness was Lindi Beaudreault, the lawyer who represented Sedna and later Galleon in the proceedings before the SEC. Beaudreault told the court that Galleon and Rajaratnam complied with all the document requests and subpoenas the SEC served it between November 2003 and July 2007. In response to two subpoenas alone, on May 14 and June 8, 2007, Galleon and Rajaratnam produced 4.1 million documents that included among other items emails and instant messages. By putting Beaudreault on the stand, Dowd was trying to show the court that Galleon and Rajaratnam met the SEC's exhaustive investigative requests and in doing so, they obviated the need for wiretaps.

But Michaelson painted a different picture, showing that even though the SEC's efforts generated countless leads, they were not enough to crack the case. "We kept pushing trying to get these boulders to the top of the hill," he said. "We kept at it." Before the wiretaps went up in March 2008, Michaelson said that he had not even identified McKinsey's Anil Kumar as a source of inside information.

On October 7, the hearing ended.

As the SEC lawyers and federal prosecutors who'd been working the case for years nervously awaited Judge Holwell's ruling, the Manhattan US attorney took to trumpeting the virtues of wiretaps. Standing before some two hundred lawyers at the New York City Bar Association on October 20, Preet Bharara spoke for the government: "It does not take a rocket scientist to understand that it would be helpful to have the actual recording of the communication. Recordings are the absolute best evidence and so we will not shrink from using them."

In a veiled reference to the Rajaratnam case, Bharara said, "On October 4th, a well-known criminal defense lawyer was arguing to a judge in connection with one of our more well-known cases that a wiretap should be suppressed because the Government could not meet the burden of showing the necessity of the tap in an insider trading case." Some in the audience were struck by Bharara's oblique reference to the Rajaratnam case. It was unclear yet if the wiretaps would be allowed. Only a month later, on November 24, did Judge Holwell, after excoriating the government for its omissions, rule that the wiretaps were admissible at trial.

With the recordings in, Jon Streeter and his colleague Reed Brodsky began focusing on the evidence they would present in the US attorney's criminal case against Rajaratnam and his cohorts. A trial date had been set for March 8, 2011. Over the holidays and into the New Year, he and Brodsky sat in their drab offices, both with headphones on, listening to roughly four hundred calls that had been culled from more than a thousand. Their colleague Michaelson was intimately familiar with them because he had built the investigative case, but Streeter and Brodsky, who were to lead the government at trial, were tuning into the recordings for the first time. They were blown away by the Goldman calls. The most incriminating one was on October 24, 2008, just a day after Blankfein told Goldman's board that the bank was going to lose money in the fourth quarter.

"I heard yesterday from somebody who's on the board of Goldman Sachs, that they are gonna lose $2 per share," Rajaratnam told David Lau, a lieutenant in Singapore. The call was compelling to the prosecutors: it's rare for someone to lie and implicate himself in a crime.

When the Manhattan US attorney's office first indicted Rajaratnam on December 15, 2009, it formally charged the Galleon chief with trading on inside information in Polycom, Hilton Hotels, and Akamai Technologies, among other stocks. Galleon's profitable trading in the shares of Goldman was not part of the original indictment. Though it was on prosecutors' radar screens, evidence on other stocks was more compelling at the time. Not anymore.

Besides the powerful tapes, there was also compelling circumstantial evidence, much of it ginned up by the SEC, showing a pattern of Gupta hanging up from board of directors calls and telephoning Rajaratnam immediately. Convinced that Rajaratnam's trading in Goldman was central to the criminal case it would put on in the spring, Streeter decided it was essential for prosecutors to join the Blankfein interview orchestrated through Steve Peikin at the SEC in a few days.

* * *

When Streeter called Peikin at home, he got straight to the point with his old chief, who was now Goldman's lawyer at Sullivan & Cromwell.

"Don't freak out, there are going to be three AUSAs [assistant US attorneys] and one FBI agent" at the Blankfein interview. Streeter assured Peikin that they were not attending because "they were starfuckers." Blankfein was simply the best witness to testify about what he told Gupta about developments at the investment bank.

After he hung up with Peikin, Streeter telephoned Wadhwa and told him that prosecutors were planning to join the Blankfein interview the next morning.

"You had better tell Peikin," Wadhwa said. When Streeter said he already had, Wadhwa was livid. The Indian-born lawyer was not given to open flashes of temper, but Streeter could tell over the phone that he was steaming. The SEC had painstakingly built up the circumstantial case against Gupta, and now Streeter and the prosecutors from the Southern District had the nerve to gate-crash the biggest interview in the case without even asking him before doing so?

Neither Streeter nor Wadhwa mentioned it, but both knew that Bharara's press offensive had strained relations between attorneys at the SEC and the US attorney's office, making the SEC a little more sensitive than usual to something that would not have been out-of-the-ordinary behavior in normal circumstances. Prosecutors from the US attorney's office are always sitting in on interviews conducted by the SEC and vice versa.

"You need to do a little bit more than pay lip service to our role here," Wadhwa told Streeter.

The slight was unintentional, Streeter said. "I just go back a long way with Peikin," he told Wadhwa. He could tell Wadhwa was angry, though, so he didn't make any excuses. He just apologized again and again.

On January 7, 2011, Lloyd Blankfein, accompanied by a phalanx of lawyers, arrived at the SEC. After passing through security, he headed to a testimony room on the fourth floor, where he was met by more lawyers: Wadhwa and Friedman among others from the SEC; and Streeter, Brodsky, and Michaelson from the US attorney's office. B. J. Kang, the FBI agent on the case, was the designated note-taker. After walking Blankfein through the preliminaries, the SEC's Friedman got to the crux of the matter. What did Blankfein tell Goldman's board on the October 23 call?

"I would have told the board as of now Goldman is down 2 bucks a share," Blankfein said. Friedman asked the question again, in a different way, and Blankfein's answer was the same. Every way Friedman asked the question, Blankfein provided the same answer.

Friedman and Wadhwa felt they were on to something: Blankfein's words—"Goldman is down two bucks a share"—mimicked Rajaratnam's language on the wiretap.

On January 21, two weeks after Blankfein's interview, the US attorney's office unveiled a new indictment against Rajaratnam and cited seven additional stocks that were part of Rajaratnam's alleged conspiracy to commit securities fraud. One of the stocks was Goldman Sachs.

As prosecutors geared up for the Rajaratnam trial, Wadhwa—out of the office for a few days for the birth of his first son, Kiran—spent much of the time on his cell phone. Standing outside the hospital room where his wife, Judy, had just given birth, he discussed whether to pursue a civil case against Gupta with Canellos, the SEC's New York regional chief, and staff attorney Friedman. On January 28, the SEC sent Gupta's attorney Naftalis a so-called Wells notice, informing him of the SEC's imminent plans to charge Gupta. In most cases, where there is a parallel criminal investigation, the SEC does not "Wells" a potential defendant for fear of flight risk and tipping the person to theories civil and criminal authorities might use in a future case. But when George Canellos learned that his counterpart at the US attorney's office, Bharara, planned to give Gupta's lawyers an audience if prosecutors later pursued a criminal case, he decided that the SEC would give Gupta a chance to respond to the charges against him.

Upon receiving the Wells notice, Naftalis sought a meeting with Canellos. Naftalis knew Canellos when they were both on the same side, working as defense lawyers. Repeating the same arguments that he had made with Canellos's underlings, Naftalis questioned the motivation for his client Gupta to pass inside information to Rajaratnam.

"He has lived a life of probity," said Naftalis. "Why would he do this in the seventh decade of his life?" The phone calls the SEC lawyers were focused on had nothing to do with Gupta passing inside information to Rajaratnam. Rather, they had everything to do with Gupta tracking down his $10 million investment in a vehicle Rajaratnam managed.

At the full-day meeting attended by Wadhwa and the staff attorneys on the Gupta case, Canellos listened and then told Naftalis that based on the evidence, "the question of whether we are charging Rajat Gupta is not a close call...

"Gary, if we don't take a shot at this case, when would we ever take a shot?"

Naftalis, as it happened, was not the only one opposed to the SEC's move to file a civil action against Gupta. Prosecutors preparing to try the Rajaratnam case at the US attorney's office in Manhattan were livid too. Charging Gupta on the eve of the Rajaratnam trial, they feared, would make prosecutors vulnerable to accusations that they were tainting the jury pool. A civil action against Gupta would mean Rajaratnam was back in the news in a negative way again. It could anger Judge Holwell. The SEC maneuver would be seen as a government dirty trick, an attempt to smear Rajaratnam. But the SEC, smarting from missing out on the public relations bonanza from the Rajaratnam case and intent on fulfilling its role as corporate watchdog, would not back down.

"We're ready to go," asserted Wadhwa. In a concession to criminal authorities and to avoid compromising the Rajaratnam trial, the SEC agreed to file an administrative action against Gupta, which carries less onerous discovery requirements than a civil proceeding.

In late February, Gupta was in Bangalore with his New Silk Route partner Parag Saxena watching England and India face off in the World Cup cricket tournament when he learned that the SEC was planning to file charges against him. He couldn't believe it was actually coming to pass. His lawyers had just filed their response to the SEC's Wells notice—at around 10:45 p.m. on Friday, February 25. The agency would barely have had time to read their arguments. As thrilling as the cricket match was—the game ended in a dramatic tie—Gupta's mind was elsewhere.

On Tuesday, March 1, 2011, three months after Gupta had taken the Fifth Amendment at SEC headquarters and a week before the start of the Rajaratnam trial, the SEC filed its civil action against Rajat Gupta, alleging that he passed insider tips about Goldman (and Procter & Gamble) to the Galleon chief.

In New York, when Sanjay Wadhwa's father heard of the SEC move, he telephoned his son.

"Rajat Gupta. Really, Rajat Gupta?" he asked. "I hope you guys know what you are doing." Arjun Wadhwa was Sanjay's biggest cheerleader and was deeply protective of his son. Gupta was so prominent, a far bigger name in his mind than the other South Asians that the SEC had charged by now, that he wanted to make sure there was no risk that his son and the team he led was wrong in bringing charges.

Hours before the SEC's action, Gupta sent an email to business associates, friends, and partners.

"I am stunned and shocked by the proposed action," he wrote. "Let me assure you. I have done nothing wrong. The SEC's allegations are totally baseless. I am informed by my lawyers that the case is based on speculation and unreliable third hand hearsay."

Then he added: "Just to be clear: there are no tapes or any other direct evidence of my tipping Mr. Rajaratnam."

Within two weeks, that last line would come to haunt him.

CHAPTER THIRTY-SIX

Kumar Sings

"Greed and corruption—that's what this case is all about."

On the afternoon of Wednesday, March 9, 2011, as the sun peeked into a mahogany-paneled courtroom in Lower Manhattan, a boyish-looking brown-haired prosecutor stood before a jury of nine women and three men and with a few plainly spoken words kicked off the biggest insider trading case in more than a generation. Jonathan Streeter was still in college when Rudolph Giuliani, then the US attorney for the Southern District of New York, launched the first big criminal crackdown on Wall Street with a spree of high-profile arrests that dethroned some of the biggest kingmakers of the era. Their names had receded from the headlines by the time Streeter arrived at the US attorney's office at One St. Andrew's Plaza, but in the annals of financial history the glittering epitaphs of men like Ivan Boesky would be indelibly checkered by the financial crimes they committed. They were crimes that Streeter, the youngest son of a Cleveland lawyer, knew intimately well. Over the years as an assistant US attorney in Manhattan he had prosecuted a number of securities fraud cases, and now he was leading the government in the granddaddy of them all, the *United States of America v. Raj Rajaratnam*.

For weeks, there was growing anticipation about a trial, but few expected a live slugfest would actually take place. In legal circles, *US v. Raj Rajaratnam* was considered a non-triable case, a somewhat misleading phrase to a layperson. Far from suggesting a glaring weakness in the government's brief, it pointed to the opposite. The prevailing view among seasoned lawyers was that the evidence prosecutors assembled was so overwhelming that Rajaratnam would likely settle even if folding so late in the day would buy him little in the way of a reduced sentence. By the time the trial started, of the forty-seven coconspirators the government had charged, twenty-three had pleaded guilty, foremost among them Anil Kumar and Danielle Chiesi.

Kumar, the former McKinsey star and Rajaratnam's acquaintance from Wharton, was the first to cave. On the afternoon of Thursday, January 7, 2010, he pleaded guilty to conspiracy to commit securities fraud and securities fraud—crimes that carry a maximum prison sentence of twenty-five years. Though Kumar was seeing a psychiatrist and taking prescription drugs for anxiety and depression, he told then Manhattan federal judge Denny Chin that his mind was clear and he was prepared to waive indictment. After Kumar admitted to receiving $1.7 million from Rajaratnam in exchange for divulging confidential information and detailed his crimes—the winning scoop about AMD's acquisition of ATI—Judge Chin asked him:

"You had an understanding or agreement with Mr. Rajaratnam, is that true?"

"Yes," replied Kumar.

"To commit securities fraud?" asked the judge.

"Yes," answered Kumar.

"And you understand that he would be taking this confidential information that you were providing him with, and that he would trade in securities using that information, correct?" the judge continued.

"Yes, sir," replied Kumar.

"And you knew that he was intending to defraud people with whom he was making those trades," asked Judge Chin.

"Yes, Your Honor," he confirmed.

Over the years, Kumar had tried to delude himself into believing there was nothing wrong with the scheme he'd cooked up with Rajaratnam. But now he could not run away from it: the crime was staring him straight in the face.

A year after Kumar's plea and weeks before the Rajaratnam case was to be heard in open court, Chiesi, strapped for cash to fight the government, pleaded guilty too, stripping the case of its most colorful defendant. Even in the thick of the fight, Chiesi, a former teen beauty queen, could not resist playing court coquette. In November 2010, after a hearing on whether her Miranda rights were violated when she was arrested, Andrew Michaelson was waiting for the elevator when the doors opened. Inside were Chiesi, her lawyer Alan Kaufman, and her mother. Wanting to sidestep any awkwardness, the boyish and earnest-looking Michaelson waited. He planned to take the next elevator down when Chiesi and her mother sweetly beckoned: "Come in, we don't bite." Inside the elevator, Chiesi's mother needled him: "Stop doing such a good job," she said. "You are putting my daughter in jail."

Michaelson was not the only one to have a brush with the Chiesis. In the Upper West Side building where Streeter lived, it seemed like everyone knew before the trial that Streeter was the one putting away the sister of Alex Chiesi, a resident. Everyone but Streeter. One night during the trial, as Streeter was getting into the elevator, a drunken neighbor declared, "You're the guy who is prosecuting Alex Chiesi's sister." Streeter was stumped until the woman explained that Alex Chiesi was Danielle's brother. Streeter and Alex Chiesi had at one time literally lived next to each other, and Alex had even invited Streeter to his family's lakeside house in Connecticut, the same one that IBM executive Robert Moffat had been brought to by his sister. Streeter declined the invitation.

On the first day of *United States of America v. Raj Rajaratnam*, Streeter kicked off by describing how the defendant "knew tomorrow's business news today and traded on it." Yards from where Streeter stood sat Rajaratnam, flanked by six lawyers, at the center of the defense table. He was literally and figuratively a shadow of his former self. During his heyday as a hedge fund giant, Rajaratnam could be generously described as portly. Overweight, with a self-satisfied toothy grin, the Galleon Group manager seemed to epitomize all the excesses and arrogance of the hedge fund world in his very body. Now, almost a year and a half after his arrest, he looked astonishingly lean and cowed.

Rajaratnam stared impassively as Streeter recited a litany of charges against him.

It was the most controversial case the forty-three-year-old assistant US attorney had tried in his ten-year career as a public prosecutor. All his previous convictions—Anthony Cuti, the former Duane Reade executive; and Marc Dreier—seemed to be warm-up bouts on an impressive record as he approached the showdown with Rajaratnam's lawyers. A battery of nearly a dozen attorneys and paralegals outmanned the government in number and experience.

Leading the defense brigade was John Dowd, a folksy litigator approaching seventy, from Washington, DC. A former government prosecutor who made his name on mob-related cases, Dowd was known for having something of a Jekyll-and-Hyde personality. At times he seemed like everybody's favorite uncle, the kind of man who enjoyed regaling those around him with war stories—even the ones that left him scarred, like his unsuccessful bid in 1974 to convict Meyer Lansky, the Jewish organized crime bigwig. He liked to needle up-and-coming prosecutors, often teasing them about the black binders they used to display their court exhibits. The dark covers stood in stark contrast to the defense team's white binders signifying purity and goodness, Dowd liked to point out, much to Streeter's amusement.

More often than not, though, the balding and portly Dowd came across as cantankerous and curmudgeonly. Midway through the trial, Dowd would fire off an expletive-filled email to *Wall Street Journal* reporter Chad Bray, who wrote an article suggesting that the defense had been blindsided by the cross-examination of one of its witnesses. "This is the worst piece of whoring journalism I have read in a long time. How long are you going to suck Preet's teat? Preet is scared shitless he is going to lose this case so he feeds his whores at the WSJ."

As Streeter took the jury through the government's case, sitting in the back of the courtroom on a wooden bench usually reserved for the government and listening as intently as the defendant himself was Streeter's boss, and the man Dowd reserved his choicest language for: Preetinder Singh Bharara. Basking in the afterglow of the

Rajaratnam charges and the victory on the wiretaps, Bharara would soon come to be dubbed "the New Sheriff of Wall Street," even though the case playing out in front of him had been built well before he arrived at the Manhattan US attorney's office—a fact that his closest friends would rib him about from time to time. Ultimately, the public relations blitz would catapult Bharara onto the pages of mainstream magazines like the *New Yorker* and *Time*, which in 2012 would name him one of its "100 Most Influential People."

Ever since he started as a lawyer, Preet Bharara's dream job was to be the US attorney for the Southern District of New York. Over the years, as law school classmates pursued profitable careers in private practice, he made conscious choices to put himself in a position to get the job of running the second biggest US attorney's office outside Washington, DC. (The US attorney's office in Washington serves as both the local and federal prosecutor for the nation's capital.) In 2005, Bharara was picked from relative obscurity to be chief counsel to New York senator Charles Schumer. He stayed under the radar until 2006, when he led the Senate Judiciary Committee's investigation into whether the firings of eight US attorneys during the Bush administration were politically motivated. No charges were brought after the two-year investigation, and Bharara was credited for his evenhanded approach to the politically charged probe.

The Senate confirmed him for the Manhattan US attorney job in August 2009 after he was handpicked by President Obama. Even Bharara's daughter, who was too young to know precisely what being a US attorney means, sensed its importance. When she visited his new office, she noticed that it was "humongo."

At his swearing-in reception, on October 13, Bharara spoke of the varying influences on his approach to the law. "My mother is the kindest and most forgiving person I know...If she were a federal prosecutor, she would likely favor the deferred prosecution," in which a company or individual is granted amnesty in exchange for following certain steps. "I can see from your expressions that many of you are now wondering whether I take after my mother. Well, the answer is: sometimes. My father, on the other hand, is more of an upward departure kind of guy" (by which Bharara meant that if his father were a judge, he would exceed sentencing guidelines and dole out harsh punishments).

Almost a year into his new job, as he was juggling a full docket of high-profile cases, including some like the Rajaratnam case that had thrust him into the crosshairs of controversy, Bharara confessed to loftier aspirations. "There are only two jobs I could see wanting to have." Out one night with an old friend whom he has known for more than twenty years, Bharara said that he was "constitutionally barred from" one of the jobs. He was alluding to the fact that to be president of the United States a person has to be a natural-born citizen. Bharara was born in India and came to live in America when his parents immigrated to the United States some forty years ago. The other job that piqued his interest, he confided, was being one of the justices in the hallowed chambers of the Supreme Court of the United States. (Bharara, through a spokesperson, said he has no recollection of this.)

Before Bharara could even consider higher office, he needed a career-defining case, and in *US v. Rajaratnam*, he had a very good shot at one. The forty-four-year-old Bharara, who can come across as a Boy Scout, takes insider trading seriously. Some legal scholars contend that it is a victimless crime, often involving minuscule amounts of money. In the Galleon case, for instance, the government alleged that Rajaratnam pocketed as much as $75 million from his illegal trades. Compared to Rajaratnam's net worth of $1.3 billion at one time, the sum pales. What galled Bharara, whose father is a doctor and whose mother is a homemaker, was that the Rajaratnam case boiled down to people with lots of money trying to game the system. "Disturbingly, many of the people who are going to such lengths to obtain inside information for a trading advantage are already among the most advantaged, privileged and wealthy insiders in modern finance," he told a packed crowd at the New York City Bar Association in October 2010. "But for them material nonpublic information is akin to a performance-enhancing drug."

The South Asians who have been prosecuted by Bharara's office are by and large first-generation immigrants, born and bred outside the United States. Bharara, whose first name, Preetinder, is a Sikh name meaning "the one who loves God," is of a different generation. He was born in 1968 in Ferozepur, India, an ancient city not far from the Indo-Pakistani border, but came to the United States when he was a toddler. Mirroring a journey taken by hundreds of thousands of Indian immigrants, his father, Jagdish, a Sikh, and his mother, Desh, a Hindu, migrated to Eatontown, New Jersey, in 1970. When the Bhararas arrived in Eatontown, it had only about two dozen South Asian families.

Jagdish Bharara, a pediatrician with a medical degree from Amritsar Medical College in Punjab, quickly poured his energies into retraining as a doctor so he could practice medicine in the United States. He started a practice in Asbury Park, New Jersey, home to the blue-collar poet Bruce Springsteen, a lifelong idol of Preet's. On the side, the family and others owned an Indian restaurant for a short time, where Preet washed dishes and waited on tables. Weekend evenings were spent socializing with the small group of Indians in Eatontown or with Jagdish Bharara's classmates from Amritsar and their families. Like the Bhararas, they had come to America to stake out a new future.

Bharara's father was typical of the early wave of Indian immigrants. He pushed his children to excel. The Bharara boys were not expected to come home with anything less than a perfect score on tests. "My dad was more of a tiger dad—if there is such a thing," Bharara told NDTV, an Indian television station. Though money was tight, the Bhararas splurged on one luxury: a private school education at the Ranney School in Tinton Falls, New Jersey, for their oldest son, Preet, and his younger brother, Vinit, born not long after their arrival in America. Vinit went on to cofound an online retailer—its businesses include Diapers.com—which he and his partner would sell for $540 million to Amazon.

Preet shone at Ranney, making his mark in everything from ballroom dancing to art history. One time, for a difficult art history test in eighth grade, Bharara simply handed in an outline. He got an A-plus. "Mrs. Tomlinson held it up in class and said, 'Look what Preetie did,'" says Christine Gasiorowski, a classmate. "If it was anyone else, I would be really mad." But Bharara was so unassuming and low-key about his achievements that he was well liked despite having a reputation as something of a teacher's pet. Whenever he did well, he shrugged it off, telling friends, "Oh, I was just lucky." His modesty was endearing. More important, it sheathed a great ambition.

After graduating from Ranney as valedictorian, Bharara headed to Harvard College in the fall of 1986 to major in government, with a specialty in political theory. He was a nerd with a serious girlfriend at Wellesley College, with whom he spent almost every weekend. Bharara entered Harvard with sophomore standing, meaning he was eligible to graduate in three years because he did sufficiently well on the required number of AP tests in high school. His freshman roommate, Chip Clark, remembers being blown away by Bharara when the two took political science professor Joseph Nye's class together. "We decided to study together and we found a quiet place, and all he did was bring the syllabus," recalls Clark. "And he stared at the syllabus for forty-five minutes and he said, 'Okay, this is what the questions are going to be.'" Clark and Bharara were sitting next to each other when the exam questions were passed out, and Clark heard Bharara say under his breath, "You're welcome."

At Harvard, Bharara bonded with Viet Dinh, the conservative legal scholar and former assistant attorney general under George W. Bush, when they were both in the same sophomore tutorial. The two started arguing in class about whether the founding fathers considered man to be inherently good or evil. Their debate raged until 9 a.m. the next day. "I really think they considered themselves intellectual peers," says Clark. Socially and politically, though, they were different. Dinh wanted Bharara to join the Phoenix Club, one of eight exclusive all-male final clubs at Harvard. Bharara demurred. "I do think he just didn't think it was the right thing," says Clark. After Harvard, Bharara headed to Columbia Law School, where he got a law degree and found a wife in Legal Method class. The couple live in Westchester County today with their three kids.

As Bharara watched, Rajaratnam's lawyer, John Dowd, painted a very different picture of the case in his opening remarks. The "evidence will show that the government has it wrong. And the government has it wrong because it believed the word of unbelievable people." One of the "unbelievable people" Dowd clearly had in mind was Anil Kumar, the former McKinsey consultant. The contempt Dowd displayed toward Kumar came straight from his client Rajaratnam. Before the trial, Rajaratnam gloated to friends that the government's case would crumble under Kumar. "He's a wimp," declared Rajaratnam. "He will crack on the stand."

Kumar was the government's star witness, and on March 10, 2011, he took the witness stand wearing a charcoal suit, white shirt, and blue tie. He appeared to be nervous. He did not broach a smile or look at his onetime friend Rajaratnam. He simply bowed his head and put his hands together and composed himself. He was determined to excel as the state's witness just as he had in every undertaking since he was a schoolboy.

As Streeter led Kumar through a series of biographical questions that centered on his former professional life as a consultant at McKinsey, he grew more at ease. His face lit up when Streeter asked him to explain basic concepts. In defining the term "hedge fund," Kumar gave jurors a tutorial explaining that the name was derived from the fact that they hedge their risk and that virtually anything could be hedged today.

Even when the reality of his present situation intruded into his testimony, Kumar was articulate and forthright. Knowing that the defense would seek to paint Kumar as a liar who was testifying only because he had signed a cooperation agreement with the government in the hope of leniency at sentencing, Streeter asked him to tell the jury the consequences of lying on the witness stand.

"That would be a very big mess," said Kumar. "That would be like a huge crime—maybe perjury or something like that." For a moment, he sounded like he was back at the Doon School considering the punishment he would receive if he went "out of bounds."

Kumar's testimony against Rajaratnam proved devastating. He painted a clear and astonishingly detailed picture of his tipping Rajaratnam on the AMD-ATI deal, among others. His testimony about the payments he received for his moonlighting and the admonishments he got from Rajaratnam when his tips didn't pan out seemed credible. He provided color and context for the jury on several wire-tapped conversations that offered a rare window into the life of a hedge fund manager in the midst of a financial crisis. In one memorable wiretap, Rajaratnam asked Galleon portfolio manager Adam Smith how the market was treating him that day.

"Ahhh...like a baby treats a diaper," replied Smith.

Rajaratnam would never take the stand in his defense during the course of the two-month trial, but almost every day his cool, calm voice would emanate from the crackly wiretaps.

Though Kumar's testimony was convincing, his explanations for his own motives in deviating from a life of probity were less believable. By pleading guilty he had taken responsibility for his actions in the eyes of the government. But on the witness stand he seemed to blame Rajaratnam for leading him into a half-life of crime. And away from the scrutiny of the government lawyers, he appeared to act as if nothing extraordinary had happened. After receiving sanction from the court, he got back his passport and resumed his whizzing around the world. He was a regular passenger in the first-class cabin of the British Airways flight from Delhi to London. When he ran into old friends, he was as high-handed and arrogant as they remembered him.

The kindest explanation they could offer was that it was all an elaborate facade—a desperate bid to hide the emotional scar tissue beneath. Six months after his arrest, his mother, who was caring for his ill father, suddenly died. Kumar confided in friends that he was having a terrible time coping. She believed in him as only a mother could—unconditionally. He knew his father was too sick to appreciate what had happened to him, but his mother understood the gravity of his situation. Intelligent as he was, he had to wonder if she died because she could not bear the shame of it all.

The hardest person Kumar had to face was his own son. After his arrest, Aman asked his father, "Why?" He did not have to say more. His father knew exactly what he was asking. Why, with everything he had going for him, did he have to resort to selling corporate secrets?

"Someday I will have to explain to Aman," Kumar confided to an associate. "But for now I don't know."

On March 15, the third day of Kumar's testimony, assistant US attorney Jon Streeter dropped a bombshell. It was exactly two weeks after Gupta had sent hundreds of friends and business associates an email saying that there were no tapes showing him tipping Rajaratnam. Streeter introduced into evidence the wiretapped conversation between Gupta and Rajaratnam on July 29, 2008, more than a month after Goldman's board meeting in St. Petersburg, Russia.

In a way, the information Gupta transmitted about Goldman was the most innocuous part of the call. When Rajaratnam asked Gupta about a rumor he had heard about Goldman looking to buy a commercial bank, Gupta confirmed that there had been a big discussion at the board meeting about Goldman acquiring a bank or even an insurer and threw out a couple of names. It was hardly information on which Rajaratnam could place a trade. However, during their rambling conversation, Rajaratnam confessed that he had been paying Kumar, still employed at McKinsey, "a million dollars a year for doing literally nothing."

"I think you're being very generous...he should sometimes say thank you for that, you know?" replied Gupta.

For a while, the two kibitzed about their greedy pal Kumar and his aggressive push to get an equity stake in New Silk Route. Then Rajaratnam returned to the subject of his paying Kumar a million bucks a year for about four or five years. The money, Rajaratnam said, was "after taxes, offshore cash."

Gupta, the former three-time managing director of McKinsey, did not flinch. "Yeah. Yeah," he replied, seemingly unperturbed by Rajaratnam's disbursements to Kumar, which at the very least would have been inappropriate in Kumar's role as a full-time consultant for McKinsey and, though ambiguously worded, could have represented an evasion of US taxes.

Gupta's nonchalance was damning and the repercussions of the public release of the tape were swift and severe. A few days before it was unveiled, Gupta took a leave of absence from his own private equity fund, New Silk Route. Soon after it was played in court, McKinsey moved to cut all its ties with its former managing partner. By the end of March, Gupta also stepped down as an adviser to the

Bill and Melinda Gates Foundation, one of the last high-profile positions he still held. Unfortunately for Gupta, it was not the last time the jury would hear the tape.

When it came time to cross-examine Kumar, John Dowd could not hide his disdain. Like an aging heavyweight fighter, the lumbering Dowd threw punch after punch with remarkable effect. He walked Kumar through the embarrassing steps he took to craft an Indian identity for his housekeeper, Manju Das, who lived in California.

"You wrote here that it was going to be tricky to get the information Shireen was asking for, right?" Dowd hectored. "Tricky because Galleon and Morgan Stanley were requiring proof that Manju Das lived in India when she, in fact, lived in California with you. That's what you meant by tricky, right?"

"Correct, sir," Kumar conceded.

But he did not crumble. After he stepped down from the stand, Rajaratnam's friends sensed that the Galleon chief for the first time was contemplating defeat. He reviewed his assets to figure out the amount his family would need to survive if he was sent to jail and the sum he could reserve for fighting the costly legal battle. And he talked about taking the case to the Supreme Court.

On March 23, 2011, Goldman Sachs chief executive Lloyd Blankfein arrived at the federal courthouse to testify for the prosecution. Blankfein has a bald pate and elephantine ears, but based on the anticipation surrounding his appearance, he might as well have been a supermodel. US attorney Preet Bharara, who had been attending the trial regularly, was in the courtroom with four of his deputies. Andrew Ross Sorkin, the *New York Times* writer and author of the best-selling book *Too Big to Fail,* made a cameo. The only person unfazed by Blankfein's appearance seemed to be Judge Holwell, who, a couple of weeks earlier, when lawyers were picking a jury for the case, mispronounced Blankfein's name. He rhymed the second syllable with "bean" rather than "fine."

The task of drawing testimony from Blankfein fell to Andrew Michaelson, a moment in the sun for an attorney who had worked the case for both the SEC and the US attorney's office. Michaelson quickly laid the groundwork and then went to the wiretap of the July

29 conversation between Gupta and Rajaratnam. After playing an excerpt, he asked Blankfein, "Did Gupta violate his duties as a board member?"

Blankfein hesitated and then said, "My sense of it, yes." He didn't have to say any more.

Then Michaelson honed in on two events at Goldman, the $5 billion investment by Berkshire Hathaway on September 23, 2008, and a call a month later in which Blankfein disclosed that Goldman was losing money. Michaelson asked the Goldman chief the significance of both events. The October 23 call, Blankfein testified, was important because "we were losing money...We generally make money." The jury and spectators laughed.

Unlike with Kumar, when it came to cross-examining Blankfein, Dowd treated the Goldman chief with kid gloves. He was almost deferential. He asked if Blankfein knew if Rajaratnam traded on information about Goldman. Blankfein said he didn't. He also asked Blankfein about the Troubled Asset Relief Program (TARP) and whether Goldman received any money under the government plan. One of the defense's arguments was that Rajaratnam bought Goldman shares on September 23 because of growing signs that TARP would be enacted.

As he was leaving the courtroom after testifying, Blankfein walked over and extended his hand to Rajaratnam, his former client. The two spoke briefly before Blankfein walked away. Rajaratnam was beaming.

Over the course of five weeks, and before resting its case on Wednesday, April 6, the government would trot out eighteen witnesses, among them Adam Smith, a clean-cut Galleon portfolio manager who turned cooperator after being confronted with incriminating wiretapped conversations. In his testimony, Smith completed the story Kumar had started to tell, regaling the court with an insider's view of the corrupted culture at Galleon. The firm's practice, he told jurors, was "to do your homework but to still cheat on the test."

When making trades, Galleon portfolio managers liked to "have two torpedoes in the water," one for buying or selling shares on information that was in the public domain and lawful and the other for making trades on inside or unlawfully obtained information. His insights into Galleon would stand in sharp contrast to the one Galleon witness the defense called, Richard Schutte, a top executive at the hedge fund who came off as measured and mature, someone to be believed.

Taking the stand more than a week after Smith, Galleon president Schutte testified in excruciating detail to research reports showing that the hedge fund's winning trades were grounded in deep and rigorous investment analysis. He cast the research effort at Galleon as a disciplined process during which analysts routinely went on bus tours to visit with companies' management and wrote weekly reports, which were due every Friday at 5 p.m. Most important, he described Rajaratnam as a well-prepared investor who was on top of the companies in Galleon's portfolio. "He knew what questions to ask...It was impressive to watch," Schutte testified.

But Schutte's credibility was shattered on cross-examination. In questioning him, Brodsky elicited that Rajaratnam had invested $10 million in the fall of 2010 in a fledgling hedge fund Schutte had founded, called SpotTail, and that Rajaratnam's family had wired another $15 million only eight weeks before the trial started. With $25 million, the Rajaratnams were the largest single investor in SpotTail, which had less than $35 million in assets. Like most hedge fund managers, Schutte charged a 2 percent management fee and a 20 percent performance fee on assets managed, meaning that at the very least he would earn $500,000 a year if the Rajaratnams kept their money in. Schutte, who at first struck a marked contrast to Smith, the calculating cooperator, wound up looking much like him. He was stunned by the public smearing over SpotTail; in preparation for his testimony he had discussed it with Rajaratnam's lawyers and expected to be "questioned" about it on direct examination.

Compared to the prosecution, the defense case was surprisingly swift. Rajaratnam's team called only five witnesses.

Rajaratnam's most powerful witness was Geoffrey Canada, the chief executive of the Harlem Children's Zone, who took the stand for only ten minutes but transfixed the racially diverse jury. Canada testified that he had met Rajaratnam seven years before and the two "hit it off right away. His wish was that we could level the playing field for kids." Canada's personal recounting of his relationship with Rajaratnam appeared to engage the jury more fully than the tedious testimony of the defense's central witness, Gregg Jarrell, a University of Rochester professor and an expert witness for hire.

By the time he testified, Jarrell had been paid about $200,000 by the defense, and the firm that helped him with his analysis received $730,000 for work done through February 2011. Jarrell, whose role was to bolster the idea that Rajaratnam's market-beating investments were rooted in piecing together bits of a "mosaic," said he found after an exhaustive analysis that Rajaratnam's trading in the stocks at issue was "consistent" with widely available public information. To make his point, Jarrell relied on an impressive array of slides, but at times the message he delivered was lost in the blizzard of information. On Monday, April 18, a week after it started and five witnesses later, the defense rested its case.

A day earlier, on Sunday, April 17, Reed Brodsky was in the delivery room at Weill Cornell hospital waiting for his wife, a public school principal in the Bronx, to give birth and writing his summation. After she delivered a healthy baby daughter, his wife said to him, "What are you doing here? You are not really here." At 5 p.m. the prosecutor left the hospital and headed to the office. Four days later, he was standing in a packed courtroom, with his boss, Bharara, looking on, presenting the prosecution's closing arguments.

Brodsky accused Rajaratnam of wanting to "conquer the stock market at the expense of the law...In a world of uncertainty, he had certainty because he had insiders who knew tomorrow's news today." Then, using flip charts, Brodsky walked the jury through the cases of insider trading at issue in this trial. More than once, he said, "Let's go to the tapes," drawing on powerful excerpts from the wiretaps to support the prosecution's case.

Lacking scintillating wiretaps to buttress his client's arguments, Rajaratnam's defense lawyer, John Dowd, resorted to exaggeration. He called Anil Kumar "the greediest man," who "giggled" his way through his testimony. "He lied to make Raj look dirty," Dowd declared. He said Galleon portfolio manager Adam Smith's "story has changed so many times it's hard to keep it straight."

Then, referring to the provenance of the information that was at issue in the case, he delivered a simple maxim: "If it's public, you must acquit." What he was saying was that if it was information in the public realm that drove Rajaratnam's trading, then no crime had been committed. With that and an instruction from the judge, the case went to the jury.

* * *

On the morning of Wednesday, May 11, 2011, the jury in the *United States of America v. Raj Rajaratnam* trickled into a small anteroom at the back of Courtroom 17B, which fittingly overlooks the roof of the Metropolitan Correctional Center. On sunny days, inmates can be seen playing basketball on the MCC's roof.

That bright May morning, subway snafus had delayed a couple of jurors. As the others waited for the stragglers, the foreman asked for the day's lunch menu. Besides the in-house cafeteria, there are seven restaurants around the courthouse that are authorized to deliver lunches for sitting jurors. After the jurors pick a restaurant and put in their food orders, William Donald, Judge Holwell's courtroom deputy, heads downstairs to collect the food deliveries, which pass tight security: they are X-rayed. Over the past two weeks, ever since the jury had started its deliberations, word of the jury's lunch plans took on a form of legal Kremlinology. As long as the jury was ordering lunch, deliberations would likely drag into the afternoon.

At 10 a.m., the jury foreman handed back the menus. He told the court security officer they wouldn't be needing them. Twenty minutes later, the jury foreman sent a note to Judge Holwell. After eleven days of deliberations that were restarted midway because a sick juror had to be replaced, the jury of eight women and four men had reached a verdict. As the jury shuffled into the courtroom, weary after a two-month trial, five deputy US marshals took their place at the back. Judge Holwell asked the foreman if the jury had reached a unanimous verdict.

"Yes, we have, Your Honor," replied the foreman.

Then Judge Holwell asked his courtroom deputy, Donald, to read the verdict into the record.

As to count one, "Guilty," said Donald, reading from the verdict sheet. As to count two, "Guilty." He went on for twelve more counts. Each time, with deafening repetition, he sounded the same word: "Guilty."

Rajaratnam, seated at the defense table, was expressionless except for his eyes. They kept blinking over and over again.

CHAPTER THIRTY-SEVEN

An Unhappy Diwali

Manhattan US attorney Preet Bharara, soaking in the adulation from his office's victory in the Raj Rajaratnam case, urged his prosecutors not to waste any time in getting a grand jury to indict Rajat Gupta. "When are we charging Gupta?" he would ask them from time to time.

Compared to a fringe player like Rajaratnam, Rajat Gupta was the establishment. After the Rajaratnam trial, at which Gupta played a starring role as an unindicted coconspirator, the US attorney's office was bombarded with questions from the press about why Gupta had not been charged. In the wake of the 2008 market meltdown, no major Wall Street figure had been sent to jail, and Bharara was sensitive to the criticism that he had not taken on the architects of the worst financial crisis since the Great Depression. In an article in the June 27, 2011, issue of the *New Yorker*, George Packer wrote that when he asked Bharara about the lack of financial crisis prosecutions, "his even manner gave way to pent-up annoyance at 'ideologues.'" Then Bharara said, "It bothers me a little bit when people suggest, without knowing anything, that we're not even bothering to look." Getting a grand jury to indict Rajat Gupta would certainly not answer the critics looking for a big bank scalp. But by not charging Gupta, the Manhattan US attorney could open himself up to worse: critics clamoring that he wasn't doing his job.

With the Rajaratnam conviction nailed, everyone in the office expected Jon Streeter to exit for private practice, making Reed Brodsky the lead prosecutor on the Gupta case. Before bringing charges, Brodsky wanted to conduct a full-blown investigation. He asked Goldman and Procter & Gamble to make available all their board members so he could interview each and every one. At first, P&G asked if it would be sufficient for prosecutors to question just one director.

"No," said Brodsky, who has a reputation as a workaholic and a tireless digger. It was Brodsky who during the Rajaratnam trial discovered the well-timed investments by Rajaratnam and his family in the fledgling hedge fund started by Richard Schutte, Galleon's president and a key defense witness. On the Friday before Schutte was set to testify, Brodsky, over the grumbling of his colleagues, started rooting around in his background. He learned from Adam Smith, a cooperator, that Schutte had started a hedge fund called SpotTail. Smith didn't know a lot about SpotTail, but he gave Brodsky a presentation about the fund. On it was the name of the fund's outside auditor. Brodsky subpoenaed the auditor for information on the fund and its investors, and two days later, on a Sunday, he dispatched FBI agent Kang to pick up the documents from the auditor's home. By going the extra mile, Brodsky had succeeded in discrediting one of Rajaratnam's best defense witnesses.

In insider trading cases, besides showing that nonpublic information was passed, prosecutors have to prove two elements: the tipper violated his duties in disseminating the information, and the tipper received some benefit as a result. In the Gupta case, the benefit was nebulous. Even if Gupta had given Rajaratnam inside information, what had he received in exchange? There was no money trail linking the two as there was with Kumar and Rajaratnam. There was no clear tit for tat. Brodsky would have to use the business ties between Gupta and Rajaratnam to show that there were a variety of ways that Gupta benefited from his relationship with Rajaratnam. The most tangible way was through the role Gupta played at Galleon International.

After the Rajaratnam trial, Brodsky took two days off. By Monday, May 23, 2011, he and Michaelson were back to putting in eighty-hour workweeks to build the case against Gupta. To paint a clearer picture of the relationship between Gupta and Rajaratnam, Brodsky told Michaelson, "Let's talk to the secretaries." In July 2011, they met with Rajaratnam's executive assistant, Caryn Eisenberg, and asked her if she remembered anything about the afternoon of September 23, 2008, the day of the Buffett investment in Goldman.

"I remember it very clearly," she replied. Then she went on to tell a riveting story of the events on that fall afternoon. Brodsky and Michaelson were nonchalant as she spoke, but at that moment they knew they had their star witness in the Gupta case.

Some of the witnesses they wanted to interview were harder to pin down. Galleon marketing executive Ayad Alhadi was always on a plane and never at home. It took two FBI agents showing up at his home at 6:42 a.m. one day in early August before Alhadi would sit down with prosecutors. Alhadi turned out to be important for the government's case because he was one of the few Galleon executives who could testify to Gupta's work for Galleon International, telling of a marketing trip he took to the Middle East in late March 2008 during which Gupta joined meetings one day.

In the weeks leading up to their decision to charge Gupta, prosecutors redoubled their efforts. They focused on Kumar, the star witness in the Rajaratnam trial, who met with the government more than ten times, making seven visits from California to New York in connection with the Gupta case. Gupta had stayed in touch with Kumar even after his arrest, and at times when Kumar came to Manhattan and needed a place to stay, he would camp out at Gupta's place on Central Park West. Prosecutors felt that as Gupta's longtime protégé, he more than anyone could speak to his mentor's relationship with Rajaratnam and shed light on the dispute between the two men over the failed investment in Voyager. Through Kumar, prosecutors learned of meetings and calls in which the future of Galleon and Gupta's potential role in it were discussed. Kumar also had been approached by Gupta several times starting in mid-October 2008 about Gupta's money-losing investment in Voyager; the timing of the approach would be critical to the prosecution's trying to blunt the defense's arguments that by late September 2008 Gupta was in a dispute with Rajaratnam.

In late August, Brodsky and Jon Streeter met with Terence J. Lynam and Samidh Guha, two of Rajaratnam's lawyers. It was two months before their client was to be sentenced, and prosecutors were asking for a prison sentence of as many as twenty-four and a half years. Lynam and Guha urged the government not to ask for a long prison sentence for Rajaratnam, saying a lengthy jail term would almost certainly kill him. Rajaratnam had diabetes; there was a strong chance he would need a kidney transplant in the next couple of years.

At the meeting, Brodsky made an unusual off-the-cuff offer. "Why doesn't Raj cooperate now?" he asked. He didn't divulge the type of cooperation he was seeking, but he didn't have to spell it out. It was well known to everyone after the Rajaratnam conviction that one of the top priorities of the US attorney's office was charging Gupta. Among prosecutors, "cooperation" is a formal word with a specific meaning, and any cooperation with a convicted felon would have required the approval of Bharara in a high-profile case like this. As soon as Brodsky uttered the words, his colleague Streeter shot him a look. Brodsky, as he admitted to Rajaratnam's lawyers, did not have the authority to make the overture and it was unlikely to have any legs.

"We will take it back to our client," said Lynam. He and Guha had talked to Rajaratnam in the past about cooperation, but he was not interested. In any case, chances were slim that Bharara would be willing to consider leniency for someone like Rajaratnam, who had fought the government tooth and nail all the way.

* * *

On October 13, more than sixty people packed into a courtroom on the seventeenth floor of 500 Pearl Street to watch Judge Holwell pass sentence over one of the most colorful personalities of the hedge fund world. For the first time, Rajaratnam's wife was in the courtroom. Rajaratnam declined the opportunity to speak at his sentencing, but

Judge Holwell did. He made it clear that he thought the crime Rajaratnam was convicted of was endemic.

It reflects "a virus in our business culture that needs to be eradicated," said Judge Holwell. "Simply, justice requires a lengthy sentence." As Rajaratnam stood, the judge sentenced him to eleven years in prison, the longest sentence ever for an insider trading case. He was impassive, just as he had been during his two-month trial.

Less than a month earlier, on September 19, in a final appeal to sway the government not to charge Gupta, Naftalis had met with Bharara. He was accompanied by Bharara's first boss in the office, Mary Jo White, who was the former US attorney for the Southern District of New York when Bharara started there as a young prosecutor in 2000. Naftalis sounded the same legal high notes—Gupta's "life of probity"—that he had with Canellos at the SEC nine months earlier and in one-on-one conversations with Bharara's prosecutors over the summer.

It was vigorous legal advocacy, but it didn't sway Bharara and his lieutenants. There was one wiretapped call in which Gupta gave information freely to Rajaratnam, and there were countless other instances of circumstantial evidence—board meetings followed by calls to Rajaratnam. It was hard to argue there was no smoke.

White, whom all the lawyers in the room deeply respected, at least acknowledged the government's case. "For the sake of argument, even if what you say he did is true, it isn't criminal," she said. Besides showing benefit and breach of duty in an insider trading case, a prosecutor has to demonstrate that there is criminal intent. After meeting for about an hour, Naftalis, White, and an army of lawyers left.

Late on the afternoon of Tuesday, October 25, Naftalis got a call from Brodsky. The prosecutor confirmed what Naftalis had heard a little while earlier from a *New York Times* reporter. Gupta had been indicted and the government was planning to unseal the indictment the next day. "We are not looking to have a perp-walk kind of thing," Brodsky told Naftalis. But "you need to come in and have him surrender." If he didn't, Brodsky said, FBI agents would go out and arrest him. Brodsky didn't tell Naftalis that there had been some behind-the-scenes griping at the FBI about Gupta being allowed to turn himself in. Arresting high-profile defendants and parading them in handcuffs are among the few things FBI agents do that get public visibility.

When the Guptas learned of the indictment, they were stunned—and not just because the government was planning to charge Gupta criminally. His family had been aware for some time that there was a very real possibility that Gupta would be indicted. The only bright spot in a summer of bad news was on August 4 when the SEC dismissed its administrative proceeding against Gupta. The dismissal came in response to a civil lawsuit Gupta had filed in March after the SEC's action. In his suit, Gupta accused the SEC of denying him his right to a jury trial and treating him differently from the other defendants in the Rajaratnam case, who were all sued in federal court.

In July 2011, federal judge Jed S. Rakoff ruled that Gupta's suit could proceed and criticized the SEC for bringing an administrative action. Naftalis welcomed the news: "Mr. Gupta is very pleased that as a result of his lawsuit, the SEC has dismissed its administrative proceeding and he will no longer be singled out for disparate treatment." The victory was a hollow one, though, because the criminal probe was heating up. The SEC action was the least of Gupta's worries.

What really upset the Gupta family was that the government was planning to indict Gupta on the biggest Hindu religious holiday, Diwali, the festival of lights. It struck the Guptas as insensitive, especially coming from a US attorney who was Indian. Kanchan Gupta, Rajat's younger brother, was driving home from work when his brother called to tell him the news. He quickly went home and collected his wife, who was a doctor, just as he was, and headed to the Gupta homestead in Westport. When they arrived, the mood of his sister-in-law Anita and his nieces was very somber. The family already felt that the government had treated Gupta shoddily. Its latest move left them fuming. But Gupta was surprisingly calm. As telephone calls streamed into the house, he reassured the anxious callers. When Bharara later got wind that the Guptas and other Indians, including his own father, were upset that Gupta had been indicted on Diwali, he confessed that it was unintentional. He didn't know it was Diwali and Naftalis had not enlightened Brodsky. (Naftalis wasn't aware it was Diwali either.)

On Wednesday, October 26, 2011, Rajat Gupta left his home in Westport, Connecticut, at daybreak. He was accompanied by his wife, daughters, brother, and other members of his immediate family. Together the group made their way to his pied-à-terre on the twenty-second floor of the Century Building, which he'd bought in 2000 for $1.65 million. The understated art deco Century stands next to one of the most venerated addresses in New York: 15 Central Park West, home to hedge fund impresarios including Daniel Loeb and Wall Street titans Goldman chief executive Lloyd Blankfein and Citigroup's Sandy Weill. Shortly before 8 a.m., Gupta hugged and kissed his family good-bye. Expecting his appearance in court would trigger a media circus, he asked his loved ones to remain in the apartment. All his life, from the time he was a young boy, he put his family first; he wasn't going to change that even in his darkest hour.

Then, impeccably dressed in a blue suit and salmon-colored Hermès tie, he walked out of the bank-vault-like doors of the Century, jumped into a car with his lawyers, and headed downtown to surrender to the FBI.

CHAPTER THIRTY-EIGHT

Et Tu, Kumar?

Amid a heavy downpour of summer rain, Rajat Kumar Gupta arrived at the federal courthouse at 500 Pearl Street on the morning of Monday, May 21, 2012. As soon as he stepped out of his black sedan, carrying a big dark umbrella, it was clear that the ordeal that had begun with a call from Goldman's general counsel two years earlier had sapped him. In the months leading up to the trial, he had been exercising and doing yoga. He had lost ten pounds and had to buy new clothes, but they didn't hide the strain. For the first time in his life, he appeared old. At one time, he had an inspiring look of quiet confidence, a steady calm that reassured. In its place now was a deep weariness. The only thing that seemed to sustain him was a stoic determination to clear his name.

Seven months earlier, he had been arraigned in this courthouse on one count of conspiracy to commit securities fraud and five counts of securities fraud. The charges related to his tipping Rajaratnam about material, nonpublic information in two stocks, Goldman and Procter & Gamble. Since then, well-meaning friends would suggest he plead guilty to the charges—fighting the US government was costly and it ran the risk of a longer prison term if he was convicted. But Gupta would not think of it. He passionately believed in his innocence and was quietly optimistic that he would prevail in court. From the beginning, his lawyer Naftalis had said that he had never seen a case with such a paucity of evidence. Now, after enduring a very public two-year government investigation, he welcomed the opportunity to defend himself.

Since the government had first charged Gupta in October 2011, it had expanded its case. In February 2012, it unveiled a new indictment contending that in March 2007 Gupta called into a Goldman audit committee meeting from Galleon's offices. During the call, the members of the panel previewed Goldman's first-quarter earnings, set to be released the next day. About twenty-five minutes after Gupta hung up the phone, Galleon bought approximately $70 million of Goldman stock.

The new indictment appeared to strike at the heart of Gupta's defense. Gupta's lawyers had been arguing that by the time the government's allegations of insider trading activity occurred in the fall of 2008, their client was in a dispute with Rajaratnam over Gupta's $10 million loss. But in March 2007, Gupta felt comfortable using a Galleon phone to call in to hear confidential reports from Goldman Sachs. It would appear that the two men were still amicable business partners.

In a way, the new charges didn't matter. When the tape of Gupta's conversation with Rajaratnam about discussions at a Goldman board meeting had been aired at the Rajaratnam trial a year earlier, McKinsey and its partners turned on him. Old friends whom he had entertained in his own home and whose children he had helped stopped taking his calls.

One of many stinging betrayals came from Adil Zainulbhai, the chairman of McKinsey India, whom Gupta had personally mentored when they were both in Chicago. Gupta recommended each of Zainulbhai's children for the University of Chicago, whose board he was on, and he later helped guide them in their search for jobs. But when the Gupta-Rajaratnam tape surfaced, Zainulbhai went into overdrive with his clients, telephoning and sending emails saying that Gupta no longer had any ties to the firm and had not been an active partner for years. McKinsey also quickly moved to sever its links with its three-time managing director. After a meeting lasting no more than an hour with his successor and friend Ian Davis, Gupta learned that McKinsey was moving to take away all his benefits—right down to his secretary and his phones. He was even removed from the McKinsey alumni directory. Gupta was devastated. He told friends that he could not believe an unblemished thirty-year career was wiped out in a short meeting.

"During these times, you get to know your real friends," he wrote in an email. What he didn't appreciate was that his former colleagues felt equally betrayed. As bad as his actions were, what was more disappointing was that he showed no contrition.

Even among the Indian community, where there seemed to be greater sympathy for Gupta than outside it, some leading lights distanced themselves. Earlier in the year, when friends of Gupta's started a campaign to solicit signatories for a website supporting him, Vinod Khosla, the renowned venture capitalist and fellow IIT alumnus, asked the organizers of the website not to use his name. He was upset that Gupta's actions had sullied the reputation of the Indian diaspora in America.

Aside from these professional humiliations, there were legal setbacks. On May 16, Jed S. Rakoff, the federal judge presiding over the case, said he intended to allow the jury to hear three potentially incriminating wiretapped recordings between Rajaratnam and his lieutenants. Gupta's lawyers had argued that these conversations should be deemed inadmissible, hearsay evidence. But Judge Rakoff subscribed to the government's argument that the wiretaps were allowable because they reflected conversations of a coconspirator in furtherance of an insider trading scheme. The ruling would turn out to be a blow for Gupta.

As he approached the biggest test in his adult life, Gupta seemed calm and unflappable. "Today is Friday, May 18th, and my trial starts on Monday, May 21st. As I sit here in my office reflecting on the last year, I am filled with emotions. The overwhelming one is God is putting me through a test, and my duty is to do the very best I can and be prepared to accept whatever outcomes. I know I have done nothing wrong and expect to be fully vindicated."

In the same federal courthouse that has seen its share of high-profile cases against boldface names—Martha Stewart and the two

Bernies, Madoff and Ebbers—the trial of the *United States of America v. Rajat K. Gupta* stood out. It was the most uncomfortable trial in recent memory. It pitted one corner of the establishment, represented by Gupta, the former three-time managing director of McKinsey, against the other corner of the establishment, Goldman Sachs & Co. There was no love lost between the two. In the months before the trial, Gupta had come to distrust his relationship with Goldman and view Blankfein with great disdain. On February 24, 2012, Blankfein, accompanied by his usual coterie of lawyers, arrived at the midtown offices of Kramer Levin to be deposed by Naftalis in connection with the SEC's civil case against Gupta, which after being dropped in August 2011 was filed in federal court on October 26, 2011, the same day that criminal authorities unsealed their indictment against Gupta. When Blankfein entered the conference room, he was taken aback. There sat his former board member Rajat Kumar Gupta. The two men didn't say a word to each other, but in an unusual move, Gupta sat for nine hours and listened in on Blankfein's deposition.

Although the Gupta case was to be decided by a twelve-person jury, it was clear from the beginning that the indomitable Judge Rakoff would be dominating proceedings in Courtroom 14B. Never one to shy away from controversy, Judge Rakoff reined in lawyers when they strayed from the law and jumped in and elicited testimony when they got tongue-tied. Through it all, he entertained the spectators and jury with his witty rejoinders.

"You look so much taller than Napoleon," Judge Rakoff said as the lead prosecutor, Reed Brodsky, rose to speak on the first day of the trial. The courtroom broke into quiet laughter. Just that morning, the *Wall Street Journal* had run a profile of Brodsky noting that his dogged pursuit of a conviction of Rajaratnam had prompted jurors in that case to nickname the fresh-faced, dark-haired, five-foot-nine-inch prosecutor from Long Island "Napoleon."

Some of the best banter, though, occurred between Judge Rakoff and Gupta's lawyer Gary Naftalis, who are old friends. Before Naftalis started his opening arguments, Brodsky sought to confirm that his adversary would not be able to speak at length about Gupta's many philanthropic pursuits. Naftalis had wanted some leeway to expound on Gupta's charitable endeavors to dispel "the phony picture" created by the prosecution.

"Your Honor, just to be clear, he won't mention AIDS, malaria or tuberculosis," said Brodsky.

"Or the bubonic plague," shot back Judge Rakoff.

"Or even scurvy," piped up Naftalis. Even the impassive-looking Gupta cracked a smile.

In the large and clubby New York Bar, it is common for prominent and powerful attorneys to know judges well, and it was no secret that Naftalis and Judge Rakoff went back a long way. Judge Rakoff joined the US attorney's office in Manhattan in 1973, fresh from Harvard Law School and a master's in philosophy from Balliol College, Oxford University, where he studied Indian history. Naftalis, then assistant chief of the Criminal Division, was Rakoff's boss. The two overlapped for a year—Naftalis left the office in 1974—but have been friends ever since. In 2009, Judge Rakoff presided over the wedding of one of Naftalis's sons, who had clerked for him.

The sixty-nine-year-old Judge Rakoff, with his snowy white hair and beard, is an old pro at insider trading cases. He's seen them from all sides, as a judge, a prosecutor, and a defense lawyer. Twenty-five years ago, Rakoff, then a defense lawyer, was hired by former Kidder, Peabody & Co. mergers and acquisitions banker Martin Siegel to represent him in the headline insider trading case of the time. Siegel, who pleaded guilty to securities fraud, was accused of passing inside information to arbitrageur Ivan Boesky in exchange for briefcases filled with dollar bills. The case against Gupta, who had never received cold cash from Rajaratnam for the alleged insider tips he provided, was downright dull in comparison.

By 2 p.m., a jury of four men and eight women were seated. Among the New Yorkers deciding Gupta's fate were an executive at a nonprofit organization, a fourth-grade teacher, a nurse, and a freelance beauty consultant. Gupta, who knew his way around the corporate boardrooms of America, appeared unsure of the customs of a courtroom. When the jury first walked in, he did not rise from his chair. Only when one of Naftalis's colleagues, Alan Friedman, signaled for him to get up did he quickly comply. It was a slipup he wouldn't make again.

In their opening arguments, the lawyers painted two competing pictures of Gupta's life. As his wife, Anita, and their four daughters looked on, Reed Brodsky took the floor and declared, "This is a case about illegal insider trading." Then, pointing to an expressionless Gupta, he said, "It is about how this man, Rajat Gupta, violated his duties and abused his position as a corporate insider" so his friends could make money on the financial crisis.

Seeking to leave no doubt that Gupta benefited from his relationship with Rajaratnam, Brodsky told the jury that "the more money Galleon funds made, the more money Gupta and Rajaratnam made in Voyager." By tipping off Rajaratnam, "Gupta cheated. Gupta violated his duty to those public companies and their shareholders. That is called insider trading. It is securities fraud. It is a serious crime."

In his opening, Naftalis countered, saying the government was offering the jury a "cropped photo" of Gupta.

"He is not an insider trader...He has not defrauded anybody. He has not cheated anybody. He doesn't belong in this courtroom." Naftalis said the government's case was characterized by an "absence of real hard direct evidence...Indeed this is a very strange insider trading case because the evidence will show that Rajat Gupta did no insider trading. Let me repeat it. Rajat Gupta did no insider trading." There are no wiretapped conversations, firsthand testimony from any witnesses of Gupta giving them inside information, or documents showing him tipping off Rajaratnam. "Zero," emphatically asserted Naftalis. "Strike out there as well." Rather, the prosecution's case was based on "speculation" and "guesswork."

"We don't guess people into guilt in America," intoned Naftalis. "Even if there was a crime, Rajat Gupta had nothing to do with it. You have the wrong man on trial here."

Sitting in the back of the room as Brodsky and Naftalis spoke was the SEC's Sanjay Wadhwa. With his backpack slung over his shoulder, he had made the fifteen-minute crosstown trek from his office at Three World Financial Center even though he and his team were busier than ever. As prosecutors were preparing for the Gupta trial,

Wadhwa and his colleagues were building a civil case against SAC Capital. In May, they deposed SAC Capital's founder, Steve Cohen, for seven hours; it would be a first step leading to SAC paying a huge $616 million civil penalty to settle two insider trading cases. When SAC first learned in 2012 of possible charges against the firm, Cohen said he acted appropriately.

Unlike Manhattan US attorney Bharara, Wadhwa didn't have to worry about anyone noticing him. Barely anyone knew who he was. He didn't attract a media spectacle whenever he stepped into the public eye, but he was keen to be present for the opening arguments because he and his team of lawyers had assembled much of the circumstantial evidence at the heart of the government's case. Unlike with Rajaratnam, the government had only one wiretap on which Gupta was heard relaying discussions at a Goldman board meeting to Rajaratnam. Most of the case was rooted in evidence of board meetings followed quickly by phone calls and wiretap recordings of Rajaratnam boasting to associates that he had received information from a Goldman board member, the "hearsay" evidence that Gupta's lawyers had tried to get Judge Rakoff to exclude.

Meanwhile, Bharara, who studiously attended the Rajaratnam trial, appearing for both opening and closing arguments, was noticeably absent in the Gupta case. On one occasion in the middle of the trial, he stopped by. When he walked into the well during a break to consult with his prosecutors, Rajat Gupta was standing alone nearby. As soon as Gupta caught a glimpse of Bharara, he walked out of the well.

On Tuesday, May 22, the first day of evidence in the trial, the government called Caryn Eisenberg, Rajaratnam's executive assistant. Eisenberg, dressed in a black halter top and sequined cardigan, walked to the witness stand and was sworn in. Soon after starting her testimony, she dropped a bombshell. A few days before the trial was set to begin, Eisenberg found a red notebook in which she had scribbled Rajaratnam's VIP callers—the people who were so important that Rajaratnam had told her to find him if they called.

Gupta's name was second on the list, just after Rajiv Goel, the former Intel Treasury executive and Rajaratnam informant who had pleaded guilty.

Among the others: Parag Saxena; Stanley Druckenmiller, whose name Eisenberg had starred, though she could not remember why; and Anil Kumar. Ironically, the notebook, which surfaced in response to a defense subpoena of documents from Eisenberg, bolstered the government's contention that Gupta and Rajaratnam were far closer than Gupta was willing to admit.

It got worse for Gupta.

Eisenberg testified that on the afternoon of September 23, 2008, she remembered getting a call about ten minutes before the market closed. The caller, a man, said it was "urgent" and that he needed to speak to Rajaratnam. Eisenberg said she recognized the man's voice as someone who was on the list of important callers, a person who telephoned frequently, but she could not recall his name. She put the call on hold and went to find Rajaratnam. He returned to his office quickly, closed the door, and had a brief conversation with the man.

Eisenberg testified that moments later Rajaratnam called his lieutenant Gary Rosenbach into his office. The door was closed again and Eisenberg could not hear their conversation, but when Rosenbach walked out of Rajaratnam's office, he barked an order to the entire trading desk: "Buy Goldman Sachs." Eisenberg said she heard Rosenbach repeat the order a few times and, for emphasis, she said it again: "Buy Goldman Sachs. Buy Goldman Sachs."

The trial had hit a fever pitch on its first day of evidence. Minutes after her testimony, the words "buy Goldman Sachs, buy Goldman Sachs" echoed through the quiet, high-ceilinged courtroom. After Rajaratnam received the call, he was "smiling more," Eisenberg added. It was a small detail that seemed to take away from the credibility of her testimony rather than add to it.

Under cross-examination, David Frankel, a soft-spoken defense lawyer who contemplated a PhD in English before settling on being an attorney, tried to undermine Eisenberg. The best he could do was to elicit that she had worked as a party planner for a year after college. But he succeeded in drawing out that a Goldman salesman, David Loeb, was also on her list of important callers. Loeb was under investigation by the government for passing inside information about Intel, Apple, and Hewlett-Packard to Rajaratnam. He has not been charged with any wrongdoing, and since the trial ended the investigation into Loeb has been closed. But Loeb quietly left Goldman in early 2013.

In a bid to show that the government had the "wrong man on trial," the defense suggested that the tip-off to Rajaratnam could have come from Loeb. Eisenberg swiftly doused that theory. When Loeb called, "he always said hello to me and was extremely friendly," she recalled. The manner and style of the person who called just before the market closed was different.

The drama continued. Some of the witnesses the government put on during its three-week case appeared to walk out of central casting. Ananth Muniyappa, a Galleon employee who provided important testimony about getting an order from Rajaratnam to buy Goldman stock just before the market closed on September 23, 2008, played the part of the cocky young hedge fund trader. He took the stand wearing an untucked plaid shirt and sporting designer jeans. Byron Trott, the Goldman banker who had helped craft Warren Buffett's investment in the firm, was predictably tall, handsome, and smooth-talking. He came to court dressed in a dark suit, tie, and white shirt. In an amusing and somewhat absurd sidebar that highlighted the familiar give-and-take between Naftalis and Judge Rakoff, Naftalis took issue with Trott's characterization of Buffett.

"I don't think it is appropriate for this witness and the prosecution to be characterizing Warren Buffett as the most respected investor in the world," joked Naftalis.

"Well, we corrected that, and I know your broker disagrees strongly," countered Judge Rakoff.

"Warren has not done so well lately, we all know. He is a little played out," said Naftalis. Few in the courtroom knew it, but in the early nineties, when Naftalis represented Salomon Brothers, which was embroiled in a Treasury bond rigging scandal, he accompanied Buffett and two top Salomon lawyers to make a presentation to Manhattan US attorney Otto Obermaier, successfully persuading him not to indict Salomon.

On May 25, the fifth day of the trial, the government called to the witness stand Goldman board member William George. Just weeks before the trial started, he was substituted for John Bryan, the director who was closest to Gupta, as the Goldman board witness. On May 4, Brodsky, the lead prosecutor in the Gupta trial, sent Naftalis and his team of lawyers a letter via email advising that in a meeting on April 30, Bryan said he did not recall "one way or another" if he learned Goldman was losing nearly $2 a share in a board posting call on October 23, 2008. The previous summer in a videoconference interview, Bryan, who lives in Chicago, had indicated to Brodsky that he remembered Blankfein saying Goldman was losing $2 a share in the October call. His lapse in memory—or perhaps his reluctance to testify against his good friend Gupta—posed a big problem for the prosecution. If the government put Bryan on the stand, the defense could grill him on the inconsistencies between his first and second interviews with the government.

To avoid that, the prosecution decided to put George on the witness stand, even though it knew that he could not testify to hearing Blankfein tell the board that Goldman was going to lose $2 a share. The $2 number was important because it dovetailed with the comment Rajaratnam made the next day to his lieutenant in Singapore. But the best recollection George had of the October 23, 2008, board call was simply that Goldman was going to lose money.

By Friday, June 1, the ninth day of the trial, the strains of the taxing case began to take their toll on the Gupta family. The day kicked off with a discussion outside the presence of the jury of whether to admit the notes of Heather Webster, a J.P. Morgan private banker who met with the Guptas in April 2008. Webster's notes, taken during a meeting in the study of Gupta's waterfront home in Westport, offered a rare peek into the family's wealth. At the time, Gupta and his wife had assets of $134 million—a net worth of $84 million, an irrevocable trust of $38.5 million, and $11.2 million in cash and liquid assets. Under the section in her notes regarding estate planning, Webster had noted that the Guptas wanted to give 80 percent of their money to charity.

The prosecution sought to admit Webster's notes because in her financial review of the Guptas she had asked for an update on his sources of income. In the notes she took at the time, she wrote, he was "Chairman, Galleon International, $1.3 billion, 15 percent owner, invests in long/short equity Asia, entitled to performance fees." For the prosecution, which was seeking to show the jury that Gupta was in a position to benefit from the insider tips he gave Rajaratnam—an important element of proving insider trading—Webster's notes were critical. Gupta may not have received cash in briefcases like Marty Siegel had, but he had a vested interest in Galleon's success.

Naftalis argued vehemently that Webster's notes should not be admitted because it would leave the jury with a misleading impression of Gupta's role at Galleon. He had an informal arrangement with the hedge fund, and he and Rajaratnam had never reached a signed agreement about Gupta becoming chairman of Galleon International. "Nothing was agreed and nothing ever happened," said Naftalis. The only part of the notes Naftalis would have admitted was the reference to Gupta's desire to give most of his money to charity.

At one point, Judge Rakoff, who stepped in to elicit testimony from Webster, asked the prosecutor Brodsky whether Gupta's arrangement to be chairman and work for Galleon International happened or not.

"It is both," replied Brodsky.

"You think it was like science fiction? It was and it wasn't," Judge Rakoff asked.

Brodsky said Gupta was negotiating for a 20 percent stake in Galleon International—more than promised by Rajaratnam. The matter had not been settled. Judge Rakoff ultimately ruled that the notes could be admitted, but he disallowed testimony on Gupta's philanthropic plans, saying, "The annals of white-collar crime in this district are filled with people who wanted to make themselves respected, powerful members of society by giving to charity."

In one of his rare displays of emotion, Gupta shook his head, clasped his hands in resignation, and looked up. Anita Gupta, flanked by two of her daughters, bowed her head and then left the courtroom.

That afternoon, Anil Kumar, Gupta's friend and longtime protégé, took the stand. A pro by now at testifying for the government, he came to court without his lawyer, Greg Morvillo. (In December 2011, Greg's father, Robert, passed away.) As Kumar walked into the well, his head bowed, Gupta's eyes followed him. He raised his eyebrows and looked back at his wife, who was sitting in the first row of the spectators' gallery. Kumar was a star witness for the government in the Rajaratnam case. But how would he perform in the case against his old boss, Gupta?

As the courtroom deputy swore Kumar in and he spelled his name, his voice cracked. During a sidebar later, his discomfort showed. He looked everywhere—at the judge's bench, under the computer monitor before him—everywhere but at Gupta, who was seated directly in front of him. Gupta stared straight ahead, avoiding eye contact with Kumar.

After rehashing some of the testimony he had served up at the Rajaratnam trial, Kumar testified about the business dealings between Rajaratnam and Gupta, particularly how they came to start New Silk Route. He told the jury how in mid- to late October 2008 he heard from Gupta that he had lost his $10 million investment in Voyager. Brodsky was trying to establish the timing of Gupta's dispute with Rajaratnam over Voyager. If Kumar was to be believed, the dispute came after the insider tips on Goldman and Procter & Gamble.

In his questioning of Kumar on Monday, June 4, defense lawyer Naftalis tried to show that the statements Kumar had made in previous interviews with the government were consistent with Gupta's defense.

"Did you tell the government that Mr. Gupta felt that Mr. Rajaratnam had not kept a straight book?" asked Naftalis.

"Yes, sir," responded Kumar.

During the middle of the lunch break, a black Mercedes-Benz SUV with blacked-out windows pulled up outside the entrance of the federal courthouse. A swarm of photographers and cameramen rushed to the car. Everyone was expecting Goldman's chief executive, Lloyd Blankfein, who was scheduled to testify that afternoon at the Gupta trial. But when the door opened, a scrawny leg protruded. A bouncer appeared and shouted: "Stand back, stand back."

Emerging from the SUV was Paris Hilton, dressed in a blue suit, blue stockings, and her famous outsized white sunglasses—not that she needed them amid the cloudy skies. She had arrived for a settlement conference involving a dispute with an Italian lingerie company. Before she strode into the courthouse, she smiled and posed for photos.

Blankfein, meanwhile, dressed more conservatively in a white shirt, blue suit, and red tie, was already upstairs waiting to testify. He had permission to come into the courthouse via its underground parking garage. After he was sworn in, Judge Rakoff couldn't resist the opportunity to question Blankfein. In asking Blankfein some routine biographical questions, Brodsky skipped over his brief career as a lawyer some thirty years before. Judge Rakoff jumped in to correct the omission.

"I'm sure you want to hide the fact that this witness is a lawyer," said Judge Rakoff. Then he turned to Blankfein and asked, "Did you go to law school?"

Blankfein said he had worked for a law firm for four and a half years as a corporate tax lawyer.

"Then you got religion," said Judge Rakoff.

"It was a mutual decision," quipped Blankfein.

The Goldman chief executive was the star of the government's case. And his wattage again ensured a packed courtroom. But much of what Blankfein said was a replay of the testimony he'd delivered the previous year at the Rajaratnam trial. During one sidebar between the attorneys and the judge, he grinned at the jury, craned his head to see what the lawyers were discussing, and fidgeted, looking everywhere but directly ahead at Gupta.

The former Goldman board member seemed equally uncomfortable during Blankfein's testimony. He often glanced back at his wife, Anita, and during one sidebar, he even got up from his chair and leaned over to speak to his wife. She stretched out her hand in a show of solidarity.

Blankfein offered tutorials to the jury on the basics of corporate finance. Asked what it meant when Goldman posted record profits one quarter, he said, "That means it's better than it has ever been before." The one area where he shed new light was recalling his conversations with Gupta about taking up an advisory position at the private equity firm Kohlberg Kravis Roberts & Co.

Blankfein testified that when Gupta told him that he was thinking of accepting the KKR role, Blankfein said it "presented certain conflicts" to Goldman. Gupta disagreed, and the two were set to part ways. A draft press release was prepared announcing Gupta's resignation from the Goldman board and celebrating his tenure on it. To mark his time as a board member, Goldman gave him some cuff links.

But unexpected events intervened. In September 2008, when Lehman Brothers "quite famously went bankrupt," Blankfein said he asked Gupta to withdraw his resignation and remain on the board. With the markets in turmoil, it didn't seem like a lot of private equity business was going to get done, and the conflict didn't "loom as large," said Blankfein. Gupta remained on the Goldman board and took up the advisory position at KKR.

At one point, Brodsky asked Blankfein if he knew how much Gupta was going to earn at KKR. The defense objected, but just as Judge Rakoff said, "You may answer yes or no," Blankfein uttered "Five," clearly meaning $5 million. Gupta's jaw dropped.

Blankfein's testimony had to be spread over the course of a week because he had an important engagement midweek: his daughter was graduating from Fieldston School, a leafy private school north of Manhattan. Blankfein told Judge Rakoff that it would be hard to get to the courthouse after the celebratory lunch he planned to attend in Yonkers.

"I live in Yonkers, so I know," said Judge Rakoff.

"I am going to a restaurant in Yonkers which you probably know," said Blankfein.

"If it's the one I am thinking of, I can't afford it," retorted Judge Rakoff. (The proprietor of the restaurant told Blankfein that Judge Rakoff is a regular.)

Naftalis, in his cross-examination of Blankfein, tried to show that Gupta was so loyal to Goldman that when Blankfein asked him to stay in the midst of the financial crisis, he readily agreed, doing Goldman a favor. "It wasn't going to be helpful to have a director resign from the firm if it was going to be construed that there was a problem at the firm, which there wasn't," conceded Blankfein.

It was clear from the start that Naftalis's cross-examination of Blankfein was going to be testy. Naftalis asked Blankfein if he was number one at Goldman Sachs.

"No. 1 is not an official title," said Blankfein, smiling. "Chairman and CEO" was his title. Then Naftalis asked if Blankfein succeeded someone called Henry Paulson. "His name is Hank Paulson," said the wisecracking Blankfein.

Naftalis, trying to undercut the prosecution's contention that Gupta leaked information on October 23, 2008, about Goldman's fourth-quarter loss, showed an exhibit of a *Wall Street Journal* story that morning saying Goldman was planning to cut 10 percent of its workforce. Naftalis suggested that was the reason Goldman's stock started to slide. But Blankfein said he did not remember the downsizing article. Naftalis would seize on Blankfein's remark to unleash an unusual attack on the Goldman chief executive in his closing arguments.

When Blankfein left the courtroom, he acknowledged Gupta with a smile. Gupta didn't return it.

On Friday, June 8, after calling twenty witnesses over twelve days, the government rested its case. Although the defense had submitted the names of a number of character witnesses it planned to call to testify on Gupta's behalf, there was still no word on whether Gupta himself would take the stand. Since the trial started, Naftalis had held it out as a possibility. After the jury left for the weekend, Naftalis said it was "highly likely" that Gupta would testify the following week. It was a risky gambit. Most lawyers advise a criminal defendant not to take the stand because it can open up the person to wide-ranging questioning from prosecutors. Gupta wanted to explain to the jury his version of events, but by Sunday, he and his lawyers decided against it, a move he would later come to second-guess.

Instead, his eldest daughter, Geetanjali, an accomplished Gupta in her own right—she is a graduate of both Harvard Law School and Harvard Business School, has a bachelor's in applied math from Harvard College, and works for the Harvard endowment—told his story. At 4:30 p.m. on Monday, June 11, the fifteenth day of the trial, Geetanjali, wearing a simple gray dress and jacket and black high-heeled shoes, her long hair sensibly pulled back, walked calmly to the witness stand. In a forthright and compelling fashion, she testified about the events around September 20, 2008. It was an important weekend for her. On September 20, she celebrated her thirtieth birthday, and the next day was her mother's birthday. Geetanjali told the rapt jury that her father was very upset that weekend about an investment he had with Rajaratnam. "He was running his hand through his hair, which he does when he is stressed," she recalled.

By Thanksgiving, when the family gathered at her parents' house in Westport, her father was "quite different from his normal self…He was quite depressed, withdrawn and not himself." The failed investment was well known within the family. Geetanjali Gupta's testimony was critical for the defense, as it sought to show that at the time of the alleged insider tipping, Gupta's relationship with Rajaratnam had so deteriorated that he had no incentive to give him inside information.

Like her father, Geetanjali came off as poised and articulate and her testimony credible.

On cross-examination, prosecutor Reed Brodsky, known for his theatrics in the courtroom, lowered his voice to a barely audible whisper and asked her just two questions:

"Do you love your father?"

"Yes," she replied.

"Would you do anything for your father?"

"I would do anything for my father, but I would not lie, though, on the stand," she replied.

After the jury left the courtroom, Geetanjali walked toward her father, who was seated at the defense table. The two embraced. For the first time since the trial had started a month earlier, Gupta was overtaken with emotion: his eyes were moist with tears.

Just before Geetanjali took the stand, Suprotik Basu, a cocksure thirty-four-year-old United Nations executive working on a project to eradicate malaria, testified. When asked how he met Gupta, Basu said that in May 2007 he got an "urgent call" from a colleague in New York who said there was a businessman who "wanted to end all childhood deaths from malaria by 2025."

A prosecutor sprang up and objected. Judge Rakoff agreed and the testimony was struck.

Basu then testified that he was meeting with Gupta on the afternoon of September 23, 2008, the day of the Buffett investment in Goldman. He traveled with Gupta for a dinner they were attending that evening with the Ethiopian health minister. He had no conversations about Goldman or Warren Buffett with Gupta. "We were focused on our meetings...to close our malaria funding gap," said Basu.

When asked by the prosecutor Brodsky, Basu said he was not in the room when Gupta took part in the Goldman board call or when a call was placed from a McKinsey conference room, which Gupta was using that day, to Rajaratnam's direct work line. However, Basu sought to bolster the defense team's argument that Gupta's call to Rajaratnam was simply a matter of habit: he was always returning calls between engagements.

"My picture of him is with a earpiece in his ear constantly returning phone calls between meetings," said Basu.

The defense case took just two and a half days. That was in large part because Judge Rakoff limited the number of character witnesses Gupta could call. And he rejected a major thrust of the defense: Rajaratnam wasn't tipped by Gupta but by one of Goldman's own, David Loeb, the head of Asia equity sales. After Geetanjali Gupta finished testifying, lawyers for Gupta worked late into the evening trying to persuade Judge Rakoff to allow them to play two wiretapped phone conversations between Rajaratnam and David Loeb in August 2008. In the calls, Loeb is said to have passed information about Intel and Apple to Rajaratnam. Judge Rakoff ruled against allowing the Loeb tapes in.

On the morning of Tuesday, June 12, Goldman's outside lawyer Steve Peikin got an email from Loeb's attorney. Loeb was headed to the courthouse because the defense planned to call him as a witness. "Are you calling Loeb?" Peikin asked Naftalis. Keeping his cards close to the vest, Naftalis didn't answer. During the morning break, Peikin broached the issue with prosecutor Brodsky who didn't know either. But the next time Peikin saw Naftalis, he seemed annoyed and asked him: "Are you a government stooge?" The relationship between Goldman and Gupta was so frayed by now that the normally affable Naftalis incorrectly perceived Peikin's move as a way to telegraph the defense's strategy to the government.

Just before the defense rested its case, it played a tape of Rajaratnam speaking to one of his lieutenants in which he appeared to confirm Gupta's allegation that he had cheated in Voyager Capital Partners, the investment vehicle the two men had invested in together.

"When you take leverage you, you know. My problem is, I'm a big boy. I hope Rajat is a big boy. You know?" Rajaratnam told Galleon portfolio manager Sanjay Santhanam in a phone call on October 2, 2008. "And then I didn't, I, I, I didn't tell him that I took that equity out, right." The tape bolstered earlier evidence presented by the defense showing an internal Galleon document that appeared to indicate that Rajaratnam took $25.2 million from Voyager in December 2007.

On June 13, the prosecution and the defense concluded the trial much as they had begun, by offering two polar opposite pictures of Gupta. In his closing argument, assistant US attorney Richard Tarlowe walked through the evidence piece by piece. He said that in the last ten minutes of the trading day on September 23, 2008, there was only one call to Rajaratnam's direct line, and that call was from Gupta.

"That evidence is devastating for the defendant...If you believe Ms. Eisenberg, it is over, it is over, the defendant is guilty of illegally tipping." Later, his colleague Reed Brodsky said that Gupta would have to be "one of the unluckiest men in the world" if jurors were to buy defense arguments that he didn't leak information to Rajaratnam despite a pattern of him calling the Galleon hedge fund manager after board meetings and Rajaratnam trading shortly after the calls.

Naftalis sounded the same themes he had at the start. He said that Gupta had legitimate business reasons for speaking with Rajaratnam and "never did any insider trading, period, zero, none." If Rajaratnam so relied on Gupta's insider tips, he would have asked Gupta to remain on the Goldman board rather than take up the position at KKR. He would have said, "You're my meal ticket there," said Naftalis. Instead, he told Gupta to take the KKR job "in a heartbeat."

After walking the jury through the evidence, Naftalis, his voice falling to a faint whisper, appealed to the jury to consider their verdict carefully in the context of a great man's life: "In a few weeks this case will be a dim memory to you...But for Rajat Gupta this is the only case, and whatever you do here will mark whatever future he has left."

At 11 a.m. on Friday, June 15, 2012, word trickled out that there was a note from the jury. No one paid much attention at first. An hour earlier, the jury had placed its lunch orders with Judge Rakoff's court deputy, suggesting that deliberations were set to go into the afternoon. Since the start of the trial, there had been twenty-five notes from the jury for everything from smoking breaks to juror number 6 telling the judge that she knew Goldman president Gary Cohn's daughter, who attended the Trevor Day School, where she worked.

Reed Brodsky, the prosecutor, saw the court security officer, a tall man with a black goatee, walk into the jury room and come back out. He had nothing in his hands. Evidently he had stuffed the envelope with the word "verdict" written all over it into his pocket. Then he walked into the courtroom. Not seeing Judge Rakoff's courtroom deputy, Linda Kotowski, in sight, he stood outside the door to Judge Rakoff's chambers and waited.

Kotowski at that moment was meeting with Stephanie Cirkovich, the press officer for the Manhattan federal court, and Judge Rakoff to discuss press procedures for the jurors in the event of a verdict. The three met for twenty minutes, with some issues left undecided.

"We'll see when the verdict comes in," said Judge Rakoff as Cirkovich was leaving his chambers. When she and Kotowski opened the door into the courtroom, the court security officer was standing outside with an envelope. He gave it to Kotowski.

By now, a nervous energy was starting to build in the courtroom. Gupta, dressed in a navy suit, white shirt, and orange-red tie, had returned to the defense table to sit in his usual spot in the third seat. A half hour earlier, he was sitting in the courthouse cafeteria playing cards with a couple of his daughters. No one seemed to know what the jury note was about—or at least they weren't telling. But when a US marshal appeared, seasoned court observers suspected that there might be a verdict.

Another sign that the jury note might be important came when Alan Friedman, a lawyer at Naftalis's firm, Kramer Levin, walked over to the press side and pulled away his public relations manager. The two huddled at the back of the room. Then Naftalis returned to the courtroom. He walked straight into the well, skipping his usual banter with the press. He seemed unusually serious. If indeed it was a verdict, it was not a good sign.

Typically, quick verdicts favor the government. David Frankel, Naftalis's colleague, rose from his position in the second chair and gave his seat to Gupta. It seemed like something deadly serious was about to happen.

At 11:30 a.m., Judge Rakoff entered the courtroom for the penultimate scene. He confirmed what everybody already knew. Gupta sat stoically, as he had every day, at the defense table. Behind him were his wife, Anita, and three of their daughters. The oldest, Geetanjali, who had testified so eloquently a few days earlier, was noticeably absent. She was at the Starbucks coffee shop on the corner of Worth and Lafayette Streets. She had work and needed an Internet connection.

At 11:28 a.m., *New York Times* reporter Peter Lattman, who was also at the Starbucks, received an email on his BlackBerry that a verdict had been reached. He yelled to a colleague, "They've reached a verdict," and then he turned to Geetanjali and delivered the same news. She looked up from her laptop, startled. The three raced to the courthouse, a block away. Geetanjali managed to slip in just before the jury filed in and sat with her hand on her mother's shoulder.

At 11:35 a.m., the jury filed into the courtroom. Judge Rakoff reviewed the verdict to make sure it was in proper form. Then Rakoff's courtroom deputy played her role. "Mr. Foreman, please rise. You say you have agreed upon a verdict," she said.

"Yes," he replied.

"On Count 2...not guilty," he said.

For a moment, it seemed like the jury had found Gupta not guilty. But then the foreman reeled off a string of "guiltys."

Gupta sat expressionless, his face as constricted as his future.

In the visitors' gallery, two of his daughters cried, the younger of the two sobbing loudly. A third Gupta girl embraced them both, tenderly stroking one of her sisters' hair.

Rajat Gupta's wife, Anita Mattoo, covered her head in her hands and lowered it. As the jury filed out, the courtroom stood up at once—except the Gupta girls and their mother.

After Judge Rakoff left the courtroom, Gupta hugged his lawyers. He then turned to his family.

He walked out of the well and locked arms with his daughters and wife in a huge, long embrace. It was sacred ground: a show of private grief in a very public place.

Throughout the trial, Gupta's wife and daughters gave him strength. They held out a comforting hand or acknowledged a nod when he looked back from the defense table with a warm smile.

The love the family felt for each other had so moved the jurors that when they left the courtroom, some were teary-eyed. They wanted to see Gupta walk out a free man. Now, in his darkest hour, it was Rajat Gupta, like his father, who was the rock.

He extended his hand to his wife, who, as hard as she tried, could not mask her feelings. She had flung her head back at first when she heard the guilty verdicts. She was disgusted by it all. The man she knew and the principles he stood for did not emerge during the four-week trial she had attended day after day. In his hands, Gupta cradled the head of one of his younger daughters, who seemed the most visibly upset by the verdict. He consoled her, stroking her head as she sobbed loudly. Just as he had when he was a young boy and he and his brothers and sisters lost their parents, he found in himself the strength to stand tall.

CHAPTER THIRTY-NINE

A Family Secret

Gupta spent the summer between his conviction and his sentencing trying to avoid second-guessing the decision he and his lawyers had made not to have him testify in his defense. He kept busy, spending time with family and friends, officiating at a wedding, contemplating building a tree house for his grandkids, and reaching out to people in his vast circle to write letters on his behalf for his upcoming sentencing. The letters turned into a litmus test of loyalty. When old colleagues from McKinsey came to visit, the seemingly immovable Gupta would detail the people whose careers he had nurtured—his lieutenant Jerome Vascellaro and his former coworkers from Scandinavia—who now were not willing to pick up a pen and write a letter on his behalf. He felt that he had been made a scapegoat for the public's anger toward Wall Street and he wondered if his friends who now cast stones were sitting in self-made glass houses. "Can you imagine if everyone's phone was wiretapped?" he asked a friend, suggesting that he would not be the only one facing criminal charges.

For most of his career, Gupta had lived outside the epicenter of capitalism, New York City, where one's net worth and job title had a lot to do with which doors were open or closed to a newcomer. His stepping down as managing director of McKinsey came just as he was settling into life in the Big Apple, where the yardsticks of success were different from those in Chicago or Scandinavia. And the circles he traveled in only served as a reminder of the chasm between him and them—the Rajaratnams of the world, whose wealth allowed them single-handedly to bankroll the causes that Gupta collected checks for. For an achievement-driven man like Gupta, it appeared that keeping up with the Rajaratnams was important. It was too hard to resist even if it meant bending the rules.

This desire to play in a very elite sandbox was perhaps just one of the inducements to breaking the law, but since Gupta is a man who keeps his own conscience, it is unlikely that we will ever really know what he felt deep inside. Was it a sense that passing along a bit of inside information was no more reprehensible an act than driving seventy miles per hour in a sixty-five-mile-per-hour speed zone? Was it that for the first time in his life Gupta was flying without a manual? (There was no HBS handbook or McKinsey code of conduct to comply with anymore.) Or was it that everyone else around him seemed to be doing it? After all, some of his own friends had had regulatory scrapes before and emerged with hardly a bruise.

In the weeks after his conviction, Gupta's daughters, who relied on their father for everything from getting through a painful breakup to forging a new career path, now found themselves in the position of trying to be a rock for the biggest rock of all, their dad. At times during the summer between his conviction and his sentencing, his second daughter, Megha, spotted an "unfamiliar look of fear on his face." When that happened, she would put her arm on his shoulder and say, "Don't worry, Baba." Deeply private and dignified even with his own family, her father would move quickly to compose himself. "I'll be all right, baby," he would say. "Are you all right?...If my babies are all right, I'll be all right." It was a salient quality of her father's: even in times of stress, his concern lay not with himself but with others.

Unlike the stoic Gupta, his wife, Anita, freely gave way to her emotions. She was stunned by the verdict. "Every single lawyer told us this case was not going to go forward," she declared to a visitor. But "as soon as the judge gave the instruction, I knew it was over." It was not the words but the judge's tone that made it clear to her that the jury would come back with a guilty verdict. Even at times when his wife would break down in tears, Gupta managed to keep an even keel.

"Life is just a journey," he said philosophically.

"I want off this journey," shot back Anita, sobbing as she spoke.

After the verdict, some friends were in such disbelief that they questioned the jury's decision with the analytical power worthy of a McKinsey consultant. "As I listened to the evidence, particularly the evidence about the 3 board meetings in which he was charged with passing information, all I could think of was, but what about the other 49 Board meetings" (where material information was discussed, but no trade followed), wrote former McKinsey consultant Purnendu Chatterjee in a letter sent on Gupta's behalf to Judge Rakoff. "I may be biased in interpreting this data, but I do know from my PhD work in Statistics that prior basis has a significant impact on conclusion in a multivariate scenario where due to Press and other reasons, there could have been a strong prior bias about 'Wall Street' people." Chatterjee's letter was one of more than four hundred submitted to Judge Rakoff on Gupta's behalf before his sentencing. Besides letters from global luminaries such as Microsoft founder and billionaire Bill Gates, who called him a "dogged advocate for the world's poor," and former UN secretary-general Kofi Annan, there were hundreds of heartfelt and moving letters from friends, cousins, nephews, nieces, and his wife and children.

Even Aman Kumar, whose father, Anil, had testified against Gupta at trial, felt compelled to write for the man he simply knew as "Rajat uncle." Gupta is no relation to Kumar; "uncle" is just an affectionate appellation young Indians often use to address their elders. Aman Kumar said some of his "most treasured childhood memories are of falling into the Colorado River while fly fishing with Rajat uncle, or of Rajat uncle excitedly telling former President Clinton about an award I had received that week from then President Bush, or of lazy walks together on the beach talking about middle school classes and crushes."

A week after the jury rendered its decision, Gupta headed to Boston to help his eldest daughter, Geetanjali, rearrange her house to create a new playroom for her twin daughters, Meera and Nisa. They adored their grandfather. It was he who danced with them and made them smile when they were feeling out of sorts. Gupta could not change the outcome of the trial, but he could see to it that his family was as settled as possible if and when he had to leave them. He focused on getting his financial house in order. His associates at New Silk Route wanted him to sever his ties with the private equity firm he helped start. But Gupta was not going to accept a lowball offer for his stake in the company. There was no way of knowing how long he would be away or how much of his legal defense he ultimately would be forced to pay for. (Goldman had advanced him money to pay his legal bills, which by the end of the trial amounted to $30 million. But a week before his sentencing, Gupta learned that Goldman was moving to recoup nearly $7 million of legal fees and monies spent on investigating the case. Gupta balked at the request.)

For a man to whom reputation was everything, the public humiliation was hard to bear. Harder still was the thought that his lapse in judgment had brought anguish to his wife and four daughters, whom he dearly loved, whom he had devoted his entire life to protecting. Every day seemed to bring a new ignominy—and not necessarily for him.

Belatedly, he learned of the slights faced by his third daughter, Aditi, whose graduation from his alma mater Harvard Business School he missed because of the trial. Soon after his legal problems came to light, news articles chronicling them "magically appeared" in her on-campus mailbox. A nasty email made the rounds at HBS calling for the school to cut its ties with her father. Gupta was on the HBS board of dean's advisers, a group of businesspeople, not all alumni, who meet informally as a group with the dean each year, and on the advisory board of the school's India Research Center in Mumbai. And during one of his daughter's classes in her first year at HBS, Aditi had to sit and struggle to keep an even keel as Preet Bharara, the US attorney for the Southern District of New York, whose office brought the case against her father, spoke for more than an hour about his fight against white-collar crime.

Try as he might, Gupta still found it hard to accept the verdict. In July, a month after his conviction, he hosted two dozen couples, friends from his IIT mechanical engineering class of 1971. The close-knit group met every year, but their gatherings for the past two years had been marred by the news that one of their most admired friends was being investigated for a crime they simply could not contemplate him committing. Naturally, when they met, the verdict was at the forefront of Gupta's mind. Even after the conviction, Gupta still believed passionately that he was innocent. He felt he had been unfairly lumped into a sprawling network of people who regularly fed Rajaratnam inside information.

Even if, for the sake of argument, a couple of words had slipped from his mouth to Rajaratnam after the Goldman meeting, it was never his intention to pass along inside information, and he certainly never expected Rajaratnam to trade on it. "I can't be responsible for someone else's actions," he asserted to his friends. After all, as he reminded them, he had not made a dime from any of it.

Gupta revealed to his friends his disappointment with the fact that the judge presiding over the case had not allowed his lawyers to present an alternative theory about how Rajaratnam had learned about Warren Buffett riding to the rescue of Goldman Sachs. Judge Rakoff had blocked Gupta's legal team from presenting evidence that would have opened up the possibility of a senior Goldman executive tipping Rajaratnam. And after all his hopes for a fair hearing of his case, Gupta felt the members of the jury had not weighed the facts with the gravity he expected. Their deliberations had ended so quickly, so abruptly, that it was hard to believe that they had taken enough time to carefully consider the evidence before them.

* * *

Shortly before 2 p.m., on Wednesday, October 24, 2012, Gupta returned to Honorable Judge Jed S. Rakoff's courtroom, a changed man from the one who had sat stoically through his trial. If he had once been the confidant of CEOs and a keeper of corporate secrets, he now stood convicted of giving them away. After embracing his wife, Anita, who had come to court wearing dark sunglasses, and hugging his four daughters, he walked into the well to be sentenced.

As the courtroom deputy intoned, "All rise," Judge Rakoff entered the courtroom. After some preliminary remarks, Judge Rakoff turned to Naftalis to make his case for probation rather than a prison sentence.

"I think it is fair to say Rajat Gupta's life has been an extraordinary one, and he has lived a life well-lived, a life devoted to giving back," said Naftalis. He pointed to the probation officer's report, which said that Gupta's charity work arose "out of a true devotion to their causes" and not out of any sense of obligation "because of the prominence of his wealth." As Naftalis spoke, Gupta's eldest daughter, Geetanjali, whose poise on the witness stand during the trial was impressive to watch, dabbed her eyes with a tissue. Seated next to her mother, she was dressed simply in a black suit with two strands of pearls.

"This is as laudatory a description of someone at the bar of justice as I have ever seen," Naftalis said.

Judge Rakoff agreed but then offered a glimpse into the competing arguments he must weigh. "I have received some suggestions that this is just a rich man who through his connections could get a lot of people to write good letters. I think that's totally wrong," said Judge Rakoff. The record, he noted, "bears out that he is a good man. But the history of this country, and the history of the world, I'm afraid is full of examples of good men who do bad things. So that's not the end of the subject."

Naftalis countered, arguing that the offense is "one piece but one piece of a larger puzzle." It was "aberrational behavior."

Again Judge Rakoff agreed but then raised a salient point. "If the aberrant misbehavior in some hypothetical case was a murder, the fact that the person had otherwise led a blameless or even totally lawful life would not mean that you didn't have to impose serious punishment for the murder," he noted.

In case the judge was inclined to sentence Gupta to prison, simply for the general deterrence effect, Naftalis was quick to point out that Gupta was "a man who has suffered punishment far worse than prison already. The fall from grace that Mr. Gupta has suffered or experienced as a result of this matter is as steep as I have ever seen anyone in any case that I have ever been in" as a prosecutor and defense lawyer. "I mean this was an iconic figure, someone who had been a role model for countless people around the globe...I mean this is a fall from grace of Greek tragic proportions." Unbeknownst to everyone else in the courtroom, Gupta's fall was not so much a Greek tragedy as it was an echo of a deep, dark family secret that Rajat had spent his life running from.

* * *

"A great deal of sensation" has *"prevailed over this case in newspapers... It is not a case of pickpocketing by one having a dozen previous convictions. But in it concerns a career of a brilliant intellectual, a young man... Even if a fine of one rupee is imposed on him, then his career, his life, his all will be doomed—doomed for ever."*

With those words, on Monday, November 25, 1935, S. K. Sen, one of Calcutta's best defense lawyers, presented his closing arguments in a highly celebrated case that pitted the Crown against Ashwini Kumar Gupta, Rajat Gupta's father. Not even thirty years old, Ashwini Gupta had a promising academic career ahead of him, but the case that had its beginnings on Tuesday, April 9, 1935, would change the course of his life forever.

Around 2 p.m., about three hundred students, mostly men, dressed in shirts and dhotis, filed into a large hall on the second floor of Calcutta University's Ashutosh Building, a dignified colonial-era edifice. The students had assembled that afternoon to take their final paper for the bachelor of arts degree in economics.

It had been a grueling day. In the morning, amid the sweltering one-hundred-plus-degree temperature, the students had written their answers for the first part of the exam. Apart from a few empty seats, the hall was packed. Between thirty and forty guards and a number of proctors policed the room.

Shortly after the exam started, a proctor spotted something curious. A student with the identification number 160 was sitting in a different seat than his assigned one, where he had been sitting all morning. For the afternoon session, he had moved into the place of a candidate who was absent that day for the exam. It was a seat that was quite far away from the one he had been given. He was dressed in a fine dhoti with an elaborately embroidered border. A proctor started watching the student and suspected that he was wearing a false mustache and a pair of sunglasses. When the proctor quizzed the student, he said he could not bear the glare of the sun and so he had changed his place. The proctor told the student to return to his own seat, which he did.

After consulting with one of his colleagues, the proctor decided to ask the student for his signature to see if it would tally up with the signature on file for the student. To prevent cheating and reduce the risk of someone else sitting in for a student at an examination, the university typically asked students before an exam for their signatures, which were kept in case they needed to verify someone's identity. The proctor found that the signatures did not match.

The view among the proctors was that the man was not the real candidate but someone impersonating him. One asked the student to fill in a blank application form when he submitted his answer papers at about 4 p.m. When he did, two of the proctors advised the student to see the presiding officer in charge of the exam hall that afternoon before taking his leave. But the student paid no heed and hurried down the staircase, taking off along Colootolla Street, a busy thoroughfare.

The proctors gave chase, one of them yelling, "Thief, thief," as the student ran out of the building. They followed him until he slipped and fell on the pavement outside. When the three proctors pinned him down, they found that his mustache and sunglasses were gone. The proctors escorted the man to the office of the university controller. After the proctors filled the controller in on what had transpired, he asked the young man his name.

"Ashwini Kumar Gupta," he replied.

On questioning, Gupta admitted that during the final two papers of the economics examination for the bachelor of arts degree, he had impersonated a student who was assigned the identification number 160. When the controller asked Gupta why he sat in the student's place for the exam, Gupta said the boy, whom he tutored privately in economics, had asked him to do so. Gupta was sent home to wait.

A few days later, the police visited Gupta at his home in North

Calcutta and arrested him. In his possession they found, among other things, a dhoti and one Calcutta University examination admission card with the identification number 160, which belonged to the student who was supposed to be taking the exam that day. The "dhobi mark" on his clothes—the telltale sign left by Indian washermen to show which clothes belong to different clients—matched the same mark on the clothes that Gupta's student was wearing when he surrendered a few days later. The similar marks suggested that Gupta was wearing his student's clothes in an effort to appear like him. As the police dug into the case, they found that on the morning of the exam, Gupta had asked his bosses at Ripon College for casual leave because he was suffering from diarrhea. He had earlier gone to his barber, where he had his hair dyed, clipped, and curled, ostensibly to conceal his real identity.

The subsequent case was a cause célèbre in Calcutta. For two weeks, newspaper readers feasted on daily reports of the happenings in court, which one paper carried under the headline "Professor and Pupil on Trial."

Gupta denied all the charges and said he had been framed. Nevertheless, on December 4, 1935, a Calcutta magistrate found Gupta guilty of both counts on which he was charged: cheating the registrar of Calcutta University by pretending to be someone else, and forging the economics examination papers. Gupta was sentenced to six months' hard labor. Gupta appealed, but in April 1936, his sentence was upheld by the Calcutta High Court. The appellant took a "defense which was entirely false and unworthy of a person of his status in society," the court ruled.

What the court and the public didn't know was that his defense may have been the only course open to an honorable man. Gupta had stood in for his student, who paid him 50 rupees a month to be tutored, in the Calcutta University exam. Gupta had accepted the payment in an apparent effort to help raise money for the Socialist Party. Ashwini Gupta appeared to have committed an ignoble act for what only his close associates knew to be a noble cause, love of country, while three-quarters of a century later his son would throw away a noble reputation for an ignoble cause.

* * *

Before Judge Rakoff prepared to pass sentence, Gupta moved to the second chair at the defense table and addressed the court.

"The last eighteen months have been the most challenging period of my life since I lost my parents as a teenager," he said, looking strained as he spoke. "I have lost my reputation that I have built over a lifetime. The verdict was devastating to my family, my friends and me. Its implications to all aspects of my life—personal, professional and financial—are profound... Anita's and my daughters' happiness means more to me than anything else... We are a close and loving family. They have had to endure a barrage of negative press about their father and husband, unkind comments from their colleagues and classmates, uncertain prospects for their future careers and a host of other negative outcomes. It is unbearable to me to see how much they have suffered. I just feel terribly that I have put them through this."

As he came before the court to be sentenced, Gupta said, "The overwhelming feelings in my heart are of acceptance of what has happened, of gratitude to my family and friends, and of seeking forgiveness from them all."

After a short break, Judge Rakoff returned. The government was seeking a term of incarceration of as many as ten years. In lieu of a prison term, Gupta wanted to be sent to Rwanda so that he could "work with rural districts to ensure that the needs to end HIV, malaria, extreme poverty and food security are implemented."

Judge Rakoff rejected both recommendations. The immense loss of stature Gupta had suffered meant that severe punishment was unnecessary to keep Gupta from transgressing again; however, a sentence of probation alone would not have the desired effect of deterring others to commit similar acts in the future. While there was no need to prove motive at trial, Judge Rakoff speculated on it in his sentence, saying that Gupta, for all his charitable works, "may have felt frustrated in not finding new business worlds to conquer." In Judge Rakoff's mind, "there is no doubt that Gupta, though not immediately profiting from tipping Rajaratnam, viewed it as an avenue to future benefits, opportunities and even excitement."

As he arrived at his sentence, the judge touched on the seemingly contradictory and perplexing threads in the life of the defendant who stood before him.

"The Court can say without exaggeration that it has never encountered a defendant whose prior history suggests such an extraordinary devotion, not only to humanity writ large, but also to individual human beings in their time of need," Judge Rakoff pronounced. "But when one looks at the nature and the circumstances of the offense, the picture darkens considerably. In the Court's view, the evidence at trial established, to a virtual certainty, that Mr. Gupta, well knowing his fiduciary responsibilities to Goldman Sachs, brazenly disclosed material, non-public information to Mr. Rajaratnam at the very time, September and October 2008, when our financial institutions were in immense distress, and most in need of stability, repose and trust." Gupta's tipping of Rajaratnam of the $5 billion investment by Warren Buffett "was the functional equivalent of stabbing Goldman in the back."

At 4 p.m., two hours after Gupta had first entered the courtroom, Judge Rakoff imposed his sentence: two years in prison. Then he picked up a stack of papers and walked off the bench with a flourish, leaving Gupta and his glittering accomplishments—IIT, HBS, McKinsey—forever tarnished. As Gupta sat expressionless next to his lead lawyer, Naftalis, he was as lost and laid bare as he'd been when he cremated his father at the age of fifteen. Ashwini Gupta had begun his career with a disgrace and ended it as an intimate of the first prime minister of independent India. Five thousand miles away and fifty years later, his son would rise to become a confidant of CEOs and heads of state yet end up disgraced in America. He would be remembered as a disappointment to the Indians to whom he had once been an inspiration, and he would turn into an all-too-easy excuse for prejudicial Americans to dismiss his moral lapse as indicative of the Indian national character. Far from the charmed life of the twice blessed, he would be cursed to live out a sentence of life-long regret and self-reproach, a punishment more onerous than any a judge could impose.

AFTERWORD

At 12:30 p.m. on December 5, 2011, Raj Rajaratnam surrendered to authorities at the Federal Medical Center Devens, forty miles west of Boston. Upon arrival he was fingerprinted, photographed, strip-searched, and issued a number that in his new life would serve as his identity. He was then led to his living quarters, a ten-foot-by-ten-foot cell with a desk, seat, toilet, sink, wall locker, and bed. Seven months into his sentence, it appeared that prison was having a salubrious effect on him: overweight most of his adult life, Rajaratnam is looking lighter these days, reported a visitor.

During his heyday as a hedge fund titan, Rajaratnam was bombarded with callers and visitors every day. Now in prison he bemoans the fact that his rich and powerful pals no longer visit or take the time to stay in touch. Their reticence is a reflection in part of the fickle world of Wall Street's transactional friendship, but it is also a fear of taint by association. Rajaratnam's friends know that the government's probe into insider trading at hedge funds is far from over. Since Rajaratnam's imprisonment, the Manhattan U.S. Attorney's office has won more than two dozen insider trading cases, and, as part of its overall crackdown on insider trading, has obtained convictions against eight former money managers and analysts at the hedge fund formerly known as SAC Capital Advisors, started by the enigmatic trader Steven A. Cohen. Despite its success in locking up some of Cohen's lieutenants, the government failed in its effort to bring criminal charges against Cohen himself. But his firm wound up pleading guilty to insider trading and was forced to stop managing money for outside investors. The government also was unsuccessful in its attempt to send to prison Rajaratnam's brother, Rengan. In July 2014, a jury acquitted Rengan of conspiring to trade on confidential corporate information in an insider trading ring led by his brother, Raj. It was the government's first defeat in the crackdown on insider trading that started in 2009 with the arrest of Rajaratnam.

At one time, being a friend of Rajaratnam's was a point of pride, but today it is a liability, so much so that rival hedge fund managers get their handlers to call the press to play down any suggestion of a relationship. The irony, of course, is had it not been for Rajaratnam's notion of "honor," a bond among thieves, they too could be sitting exactly where Rajaratnam is—in a lonely jail cell. Even with his own future at stake, Rajaratnam refused to cooperate with the government. In an interview he granted after he was arrested, he assailed the South Asians swept up in the case, singling them out for their lack of honor.

"The Americans stood their ground. Every bloody Indian co-operated—Goel, Khan, Kumar," he railed in *Newsweek* magazine. (Rajaratnam was not entirely correct; one of his carefully groomed protégés, Adam Smith, cooperated and testified at his trial, but he was never one to let the facts get in the way of a good story.)

Nearly a year into Rajaratnam's sentence, the newest heavy hitter on his legal team, Patricia Ann Millett, stood in a large ceremonial courtroom in the federal courthouse at 500 Pearl Street and made the case for a reversal of his conviction. Millett was impressive. "In this case, you had cascading errors" in the wiretap affidavit, she declared. One of the most glaring, a central pillar on which Rajaratnam's lawyers were seeking a reversal, was the "wholesale omission" of the SEC investigation of Galleon and the results of the probe. Just as Manhattan US attorney Rudolph Giuliani pioneered the use of the racketeering statute to go after bankers and traders, the Rajaratnam case was the first time prosecutors had ever resorted to wiretaps to snare a white-collar defendant. Since Rajaratnam's arrest, the government had gone to the wiretaps time and time again to build cases against a new and even bigger set of names in the hedge fund industry. And without the wiretaps, the government may not have succeeded in the Gupta case. Gupta was acquitted on two counts where there were no wiretaps.

As Millett spoke, a lawyer who spearheaded the government's defense of its recordings of Rajaratnam and his ring sat in the back of the room and listened intently. By October 2012, Jon Streeter was playing for the other side as a white-collar defense lawyer at Dechert LLP. But the ruling by the panel of three appeals court judges was as important to him in his new life as it was when he was defending the wiretaps as a prosecutor. The Galleon case had revolutionized the way white-collar crimes were investigated in the United States. If the conviction and wiretaps were upheld, it would open up a gusher of new cases for attorneys like Streeter. And it would change the way they fought them. With the hard-to-dispute wiretaps to defend against, rather than the more nebulous circumstantial evidence, the case for plea bargaining was likely to be a more attractive course for all but the wealthiest of white-collar defendants. Though Rajaratnam was not in the courtroom as his lawyer Millett spoke, he had the most at stake. In June 2014, two-and-a-half years after Rajaratnam went to prison, the U.S. Supreme Court declined to consider his challenge to his conviction. With all his appeals exhausted, Rajaratnam will have to be content with living in a ten-by-ten cell until at least 2021.

In the summer of 2012, Rajaratnam's nemesis, Anil Kumar, who provided powerful testimony against his onetime friend, was sentenced to probation. His noncustodial sentence came after prosecutors spoke at length of his "extraordinary" cooperation in helping convict Rajaratnam and his former mentor, Rajat Gupta.

After the sentencing, Kumar walked out of the federal courthouse at 500 Pearl Street a free man, with a smile on his face and holding the hand of his wife, Malvika. Their happy faces masked the fact that Kumar's life would never be the same again. "My ability to return to my prior professional business world has disappeared totally," he said. "I have become a pariah in that world and am followed by questions and whispers. Probity, reputation and trust were the bedrock of my life and in that I and my family have lost everything."

Organizations that would have once boasted of his services when he was a McKinsey consultant now stayed clear of any association with him. His offers to help schools for the disadvantaged in Silicon Valley were rejected outright, and promises were broken at the eleventh hour.

In 2010, Kumar volunteered to consult pro bono to the Baylor College of Medicine in Houston, Texas, which was in financial trouble. Baylor's president and chief executive, Dr. Paul Klotman, told Kumar that he would write a letter to the court at the time of sentencing describing the work Kumar did for the school. But when it came time to write the letter, lawyers precluded Klotman from signing it—the potential negative press for Baylor was too great.

In India, Kumar faced a warmer reception and an opportunity for rehabilitation. His old friend from the Doon School, Analjit Singh, tapped Kumar to establish a medical education initiative between his company, Max India, which offers health-care services and runs insurance companies, and Baylor. One day in the fall of 2012, just days before Gupta was to be sentenced, Kumar stopped by a friend's house in New Delhi. He was back to his old self, regaling the friend and his guests about the inordinately long hours he was working.

Almost three years after he was arrested at his home in California, Rajiv Goel was sentenced on September 24, 2012, to probation. He had exhausted his savings paying his legal bills and was forced to sell his house in Los Altos, California, to stay afloat. Fired from Intel after his arrest, Goel has had a hard time finding a new job. In the meantime, loans from his family in India have allowed two of his children to attend the universities of their choice.

Roomy Khan, the former Intel employee who had a hard time telling FBI agents the truth, emerged from prison in 2014 determined to rebuild her tattered life. Since she started cooperating with the government in early 2008, much had happened to the fifty-six-year-old Khan. In 2009, she sold her house in Atherton at a loss and moved to Fort Lauderdale, Florida. Despite some ups and downs, she and her husband, Sakhawat, remain married. Away from the stressful life of wheeling and dealing and nonstop entertaining she once led, Khan has lost weight. Like Goel, she too is eager to work, but for the last few years it's only government prosecutors who need her help. And they don't pay.

In August 2012, she made her debut on the witness stand in the trial of *US v. Doug Whitman*. Khan turned in a superb performance for the government. Whitman, Khan's former neighbor in Atherton, was convicted on two counts of conspiracy and two counts of securities fraud. But her star turn for the government was not sufficient to keep her out of jail. On January 31, 2013, Judge Rakoff sentenced her to one year in prison, saying, "This is too serious. You cannot have it both ways—to cooperate and then obstruct justice." Khan, freed from prison in April 2014, is now at home charting her second act. A working woman all her life, Khan is looking to turn her experience into something others can learn from and she can live on.

On Tuesday, November 20, 2012, the US attorney's office in Manhattan and the SEC brought criminal and civil charges against Mathew Martoma, a former portfolio manager for SAC Capital Advisors. Among the South Asian community in the United States, there was a palpable sigh of relief. After three years of unremittingly bad press about some of the community's shining lights, it appeared that prosecutors had moved on. Judging by his name, it looked like their newest target was someone in mainstream American society. Their euphoria turned out to be short-lived. By the end of the week, Bloomberg News reported that Martoma was born Ajai Mathew Mariamdani Thomas. He was the son of Indian immigrants and had changed his name in 2003. Martoma was convicted in February 2014 of using inside information about a failed Alzheimer's drug trial as a basis for selling shares in two drug-makers. In November, he started serving his nine-year prison term in a "low security" facility in Miami.

The fall from grace of Raj Rajaratnam, Anil Kumar, Mathew Martoma and, most important, Rajat Gupta was not just a pivotal turning point in the lives of three individuals and their families. It was an important stepping-stone in the odyssey of the twice blessed. For four decades, the South Asian diaspora in the United States had enjoyed unrivaled success. Its members were considered the new "model minority," a community that had come to the United States with very little and, within the span of two decades, had vaulted to the highest echelons of society.

When Rajat Gupta was indicted in October 2011, Gurchuran Das, the former chief executive officer of Procter & Gamble India and the author of *India Unbound*, one of the first books highlighting India's resurgence, articulated a worry that many Indian corporate executives in the West harbor but dare not utter.

"He has stained the India story," Das declared.

Over the years, Indians had developed a reputation in the West as being highly effective managers. Their leadership skills were fodder for new frontiers in academic research. One book written by four Wharton School professors and entitled *The India Way* purported to tell "how India's top business leaders are revolutionizing management." Now, with one of the country's most beloved icons convicted of a crime, there was hand-wringing behind the scenes about how Indians would be perceived in the future. Would the rose-colored glasses come off?

David Ben-Gurion, considered the founder of the state of Israel, reportedly once said, "In order for Israel to be counted among the nations of the world, it has to have its own burglars and prostitutes." It is an apt analogy for the South Asian community in the United States today. When South Asians first started streaming into America in growing numbers after the Hart-Cellar Act was passed in 1965, there was a natural patriotism, a penchant for flag-waving. Ethnic newspapers like *India Abroad* sprang up celebrating Indian achievements. Among South Asians in the United States, Indians make up the single largest group.

Today, after forty years of steady and growing immigration, the community is vibrant, rich in diversity, and strong in numbers. There is no better example than Edison, New Jersey, where Sanjay Wadhwa's parents, Arjun and Rashmi, now live. Its central thoroughfare, Oak Tree Road, is called "Little India." Every store on the street—even the auto repair shop—is owned by an Indian-American.

Much like the Irish-Americans and the Italian-Americans in the first half of the twentieth century, Indian-Americans in the twenty-first century have emerged as a force to be reckoned with in the

United States. They no longer are confined to walking the corridors of corporate America; they now stalk the halls of justice. Forty years ago, when Rajat Gupta arrived in the United States, or even twenty years ago when he ascended to the helm of McKinsey, Indian-Americans were too small in number and too invisible a group to matter. Today, as tragic and heartbreaking as Gupta's fall from grace is, it is a sign that Indians, much like the immigrant groups before them, have attained a certain security and once unimaginable position in American society. They are large enough in number to be counted and, more important, they constitute a diverse collection of voices. No longer fearful of standing out, the children of the twice blessed are all too eager to stand up.

ACKNOWLEDGMENTS

This book would not have been possible without the ambitious vision of Shawn Coyne. From the beginning, Shawn, my agent, saw that this book was much more than a book about insider trading. He realized early on that the Galleon case was the perfect way to tell the story that I had been wrestling with for years: the rise and maturation of the South Asian diaspora in the United States. Shawn worked with me every step of the way, serving as editorial counsel on the project and guiding me as I navigated the twists and turns of this complex tale. John Brodie, my editor at Business Plus, enhanced the manuscript with his deft touch and keen appreciation of the important ingredients of a great story, honed by over twenty years as a working journalist. He, Meredith Haggerty, Carolyn Kurek, and the entire team at Grand Central did everything they could to make my first book a smooth journey.

A few others played a great role in producing this book. Sue Radlauer, the librarian at *Forbes*, devoted hours and hours of her own time, too immeasurable to count, to unearthing sources for me, finding research by academics, and tracking down articles that offered a key nugget or two. Like all librarians, Sue is a prodigious digger and invariably produced far more than I asked for, often going the extra mile to put the information she gleaned in context for me.

N. Ram, the former editor in chief of the *Hindu*, the largest newspaper in South India, opened up to me the most valuable possession a journalist has: his Rolodex, which he had cultivated through a remarkable forty-six-year career as one of the country's finest journalists. Ram read the manuscript and offered constructive suggestions on how to strengthen it. Although he knew of me only through his daughter Vidya, with whom I worked at *Forbes*, I am grateful that he had the faith to believe in me and trust me with his contacts. I am also indebted to Vidya for introductions in her ever-widening circle of sources.

A close friend in London, Uma Waide, who edits books, made gentle but important suggestions to the manuscript. I have always respected Uma as a friend. In the past two years, I have come to admire her as an editor.

Seena Simon, an old friend from my early days in New York, read the manuscript with a critical eye. A number of former colleagues from *Forbes* were invaluable too. Kai Falkenberg was unflinching in her advice on legal issues, Naazneen Karmali helped open doors in India, Janet Novack assisted in all things Washington, and Tom Post got the ball rolling by championing a piece about Raj Rajaratnam for the Forbes 400 more than two years ago.

I am grateful to my fact checker and researcher, Matthew Resignola, who was tireless in chasing down people and checking memos, even offering to help during the Christmas holidays.

Much of the reporting for this book was done in New York, which once was my home. A number of old friends and some new ones eased my reentry to the city. First and foremost, I want to thank my old colleague from the *Wall Street Journal*, Ianthe Dugan, who made her home "a home away from home"; the Southworths and their daughter Leela; Dave Smith and Amy Stiller, my friends from my old building who made me feel as if I had never left; and my cousins.

Several others helped in this endeavor in various ways: Peter Lattman, George Packer, Andrew Sorkin, Kaja Whitehouse, Scott DeCarlo, Quinn Martin, Vai Rajan, Azam Ahmed, David Glovin, Patricia Hurtado, Chad Bray, Kara Scannell, Parmy Olson, Juju Menon, Raghu Kumar, Shaku Sindle, Anjollie Feradov, and my old friends at home in London, Shonu Das, Sara Calian, Amanda Partridge, and Stephen Macmillan. Finally, a special thanks to my former editor at the *Wall Street Journal*, Michael Siconolfi, for teaching me how to fish.

Writing a book is a lonely experience, and I would not have survived had it not been for Martin, who has accompanied me on this journey. His quirky sense of humor made me laugh when all I wanted to do was cry, and his love has nourished me when I flagged. All I hope is that one day I can do the same for him.

My father came to the United States in 1958 to study for his doctorate at Princeton University, and my mother came a year later on her own for an internship at the Brooklyn Public Library. Even at eighty-two, she is still a librarian at heart, eager to dig up a book or find a source for me. Like many in this story, my parents are symbols of Indian achievement in the United States. I am grateful to them for their love and support and, most important, for the values they instilled in me. No one could be blessed with more wonderful parents.

A NOTE ON METHODOLOGY

This book was born with the arrests on October 16, 2009, of Raj Rajaratnam, Anil Kumar, and Rajiv Goel. Ever since I wrote a piece for the *Wall Street Journal* in 2006 about the Doon School and its graduates who had made it to the highest echelons of corporate America, I had been struggling to find an engaging way to write about the South Asian diaspora in the United States. The Galleon arrests provided the perfect vehicle. What is remarkable about the case is that it told many stories in a single story. It was a tale of the early migration of Indians to the United States, their breathtakingly swift rise and heady success in America, and last but most important, the emergence of a second generation of Indians who would ignore the blind loyalties their fathers held to kin and country and serve as a model of assimilated Indians in America. Of course, when I started on this odyssey I had no way of knowing that the story would also offer a compelling tale of India under the rule of the British and a window into the sacrifices that men like Rajat's father made so that every Indian today has the privilege to live in an independent and free country.

This book is based on more than two hundred interviews in three countries: the United States, the United Kingdom, and India. To understand the forces that influenced Gupta, I traveled to Calcutta, now Kolkata, where I visited his uncle's house, and interviewed his cousins, one of whom lives in the very same house where Rajat's father was brought after his death. I also examined police records and spoke to journalists who knew his father, which helped round out the picture of Gupta's father that I had started to form by trolling through records in the British Library and the Library of Congress.

A word is necessary on the spelling of an important name in the book. Rajat Gupta spells his father's name Ashwini, which is the way his name would have been pronounced in Bengali. However, the account of Gupta's father's freedom-fighting crimes is drawn from historical sources and newspaper articles in which his name is given as Aswini. Such inconsistencies in name spellings are not uncommon in India and arise from the challenge of translating Indian names into English. My research establishes that Rajat's father and the Aswini Gupta depicted in historical records and newspapers are one and the same person. A piece entitled "Aswini Gupta: A Life Sketch" that ran in the *Hindusthan Standard* on November 5, 1964, says that Gupta, the head of its news bureau in Delhi, was the younger brother of Mrs. Tatini Das, a former principal of Bethune College, Calcutta. He is similarly identified as the brother of Mrs. Tatini Das in newspaper reports in the mid-1930s on a crime and conviction case that was a cause célèbre in Calcutta. Finally, Indian cities in the book are referred to by their names at the time of the events in the story with a few exceptions, such as Pondicherry, which, despite its official name change, still goes by its old colonial name.

My research on Gupta continued in Delhi, which I visited three times. There I began to form an impression of the adolescent Gupta, and through the sources I cultivated for the *Journal* story on the Doon School, I was able to track Anil Kumar's metamorphosis from quiet, unassuming schoolboy to master-of-the-universe wannabe.

In a sense, like the characters in my book, I was twice blessed in my reporting. This is the first book on an insider trading case written with the aid of nearly fifty wiretapped calls, some of which run nearly 30 minutes. The wiretaps offered an extraordinary glimpse into white-collar crimes, typically shrouded from public view, being perpetrated in real time. More important for me as a writer, the wiretaps were key in developing an understanding of a protagonist's real character and a person's state of mind. In situations where a person's thinking could not be drawn from a direct interview of the subject, the wiretaps were invaluable.

All quoted conversations from these recordings are footnoted as coming from the relevant recordings and reflect the actual words spoken by the participants in the exchange. Other quoted conversations re-created in the book do not necessarily come from the individuals party to the conversations but rather reflect remarks heard by others or are contained in testimony or court documents such as FBI interview notes. Unlike the wiretaps, these re-created but quoted conversations in some cases rely on the individuals' memories and represent their best recollections. Like the wiretaps, though, these sources were important in painting a scene or providing a window into a person's thinking. Invariably, in a story like this, individuals try to retouch the truth after the fact or in their public declarations. This book relies to a large extent on conversations some of the key players had with their close circle of friends. In my view, it is in these private, unguarded moments that the closest semblance of the "truth" emerges.

In instances where there are two competing versions of events, I have footnoted the conflicting account and explained the reason I chose the version that appears in the text. Typical is the recounting of Anil Kumar's role in the growth of the McKinsey Knowledge Center. My reporting points to Kumar's playing a pivotal role in getting the Knowledge Center off the ground and leveraging his relationship with Gupta to secure approval from McKinsey's Shareholder Committee. McKinsey disagrees. A spokesman flatly says, "That is not accurate. To our knowledge, Anil Kumar did not play such a role in getting support for the knowledge initiative." My decision to follow my reporting in the text is based on interviews I conducted with individuals who were involved in the setup of the center at the time and who, in my mind, don't have a vested interest in the way Kumar is portrayed. These individuals, while conceding that they were not fans of Kumar's, said he was instrumental in the creation of the center.

This book was enriched by two trials, which I attended, one involving Raj Rajaratnam and the other Rajat Gupta, and two hearings that produced a huge volume of court testimony and documents including contemporaneous FBI interview notes of witnesses. While neither Rajaratnam nor Gupta took the stand in their defense at their trials, this gold mine of information combined with the wiretaps offered a penetrating portrait of both men. In addition, in the case of Gupta, my reporting was enhanced by two sources: a remarkably revealing three-hour taped talk Gupta gave to a class entitled Creativity and Personal Mastery taught by Srikumar Rao and a self-published history of McKinsey, *A History of the Firm*, by George David Smith, John T. Seaman Jr., and Morgen Witzel. Those two sources, along with more than eight hundred pages of letters that were submitted on Gupta's behalf before his sentencing, helped pierce the veil of a deeply private man with a well-cultivated public persona. (The letters were made available under an order by Judge Rakoff in response to a request by the *Wall Street Journal*.)

I am grateful to my colleagues in business journalism for some stellar reporting on this case. A handful of stories stand out. On the investigation, Susan Pulliam of the *Wall Street Journal* led the way with her early story, "The Network: The Feds Close In: Fund Chief Snared by Taps, Turncoats—Prosecutors Stalk Galleon's Rajaratnam After Finding a Revelatory Text Message." George Packer of the *New Yorker* enriched the story with his piece "A Dirty Business: New York City's Top Prosecutor Takes on Wall Street Crime." By far the best reporting on Raj Rajaratnam came from a *Wall Street Journal* story on December 29, 2009, by Robert A. Guth and Justin Scheck, entitled "The Network: The Rise of Raj: The Man Who Wired Silicon Valley—Fund Boss Built Empire on Charm, Smarts and Information." Peter Lattman, at the *New York Times*, who has a keen eye for everything from legal maneuvers to sartorial style, served up some of the most riveting reporting on the two trials.

David Glovin and Patricia Hurtado of Bloomberg News left no stone unturned in their coverage of the Gupta and Rajaratnam cases. And finally, as I delved into the life of Rajat Gupta, I found myself turning again and again to a story written nearly two decades ago about him by Sreenath Sreenivasan.

Although I am a member of the South Asian diaspora, this story was as hard to report as any in my twenty-four-year career as a journalist. The Galleon case was the first black mark on a community that had enjoyed unflinchingly positive press. Like any immigrant group thrust into the limelight, South Asians were reluctant to air their dirty laundry in public. A few were aghast at the actions of their friends and spoke on the record. But many more were bewildered and hesitated to speak for attribution. They were worried about jeopardizing the legal outcomes; even as this book was being finished, two of the central characters, Gupta and Rajaratnam, were appealing their cases. As a result, much of the storytelling in the latter part of the book relies on anonymous sources, mostly declared friends of some of the key players who followed the case both through publicly available press reports and through private exchanges with their embattled friends. Their insights, often different from the public declarations of support they offered, are reflected in the pages of this book.

NOTES

Prologue: The Twice Blessed

It was Tuesday, November 24, 2009, and other details of the White House dinner for Dr. Singh: White House, "Expected Attendees at Tonight's State Dinner," press release, November 24, 2009, http://www.whitehouse.gov/the-press-office/expected-attendees-tonights-state-dinner; Robin Givhan and Roxanne Roberts, "Marking First State Dinner, Obama Welcomes Indian Prime Minister," *Washington Post*, November 25, 2009; Bob Colacello, "The White House's Dinner Theater," *Vanity Fair*, June 1, 2010.

He sat on a handful of corporate boards: Duff McDonald, "Rajat Gupta: Touched by Scandal," *Fortune*, October 1, 2010.

Jindal, whose given name is Piyush: Adam Nossiter, "A Son of Immigrants Rises in a Deeply Southern State," *New York Times*, October 22, 2007.

Gupta's advice to Katyal: Letter written by Jody Wadhwa, Rajat Gupta's bridge partner, on Gupta's behalf before his sentencing and interview with Wadhwa, November 1, 2012.

Katyal's position: At the time of the dinner, Katyal was principal deputy solicitor general. He became acting solicitor general in 2010 and is now in private practice.

"As you looked around the room": Interview with Timothy Roemer, November 3, 2012.

A generation dubbed the "twice blessed": Interview with Vijay Prashad, October 13, 2010.

US immigration policies in the twentieth century and growth in Indian immigration: "The Passage from India," Immigration Policy Center, June 2, 2002, says the Luce-Cellar bill of 1946 provided for the admission of one hundred Indians each year and allowed them to seek citizenship. See http://www.immigrationpolicy.org/sites/default/files/docs/Policy%20Report-24%20Indian%20Bkgrd.pdf.

"There is an immense, immense selectivity": Interview with Professor Marcelo M. Suarez-Orozco, July 15, 2010.

Statistics on Indian achievement in the United States: "The Rise of Asian-Americans," Pew Research Center, June 19, 2012. The Pew study says the median household income for the US population as a whole was $49,800 in 2010. http://www.pewsocialtrends.org/2012/06/19/the-rise-of-asian-americans/.

Some ran or were poised to run the nation's biggest corporations—Citigroup and MasterCard: Vikram Pandit was Citigroup's CEO at the time of the dinner but stepped down in October 2012; http://newsroom.mastercard.com/press-releases/mastercard-names-ajay-banga-president-and-chief-executive-officer-succeeding-robert-w-selander/.

Others were contenders for top jobs at all-American companies like Warren Buffett's Berkshire Hathaway: Ajit Jain, who is the head of Berkshire Hathaway's reinsurance group, has been widely mentioned as a successor to Buffett. Jason Zweig, "And Buffett's Successor," *Wall Street Journal*, April 23, 2012.

The absences—the most notable being Citigroup chief Vikram Pandit: John Shazar, "Noted Corporate Welfare Recipient Not Welcome at White House Dinner," Dealbreaker.com, November 25, 2009.

Mukesh Ambani's views of Gupta: Letter written by Mukesh Ambani, head of Reliance Industries, on behalf of Rajat Gupta before his sentencing.

Tata, whose holdings run the gamut from cars—Jaguar Land Rover—to hotels: See http://www.tata.com/company/index.aspx?sectid=21vxqwHGkoo= and http://www.tata.com/company/profile.aspx?sectid=QqiuFWVxL/g=.

Tata worked early on to help Gupta turn his dream of an Indian business school into a reality: Gupta spoke of Tata's role in his graduation address to the Indian School of Business in April 2006, http://www.isb.edu/gradday2006/Transcript_Rajat.html.

Gupta's most important relationship was with Dr. Manmohan Singh: Author interviews and letters written by Gupta's friends before his sentencing confirm his relationship with Dr. Singh. Adil Zainulbhai, the chairman of McKinsey India, recalled being at a meeting with Dr. Singh where he said to Gupta, "I thank you for the efforts in helping many institutions in India—I know you don't have to do it, but you do it for the love of your country."

Dr. Singh ushered in economic reforms that dismantled the Red Tape Raj: In his profile on the government of India website, Dr. Singh is credited with "ushering in a comprehensive policy of economic reforms," http://pmindia.gov.in/pmsprofile.php.

Building Offshore-istan: A number of firms, including General Electric, had a role in the growth of offshoring, but the author believes that McKinsey, because of its penetration of corporate America, had a more profound impact on its rise. As McKinsey's former director Anil Kumar said in "Offshoring: Spreading the Gospel," *Business Week,* by Manjeet Kriplani with Brian Grow, March 5, 2006: "We were the first to legitimize the early thinking."

One of his dinner companions was labor leader Andy Stern: Interview with Andy Stern, November 15, 2012. Stern stepped down as the union head in 2010.

Stern, whose organization spent the most money supporting Obama: The Service Employees union legally can't contribute to candidates and the Obama campaign would not take Political Action Committee money, but the union did make substantial expenditures in urging people to vote and to vote for Obama and spent the most of any nonpolitical group for Obama. See http://www.opensecrets.org/pres12/indexp.php.

Over a dinner of green curry prawns: Menu of the White House dinner, http://www.whitehouse.gov/files/documents/2009/november/state-dinner-press-preview.pdf.

Since 2002, Goldman had awarded Palm stock and options worth $67.3 million: Based on calculation by executive compensation firm Equilar Inc.

Palm's biographical details: Louise Story, "The Men Who Ended Goldman's War," *New York Times*, July 17, 2010.

Peikin worked for nearly a decade in the US attorney's office: "Leading Federal Prosecutors Join Sullivan & Cromwell," PRNewswire, November 10, 2004.

Chapter One: "Who Will Show Me the Way in the World?"

History of India under the British: A variety of sources including Larry Collins and Dominique Lapierre, *Freedom at Midnight* (New York: Simon & Schuster, 1975), 20–23; Ramachandra Guha, *India After Gandhi: The History of the World's Largest Democracy* (London: Macmillan, 2007), 3–8.

Golf (a sport that arrived in Calcutta in 1829, some sixty years before it reached New York): Collins and Lapierre, *Freedom at Midnight*, 27.

"We must at present do our best": Quoted from the text of "Minute on Indian Education" as given in M. Edwardes, *British India, 1772–1947: A Survey on the Nature and Effects of Alien Rule* (London: Sidgwick and Jackson, 1967), 381.

"What Bengal thinks today, India thinks tomorrow": Gopal Krishna Ghokale as quoted in Sugata Bose and Ayesha Jalal, *Modern South Asia: History, Culture, Political Economy*, 2nd ed. (New York: Routledge, 2004), 95.

India's English-educated elite was a rarefied group at the turn of the century, representing less than 0.1 percent of the total population: Judith E. Walsh, *A Brief History of India*, 2nd ed. (New York: Facts on File, 2011), 145, is derived from an estimate by Bruce McCully, *English Education and the Origin of Indian Nationalism* (New York: Columbia University Press, 1940), 177. McCully said that more than 48,000 Indians, or 0.03 percent of the population, had received English educations by 1887.

Ashwini Gupta's roots in Goila, his education, and his life as a freedom fighter: "Aswini Gupta: A Life Sketch," *Hindusthan Standard*, November 5, 1964.

Like all Bengalis at the time, he was a leftist: Interview with Inder Malhotra, February 17, 2011.

Ashwini Gupta's arrest in 1930: Intelligence Branch Records, no. 409/1930, serial no. 176/1930, West Bengal State Archives, lists Aswini Gupta as among the boys found in the raid of the office of the All-Bengal Students' Association on July 1, 1930. The file says he "appeared to have come there as delegate to attend the Students' Convention at Calcutta." An article the following day in *Amrita Bazar Patrika* says of the thirty men arrested at the All-Bengal Students' Association office, all but one were released later.

Apurba Maitra's encounter with Ashwini Gupta in 1932 and Maitra's story: Apurba Maitra, *We Cried Together* (Calcutta: Firma KLM, 1982), 1–13.

The reputation of Calcutta's police commissioner: Ibid.

Two years earlier, the Indian National Congress passed a resolution fixing January 26: Ramachandra Guha, *India After Gandhi: The History of the World's Largest Democracy* (London: Macmillan, 2007), 3–4.

"What is wrong with Bengal?": Michael Silvestri, " 'The Sinn Fein of India': Irish Nationalism and the Policing of Revolutionary Terrorism in Bengal," *Journal of British Studies* 39 (October 2000), 461, cites John W. Wheeler-Bennett, *John Anderson, Viscount Waverly* (London: St. Martin's Press, 1962), 126.

Ashwini Gupta's participation in the Quit India movement and his subsequent arrest: "Aswini Gupta: A Life Sketch."

Ashwini Gupta's encounter with Maitra at Presidency Jail: Maitra, *We Cried Together*, 3–15.

Ashwini Gupta had vowed not to marry: Letter written by Dr. Rajashree Sen on behalf of her younger brother before his sentencing.

The two belonged to different Hindu reform movements: According to author interviews and sentencing letters, the Guptas were followers of Brahmo Samaj, a Hindu reformist movement that eschewed Hinduism's excessive focus on idolatry and placed emphasis on learning.

Ashwini Gupta's death: Author interviews in Calcutta; Maitra, *We Cried Together*; "Aswini Gupta Dead," *Hindusthan Standard*, November 5, 1964; "Aswini Gupta: The Last Rites," *Hindusthan Standard*, November 6, 1964.

Details of Ashwini Gupta's career after independence: Author interviews in Calcutta and New Delhi.

Rajat Gupta thinking his father was alive when he arrived at the hospital: Letter written on behalf of her father ahead of his sentencing by Megha Gupta (hereafter Megha Gupta sentencing letter).

At fifty-six, Ashwini Gupta was dead of kidney failure: "Aswini Gupta Dead."

Rajat Gupta's walks with his father and what he learned: Gupta's taped remarks at Creativity and Personal Mastery class (hereafter Gupta's remarks at Creativity and Personal Mastery class), taught by Srikumar Rao at Columbia Business School, April 2004.

He was intentionally exposed to TB: Megha Gupta sentencing letter.

"He never spoke ill about anybody": Gupta's remarks at Creativity and Personal Mastery class.

"Who will show me the way in the world": Interview with Rajat Gupta's cousin Damayanti Gupta-Wicklander, October 18, 2011.

Chapter Two: "I Respectfully Decline to Answer the Question"

It was three days before Christmas 2010: Rajat K. Gupta testimony before the Securities and Exchange Commission in the Matter of Sedna Capital Management, file no. NY 7665 (hereafter Gupta SEC testimony), December 22, 2010.

Sanjay Wadhwa, the deputy chief of the SEC's Market Abuse Unit: The SEC in a press release on April 1, 2011, said that Wadhwa has been deputy chief of the Market Abuse Unit since it was created in 2010, http://www.sec.gov/news/press/2011/2011-80.htm.

Wadhwa's life and career history: Devin Leonard, "Rajaratnam Case Shows Outmanned, Outgunned SEC on a Roll," *Bloomberg Businessweek*, April 19, 2012.

The story of Sanjay Wadhwa's father and mother and their family's experience of Partition: Interview with Arjun and Rashmi Wadhwa, January 21, 2012.

Punjab Province, a collection of 17,932 towns and villages with 15 million Hindus, 16 million Muslims, and 5 million Sikhs: Larry Collins and Dominique Lapierre, *Freedom at Midnight* (New York: Simon & Schuster, 1975), 121.

Partition and the division of Punjab and Bengal: Ibid.

Partition triggered a mass migration of people, and 1 million lives were lost: Ibid. Ramachandra Guha, *India After Gandhi: The History of the World's Largest Democracy* (London: Macmillan, 2007), 32.

Jawaharlal Nehru invited the country's masses to fulfill their "tryst with destiny" and "awake to life and freedom": As quoted in "A Tryst With Destiny," guardian.co.uk., May 1, 2007.

It helped to secure a letter from a member of Parliament: Interview with N. Ram, former editor in chief of the *Hindu*, April 22, 2012.

Hundreds of thousands of files were destroyed: Michael Schroeder and Mitchell Pacelle, "Attack Destroyed SEC Enforcement Office; CFTC's New York Offices Were Also Levelled," *Wall Street Journal*, September 13, 2001.

David Markowitz introducing Wadhwa to his first case: A version of this story is reported in Leonard, "Rajaratnam Case Shows Outmanned, Outgunned SEC on a Roll."

In April 2005, Wadhwa brought his first major insider trading case: Ibid.

Sanjay Wadhwa's role in the discovery of the Reebok ring: Roger Lowenstein, "The War on Insider Trading: Market Beaters Beware," *New York Times Magazine*, September 22, 2011.

The retired seamstress who netted $2 million in profits on Reebok: Jenny Anderson, "Seamstress Makes Millions and The Law Notices," *New York Times*, April 12, 2006.

"The Zelig of the white-collar bar": Ashby Jones and Peter Lattman, "Heavy Lifters, Five Lawyers with High-Profile High-Stakes Cases in the Months Ahead," WSJ.com, 2005.

Naftalis's biography and clients: Kramer Levin Naftalis & Frankel LLP website, http://www.kramerlevin.com/gnaftalis/.

Exchange among Henderson, Gupta, and Friedman on December 22, 2010: Gupta SEC testimony.

"He got the brilliance of his father": Interview with Udayan Bhattarcharyya, November 12, 2011.

When "he decided on something, it had to happen": Interview with Damayanti Gupta-Wicklander, October 18, 2011.

Details of early family life: Author interviews in Calcutta and New Delhi; letters submitted on behalf of Rajat Gupta in connection with his sentencing; Sreenath Sreenivasan, "The Superboss: How Did McKinsey's Rajat Gupta Become the First India-Born CEO of a $1.3 Billion US Transnational?" *Business Today*, April 22, 1994.

Modern School on Barakhamba Road was founded at the height of the British Raj: See http://www.modernschool.net/history-founder.asp for the history of Modern School and its location.

It was "'the' school": Interview with Mukul Mudgal, February 2, 2011.

"Self-realization cannot be achieved by the weak-willed": See http://www.modernschool.net/history-crest.asp for Modern's motto. Other translations substitute "perfection" for "self-realization."

Details of Rajat's time in Modern: Author interviews in New Delhi; sentencing letters filed on Gupta's behalf.

His mother was diagnosed with incurable heart disease: Letter written by Jayashree Chowdhury, Gupta's younger sister, on behalf of Gupta before his sentencing (hereafter Jayashree Chowdhury sentencing letter).

Rajat's supervision of his siblings after his father's death and the family's mounting expenses: Ibid.

"He did not come from a big family that showered him with money": Interview with Debasish Bhattacharya, November 19, 2011.

In his final year at Modern, he placed fifteenth in the national entrance examination for the Indian Institutes of Technology: Sreenivasan, "The Superboss."

Chapter Three: A Family Affair

After its acquisition of ABN AMRO's prime brokerage unit in 2003: "ABN Amro Completes Sale of US Unit Prime Brokerage to UBS," Dow Jones International News, December 8, 2003.

One of the funds UBS serviced was Sedna Capital: Rajarengan Rajaratnam testimony before the Securities and Exchange Commission in the Matter of Sedna Capital Management, file no. NY 7665 (hereafter Rengan SEC testimony), December 20, 2006.

Personal details and work history of Rengan Rajaratnam: Ibid.

Description of the spat between Cohen and Rengan Rajaratnam: Ibid.

The setup of Sedna: Ibid.

Rengan floated the idea of creating a high-risk fund during a family vacation to Gila: Raj Rajaratnam testimony before the Securities and Exchange Commission in the Matter of Sedna Capital Management, file no. NY-7665 (hereafter Rajaratnam SEC testimony), June 7, 2007.

And in July 2006, Rengan opened a new fund: In his testimony to the SEC, Rengan said the fund was officially launched in August but he put money in it in late July.

"Listen, give me as much money as you are willing to lose": Rengan SEC testimony.

Rengan's $700,000 investment in the new fund and details of his family's contributions: Ibid.; *US v. Rajaratnam*, Franks hearing, Kang Exhibit 3, citing a document provided by Sedna to SEC examiners and a UBS statement.

But Rengan's older brother put in $1 million: Rajaratnam SEC testimony.

Details of Sedna's Arris trade, its profit, and Rengan's gains: *US v. Rajaratnam*, Franks hearing, Michaelson Exhibit 19, Chronology of communication and activity in Arris (hereafter *US v. Rajaratnam*, Franks hearing, Michaelson Arris chronology); Rengan SEC testimony.

After a blockbuster first month, Rengan forced investors to redeem: Rengan SEC testimony.

After it sold short $1.4 million shares of stock on July 26, the maximum allowable position: Rengan SEC testimony.

After saying he wanted to be "long into the numbers," Rengan bet heavily against Arris: Rengan SEC testimony.

On July 27, Arris's stock fell nearly 20 percent: Interactive Data via FactSet Research Systems.

Rengan, the only investor in the fund, netted $270,000: *US v. Rajaratnam*, Franks hearing, Michaelson Arris chronology said Rengan made over $250,000 and Sedna locked in a profit of more than $1.1 million.

"u r my heroine": *US v. Rajaratnam*, Franks hearing, Michaelson Arris chronology.

"It definitely feels like there are less quality women out there": "Bachelors Compete for Dwindling Supply of Bachelorettes," FoxNews.com, December 27, 2001.

"Arris [thank you] for getting us out": *US v. Rajaratnam*, Franks hearing, Michaelson Arris chronology.

Sedna was engaged in cherry picking: In *US v. Rajaratnam*, Franks hearing, October 5, 2010, Andrew Michaelson said in his testimony that the investigation at first was primarily focused on cherry picking.

Explanation of cherry picking: Ibid.

A sprawling investment metropolis of more than sixty-five hundred hedge funds managing $1.1 trillion in assets: Hedge Fund Research Inc.

Chapter Four: Drama at IIT

"Our adolescent hormones and new-found freedom formed a dangerous mixture": Harbinder Gill testimonial, Friends of Rajat Gupta website.

Details on the Gupta family after their mother died: Sreenath Sreenivasan, "The Superboss: How Did McKinsey's Rajat Gupta Become the First India-Born CEO of a $1.3 Billion US Transnational?" *Business Today*, April 22, 1994; letters written by Jayashree Chowdhury (hereafter Jayashree Chowdhury sentencing letter) and Kanchan Gupta (hereafter Kanchan Gupta sentencing letter) on behalf of their brother ahead of his sentencing; author interviews.

The description of IIT Delhi in the sixties and the change in its cachet: Drawn from interview with Shashi K. Gulhati, February 2, 2010; Gulhati, "A Double Tribute," written in 2011 for IIT's Golden Jubilee, and *The IITs: Slumping or Soaring* (Macmillan India, 2007), 4.

"When I finished IIT Delhi": Interview with Vinod Khosla by Lesley Stahl, "Imported from India," *60 Minutes*, CBS News, March 2, 2003.

The list of IIT graduates and their positions today: Chandrani Ghosh, "Boot Camp for Engineers," *Forbes*, April 16, 2001.

Narayana Murthy remark about his son: Stahl, "Imported from India."

Story about Indira Gandhi's efforts to get Rajiv Gandhi into IIT Delhi: Interview with Kanta Dogra, February 4, 2011.

Rajiv Gandhi did not receive a degree from Cambridge or Imperial College: Ved Mehta, *Rajiv Gandhi and Rama's Kingdom* (New Haven and London: Yale University Press, 1994), 70.

Gupta was one of sixty-two students: Gill testimonial.

The standoff between Dogra and the students at IIT Delhi and Gupta's role: Interview with Anjan Chatterjee, March 13, 2012. His account is confirmed by others at IIT at the time.

During his five years at IIT, he acted in seventeen plays: Sreenivasan, "The Superboss."

"You must have felt terrible": Chatterjee interview.

Anita Mattoo's family background and her impression of Rajat: Letters written by Anita Gupta on behalf of her husband ahead of his sentencing and by Girja Madan, who is related to Gupta's wife.

Indian law requiring companies to dilute their shareholdings in Indian companies to 40 percent: "India: Curbs on Foreign Investors," Facts on File News Services, November 25, 1970.

"All Rajat would talk to me about": Interview with Subramanian Swamy, April 22, 2012.

Gupta was one of two students to receive a job offer from ITC: Gupta's taped remarks at Creativity and Personal Mastery class (hereafter Gupta's remarks at Creativity and Personal Mastery class), taught by Srikumar Rao at Columbia Business School, April 2004.

ITC's history: See the company's website, http://www.itcportal.com/about-itc/profile/history-and-evolution.aspx.

Since its founding in 1935: See http://www.doonschool.com/the-school-and-campus/origins-a-history.

Doon's illustrious alumni: Anita Raghavan, "The Andover of India? Graduates from Doon Score Top U.S. Jobs—Scholastic Bootcamp for Boys Raises Stars, Faces Change; Gandhi Suffered Here Too," *Wall Street Journal*, June 3, 2006; Ed Luce, "Liberal Streak," *Financial Times*, January 2, 2003.

Gupta described a leader as "one who can motivate": Sreenivasan, "The Superboss."

Gupta's rejection of the offer from ITC and Haksar's reaction: Ibid.; Gupta's remarks at Creativity and Personal Mastery class.

Chapter Five: Birdie Trades

Description of the SEC in the Cox era: George Packer, "A Dirty Business: New York City's Top Prosecutor Takes on Wall Street Crime," *New Yorker*, June 27, 2011.

On September 21, 2006, Wadhwa received a formal order of investigation: Government's post-hearing Memorandum in Opposition to Defendant Raj Rajaratnam's Motion to Suppress Wiretaps, October 27, 2010, says that in September 2006 the SEC's Division of Enforcement began an investigation into cherry picking and insider trading at Sedna Capital Management, a hedge fund run by Rengan Rajaratnam.

Lyons, a political science graduate: Testimony of William J. Lyons III in the Matter of Sedna Capital Management LLC, file no. NY-7665 (hereafter Lyons SEC testimony), October 18, 2006.

In late July 2006, after Hewlett-Packard agreed to acquire Mercury Interactive: Hewlett-Packard, "HP to Acquire Mercury Interactive Corp.," press release, July 25, 2006, http://www.hp.com/hpinfo/newsroom/press/2006/060725a.html.

The instant-message exchanges involving the "birdie" trades: *US v. Rajaratnam*, Franks hearing, Michaelson Exhibit 19, Chronology of communication and activity in Arris (hereafter *US v. Rajaratnam*, Franks hearing, Michaelson Arris chronology).

In October, Wadhwa took testimony from Lyons: Lyons SEC testimony.

Michaelson's background: Packer, "A Dirty Business."

Rengan instant message to Andrew Quinn: *US v. Rajaratnam*, Franks hearing, Michaelson Arris chronology.

In one email to Apax: *US v. Rajaratnam*, Franks hearing, Attachment A to Kang Exhibit 3 contains email from Rengan Rajaratnam to an Apax executive on July 17, 2006.

Dhar was at Arris's headquarters in Atlanta: *US v. Rajaratnam*, Franks hearing, Government Exhibit 15, FBI memo dated June 27, 2007, to document meeting with the SEC on May 23.

It was unusual for Dhar to know Arris's earnings before they were announced: Ibid.

Dhar says he spoke to Rengan: Dhar's comment on December 12, 2012.

On July 31, 2006, Rajaratnam wired: *US v. Rajaratnam*, Franks hearing, Michaelson Exhibit 19, Chronology of trading in AMD (hereafter *US v. Rajaratnam*, Franks hearing, Michaelson AMD chronology).

That July 31 evening, at 8:32, Bloomberg News: Ibid.

The *Wall Street Journal,* citing Bloomberg, mentioned that IBM: Ibid.

"fuckers...screwing my picture": *US v. Rajaratnam,* Franks hearing, Government Exhibit 32, Chronology of Polycom activity in FBI memo dated November 6, 2007, contains an excerpt of an instant-message exchange between Rengan and Raj Rajaratnam on April 18, 2006.

"see the ibm/amd news" and subsequent IM exchange: *US v. Rajaratnam,* Franks hearing, Michaelson AMD chronology.

Dell released earnings and said it would unveil desktop computers with AMD processors: Rex Crum, "Dell Shares Fall After Weak Earnings Report," MarketWatch, August 18, 2006.

Sedna's friends and family fund sold the options for a $2.8 million gain: *US v. Rajaratnam,* Franks hearing, Kang Exhibit 3, Chronology of AMD trading.

The instant-message exchange between Read and Lyons: Ibid.

"I can't believe I am being asked to testify": Raj Rajaratnam testimony before the Securities and Exchange Commission in the Matter of Sedna Capital Management, file no. NY 7665 (hereafter Rajaratnam SEC testimony), June 7, 2007.

The SEC had been investigating Galleon on and off since 2003: *US v. Rajaratnam,* Franks hearing, Beaudreault Exhibit 1, Declaration of Lindi E. Beaudreault Esq. in Support of Defendant Raj Rajaratnam's Motion to Suppress.

In 2005, Rajaratnam paid a fine of nearly $2 million to settle an SEC case: See http://sec.gov/news/press/2005-77.htm.

On December 20, 2006, five days before Christmas, Rengan Rajaratnam, flanked by his lawyers: Rajarengan Rajaratnam testimony before the Securities and Exchange Commission in the Matter of Sedna Capital Management, file no. NY 7665 (hereafter Rengan SEC testimony), December 20, 2006.

Michaelson's questions and Rengan's responses: Ibid.

SAC Capital, run by Rengan's former boss, Steven Cohen, did not seek the SEC imprimatur until 2012: See SAC's registration details on SEC website: http://www.adviserinfo.sec.gov/iapd/content/viewform/adv/Sections/iapd_AdvRegulatorStatusSection.aspx?ORG_PK=161111&RGLTR_PK=50000&STATE_CD=&FLNG_PK=023C7D0800080166007C5BF0040FFFAD056C8CC0.

Sedna got it only in January 2006: Rengan SEC testimony.

When his brother asked how it went, he said well: Rajaratnam SEC testimony.

Chapter Six: Promises to Keep

He kept a jar of hot pickles in his room: Interview with Richard Peiser, Gupta's first-year roommate at HBS, January 11, 2013.

Notable members of HBS Class of 1973 and makeup of class: HBS Class prospectus.

"There were a lot of Brits": Interview with Grover T. Wickersham, April 6, 2011.

John Carberry's impressions of Gupta and the description of the "can group": Interview with John Carberry, April 19, 2011.

Tattered piece of paper with the lines from the Frost poem: Letter written by M. Kumar on Gupta's behalf ahead of his sentencing.

"All we ever did during those walks": Carberry interview.

The approach to teaching at HBS: Interview with Fred Sturdivant, May 24, 2011.

The incident with Townsend Clarke: Confirmed in separate interviews with Carberry and Sturdivant.

"Rajat constantly floated above this" and "if you had a problem with a case": Carberry interview.

"When you look at the guy, he is kind of a Nehru" and Wickersham's subsequent remarks: Wickersham interview.

Gupta attributing his silence to his Indian upbringing and the deal he cut with his professors: Sreenath Sreenivasan, "The Superboss: How Did McKinsey's Rajat Gupta Become the First India-Born CEO of a $1.3 Billion US Transnational?" *Business Today*, April 22, 1994; Gupta's taped remarks at Creativity and Personal Mastery class, taught by Srikumar Rao at Columbia Business School, April 2004.

Carberry's recollections of Gupta watching American football and Carson: Carberry interview.

John Hook's recollection of Gupta: Interview with John Hook, May 30, 2011.

Chapter Seven: The Good Ship Galleon

On the morning of Monday, February 12, 2007: *US v. Rajaratnam*, Franks hearing, Testimony of Lindi Beaudreault, October 4, 2010, provides details about the meeting.

She told the examiners that Galleon adhered to a very detailed policy on insider trading: *US v. Rajaratnam*, Franks hearing, Government Exhibit 150, notes of the SEC examination staff's interview of Lindi Beaudreault and others.

Chat between Rajaratnam and Quint Slattery: *US v. Rajaratnam*, Franks hearing, Government Exhibit 17, Email from Andrew Michaelson to Lauren Goldberg and Brian Coad on June 18, 2007, with instant-message exchange between Rajaratnam and Slattery attached.

Michaelson's probe of Rajaratnam's possible source on Computer Associates: *US v. Rajaratnam*, Franks hearing, Testimony of Andrew Michaelson, October 5, 2010.

At the same time, an anonymous letter arrived: *US v. Rajaratnam*, Franks hearing, Government Exhibit 4, Copy of the letter.

"Is this an investigation of Galleon or an investigation of Sedna?": *US v. Rajaratnam*, Franks hearing, Defense Exhibit 48, Deposition of Paul Yook.

Wadhwa did not answer: Ibid.

Its employees were absorbed by Galleon: *US v. Rajaratnam*, Franks hearing, Beaudreault testimony.

On May 14, 2007, the SEC issued a subpoena to Galleon: *US v. Rajaratnam*, Franks hearing, Testimony of Lindi Beaudreault, October 4, 2010.

The firm's lawyers canceled a scheduled SEC interview with Tom Fernandez: On October 4, 2010, at the Franks hearing, Beaudreault testified that she telephoned Andrew Michaelson and said if he was subpoenaing witnesses she would prefer if they met once with the enforcement staff rather than have two meetings. She said her recollection was that the examination ended in late May, not in mid-May when the subpoena was issued.

The staffer found "some interesting" chatter: George Packer, "A Dirty Business: New York City's Top Prosecutor Takes on Wall Street Crime," *New Yorker*, June 27, 2011.

Devised a way of asking Rajaratnam about roomy81: Ibid.

At 10 a.m., Rajaratnam, flanked by the same two lawyers: Raj Rajaratnam testimony before the Securities and Exchange Commission in the Matter of Sedna Capital Management, file no. NY 7665 (hereafter Rajaratnam SEC testimony), June 7, 2007.

During the course of the seven-hour deposition: The transcript of Raj Rajaratnam's SEC testimony says it started at 10:12 a.m. and ended at 4:54 p.m.

Michaelson's questions and Rajaratnam's answers: Rajaratnam SEC testimony.

The hedge funds Rajaratnam was invested in: Ibid.

At about 12:30, Isenberg requested a break: Ibid.

Rajaratnam's explanations for his AMD trades: Rajaratnam SEC testimony.

The hedge fund paid between $30 million and $60 million to its analysts: Ibid.; Devin Leonard,

"Rajaratnam Case Shows Outmanned, Outgunned SEC on a Roll," Bloomberg, April 19, 2012.

Michaelson's questioning regarding roomy81 and Rajaratnam's instant-message exchange with Apjit Walia: Rajaratnam SEC testimony.

"Package B": What was meant by package B was never conclusively established and there is potential contradictory evidence. Tickets to the 2007 ICC Cricket World Cup went on sale to the public in May 2006, a few months before the IM exchange and there was a package B offered. Walia in his voluntary testimony said he never traded stocks or options in his personal capacity and that he did not have any investments in hedge funds.

The next day, June 8, 2007, the SEC issued a five-page subpoena to Galleon: Lindi Beaudreault in her testimony on October 4, 2010, testified to the date and contents of the SEC subpoena.

Chapter Eight: No Ask Backs

Walter Salmon had just wrapped up a class at Harvard Business School in the spring term of 1973; his impressions of Gupta: Interview with Walter Salmon, January 30, 2012.

Salmon's sitting on the boards of Hannaford Brothers and Stride Rite: Form 10-K, Hannaford Brothers Co., January 1, 2000; and Proxy Statement, Stride Rite, February 28, 1991.

Recruiting at HBS in the 1970s: Interview with John Carberry, April 19, 2011.

The change in American business culture in the early 1970s and the rise of companies like consulting firms that sold advice: David Leonhardt, "Consultant Nation," *New York Times,* December 10, 2011.

McKinsey saw an opportunity to counsel managers when he worked in the Army Ordnance Department; early history of McKinsey and its work for Marshall Field: From Amar V. Bhide, "Building the Professional Firm: McKinsey & Co.: 1939–1968"; John Huey, "How McKinsey Does It: The World's Most Powerful Consulting Firm Commands Unrivaled Respect—and Prices—but Is Being Buffeted by a Host of New Challenges," *Fortune,* November 1, 1993.

"BCG and Bain hired 'the best and the brightest'": Jeffrey Skilling email, March 4, 2012.

Bruce D. Henderson, a onetime Bible salesman and Harvard Business School graduate, founded the Boston Consulting Group in 1963: www.bcg.com.

It started with just two consultants and in its first month racked up $500 in billings: Ibid.

By 1973, Boston Consulting had grown to 142 consultants: Ibid.

And like McKinsey, it had offices in London and Paris: Ibid.

So-called Baker Scholars such as unsuccessful presidential candidate Mitt Romney: Leonhardt, "Consultant Nation."

Harvey Golub, Michael Jordan, and Louis Gerstner Jr. went on to jobs at American Express, Westinghouse, and IBM: John A. Byrne, "The McKinsey Mystique," *Business Week,* September 19, 1993.

USA Today study: The *USA Today* study is cited by Duff McDonald in "The Answer Men," *New York Magazine,* July 26, 2009.

Gupta being awarded perfect grades but striking out in his first effort to be hired by McKinsey: Sreenath Sreenivasan, "The Superboss: How Did McKinsey's Rajat Gupta Become the First India-Born CEO of a $1.3 Billion US Transnational?" *Business Today,* April 22, 1994.

Anita Mattoo thought she would not see Gupta: Letter written by Anita Gupta on behalf of her husband ahead of his sentencing.

In his wallet, he kept a five-rupee note: Letter written by M. Kumar on behalf of Gupta ahead of his sentencing.

Anita winning the director's gold medal at IIT: Sreenivasan, "The Superboss."

Rajat's summer job at the food-processing plant: Interview with Doug Manly, December 23, 2012.

"If you didn't have a US citizenship": Gupta's taped remarks at Creativity and Personal Mastery class (hereafter Gupta's remarks at Creativity and Personal Mastery class), taught by Srikumar Rao at Columbia Business School, April 2004.

Bill Clemens's words to Gupta: Sreenivasan, "The Superboss."

"Nobody else is interviewing me": Gupta's remarks at Creativity and Personal Mastery class.

At one point, more than a third of McKinsey's consultants held a Harvard MBA: McDonald, "The Answer Men."

"You guys do great work": Interview with Anjan Chatterjee, March 13, 2012.

"That surprises me given your work in my class" and Salmon's subsequent remarks to Gupta and Daniel: Salmon interview.

Chapter Nine: "The Tamil Tiger" of Wall Street

Rajaratnam's hiring by Chase and his starting salary of $34,000: Anita Raghavan, "Power and Pleasure," *Forbes*, October 11, 2010.

"Wall Street was tough to get into for us": Suketu Mehta, "The Outsider," *Newsweek*, October 23, 2011.

Rajaratnam's early years at Chase: Raghavan, "Power and Pleasure."

"Give me a Quotron": Ibid.

"After a while money is not the motivation": Lois Peltz, *The New Investment Superstars: 13 Great Investors and Their Strategies for Superior Returns* (Hoboken, NJ: John Wiley & Sons, 2001).

In 1985, Rajaratnam quit Chase for Needham: Raghavan, "Power and Pleasure."

"I hire one-legged men": Robert A. Guth and Justin Scheck, "The Network: The Rise of Raj: The Man Who Wired Silicon Valley—Fund Boss Built Empire on Charm, Smarts and Information," *Wall Street Journal*, December 29, 2009.

Required to take red-eye flights: Ibid.

When US semiconductor companies were struggling: Ibid.

He told them his first name meant "king" in Hindi: Ibid.

"He would tell about his experience with the Tamil Tigers": Raghavan, "Power and Pleasure."

"When you are presenting a highly technical story": Interview with Bob Anderson, August 10, 2010.

"Raj sort of had a South Asian mafia": Raghavan, "Power and Pleasure."

At Needham, he was "pretty much the same guy you see now": Ibid.

In 1988, he and Asha Pabla were married: *US v. Rajaratnam*, Sentencing Memorandum on behalf of Raj Rajaratnam (hereafter Rajaratnam sentencing memo).

In 1991, George Needham promoted Rajaratnam to president: Guth and Scheck, "The Network."

Rajaratnam's bet that he could handle any spicy sauce: Ibid.

By the beginning of 1994, Rajaratnam owned 17 percent of Needham: Ibid.

Needham confronting Rajaratnam about his South Asian hires: Suketu Mehta, "The Outsider," *Newsweek*, October 23, 2011.

In 1992, Rajaratnam started a small hedge fund at Needham: Rajaratnam sentencing memo.

Between 1993 and 1996, at least five Needham executives: Guth and Scheck, "The Network."

"I greatly regret that Raj Rajaratnam": Ibid.

How do I get these guys to call me?: Raghavan, "Power and Pleasure."

Chapter Ten: Up or Out at McKinsey

Gupta's impressions of his early years at McKinsey: Gupta's taped remarks at Creativity and Personal Mastery class (hereafter Gupta's remarks at Creativity and Personal Mastery class), taught by Srikumar Rao at Columbia Business School, April 2004.

"I was sitting there and wondering": Ibid. McKinsey says Gupta became an engagement manager less than three years after joining the firm.

"Rajat did not seem overwhelmed at all" and subsequent remarks by Wyss: Interview with Karl Wyss, October 31, 2012.

Bob Waterman's impressions of the young Gupta: Interview with Robert Waterman Jr., May 20, 2011.

Skilling's observations of McKinsey in the 1970s: Email from Jeffrey Skilling, March 4, 2012.

"The new markets were blocked by the new guys": Email from Jeffrey Skilling, March 7, 2012.

Gupta's encounter with Bud Miles and the advice he received from a partner: Gupta's remarks at Creativity and Personal Mastery class.

An electrical engineer, Gluck arrived in 1967 after a stint at Bell Labs, where he was program manager for the Spartan missile: Walter Kiechel III, *The Lords of Strategy: The Secret Intellectual History of the New Corporate World* (Boston: Harvard Business Press, 2010).

"The whole place moved": Interview with Anjan Chatterjee, March 13, 2012.

Henzler made principal in four and a half years: Herbert Henzler, *Immer am Limit* (Berlin: Econ, 2011), 89.

Gupta being late in making principal: Gupta's remarks at Creativity and Personal Mastery class.

He bought $2 shirts at Filene's Basement and sent money for his siblings to buy a house: Letter written by Jayashree Chowdhury on behalf of her brother ahead of his sentencing.

"I spent my first night": Chatterjee interview.

Gupta's expectation that his wife would give him the cover to turn down Scandinavia and her surprising reaction: Gupta's remarks at Creativity and Personal Mastery class.

Anita's job at Bell Labs: Ibid.

Purchase of house for $75,000 in Middletown, NJ: Monmouth County Clerk's Office.

Naming his daughter after the Tagore epic: Letter written by Gupta's IIT friend Ashok K. Manchanda on his behalf before Gupta's sentencing.

Gupta's reaction to McKinsey's offer for him to visit Scandinavia, his first house-hunting trip there, and his colleagues' buying his house there: Gupta's remarks at Creativity and Personal Mastery class.

Scandinavia was "a very homogeneous environment": Ibid.

The Scandinavian office manager's drinking problem and Gupta's reflections on it: Ibid.; the episode is also confirmed and elaborated upon by other McKinsey partners and is described in George David Smith, John T. Seaman Jr., and Morgen Witzel, *A History of the Firm* (privately published by McKinsey in 2010).

"Office managers had a lot of power": Chatterjee interview.

Gupta was one of the youngest office managers: Sreenath Sreenivasan, "The Superboss: How Did McKinsey's Rajat Gupta Become the First India-Born CEO of a $1.3 Billion US Transnational?" *Business Today*, April 22, 1994.

Christian Caspar's recollection of Gupta: John A. Byrne, "A 'Global Citizen' for a Global McKinsey," *BusinessWeek*, April 10, 1994.

"What a change": Skilling email, March 4, 2012.

Skilling's experience with Gupta in Scandinavia: Email from Jeffrey Skilling, March 6, 2012.

Grown the practice in Scandinavia from 15 to 125: Gupta's remarks at Creativity and Personal Mastery class.

"To this day our competitors find it hard to compete": R. Sridharan, "Change Agent," *Business Today,* August 12, 2007.

Gupta's approach in Scandinavia "probably foreshadowed McKinsey's phenomenal worldwide success": Skilling email, March 4, 2012.

The story about Marvin Bower as Santa Claus: Smith, Seaman, and Witzel, *A History of the Firm,* 118.

Chapter Eleven: The Camera Never Lies

In the spring of 1998 Intel installed a hidden video camera: *US v. Roomy Khan* CR-01-20029-JW, Government Sentencing Memorandum and Motion for Downward Departure, July 1, 2002.

By design, the fax feeder required that documents be laid faceup on the machine: Interview with former FBI agent Russell Atkinson, May 17, 2012, and September 14, 2012.

Intel also installed a camera in a fabric divider panel: Ibid.

The time clock on the camera was synchronized with the clock on the fax: Ibid.

After complaints two years earlier from investors: *US v. Rajaratnam*, Franks hearing, Government Exhibit 2, Electronic Communication dated April 29, 1998, from FBI San Francisco to FBI headquarters.

Preliminary investigations of its phone records: Ibid.

"If you sell this information you can get real money for it": Justin Scheck, Robert A. Guth, and Ben Charny, "Rajaratnam Investigated Decade Ago—Probe Adds Another Missed Opportunity by Securities Regulators and Government Prosecutors," *Wall Street Journal,* December 4, 2009.

Investors had been complaining to Intel since 1996 of their suspicions that information was leaking to Rajaratnam's newsletter: *US v. Rajaratnam*, Franks hearing, Government Exhibit 2.

Just a year earlier, Rajaratnam had struck out on his own: *US v. Rajaratnam*, Sentencing Memorandum on behalf of Raj Rajaratnam (hereafter Rajaratnam sentencing memo).

"I was spending two or three hours a day as a shrink": *US v. Rajaratnam*, Franks hearing, Government Exhibit 169, Raj Rajaratnam, the Galleon Group, interview with Antoine Bernheim, *HedgeFund News* publisher, April 1997.

In January, he and three lieutenants from Needham: Lois Peltz, *The New Investment Superstars: 13 Great Investors and Their Strategies for Superior Returns* (Hoboken, NJ: John Wiley & Sons, 2001), says that Gary Rosenbach, Krishen Sud, and Ari Arjavalingam joined Rajaratnam at Galleon.

Within a decade after he set up Galleon, assets at hedge funds would swell to $1.5 trillion: Hedge Fund Research Inc.

Steven Cohen, founder of SAC Capital, ranks fortieth on the Forbes 400 list and is a Wharton grad: See http://www.forbes.com/profile/steve-cohen/.

Cohen grew SAC from $25 million in assets: Ibid.

Cohen's estate: First described by Susan Pulliam in "Private Money: The New Financial Order—The Hedge-Fund King Is Getting Nervous—Inside Billionaire Steven Cohen's Hidden World of Massive Trading and Lavish Art; Is the Party Over?—At Home with Van Gogh, Gauguin and a Skating Rink," *Wall Street Journal,* September 16, 2006. Bryan Burroughs, "What's Eating Steve Cohen?" *Vanity Fair,* July 2010.

Office on Lexington and Fifty-Seventh Street, about a block from his old firm: Robert A. Guth and Justin Scheck, "The Network: The Rise of Raj: The Man Who Wired Silicon Valley—Fund Boss Built Empire on Charm, Smarts and Information," *Wall Street Journal,* December 29, 2009.

Managing about $350 million that he cobbled together from close friends and family: Peltz, *New Investment Superstars.*

His firm was called Galleon Group after the large ships that traded in spices and ivory with Sri Lanka, his birthplace, known long ago as the Isle of Serendip: Suketu Mehta, "The Outsider," *Newsweek*, October 23, 2011.

It traded on Rajaratnam's expertise, technology stocks: Peltz, *New Investment Superstars.*

On the walls of his new office, he hung: Ibid.

Investors were Ken Levy, Neil Bonke, and Kris Chellam: Raj Rajaratnam testimony before the Securities and Exchange Commission in the Matter of Sedna Capital Management, June 7, 2007; author interviews.

He and his wife lived with their son: *US v. Rajaratnam*, Rajaratnam sentencing memo.

At one time Marilyn Monroe lived at the address: "Playwright wins Marilyn," *Long Beach Independent*, June 22, 1956; Donald Spoto, *Marilyn Monroe: The Biography* (New York: HarperCollins, 1993).

And today it counts among its famous residents Mario Cuomo: Christine Haughney, "The Appraisal; From Queens Roots, Cuomo Clan Branched Out," *New York Times*, May 3, 2010.

In 2000, when he moved to combine the two apartments and have two kitchens, he cited "adherence to Jewish traditions": Anita Raghavan, "Power and Pleasure," *Forbes*, October 11, 2010.

So he stacked its board of advisers with impressive names including hedge fund titan Stanley Druckenmiller and Paine Webber chief Don Marron: Peltz, *New Investment Superstars*, 204.

He generally walked to work from his apartment: Ibid., 203.

Galleon's 8:30 a.m. meeting and the fine for latecomers: Robert A. Guth and Justin Scheck, "The Network: The Rise of Raj: The Man Who Wired Silicon Valley," *Wall Street Journal*, first reported on the $25 fine.

Rajaratnam's focus on bottoms-up research carried out by a team of analysts visiting more than three hundred companies: Peltz, *New Investment Superstars*, 201.

Rajaratnam's requirement that his analysts' travel expenses would be reimbursed only if they sent an explanation of what they learned: Ibid., 202.

Eight of ten analysts were engineers by training, and Rajaratnam liked to boast his analysts weren't "blindsided by the marketing hype": Ibid.

He said it was easier to teach an engineer to pick stocks: Rajaratnam sentencing memo.

On Thursdays, employees could sign up for massages: Guth and Scheck, "The Network: The Rise of Raj: The Man who Wired Silicon Valley."

The modeling of a black Spandex outfit: A version of this story appeared in Gregory Zuckerman and Robert A. Guth, "Rajaratnam: Relentless Pursuit of Data," *Wall Street Journal*, October 24, 2009.

A budget for travel had to be approved before the trip: *US v. Rajaratnam*, Testimony of Adam Smith, March 29, 2011.

James Bagley met Rajaratnam in the early 1990s: A portion of the August 5, 2010, interview with Bagley first appeared in Raghavan, "Power and Pleasure."

Khan's roots in Delhi, her educational background, her meeting Rajaratnam, and their early dealings: *US v. Doug Whitman*, 12 CR.125 (JSR), Testimony of Roomy Khan, August 6, 2012. *US v. Rajaratnam and Danielle Chiesi*, S1 09 Cr. 1184 (RJH), Defendant Raj Rajaratnam's Memorandum of Law in Support of His Motion to Suppress Evidence Derived from Wiretap Interceptions of his Cellular Telephone (hereafter cited as *US v. Rajaratnam and Chiesi*, Rajaratnam Motion to Suppress Wiretaps), Exhibits A.8, A.9, and A.17, FBI 302 Memorandums of Interviews with Roomy Khan, April 27 and June 20, 2001, and December 17, 2007.

Four months after Galleon opened, it was up 3 percent: *US v. Rajaratnam*, Franks hearing, Government Exhibit 169, Rajaratnam interview with Bernheim.

"Ask around the street about the market's hottest tech investor": Eric J. Savitz, "Tech Investors Are Acting Irrationally, but a Few Guys Do Have Their Heads on Straight," *Barron's*, November 3, 1997.

The rocky waters Galleon hit in the fall of 1997 and the loss in October: Peltz, *New Investment Superstars*, 207.

Rajaratnam calling Khan for the first time for inside information on Intel and his subsequent dealings with her: Described in *US v. Rajaratnam and Danielle Chiesi*, Rajaratnam Motion to Suppress Wiretaps, Exhibit A.8, FBI 302 Memorandum of Interview with Roomy Khan, April 27, 2001.

He even offered to give her some extra money if she remained: *US v. Rajaratnam*, Rajaratnam Motion to Suppress Wiretaps, Exhibit A.9, FBI 302 Memorandum of Interview with Roomy Khan, June 20, 2001.

On March 6, 1998, Khan faxed a number of sheets and the information contained in the "book to billing" reports: *US v. Roomy Khan*, CR-01-20029-JW, Government Sentencing Memorandum and Motion for Downward Departure, June 25, 2002.

On March 24, Khan faxed several pages of handwritten notes with Intel's average selling price: Ibid.

Chapter Twelve: The Corner Office

Rajat Gupta had his pick of the next McKinsey posting: Gupta's taped remarks at Creativity and Personal Mastery class (hereafter Gupta's remarks at Creativity and Personal Mastery class), taught by Srikumar Rao at Columbia Business School, April 2004.

His colleague and his wife recommended a home for Gupta: Letter written on behalf of Gupta before his sentencing by a former McKinsey colleague in Chicago, John Patience.

The way McKinsey views internal management: Gupta's remarks at Creativity and Personal Mastery class, which are confirmed by other McKinsey partners.

Not unlike his father, who could deliver sold-out tickets: In an interview on October 17, 2011, Sukharanjan Dasgupta, a journalist in Calcutta, recalled about fifty years ago when he and some friends had difficulty getting train tickets home, they were told to approach Ashwini Gupta, who procured tickets.

His philosophy on success: Gupta's remarks at Creativity and Personal Mastery class.

The lesson he learned from attending Nehru's press conferences: Letter written on Gupta's behalf by family friend Srilata Gangulee ahead of his sentencing.

"Think of political patronage": Email from Jeffrey Skilling, March 22, 2012.

Gupta came to learn that Gluck planned to name someone else as Chicago office manager: Gupta's remarks at Creativity and Personal Mastery class; author interviews.

Gupta's ruminations about the Chicago manager job: Gupta's remarks at Creativity and Personal Mastery class.

Anita Gupta's memories of her tired husband on the couch with a baby: Letter written by Anita Gupta on behalf of her husband ahead of his sentencing.

Gupta tutoring Geetanjali in math on Saturday mornings: Letter written on Gupta's behalf by his eldest daughter, Geetanjali, ahead of his sentencing.

Gupta wanted to be with his daughters, "not merely around us": Letter written on Gupta's behalf by his daughter Aditi ahead of his sentencing.

"Moral support" was a Gupta buzzword and "If we resisted": Letter written on Gupta's behalf by his daughter Megha ahead of his sentencing.

Thanksgiving at the Guptas: Recounted in a number of letters written on Gupta's behalf ahead of his sentencing.

Amid a game of Pictionary, the quiet Gupta could outshout anyone: Letter written by Mala Gupta ahead of her brother-in-law's sentencing.

Gupta's mastery of yo-yoing: Letter written by IIT Delhi friend Veena B. Mendiratta on Gupta's behalf ahead of his sentencing.

The gifts the Guptas brought on their visits to India: Detailed in letters written on Gupta's behalf by Anita Gupta's brother Arjun Mattoo and Gupta's nephew Arvind Mattoo before his sentencing.

The role Gupta played after his father-in-law's death: Described by Anita Gupta's brother, Arvind, and her sister, Aninda, in letters they wrote on Gupta's behalf before his sentencing.

Gupta's exchange with Gluck over the Chicago job: Gupta's remarks at Creativity and Personal Mastery class.

Gluck's background: Walter Kiechel III, *The Lords of Strategy: The Secret Intellectual History of the New Corporate World* (Boston: Harvard Business Press, 2010).

Gupta's view that Gluck gave him the Chicago job "against his wishes": Gupta's remarks at Creativity and Personal Mastery class. Gluck passing over Ashley is also discussed in George David Smith, John T. Seaman Jr., and Morgen Witzel, *A History of the Firm* (privately published by McKinsey in 2010), 371.

Gupta was on the slate in 1988 and his rivals were a decade older than him: Gupta's remarks at Creativity and Personal Mastery class.

By the time Gluck was set to retire, McKinsey's revenue had grown to $1.2 billion, but 60 percent of the revenue came from overseas: John A. Byrne, "The McKinsey Mystique," *BusinessWeek,* September 19, 1993.

"Many insiders believe McKinsey may elect the first non-American": Ibid.

Lukas Muehlemann left to take the CEO job at Swiss Re: Peter Gumbel, "Swiss Reinsurance Ousts A.W. Saxer as Chief Executive," *Wall Street Journal,* April 29, 1994.

The growth of McKinsey's financial institutions practice: Smith, Seaman, and Witzel, *A History of the Firm,* 303.

"It strained the fabric of the place": John Huey, "How McKinsey Does It: The World's Most Powerful Consulting Firm Commands Unrivaled Respect—and Prices—but Is Being Buffeted by a Host of New Challenges," *Fortune,* November 1, 1993.

"By the end of the 80s, there was a growing group within the firm that felt the pendulum swung too far: Email from Jeffrey Skilling, March 5, 2012.

"Did I ever find a glass ceiling?": Gupta's remarks at Creativity and Personal Mastery class.

"He got the job because two stronger personalities were competing heavily": Interview with Bala Balachandran, May 17, 2011.

"The candidate for Managing Director has to reflect the aspirations of the firm": Emails from Jeffrey Skilling, March 4 and 5, 2012.

Chapter Thirteen: Raj's Edge

Khan quit after receiving a poor performance review: *US v. Roomy Khan,* CR-01-20029-JW, Government Sentencing Memorandum and Motion for Downward Departure, June 25, 2002, says Khan was fired by Intel. But FBI agent Russell Atkinson, who was investigating the case, says she left on her own after she was given a poor review. His account is confirmed by others.

In 1999, his flagship technology fund posted a return of 96.3 percent: Lois Peltz, *The New Investment Superstars: 13 Great Investors and Their Strategies for Superior Returns* (Hoboken, NJ: John Wiley & Sons, 2001), 208.

In June 1999, he started the Galleon New Media fund: Ibid., 205.

Assets under management swelled from $1 billion in 1998 to $5 billion: Ibid., 199.

Rajaratnam opened an office in Santa Clara with an unlisted number: *US v. Rajaratnam and Danielle Chiesi*, S1 09 Cr. 1184 (RJH), Defendant Raj Rajaratnam's Memorandum of Law in Support of His Motion to Suppress Evidence Derived from Wiretap Interceptions of His Cellular Telephone (hereafter Rajaratnam Motion to Suppress Wiretaps), May 7, 2010, Exhibit A.8, FBI 302 Memorandum of Interview with Roomy Khan, April 27, 2001.

Rajaratnam hired Khan at a starting salary of $120,000: *US v. Rajaratnam*, Rajaratnam Motion to Suppress Wiretaps, Exhibit A.9, FBI 302 Memorandum of Interview with Roomy Khan, June 20, 2001.

Rajaratnam told Khan to find contacts inside companies so they could give her 'the edge': *US v. Rajaratnam*, Rajaratnam Motion to Suppress Wiretaps, Exhibit A.8, FBI interview of Khan, April 27, 2001.

The circumstances of Khan's departure from Galleon: *US v. Whitman*, 12 CR.125 (JSR), Roomy Khan testimony, August 6, 2012; *US v. Rajaratnam*, Rajaratnam Motion to Suppress Wiretaps says in footnote 3 Khan was "terminated" in March 1999 from Galleon for trading in her personal account.

On April 15, 1999, two FBI agents showed up at Khan's house: Ibid.; *US v. Rajaratnam*, Rajaratnam Motion to Suppress Wiretaps, Exhibit A.7, FBI 302 Memorandum of Interviews with Roomy Khan, April 15, 1999. Later Khan would tell investigators she made no money giving Rajaratnam insider tips.

Chapter Fourteen: Building Offshore-istan

Kumar had been tilling over the area of remote business services: Jason Busch, in "Godfather of KPO and McKinsey director Anil Kumar Arrested," SpendMatters.com, October 16, 2009, cites Rudy Hirschheim, who edited *Information Systems Outsourcing: Enduring Themes, Global Challenges and Process Opportunities* (Berlin: Springer Verlag), as saying "The international consulting firm McKinsey initiated a project in 1995 led by Anil Kumar to exploit reductions in global telecommunications rates that would create opportunities for remote business services...this led McKinsey to establish a knowledge center in Delhi." Hirschheim's observations of Kumar's work on remote business services are confirmed by other sources.

Kumar joining McKinsey in 1986 and moving to San Jose in 1988: *US v. Anil Kumar*, 10-cr-13 (DC), Sentencing Memorandum submitted on behalf of Anil Kumar (hereafter Kumar sentencing memo), July 18, 2012.

Kumar literally pounding the pavement to get clients and the growth of the office: Ibid.

In 1992, he made principal: Ibid.

Puri and Gluck's trip to India and the creation of the India office: Based on author interviews and described in George David Smith, John T. Seaman Jr., and Morgen Witzel, *A History of the Firm* (privately published by McKinsey in 2010), 349.

No one in India knew what a management consultant actually was: Ibid.

Puri's enlisting of Vaish and McKinsey's work for Hindustan Motors: Based on author interviews; Smith, Seaman, and Witzel, *A History of the Firm*, 350–51; IBS Center for Management Research, "Hindustan Motors' Struggle for Survival," case study, 2002. See http://www.icmr india.org/casestudies/catalogue/Business%20Strategy1/Business%20Strategy%20Hindustan %20Motors%20Struggle%20for%20Survival.htm.

"We don't know what will happen": Smith, Seaman, and Witzel, *A History of the Firm*, 350.

The phlegmatic Gupta on Madh Island: Interview with former head of McKinsey Knowledge Center Amit Bhatia, May 30, 2011.

One of its partners installed the switchboard and one computer was shared between the Delhi and Mumbai offices: Smith, Seaman, and Witzel, *A History of the Firm*, 352.

One week of a McKinsey engagement equaled the salary of some Indian companies' CEOs: *US v. Anil Kumar*, Kumar sentencing memo.

In June 1991, India's reserves plummeted to $1.2 billion: "India's Election: Who, Me?," *Economist*, May 20, 2004.

The screening of *Nine Atop Everest* and the boys' reaction to it: Interview with Shomit Mitter, March 9, 2011.

"To go mountain climbing with these men" and subsequent remarks by Mitter: Ibid.

"If you were school captain or house captain": Interview with Dhruv Khanna, January 20, 2011.

"He came first in the long jump": Interview with Arjun Mahey, October 20, 2011.

"For the next year, he walked around": Dhruv Khanna interview.

Kumar's placement in the top 0.1 percent in the IIT entrance exam and his graduating third in his class: *US v. Kumar*, Kumar sentencing memo.

Winning the De Beers scholarship and accepting it after IIT Bombay's dean persuaded him to: Ibid.

Completing Imperial College's two-year program in ten months: Ibid.

Every weekend, he would make the trek: Ibid.

He also knew Kumar was a controversial consultant: *US v. Gupta*, McKinsey consultant Mark "Kito" de Boer in a letter written on Gupta's behalf before his sentencing says, "My relationship with Rajat is made more complex...because of a professional conflict I had with Anil Kumar, which forced Rajat to take sides in favor of Anil." The author has learned that this conflict related to Anil Kumar's poaching of a client from a colleague.

Bhatia's hiring and the creation of the McKinsey Knowledge Center: Based on an interview with Amit Bhatia, February 2, 2011, and confirmed by other interviews.

The McKinsey India team estimated $1 trillion of work could move to lower-cost locations: McKinsey said, "This does not seem accurate"; however, individuals on the McKinsey India team say the projection is correct.

Vinit Khanna's personal history and interaction with Kumar: Interview with Vinit Khanna, July 13, 2010.

In 2012, Khanna ran into Kumar: Interview with Vinit Khanna, February 22, 2012.

Chapter Fifteen: Partying and Polycom

Now he and his family were headed to Château Grimaldi: *US v. Rajaratnam*, Testimony of Rajiv Goel, March 23, 2011; *US v. Rajaratnam*, Government Exhibit 1078, Email from Goel to Rajaratnam, May 22, 2007.

The trip to Kenya: Anita Raghavan, "Power and Pleasure," *Forbes*, October 11, 2010.

The pot-smoking incident: Ibid.

Galleon turned over 4 million documents: *US v. Rajaratnam*, Franks hearing, Testimony of Lindi Beaudreault, October 4, 2010.

The two investor lists: *US v. Rajaratnam*, Franks hearing, Testimony of Andrew Michaelson, October 5, 2010.

When Michaelson asked Rajaratnam to identify investors who were consultants to public companies: Raj Rajaratnam testimony before the Securities and Exchange Commission in the Matter of Sedna Capital Management, June 7, 2007.

Jason Friedman joining the investigation in the summer of 2007: *US v. Rajaratnam*, Franks hearing, Michaelson testimony, October 5, 2010.

The call from Roomy Khan shortly before 4 p.m. on July 2: *US v. Whitman*, Testimony of Roomy Khan, August 6, 2012.

Khan started a consulting firm, Digital Age Capital: Ibid.

In 2000, Khan made $40 million trading Internet stocks: Ibid.

Circumstances of Khan's first meeting with Bhalla and dinner at P.F. Chang's: Ibid.

"Thanks for the tips on stocks": Email from Sunil Bhalla to Khan, August 22, 2002.

Bhalla gave Khan authority over a $50,000 account he held at Lehman: *US v. Whitman*, Khan testimony, August 7, 2012.

Bhalla wanted to grow his capital: *US v. Rajaratnam*, Government Exhibit 1472-a, Sunil Bhalla's account-opening form, October 1, 2003.

Khan doubled his money to $100,000: *US v. Whitman*, Khan testimony, August 7, 2012.

"Thanks for doing so well": Email from Bhalla to Khan, November 8, 2003.

In 2005, she lost $5 million of her money and all of Bhalla's: *US v. Rajaratnam*, Khan testimony, August 7, 2012.

"We are friends": Email from Bhalla to Khan, March 23, 2005.

During the 1990s, Sakhawat Khan was granted thirty patents: Ashlee Vance, "The Khans' Path in Silicon Valley," NYTimes.com, October 22, 2009.

When Agate was acquired for $7 million: Ibid.

In 2000, the Khans paid $10.5 million for a house in Atherton: Assessment record for San Mateo County indicates the Khans bought 168 Isabella Avenue for $10.5 million in 2000; Ashlee Vance and Michael J. de la Merced with contributors Zachery Kouwe and Dan Zehr, "Witness in Galleon Case Is Said to Have History of Passing Secrets," *New York Times*, October 24, 2009.

The description of the house: http://www.zillow.com/homedetails/168-Isabella-Ave-Atherton-CA-94027/15593703_zpid/.

Vilma Serralta's story of working for the Khans: Described by Tyche Hendricks, "The Nanny Strikes Back," *San Francisco Chronicle*, March 14, 2008.

The real estate sale that fell through: Vance and Merced with Kouwe and Zehr, "Witness in Galleon Case Is Said to Have a History of Passing Secrets"; Ben Charney, "Galleon Witness Had Long String of Financial Difficulties," Dow Jones Newswires, November 12, 2009; Paul Lewis, "Professor, Scientist, Art Collector, Crook: Jail for Conman with Millionaire Lifestyle," *Guardian*, January 21, 2006.

In 2005, Deutsche Bank sued Khan: Michael J. de la Merced, Zachery Kouwe, and Alex Berenson, "Financial Woes Plague Galleon Informant," *New York Times*, October, 21, 2009.

In April 2001, Khan pleaded guilty to wire fraud and the maximum penalties for the crime: *US v. Roomy Khan*, plea agreement, April 3, 2001.

A year later, she was given probation: *US v. Rajaratnam and Danielle Chiesi*, Defendant Raj Rajaratnam's Memorandum of Law in Support of His Motion to Suppress Evidence Derived from Wiretap Interceptions of His Cellular Telephone (hereafter cited *US v. Rajaratnam and Chiesi*, Rajaratnam Motion to Suppress Wiretaps), Exhibit A.6, Roomy Khan Final Judgment and Conditions of Probation, July 1, 2002.

Khan deserved a lighter sentence because she "has provided the United States with substantial assistance": *US v. Roomy Khan*, CR-01-20029-JW, Government Sentencing Memorandum and Motion for Downward Departure, June 25, 2002.

In mid-2005, she decided to reach out to Rajaratnam: *US v. Rajaratnam and Chiesi*, Rajaratnam Motion to Suppress Wiretaps, Exhibit A.16 and A.17, FBI 302 Memorandums of Interviews with Roomy Khan (hereafter FBI Roomy Khan interviews), November 28 and December 17, 2007.

"You are too wealthy to work for me" and the conversation between Rajaratnam and Khan: Ibid.

Rajaratnam asked Khan what companies she had an "edge" on, and Khan said Polycom: Ibid.

Khan meeting Rajaratnam in December 2005 in California and her efforts to get a job with him: Ibid.

Khan invited Bhalla and his wife for a holiday dinner: *US v. Whitman*, Khan testimony, August 7, 2012.

Her meeting with Bhalla in early January 2006: Ibid.

Khan's instant message to Rajaratnam on January 12, 2006: *US v. Rajaratnam*, Franks hearing, Government Exhibit 32, Chronology of trading and communication in Polycom by Khan, Rajaratnam, and others (hereafter Polycom chronology).

"Buy 60 PLCM": Ibid.

Two days after Khan bought 3,000 Polycom call options: *US v. Rajaratnam*, Government Exhibit 66, Roomy Khan Trading in Polycom Securities in January 2006.

At 10:36 a.m., Rajaratnam's Technology fund acquired 60,000 shares of Polycom: *US v. Rajaratnam*, Government Exhibit 65, Galleon Tech Trading in Polycom Stock (PLCM) from January 10 to January 25, 2006.

On Saturday, January 21, Rajaratnam called his brother and two days later Rengan started to acquire Polycom: *US v. Rajaratnam*, Franks hearing, Polycom chronology.

Polycom released its fourth-quarter 2005 earnings: Government Exhibit 1431, Press release from Polycom of Fourth Quarter Earnings, January 25, 2006.

"hey...tks for plcm idea": *US v. Rajaratnam*, Franks hearing, Polycom chronology.

Bhalla asking Khan to sell Polycom stock and put some winnings in his Lehman account: *US v. Rajaratnam*, Khan testimony, August 7, 2012.

Khan's tip on Polycom netted Galleon's Technology fund $482,960 in gains: *US v. Rajaratnam*, Government Exhibit 67, a calculation by the government of Galleon Tech profits from trading in Polycom stock (PLCM) in January 2006.

Rajaratnam saying he needed to confer with his head trader before giving her a job: *US v. Rajaratnam and Chiesi*, Rajaratnam Motion to Suppress Wiretaps, Exhibit A.17, FBI Roomy Khan interview.

Khan tells Rajaratnam of Blackstone takeover of Hilton: *US v. Whitman*, Khan testimony, August 7, 2012.

Khan placed a trade to buy 550 call options: *US v. Rajaratnam*, Government Exhibit 49, Roomy Khan Trading in Hilton Securities on July 2 and 3, 2007.

Galleon's trade on Hilton and the allocation of 400,000 shares to the Technology fund: *US v. Rajaratnam*, Government Exhibit 50, Galleon Technology fund trading in Hilton Stock (HLT) on July 3, 2007.

Blackstone's stock rose 6.4 percent, to $36.05: Interactive Data via FactSet Research Systems.

Blackstone said it would pay $47.50 a share for Hilton: *US v. Rajaratnam*, Government Exhibit 1486, Press release from Hilton Hotels of takeover by Blackstone.

Rajaratnam netted a profit of almost $4.1 million: *US v. Rajaratnam*, Government Exhibit 55, a calculation by the government of Galleon Technology fund's profit from trading in Hilton stock in July 2007.

A purchase of 7,500 shares was placed in Goel's Schwab account: *US v. Rajaratnam*, Government Exhibit 1276, Rajiv and Alka Goel's Charles Schwab account statement detailing purchase of 7,500 shares of Hilton on July 3, 2007.

Rajaratnam mentioned making a boatload on Hilton: *US v. Rajaratnam*, Testimony of Rajiv Goel, March 29, 2011.

7,470,686 Hilton shares changed hands, more than twice the average daily trading volume: Interactive Data via FactSet Research Systems.

Chapter Sixteen: Playing for Team USA

"Isn't this the woman you were talking about?": First reported in George Packer, "A Dirty Business: New York City's Top Prosecutor Takes on Wall Street Crime," *New Yorker*, June 27, 2011.

Michaelson scouring the blue sheets for Kumar's name and receiving three boxes of documents from Texas: *US v. Rajaratnam*, Franks hearing, Testimony of Andrew Michaelson, October 5, 2010.

Israel Friedman's involvement in the case: Ibid.

"Blackstone may have tipped Galleon": *US v. Rajaratnam*, Franks hearing, Michaelson Exhibit 73, FBI memo, July 11, 2007.

The instant-message exchange between rajatgalleon and roomy81 and the importance of it in the Galleon investigation: *US v. Rajaratnam*, Franks hearing, Government Exhibit 24, Email from Andrew Michaelson on July 10, 2007, containing instant-message exchanges between Rajaratnam and Khan; first reported by Susan Pulliam, "The Network: The Feds Close In: Fund Chief Snared by Taps, Turncoats—Prosecutors Stalk Galleon's Rajaratnam After Finding a Revelatory Text Message," *Wall Street Journal*, December 30, 2011; Packer, "A Dirty Business."

When Friedman found Polycom dragging its feet: Polycom disputes that it was slow to respond and says it cooperated with the government probe.

Rajaratnam's fiftieth-birthday bash in Kenya: Anita Raghavan, "Power and Pleasure," *Forbes*, October 11, 2010.

Kang's discovery of Khan's criminal past: Packer, "A Dirty Business."

"Intel and the FBI agree that the primary culprit": *US v. Rajaratnam*, Franks hearing, Government Exhibit 2, Electronic communication from FBI special agent Russell Atkinson, April 29, 1998.

Near the top of Michaelson's agenda was Roomy Khan: *US v. Rajaratnam*, Franks hearing, Michaelson testimony, October 5, 2010.

The FBI's approach to Khan on November 28, 2007: First reported in Pulliam, "The Network"; Packer, "A Dirty Business"; *US v. Rajaratnam*, Defendant Raj Rajaratnam's Memorandum of Law in Support of His Motion to Suppress Evidence Derived from Wiretap Interceptions of His Cellular Telephone, May 7, 2010, Exhibit A.16, FBI 302 Memorandum of Interview with Roomy Khan, November 28, 2007.

Her Atherton house was on the market for $18 million: Packer, "A Dirty Business."

"I personally have been going through very tough times": Email from Roomy Khan to Sunil Bhalla, March 29, 2007.

"Yes, personally losing all the money hurt a lot": Email from Bhalla to Khan, March 30, 2007.

Khan fled to the bathroom and returned saying, "If I don't cooperate": Packer, "A Dirty Business."

Israel Friedman sent letters to Charles Schwab: *US v. Rajaratnam*, Franks hearing, Michaelson Exhibit 67, Letter sent by Israel Friedman to Michael Gloster, Schwab, November 29, 2007.

Somebody at Galleon logged into Goel's account at Schwab: *US v. Rajaratnam*, Franks hearing, Michaelson testimony, October 5, 2010.

Bought $264,284.95 worth of Hilton stock: *US v. Rajaratnam*, Government Exhibit 1276, Rajiv and Alka Goel Charles Schwab account statement showing purchase of 7,500 shares of Hilton stock on July 3, 2007, for $264,284.95.

Made $78,000: *US v. Rajaratnam*, Government Exhibit 1277, Rajiv and Alka Goel Schwab statement showing sale of 7,500 shares of Hilton on July 6 for $342,905.80, for a profit of $78,620.85.

Chapter Seventeen: The Wharton Mafia

Rajaratnam and Kumar arrived at Wharton in 1981: *US v. Rajaratnam*, Sentencing Memorandum on behalf of Raj Rajaratnam (hereafter Rajaratnam sentencing memo); *US v. Anil Kumar*, Sentencing Memorandum submitted on behalf of Anil Kumar.

"You had this interesting demographic anomaly" and subsequent remarks by Prashad: Interview with Vijay Prashad, October 13, 2010.

America embarking on two new tracks that played to the strengths of Indian immigrants: Interview with Professor Marcelo M. Suarez-Orozco, July 15, 2010.

Indian immigration jumped to 22,600: U.S. Census Bureau, *Statistical Abstract of the United States: 1984* (104th Edition), Washington, DC, 1984: http://www2.census.gov/prod2/stat comp/documents/1984-01.pdf.

More than thirty South Asians in the class: Wharton class of 1983 list.

Rajaratnam's father joined Singer Sewing Machine: Suketu Mehta, "The Outsider," *Newsweek*, October 23, 2011, says he was the head of Singer in South Asia.

"the defining catastrophe of post-colonial Sri-Lankan history" and the Sinhala-only policy: Philip Gourevitch, "Letter from Sri Lanka, Tides of War," *New Yorker,* August 1, 2005.

Rajaratnam was the second oldest of five children: Rajaratnam sentencing memo.

The family lived in Cinnamon Gardens: C. Bryson Hull and Shihar Aneez, "In His Native Sri Lanka, Convicted Rajaratnam Is No Household Name," Reuters News, May 12, 2011.

Raj attended St. Thomas' Preparatory School: Katherine Burton and Saijel Kishan, "Raj Rajaratnam Became Billionaire Demanding Edge," Bloomberg, October 19, 2009.

When he was seventeen years old he was sent to study at Dulwich: According to an email dated February 2, 2012, from Calista M. Lucy, archivist, Dulwich College (hereafter Lucy email), Rajaratnam was at Dulwich between September 1974 and December 1976.

Dulwich is a boys' school in southeast London, better known for churning out writers like Michael Ondaatje: See http://www.english.emory.edu/Bahri/Ondaat.html; http://www.dul wich.org.uk/college/about/the-masters-welcome.

In a 2011 interview, he said he lived in the same room as P. G. Wodehouse: Mehta, "The Outsider."

By the time Rajaratnam arrived at Dulwich, Wodehouse's old dormitory was the headmaster's residence: Lucy email.

"We started pushing and shoving": Mehta, "The Outsider."

Rajaratnam stayed at Dulwich to take the Oxbridge exams and did not pass: Lucy email.

He headed to the University of Sussex, where he received a bachelor of science in engineering: Rajaratnam sentencing memo.

"He was so charismatic": Gregory Zuckerman and Robert A. Guth, "Rajaratnam: Relentless Pursuit of Data," *Wall Street Journal,* October 24, 2009.

Krishen Sud, Tom Fernandez, and David Lau: All are listed as members of the Wharton class of 1983.

The incident between Rajaratnam and Kumar after a statistics exam: Mehta, "The Outsider."

"They were both incredibly smart": Interview with Tushar Mody, August 29, 2011.

Chapter Eighteen: Reeling in Roomy

On January 3, 2008, Khan came to proffer: *US v. Rajaratnam*, Franks hearing, Testimony of Andrew Michaelson, October 5, 2010.

Khan received the information on Google from Shammara Hussain: *US v. Whitman*, Testimony of Roomy Khan, August 7, 2012.

Khan and Hussain met at a technology conference: Ibid.; first reported by Susan Pulliam, "The

Network: The Feds Close In: Fund Chief Snared by Taps, Turncoats—Prosecutors Stalk Galleon's Rajaratnam After Finding a Revelatory Text Message," *Wall Street Journal*, December, 30, 2009.

Hussain, like Khan's husband, was from Bangladesh: *US v. Whitman*, Khan testimony, August 7, 2012.

Advising her on how to dress and telling her she was like a daughter: Pulliam, "The Network."

"Saving money is boring": John Carney, "Galleon's Google Tipster Identified as Active Stock Blogger," *Business Insider*, October 27, 2009.

"Short Google" and Khan's subsequent conversations with Hussain on Google: *US v. Whitman*, Khan testimony, August 7, 2012.

Hussain seeking between $100,000 and $200,000 for her Google tip: Ibid.

Khan giving her a cell phone in the name of her cleaner: Ibid.

Rajaratnam taking a $25 million short position in Google and making millions of dollars: *US v. Rajaratnam*, Government Brief, US Court of Appeals for the Second Circuit (Docket No. 11-4416).

Khan netting a profit of more than $500,000 on Google: *US v. Whitman*, Khan testimony, August 7, 2012.

Khan said she made the Hilton trades on the advice of her broker: *US v. Rajaratnam*, Franks hearing, Michaelson testimony, October 5, 2010.

She picked Hilton because socialite Paris Hilton had been arrested: Ibid.

Neither Michaelson nor the prosecutors bought her story: Ibid.

By March 2008, Michaelson felt like he had hit a wall: Ibid.

Only two stocks, Polycom and Google, for which the authorities had direct evidence from Khan: Ibid.

Rajaratnam alone traded as many as 12 million shares a day: Rajaratnam SEC testimony.

Adam Smith joined Galleon in 2002 and was promoted to portfolio manager in 2006: *US v. Rajaratnam*, Testimony of Adam Smith, March 29, 2011.

Rajaratnam's discussions with Smith about trading around a position: Ibid.

The March 3, 2008, draft of a list of stocks with the suspected sources: *US v. Rajaratnam*, Franks hearing, Michaelson Exhibit 128, List of stocks where insider trading was suspected and possible source.

The first stock was AMD and the name next to it was Bharath Rangarajan: Ibid.

In 2008, US judges approved 1,891 phone intercepts: Dennis K. Berman, "The Game: Galleon's Legacy: Wiretapping Insider Crime," *Wall Street Journal*, May 12, 2011.

"We need a dirty call," Goldberg said: *US v. Rajaratnam*, "A dirty call" is referenced in Franks hearing, Michaelson testimony, October 5, 2010.

Khan agreed to tape some telephone conversations: *US v. Rajaratnam*, Franks hearing, Michaelson testimony, October 5, 2010.

Khan's consensually recorded call to Rajaratnam on January 14, 2008: *US v. Rajaratnam*, Franks hearing, Kang Exhibit 1, the affidavit in support of the application for authorization to intercept wire communications.

The next day Intel reported revenue up 10.5 percent: Ibid.

Three days later, on January 17, 2008, Khan telephoned Rajaratnam: Ibid.

"It should have at least been attempted": *US v. Rajaratnam*, Franks hearing, Goldberg Exhibit 20, Email from Justice Department's Michelle Swaney to Lauren Goldberg, March 3, 2008.

Kang's attempt at physical surveillance and the reason he didn't find Rajaratnam: *US v. Rajaratnam*, Kang wiretap affidavit.

"It's a fairly apparent omission": *US v. Rajaratnam*, Franks hearing, Goldberg Exhibit 20, Swaney email to Goldberg.

Chapter Nineteen: Moonlighting at McKinsey

Rajaratnam approaching Kumar at the Indian School of Business fund-raiser about moon-lighting: In *US v. Rajaratnam*, Anil Kumar testified that Rajaratnam proposed paying him for his insights while they were walking out of a charity event. Kumar did not disclose the event, and told prosecutors he does not remember where the overture was made, but the author's reporting indicates that the event was the ISB fund-raiser.

Rajaratnam's anonymous contribution of $1 million: *US v. Rajaratnam*, Testimony of Anil Kumar, June 1, 2012.

Heard Rajaratnam had profited in the dot-com boom: Ibid.

By 2001, the assets at Rajaratnam's Galleon fund made it one of the ten biggest: Katherine Burton and Saijel Kishan, "Raj Rajaratnam Became Billionaire Demanding Edge," Bloomberg, October 19, 2009.

Kumar angling to get hired by Rajaratnam: *US v. Rajaratnam*, Testimony of Anil Kumar, March 10, 2011.

Of the view he would be named as successor to Puri as office manager: *US v. Anil Kumar*, Sentencing Memorandum submitted on behalf of Anil Kumar (hereafter Kumar sentencing memo), July 18, 2012. McKinsey says it can't confirm Kumar was promised the position of India office manager.

Kumar didn't have a practice group, so he decided to set up an e-commerce practice: Kumar sentencing memo. McKinsey says it can't confirm that Kumar didn't have a practice group.

Bob Waterman's accepting of stock from Genentech and the repercussions: Interview with Bob Waterman, May 20, 2011.

Skilling's observations on accepting equity for consulting work: Emails from Jeffrey Skilling, March 31, 2002, and April 2, 2012.

Only 50 percent of fees could be taken in equity, and the committee would consider investments under $1 million: George David Smith, John T. Seaman Jr., and Morgen Witzel, *A History of the Firm* (privately published by McKinsey in 2010), 402.

Kumar's tech consulting practice would grow to 25 to 30 percent of the firm's revenue: Kumar sentencing memo.

The *New York Times* story: David Leonhardt, "Big Consultants Woo Employees by Offering a Piece of the Action," *New York Times*, October 22, 1999.

"We don't want the best talent": Ibid.

The 12 percent drop in gross revenue from the start of 2001 to end of 2002 and the 87 percent plunge in additional awards: Smith, Seaman, and Witzel, *A History of the Firm*, 413.

New arrivals rose from about 20 percent a year to the mid-to-high 30 percent range in the late nineties: Ibid., 404.

Compensation per partner is hardwired to two economic statistics: Email from Jeffrey Skilling, March 7, 2012.

Between the mid-nineties and 2000, the ratio of directors to consulting staff increased to 1:17 from 1:12: Smith, Seaman, and Witzel, *A History of the Firm*, 404.

Even as revenue grew by more than three and a half times, the partnership grew by two and a half times: Ibid.

These numbers "suggest a HUGE increase in Director compensation": Email from Jeffrey Skilling, March 29, 2012.

McKinsey's hiring practices and the number of acceptances it received in 2001: Gupta's taped remarks at Creativity and Personal Mastery class, taught by Srikumar Rao at Columbia Business School, April 2004.

"On the beach": Smith, Seaman, and Witzel, *A History of the Firm,* 414.

The firm began culling its ranks through more rigorous reviews: Ibid.

Between 2001 and 2004, its consulting staff fell from a little over seventy-five hundred to a little over fifty-five hundred: In *A History of the Firm,* Smith, Seaman, and Witzel put the exact drop from 7,631 to 5,638.

The change in Kumar's fortunes at McKinsey with the rise of Ian Davis in 2003: Author interviews and Kumar sentencing memo.

Davis had a PPE from Balliol College: See http://www.balliol.ox.ac.uk/alumni-and-friends/news/newsletters/balliol-e-news-august-2011-issue-4.

Rajaratnam said he received about $100 million a year in so-called soft dollars: *US v. Rajaratnam,* Testimony of Anil Kumar, March 14, 2011.

Many big mutual funds like Fidelity stopped accepting soft dollars: Anthony Guerra, "Hard Times for Soft Dollars," Informationweek, January 24, 2006.

On September 26, 2002, Tom Stephenson sent an eighteen-page PowerPoint presentation: *US v. Rajaratnam,* Government Exhibit 2091, Attachment to email from Stephenson to Rajaratnam, September 26, 2002.

"Good meeting with Raj": *US v. Rajaratnam,* Defense Exhibit 0015, Email from Stephenson to Kumar, Steve Klar, and Mike Nevens, September 26, 2002.

Kumar's efforts to get Rajaratnam to engage McKinsey: Described by Anil Kumar in his testimony in *US v. Rajaratnam,* March 10, 2011.

"You know you sent me that document" and subsequent exchange between Kumar and Rajaratnam: Ibid.

Rajaratnam dictated the letter and Kumar typed it: Ibid.

Chapter Twenty: A Vanaprastha on the Hudson

Definitions of the four stages of a man's life in Hinduism: Described by Ludo Rocher in *The Blackwell Companion to Hinduism,* edited by Gavin Flood (Oxford: Blackwell Publishing, 2003), 102.

Gupta's impressing on colleagues to do the right thing and not get attached to the fruits of their labors: Gupta's taped remarks at Creativity and Personal Mastery class (hereafter Gupta's remarks at Creativity and Personal Mastery class), taught by Srikumar Rao at Columbia Business School, April 2004.

Statistics of McKinsey's expanded footprint: John A. Byrne with Joann Muller and Wendy Zellner, "Inside McKinsey," *BusinessWeek,* July 7, 2002.

When Gupta was first elected, he ran the firm from Chicago: McKinsey says its personnel records show that beginning in 1994 Gupta ran the firm from New York, however, an article on July 10, 1994, by Ronald E. Yates in the *Chicago Tribune,* in which Gupta was interviewed, says his colleagues were surprised by his decision to run the firm from Chicago instead of New York.

Gupta paid $6.125 million for his waterfront estate: The *Stamford Advocate* (stamfordadvocate.com), in an article on October 26, 2011, citing records on the town of Westport's online assessor database, said the Guptas bought their eight-bedroom, eight-bath house in 1999 for $6.125 million. It also said that the home, situated on 2.28 acres, is now appraised at $12.5 million.

Gupta was earning about $5 million a year: Suzanna Andrews, in "How Rajat Gupta Came Undone," *Bloomberg Businessweek,* May 19, 2011, writes that friends estimate he was earning somewhere between $5 million and $10 million.

The pressure to take McKinsey public or seed a venture fund and where Gupta felt he "made the most impact": Gupta's remarks at Creativity and Personal Mastery class.

"I got a sense the firm had grown way too fast": Interview with Bob Waterman, May 20, 2011.

In early February 2001, just six months after President Bill Clinton invited Gupta: For details of the dinner, see http://www.indianembassy.org/UserFiles/Old-Files/october_2000.pdf.

He and an old friend, Victor Menezes: Celia Dugger, "Whatever Happened to Bill Clinton? He's Playing India," *New York Times*, April 5, 2001.

The 2008 American India Foundation spring gala and Mukesh Ambani's remarks: Indo-Asian News Service, May 1, 2008.

Gupta devoting 25 percent of his time to outside ventures and the benefits it brought: Gupta's remarks at Creativity and Personal Mastery class.

He barely got elected: "Challenge at McKinsey," *Economist*, March 4, 2000.

At one point, McKinsey's annual billings to Enron exceeded $10 million: Byrne, "Inside McKinsey."

"There are bound to be some clients who get into trouble": Ibid.

Gupta helped conceive the "one-stop shop" organization: Letter written on Gupta's behalf before his sentencing by Suprotik Basu, a United Nations executive who worked with him on eradicating malaria.

Gupta first learned about Rajaratnam from Kumar and his donations to ISB and AIF: *US v. Gupta*, Testimony of Anil Kumar, June 4, 2012, and author interviews.

In 2003, John Byrne got a call from Davis's handlers: Interview with John Byrne, January 18, 2012.

"He was feeling literally crazy" and subsequent remarks by Bala Balachandran: Interview with Bala Balachandran, May 17, 2011.

Ratan Tata's opposition to expanding the Indian School of Business: From the Balachandran interview. Gupta also alluded to it when he spoke at the ISB graduation address on April 8, 2006. Also see http://www.isb.edu/gradday2006/Transcript_Rajat.html.

"When I look at myself, yeah, I'm driven by money": Gupta remarks at Creativity and Personal Mastery class.

Chapter Twenty-One: The Dishonorable Dosco

That is "very useful information" and the talks with Dell and Hewlett-Packard: *US v. Rajaratnam*, Testimony of Anil Kumar, March 10, 2011.

Kumar's view on whether to buy AMD stock: Ibid.

AMD was founded in 1969 by colorful tech entrepreneur Jerry Sanders: See AMD website, http://www.amd.com/us/press-releases/Pages/amd_marks_its_40th-2009apr30.aspx; Don Clark, "AMD Is Making a 64-Bit Bet on Its Future," *Wall Street Journal*, April 21, 2003.

Kumar's relationship with AMD and its chief executive, Ruiz, and the rivalry between AMD and Intel: *US v. Rajaratnam*, Kumar testimony, March 14, 2011.

Kumar had a master's degree in applied mechanics: *US v. Anil Kumar*, Sentencing Memorandum submitted on behalf of Anil Kumar, July 18, 2012.

Like Ruiz who after he was widowed met his wife: Matthew Yi, "Hector de Jesus Ruiz; Passing the torch; Ruiz rises from childhood poverty in Mexico to chief executive suite at Sunnyvale's AMD," *San Francisco Chronicle*, April 21, 2002.

Ruiz, an engineer, was born in Piedras Negras and attended high school in Eagle Pass, where he graduated as valedictorian; he didn't start learning English until age sixteen: Ian King, "Ruiz's Rise to Prominence Said to Culminate in Galleon Link," Bloomberg, October 28, 2009, citing a profile of Ruiz on the Rice University website.

Ruiz known as "Hector the Dissector" at Motorola: Don Clark, "AMD Founder Bets on Hammer Chips—Outgoing CEO Jerry Sanders' Strategy Wins Support from Microsoft," *Wall Street Journal*, April 25, 2002.

Sanders personally recruited Ruiz: Yi, "Hector de Jesus Ruiz; Passing the Torch."

In November 2002, Ruiz announced that the company would lay off two thousand: Matthew Yi, "Troubleshooter; CEO Ruiz Is Shaking Up AMD to Get It Out of Red Ink While Challenging Intel," *San Francisco Chronicle*, November 17, 2002.

"I was at the heart, inside almost the body of the company" and subsequent remarks by Kumar: *US v. Rajaratnam*, Kumar testimony March 14, 2011.

The insights about the technology space that Kumar and Rajaratnam exchanged: *US v. Rajaratnam*, Kumar testimony, March 10, 2011.

The arrangement with Manju Das: Ibid.

On January 16, 2004, Pecos Trading received: Ibid.

Hewlett-Packard unveiled a $400 million trial order: *US v. Rajaratnam*, Government Exhibit 947, Press release entitled "HP, AMD Join Forces to Power Server Innovation and Performance," February 24, 2004.

The change in Rajaratnam and Kumar's relationship after the payment of money and learning about "guidance": *US v. Rajaratnam*, Kumar testimony, March 10, 2012.

"You will not remember to keep a list": Ibid.

Slipping tidbits to Rajaratnam from AMD meetings: *US v. Rajaratnam*, Kumar testimony, March 10 and 14, 2011.

Rajaratnam FedExing a package of slides on Intel to Kumar: *US v. Rajaratnam*, Kumar testimony, March 14, 2011.

Rajaratnam's offer to pay Kumar by trading on his behalf and Kumar's reaction to it: Ibid.

Rajaratnam not paying Kumar for three months and the alternative pay plan: Ibid.

The payment plan was akin to an arrangement McKinsey had with clients: Ibid.

Chapter Twenty-Two: On the New Silk Route

He owned a stake in Rosa Mexicano: Katherine Burton and Saijel Kishan, "Raj Rajaratnam Became Billionaire Demanding Edge," Bloomberg, October 19, 2009.

The investment in Deepak Chopra's daughter's company: *US v. Gupta*, Letter from Deepak Chopra on Gupta's behalf before his sentencing.

Gupta invested in Scandent: *US v. Gupta*, Testimony of Anil Kumar, June 4, 2012.

Gupta met Trehan when he rented a guesthouse from him: Michael Rothfeld, "Ex-Partner May Be Key to Gupta's Fate—Fraud Trial Could Hinge on Testimony of Longtime Friend," *Wall Street Journal*, April 25, 2012.

The creation of Voyager and details about it: *US v. Gupta*, testimony of former Galleon portfolio manager Isvari Mahadeva, June 6, 2012; Government Exhibit 2104, a Galleon worksheet on Voyager.

Three months after it was set up, Voyager's equity stood at $58,382,958: *US v. Gupta*, Government Exhibit 2055, Voyager Funds account statement as of January 11, 2006, contained in an email sent on January 12, 2006, by Phillip Shefter at BroadStreet to Rajaratnam, Gupta, and others.

Trehan selling his investment in Voyager: *US v. Gupta*, Mahadeva testimony.

Gupta's statements to Kumar about the asset management company he wanted to set up: *US v. Gupta*, Kumar testimony, June 1, 2012.

New Silk Route's $2 billion fund-raising target: Ibid.

Gupta threw in $22.5 million: *US v. Gupta*. Superseding indictment says that in 2006 Gupta made a commitment to invest about $22.5 million in a private equity fund he, Rajaratnam, and others were setting up.

Gupta's key card access to Galleon's offices: *US v. Gupta*, Government Exhibits 1980 and 1981.

Rajaratnam told his secretary to lie and tell Gupta that he wasn't there: *US v. Gupta*, Testimony of Caryn Eisenberg, May 22, 2012, Defense Exhibit 8219-A, Instant-message exchange between Eisenberg and Anita Teglasi, February 29, 2008.

The priority list of investors to target for New Silk Route and the investors Gupta and Schwartz were to reach out to: *US v. Gupta*, Government Exhibit 2152, Priority List of Investors.

Kumar had already spoken to Bronfman's brother Sam: Ibid.

In early October 2006, Kumar sent an email with the subject line "URGENT": *US v. Gupta*, Government Exhibit 2287, Email from Kumar to Schwartz, Saxena, Gupta, and Rajaratnam, October 6, 2006.

Kumar would receive a stake, albeit smaller than that of the others: *US v. Gupta*, Kumar testimony, June 1, 2012.

Gupta helped P&G's Lafley sketch the company's $57 billion for Gillette: Duff McDonald, "Rajat Gupta: Touched by Scandal," *Fortune*, October 1, 2010.

There was only one person Kilts and Lafley trusted: *US v. Gupta*, Sentencing Memorandum on behalf of Rajat K. Gupta, October 17, 2012.

"I hope you remember me": *US v. Gupta*, Government Exhibit 2193, Email on September 17, 2007, from Gupta to Devlin.

Letter to Sandy Weill: *US v. Gupta*, Government Exhibit 2266, Email from Gupta to Weill, October 9, 2007.

Gupta sent similar letters to Ajit Jain, Herb Allison, John Bryan, Bill George, Marcus Wallenberg, Indra Nooyi: *US v. Gupta*, Government Exhibits 2197; 2166; 2164; 2173; 2273; 2238, fund-raising letters via email to respective individuals.

NSR succeeded in raising $1.3 billion for its private equity arm, but its capital drive for the hedge fund side failed: *US v. Gupta*, Kumar testimony, June 1, 2012.

In late 2006, Gupta moved to exercise his option in Voyager: *US v. Gupta*, Mahadeva testimony, June 6, 2012.

Gupta and Vangal were working to buy a bank in South India: *US v. Gupta*, Anil Kumar testimony, June 4, 2012.

"We still have not received total payment for Katra Finance": *US v. Gupta*, Government Exhibit 1917, Email from Rajaratnam to Gupta, December 21, 2006.

"Our team has been chasing Ramesh's team on a daily basis": *US v. Gupta*, Government Exhibit 1918, Email from George Lau to Gupta, December 28, 2006.

"Rest assured please tell Raj": *US v. Gupta*, Government Exhibit 1918, Email from Renee Gomes on behalf of Gupta to Lau, December 28, 2006.

Chapter Twenty-Three: The Million-Dollar Man

"Anil, this can wait": *US v. Rajaratnam*, Government Exhibit 805, Email from Peg O'Malley to Anil Kumar, September 28, 2005.

The strategic challenge for AMD and Project Super Nova: *US v. Rajaratnam*, Testimony of Anil Kumar, March 14, 2011.

Required to enter into another confidentiality agreement: Ibid.

Sharing it with or copying was not permitted: *US v. Rajaratnam*, Government Exhibit 805, Email from Peg O'Malley to Anil Kumar forwarding an internal email dated September 26, 2005, from O'Malley to Hollis O'Brien.

Shift from Project Super Nova to Go Big: *US v. Rajaratnam*, Kumar testimony, March 14, 2011.

AMD had been a favorite of Rajaratnam's: Raj Rajaratnam testimony before the SEC in the Matter of Sedna Capital Management (hereafter Rajaratnam SEC testimony), June 7, 2007.

The poster board in Rajaratnam's office and "my guy from AMD": *US v. Rajaratnam*, Franks hearing, Government Exhibit 89, FBI 302 Memorandum of Interview with Ali Far on April 16, 2009.

In Galleon's lexicon, he was "the axe": Ibid.

"Are you absolutely sure?" and "C'mon I'm in the inner circle": *US v. Rajaratnam*, Kumar testimony, March 14, 2011.

ATI, the Canadian tech firm founded in the early eighties by a tourist visiting from Hong Kong: Madhavi Acharya, "Turning a Vision into a Reputation," *Toronto Star*, October 9, 1998.

Rajaratnam taunted Kumar that he, a hedge fund trader, knew more than Kumar did: *US v. Gupta*, Testimony of Anil Kumar, June 4, 2012.

Kumar's disclosures about AMD looking at ATI and Nvidia and the twists and turns of the talks with ATI: *US v. Rajaratnam*, Kumar testimony, March 14, 2011.

At Galleon, Rajaratnam honed the strategy of "arbitraging consensus": *US v. Rajaratnam*, Testimony of Adam Smith, March 29, 2011.

The code names for the deal: *US v. Rajaratnam*, Kumar testimony, March 14, 2011.

Details of the McKinsey team and the price: *US v. Rajaratnam*, Government Exhibit 846, Email from Paul Roche to Bharath Rangarajan at AMD, December 31, 2005.

Paul Roche email to Kumar on December 20, 2005: *US v. Rajaratnam*, Government Exhibit 809, Email from Roche to Kumar, December 20, 2005.

Information is "red-hot" and subsequent exchanges between Kumar and Rajaratnam over AMD-ATI: *US v. Rajaratnam*, Kumar testimony, March 14, 2011.

"Buy some atyt": *US v. Rajaratnam*, Government Exhibit 1587, Instant-message exchange between Rajaratnam and Slattery, April 19, 2006.

Quintussf was the IM handle for Slattery, who ran an unregistered hedge fund in which Rajaratnam was invested: *US v. Rajaratnam*, Franks hearing, Government Exhibit 17, Email from Andrew Michaelson to Lauren Goldberg and Brian Coad, June 18, 2007; Rajaratnam SEC testimony.

Slattery's run-in with the SEC over PeopleSoft: Ianthe Jeanne Dugan, "Instant Message on PeopleSoft Stings Manager," *Wall Street Journal*, July 30, 2001.

"U are the best on it": *US v. Rajaratnam*, Franks hearing, Government Exhibit 17, Attachment to email from Andrew Michaelson to Lauren Goldberg and Brian Coad, June 18, 2007.

Rajaratnam's investment in Wright's Paw Partners: Rajaratnam SEC testimony.

The free flow of information when Rajaratnam started on Wall Street and the change with Reg FD: Robert A. Guth and Justin Scheck, "The Network: The Rise of Raj: The Man Who Wired Silicon Valley—Fund Boss Built Empire on Charm, Smarts and Information," *Wall Street Journal*, December 29, 2009; Jeff D. Opdyke, "Deal and Dealmakers—The Big Chill: Street Feels Effect of 'Fair Disclosure' Rule—Regulation Is Altering the Way Analysts Approach Their Jobs, *Wall Street Journal*, October 23, 2000.

Smith's conversation with Rajaratnam about putting confidential information in emails: *US v. Rajaratnam*, Smith testimony, March 29, 2011.

In January 2006 Galleon had registered with the SEC: *US v. Rajaratnam*, Franks hearing, Testimony of Lindi Beaudreault, October 4, 2010.

Smith learned from his former Morgan Stanley colleague of Integrated Device Technology's acquisition of Integrated Circuit Systems: *US v. Rajaratnam*, Adam Smith testimony, March 29, 2011.

The "Two Eyes" or "Eyes" emails and what they represented: Ibid.

"The date is set for May 16": *US v. Rajaratnam*, Government Exhibit 2456, Email from Smith to Rajaratnam, April 21, 2005.

Reason for sending the email only to Rajaratnam: *US v. Rajaratnam*, Smith testimony, March 29, 2011.

On June 15, Integrated Circuit and Integrated Device unveiled a $1.7 billion merger: *US v. Rajaratnam,* Government Exhibit 1675, Integrated Device press release entitled "IDT and ICS Announce Plan to Merge; $1.7 Billion Transaction Represents Opportunity to Grow Market, Improve Efficiencies," June 15, 2005.

Galleon's $2.7 million profit on the deal: *US v. Rajaratnam*, Government Exhibit 28, Calculation by the government of Galleon Technology fund's profit on Integrated Circuit stock at time of acquisition.

Rajaratnam telling Smith that his former Morgan Stanley colleague was a good contact and Smith having a sinking feeling: *US v. Rajaratnam*, Smith testimony, March 29, 2011.

"Need to move quick": *US v. Rajaratnam*. Government Exhibit 829, Email from Paul Roche to Anil Kumar, May 31, 2006.

"This rumor surfaces occasionally": *US v. Rajaratnam*, Government Exhibit 2472, May 31, 2006, email from Galleon analyst Nadeem Janmohamed forwarding an email blast on the ATYT-AMD rumor from Genuity Capital's David Hodgson.

Rajaratnam's relationship with Walia: *US v. Rajaratnam*, Smith testimony, March 29, 2011.

Kumar told Rajaratnam AMD was very keen to do ATI: *US v. Rajaratnam*, Kumar testimony, March 14, 2011.

ATI's stock jumped 6.4 percent: Interactive Data, via FactSet Systems.

A large number of investors like Janus were opposed to the deal: In *US v. Rajaratnam*, Government Exhibit 840, Vanessa Colella in an email to Anil Kumar and others on July 12, 2006, says "There is universal negative response to a potential deal," and singled out Janus as writing a letter to Ruiz telling him a deal should happen only if "there is a good price."

Rajaratnam dropping by Smith's office on June 29 and the purpose of his visit: *US v. Rajaratnam*, Smith testimony, March 29, 2011.

In early May, Smith lunched with his former Morgan Stanley colleague who said a deal between AMD and ATI was under way: Ibid.

That morning in late June, ATI posted third-quarter earnings and said its outlook was bleak: "ATI Tech Posts Profit; Stock Falls on Disappointing Outlook," Associated Press, June 29, 2006.

Smith crafted an email entitled "ATYT—what to do": *US v. Rajaratnam*, Government Exhibit 2402, Email from Smith to Rajaratnam, June 29, 2006.

"Due to a variety of circumstances, we will need to push out the Go Big announcement": *US v. Rajaratnam*, Government Exhibit 836, Email from Anil Kumar to Luana Pereira, July 6, 2006, containing Rangarajan's original email to "stand down for the 10th."

Unbeknownst to market players, AMD and ATI were still a dollar apart on price: *US v. Rajaratnam*, Government Exhibit 840.

"So july 24 is action week!": *US v. Rajaratnam*, Government Exhibit 836, Email from Anil Kumar to Luana Pereira, July 5, 2006.

Vanessa Colella's suggestion: *US v. Rajaratnam*, Government Exhibit 840.

On July 24 AMD and ATI announced a $5.4 billion merger: *US v. Rajaratnam*, Government Exhibit 801, Press release entitled "AMD and ATI to Create Processing Powerhouse," July 24, 2006.

Rajaratnam had accumulated $89.4 million of ATI shares: *US v. Rajaratnam*, Brief for the United States of America, US Court of Appeals for the Second Circuit.

Galleon booked a profit of $23 million: *US v. Rajaratnam*, Government Exhibit 21, Calculation by the government of Galleon Technology and Diversified funds' realized profit on ATI stock held at the time of acquisition by AMD.

"We are all cheering you right now": *US v. Rajaratnam*, Kumar testimony, March 14, 2011.

In early 2007, Rajaratnam transferred $1 million from Galleon's HSBC account: *US v. Rajaratnam*, Government Exhibit 772, Fax for $1 million transfer from Galleon HSBC account to Kumar HSBC account in India.

Chapter Twenty-Four: "You've Gotta Be a Hustler"

Rajiv Goel had been Rajaratnam's buddy since Wharton: *US v. Rajaratnam*, Testimony of Rajiv Goel, March 22, 2011.

An Indian savory snack that Goel's wife, Alka, was particularly good at making: Suketu Mehta, "The Outsider," *Newsweek*, October 23, 2011.

As a thank-you for getting information on Intel's orders, Rajaratnam said he gave two women BMWs: *US v. Rajaratnam*, Goel testimony.

He tried to find replacements for Khan: *US v. Rajaratnam*, Testimony of Adam Smith, March 29, 2011.

The development of Goel's relationship with Rajaratnam: *US v. Rajaratnam*, Goel testimony, March 22, 2011.

"You're a star trader": Ibid.

"Hey, I can help you": Ibid.

He lent $100,000 to Goel, who promised to pay it back: Ibid.; Government Exhibit 1016, Email from Goel to Rajaratnam, July 20, 2005.

The purchase price of Goel's house and the loan amount: Deed Record for purchase of 12331 Stonebrook Court by Rajiv and Alka Goel.

The deepening of the relationship between Goel and Rajaratnam: *US v. Rajaratnam*, Goel testimony, March 22, 2011.

Rajaratnam wired $500,000: Goel testimony, March 22, 2011, and Government Exhibit 1023, which is Goel's Credit Suisse account statement showing that the account was opened on May 17, 2006, and received a payment of $500,000 from Rajaratnam and Asha Pabla on May 22.

The disaster with the rats: *US v. Rajaratnam*, Goel testimony, March 22, 2011.

The recapitalization of SMART Technologies and Goel's role in it: *US v. Rajaratnam*, Government Exhibit 1046, attachment to an email from Goel to Rajaratnam, March 20, 2008.

"Get me a job with one of your powerful friends, man": *US v. Rajaratnam*, Government Exhibit 504-T, Transcript of a wiretapped conversation between Goel and Rajaratnam, March 20, 2008.

In November 2006, when Goel was planning a trip: *US v. Rajaratnam*, Government Exhibit 1069, Email from Goel to Rajaratnam, November 17, 2006.

"Did you get an award or did you get cash?" and subsequent exchange between Goel and Rajaratnam: *US v. Rajaratnam*, Government Exhibit 504-T.

"The deal complexity is much higher": *US v. Rajaratnam*, Government Exhibit 1046, Email from Goel to Rajaratnam, March 20, 2008.

The holidays the Goels and Rajaratnams took: *US v. Rajaratnam*, Goel testimony, March 24, 2011.

"Dad has nobody to pick on": *US v. Rajaratnam*, Defense Exhibit 2066, email from Rajaratnam to Goel containing message from Rajaratnam's daughters to Goel's on June 24, 2008.

Chapter Twenty-Five: The Richest Maid in Silicon Valley

The exchange between Kumar and Rajaratnam on March 25, 2008: *US v. Rajaratnam*, Government Exhibit 506-T, Transcript of a wiretapped conversation between Kumar and Rajaratnam on March 24, 2008. The time on the call is 6:48 p.m., which reflects eastern standard time, though the time in the narrative reflects the time in Tokyo, which is thirteen hours ahead and almost 8 a.m. on March 25.

McKinsey's Tokyo office was in Roppongi: McKinsey & Co. website, http://www.mckinsey.com/global_locations/asia/tokyo.

Logging as many as forty thousand miles a month, being assigned offices in New York and Silicon Valley, and having two home offices: *US v. Rajaratnam*, Testimony of Anil Kumar, March 14, 2011.

"Cambodia and Angkor Wat were amazing!!": *US v. Rajaratnam*, Defense Exhibit 0071, Email from Kumar to Raj Rajaratnam, August 17, 2005.

"I'm here with...Sunil Mittal and Sunil Munjal": Government Exhibit 616-T, Transcript of a wiretapped conversation between Kumar and Rajaratnam, September 11, 2008.

He had three cell phones, ostensibly to keep McKinsey's costs down: *US v. Rajaratnam*, Kumar testimony, March 14, 2011.

He was on a list of about ten people: *US v. Gupta*, Testimony of Caryn Eisenberg, May 22, 2011.

By 2008, Rajaratnam had made the Forbes 400 list: Rajaratnam ranked 262 on the Forbes 400 list in 2008. See http://www.forbes.com/lists/2008/54/400list08_Raj-Rajaratnam_RUQ2.html.

The fantasy football league in which Rajaratnam was a member: Jon Weinbach, "Wall Street's $1 Million Fantasy League—Top Financiers Pretend to Build the Best Pretend NFL Team; Trash Talk on the Chat Board," *Wall Street Journal*, October 17, 2008.

In February, to mark the victory by Michael Daffy: *US v. Gupta*, Defense Exhibit 8340, Email from Anita Teglasi to Caryn Eisenberg on February 28, 2008, forwarding an email from Vicki Ramsey at Goldman Sachs regarding details for a trip that day to the Borgata in Atlantic City.

Rajaratnam's business card did not have his direct line: *US v. Gupta*, Eisenberg testimony, May 22, 2012.

Lenovo was in serious talks with Fujitsu and following exchange between Kumar and Rajaratnam: *US v. Rajaratnam*, Government Exhibit 506-T.

The near collapse of Bear and the bank stumping up $3 billion: Kate Kelly, "Crisis on Wall Street—Excerpt Inside the Fall of Bear Stearns—In 72 Nail-Biting Hours an Investment Bank Turned from Healthy to Nearly Insolvent," *Wall Street Journal*, May 9, 2009.

The discussion about Hindustan Oil and the subsequent conversation about Lenovo: *US v. Rajaratnam*, Government Exhibit 506-T.

Rajaratnam had originally planned to join Kumar in Singapore and following conversation: Ibid.

AMD's Asset-Lite strategy and Kumar's briefings of Rajaratnam on it: *US v. Rajaratnam*, Kumar testimony, March 14, 2011.

Kumar's new position at McKinsey leading the Asia Center: Ibid.

"It will be fantastic" and Rajaratnam's comparing it to ATI: Ibid.

"It could take two more months": *US v. Rajaratnam*, Government Exhibit 506-T.

Rajaratnam's telling Kumar of Chiesi and her alleged relationship with Ruiz: *US v. Rajaratnam*, Kumar testimony, March 14, 2011.

After she asked a Galleon analyst for an introduction: Susan Pulliam and Chad Bray, "Key Plotter Pleads Guilty in Galleon," *Wall Street Journal*, January 20, 2011.

Chiesi taking to the dance floor alone and changing in and out of slinky dresses: Anita Raghavan, "Power and Pleasure," *Forbes*, October 11, 2010.

The Kenny Rogers clambake: Robert A. Guth and Justin Scheck, "The Network: The Rise of Raj: The Man Who Wired Silicon Valley—Fund Boss Built Empire on Charm, Smarts and Information," *Wall Street Journal*, December 29, 2009.

"Your value to me is a little bit diminished" and subsequent exchange about Chiesi: *US v. Rajaratnam*, Kumar testimony, March 14, 2011.

The Business Objects tip and Rajaratnam losing money on the trade after halving his position: *US v. Rajaratnam*, Kumar testimony, March 14, 2011.

Business Objects' acquisition by SAP: "SAP Shares Drop on Business Objects Bid," Associated Press, October 8, 2007.

Galleon's loss of around $5 million and Rajaratnam being upset: *US v. Rajaratnam*, Testimony of Rick Schutte, April 12, 2011.

Morgan Stanley's push for documents attesting to Das being an offshore investor: *US v. Rajaratnam*, Defense Exhibit 1898, Email from Cliodhna Murphy, MSFS Investor Services, to Shireen Gianchandani, May 21, 2008.

"Let me look into this and see what can be done": *US v. Rajaratnam*, Defense Exhibit 1898, Email from Anil Kumar to Shireen Gianchandani, May 21, 2008.

"My concern is with Manju's mail": *US v. Rajaratnam*, Defense Exhibit 0145, Email from Reva Dayal to Anil Kumar, December 19, 2005.

In 2006, Rajaratnam started pressing Kumar to move his money out of the Das account because of possible SEC scrutiny: *US v. Rajaratnam*, Kumar testimony, March 14, 2011.

Kumar said he knew someone in Switzerland: Ibid.

"From a Morgan Stanley Fund Services perspective": *US v. Rajaratnam*, Defense Exhibit 1915, Email from Anil Kumar to Shireen Gianchandani, May 26, 2008.

Morgan Stanley required two proofs of address for Das: *US v. Rajaratnam*, Defense Exhibit 2191, Email from Shireen Gianchandani to Anil Kumar, July 17, 2008,

"Manju Das comes from a village in the remote area of Bengal": *US v. Rajaratnam*, Defense Exhibit 2193, Email from Kumar to Gianchandani, July 17, 2008.

He turned to Dr. Mathur: *US v. Rajaratnam*, Kumar testimony, March 15, 2011.

The details of Mathur's clinic, the companies he worked for, and the letter he wrote about Das: *US v. Rajaratnam*, Defense Exhibit 2490, Attachment to August 13, 2008, email from Kumar to Gianchandani.

"Dear Mr. Mahindroo": *US v. Rajaratnam*, Defense Exhibit 2333, Email from Kumar to S. P. Mahindroo, August 1, 2008.

"We will require 2 original or certified": *US v. Rajaratnam*, Defense Exhibit 2499, Email from Morgan Stanley's Sinead Hayes to Kumar, September 8, 2008.

"In India, there are not utility bills": Ibid., Email from Kumar to Sinead Hayes, September 10, 2008.

"If you can email a pdf copy immediately, that would help a lot": *US v. Rajaratnam*, Defense Exhibit 2848, Email from Kumar to HSBC, October 25, 2008.

HSBC said Das had been an account holder since October 20: *US v. Rajaratnam*, Defense Exhibit 2823, HSBC letter regarding Manju Das, October 25, 2008.

"Please resend a new letter": *US v. Rajaratnam*, Defense Exhibit 2848, Email from Kumar to HSBC, October 30, 2008.

Chapter Twenty-Six: The Wire

The conversation between Anil Kumar and Raj Rajaratnam: *US v. Rajaratnam*, Government

Exhibit 523-T, Transcript of a wiretapped conversation between Kumar and Rajaratnam, May 2, 2008.

Rajaratnam was in Washington and heading to Toronto: *US v. Rajaratnam*, Government Exhibit 524-T-R, Transcript of a wiretapped conversation between Rajaratnam, Kris Chellam, and another Galleon colleague, May 2, 2008.

Kumar and Rajaratnam were in the same Wharton class as Mukesh's younger brother, Anil: *US v. Rajaratnam*, Testimony of Anil Kumar, March 14, 2011; Wharton Alumni Directory.

The Ambani brothers lived for the longest time at Sea Wind and Mukesh moved out in 2010: Naazneen Karmali, "Anil Ambani's Taj Mahal?" Forbes.com, December 6, 2010.

Rajaratnam running into Ambani and Kumar's conversation with Ambani: *US v. Rajaratnam*, Government Exhibit 523-T.

"Do you think we should buy some Spansion?": Ibid.

Minutes after hanging up with Kumar, Rajaratnam phoned Kris Chellam and their exchange: *US v. Rajaratnam*, Government Exhibit 524-T-R.

Chellam was a regular at Rajaratnam's famous Super Bowl parties: *US v. Rajaratnam*, Franks hearing, Government Exhibit 15, FBI memo, June 27, 2007.

"Somebody is gonna put a term sheet for Spansion" and subsequent conversation with Chellam: *US v. Rajaratnam*, Government 524-T-R.

On March 7, 2008, federal judge Gerard E. Lynch: *US v. Rajaratnam*, Franks hearing, Testimony of FBI special agent B. J. Kang, October 6, 2010.

The FBI's monitoring of Rajaratnam's phone: *US v. Rajaratnam*, Testimony of FBI special agent Diane Wehner, March 10, 2011.

In mid-April, the SEC's Andrew Michaelson was lent: Michaelson testified in the Franks hearing that he went to the US attorney's office in April 2008.

On April 2, Khan admitted she made trades in Hilton and Deep Shah was her source: *US v. Rajaratnam*, Franks hearing, Testimony of Andrew Michaelson, October 5, 2010.

Khan met Shah through her cousin: *US v. Whitman*, Testimony of Roomy Khan, August 7, 2012.

One day in late 2006, Khan's cousin called and put Shah on the phone: Ibid.

Khan could not trade on Shah's first tip because it came on a Friday evening: Ibid.

The deal was announced on Monday as Shah predicted: Ibid.

She paid Shah $10,000 for the Hilton tip: *US v. Whitman*, Khan testimony, August 8, 2012.

Shah has denied being the source of the Hilton tips: Susan Pulliam, "Galleon Sinks, Informant Surfaces," *Wall Street Journal*, October, 22, 2009.

"Didi, this is happening": *US v. Whitman*, Khan testimony, August 7, 2012.

Khan getting a phone in the name of her gardener: Ibid.

After nearly two years of Sisyphean frustration: *US v. Rajaratnam*, Franks hearing, Michaelson testimony, October 5, 2010.

Starting in late March 2008, Goel began briefing Rajaratnam on the Clearwire deal and how he came to know of it: *US v. Rajaratnam*, Testimony of Rajiv Goel, March 22 and 24, 2011.

The exchange between Goel and Rajaratnam: *US v. Rajaratnam*, Government Exhibit 502-T, Transcript of a wiretapped conversation between Rajaratnam and Goel, March 19, 2008.

Goel's kids made fun of the hushed tones in which their father spoke and subsequent conversation: *US v. Rajaratnam*, Government Exhibit 503-T, Transcript of a wiretapped call between Goel and Rajaratnam, March 20, 2008.

Between March 24 and 25, Galleon bought 385,000 shares of Clearwire stock: *US v. Rajaratnam*, Government Exhibit 9, All Trading by Manager Code "TMT" in Clearwire Securities on March 24, 2008, and March 25, 2008.

"Oh dude, we're fucked" and subsequent exchange between the brothers Rajaratnam: *US v.*

Rajaratnam, Government Exhibit 509-T, Transcript of wiretapped conversation between Rengan Rajaratnam and Raj Rajaratnam, March 25, 2008.

Karpel had worked for eighteen years at Mutual Shares: Peter Lattman and William Rashbaum, "A Trader, an FBI Witness, and Then a Suicide," *New York Times*, June 2, 2011.

The call between Ephraim Karpel and Zvi Goffer: Ibid.

The FBI approach to Ephraim Karpel: Ibid.

He hanged himself in his Fifth Avenue office: Ibid.

Chapter Twenty-Seven: "I Played Him Like a Finely Tuned Piano"

The FBI agents manning the wire from 6 a.m. until midnight: *US v. Rajaratnam*, Testimony of FBI special agent Diane Wehner, March 10, 2011.

Trading corporate secrets was "like an orgasm": James Bandler and Doris Burke, "Dangerous Liaisons at IBM," *Fortune*, July 26, 2010.

Conversation between Rajaratnam and Chiesi on July 24: *US v. Rajaratnam*, Government Exhibit 532-T, Transcript of a wiretapped conversation between Rajaratnam and Chiesi, July 24, 2008.

Within Akamai, the betting was that the stock would drop to $25: Ibid.

The conversation between Chiesi and Rajaratnam on Akamai: Ibid.

Galleon diversified fund returns: *US v. Gupta*, Government Exhibit 1853, Galleon April 2008 investment presentation attached to email from Ayad Alhadi to Fernando Lamas at UBS, April 18, 2008.

In February, Rajaratnam hired Alhadi: *US v. Gupta*, Testimony of Ayad Alhadi, May 31, 2012.

The Sberbank board position paid $525,000 in 2008: Duff McDonald, "Rajat Gupta: Touched by Scandal," *Fortune*, October 1, 2010.

In 2004, the Bill and Melinda Gates Foundation gave $47 million for AIDS in India: "Bill and Melinda Gates Foundation's Avahan Initiative Announces $47 Million in Grants to Combat HIV/AIDS in India," press release, March 16, 2004, http://www.gatesfoundation.org/press-releases/Pages/grants-to-combat-hiv-aids-in-india-040316.aspx.

In March, Gupta joined Alhadi for meetings in the Middle East with investors like the Abu Dhabi Investment Council: *US v. Gupta*, Alhadi testimony; Government Exhibit 1824, Email from Alhadi to Gupta with schedule of Middle East trip as of March 31, 2008.

In late April, the Abu Dhabi Investment Council said it would invest $50 million: *US v. Gupta*, Government Exhibit 1857, Email from Alhadi to Gupta, April 28, 2008.

Larry Currie asked for a meeting with Gupta and said the National Commercial Bank would start with a $25 to $30 million investment: *US v. Gupta*, Alhadi testimony; Government Exhibit 1844, Email from Ayad Alhadi to Rajat Gupta, April 8, 2008; Government Exhibit 1856, Email from Alhadi to Gupta, April 25, 2008.

Alhadi suspected Gupta's Goldman link would help National Commercial Bank gain more comfort with Galleon: *US v. Gupta*, Government Exhibit 1852, Email from Alhadi to Gupta on April 17, 2008, where he says Currie enjoyed meeting Gupta and "I believe that meeting helped accelerate his comfort level with Galleon."

He now spoke of raising $600 million for a telecommunications fund: *US v. Gupta*, Testimony of Anil Kumar, June 1, 2012.

"It's now reached a point where it's physically": *US v. Rajaratnam*, Government Exhibit 522-T, Transcript of a wiretapped conversation between Kumar and Rajaratnam, May 28, 2008.

Gupta's discussions with KKR and Goldman's reaction to them: *US v. Gupta*, Testimony of Lloyd Blankfein, June 4, 2012.

The issue came to a head in Beijing: Letter written by Anita Gupta on behalf of her husband ahead of his sentencing.

Gupta's expected $5 million salary at KKR: *US v. Rajaratnam*, Government Exhibit 553-T-K, Transcript of wiretapped conversation on August 15, 2008, between Rajaratnam and Kumar where Rajaratnam says the KKR position would pay "about five million a year, with upside." *US v. Gupta*, Blankfein testimony, June 4, 2012.

It was Gupta's desire to be in the "billionaire [*sic*] circle": Ibid.

Schwarzman's contributions to the New York Public Library and its name change: Robin Pogrebin, "A $100 Million Donation to the New York Public Library," *New York Times*, March 11, 2008.

Rajaratnam telling Gupta to take KKR in a "heartbeat": *US v. Rajaratnam*, Government Exhibit 534-T-R, Transcript of a wiretapped conversation between Rajaratnam and Gupta, July 29, 2008.

"He'll divide his week into a hundred different parts" and following conversation with Kumar: *US v. Rajaratnam*, Government Exhibit 522-T.

Rajaratnam was mulling giving Gupta a 10 percent stake in Galleon International, but Gupta was angling for more: Rajaratnam's version of his negotiations with Gupta is supported by at least one other person who knows the two men.

On Wednesday, July 30, Akamai unveiled a pessimistic outlook: *US v. Rajaratnam*, Government Exhibit 2562, Akamai Technologies Inc. Earnings Conference Call, Thomson StreetEvents, July 30, 2008.

Akamai's stock fell 7.91, or 25 percent, to $23.34: Interactive Data via FactSet Systems.

Rajaratnam shorted 200,000 shares of Akamai, then another 375,000 shares and bought put options: *US v. Rajaratnam*, Government Exhibit 41, All Trading by Manager Code "Tam" in Akamai Securities from July 25, 2008, to July 30, 2008.

Instant-message exchange between Rajaratnam and Joe Liu: *US v. Rajaratnam*, Government Exhibits 2611 and 2612, copies of instant-message exchange between Liu and Rajaratnam, July 30, 2008.

Rajaratnam made $5,139,851 from the Akamai trade: *US v. Rajaratnam*, Government Exhibit 44, Government's calculation of Galleon Technology fund's profits from trades in Akamai Securities starting on July 25, 2008.

Chiesi's New Castle funds netted $2,437,976: *US v. Rajaratnam*, Government Exhibit 45, Government's calculation of New Castle's profit from trades in Akamai starting on July 25, 2008.

"I just wanted to say thank you," and subsequent conversation between the two: *US v. Rajaratnam*, Government 543-T, Transcript of a wiretapped conversation between Rajaratnam and Chiesi, July 30, 2008, at 5:30 p.m.

That evening, she headed to the Chinese consulate: Ibid.

Chapter Twenty-Eight: A Friend on the Board

"Raj?" said the cheerful voice: *US v. Gupta*, Government Exhibit 534-T-R, Transcript of a wiretapped call between Rajaratnam and Gupta, July, 29, 2008.

The description of Gomes and her views about Rajat: Interviews with secretaries who dealt with her.

It was early in the evening of Tuesday, July 29, 2008: *US v. Gupta*, Government Exhibit 534-T-R.

Rajaratnam, who was working from Connecticut: Ibid.

That coming Thursday at noon, he was going to be lunching with Gary Cohn: Ibid.

Rick Schutte was to join the lunch, as were a number of Goldman executives: *US v. Rajaratnam*, Testimony of Richard Schutte, April 12, 2011.

In 2008 Galleon shelled out as much as $35 million in commissions and other fees to Goldman: Ibid.

Goldman was Galleon's largest trading partner, and the hedge fund funneled the biggest volume of its transactions through Goldman: Ibid.

One of the reasons Cohn was coming to Galleon that day: Ibid.

Goldman had about $600 million of Galleon (investor) assets in custody: Ibid.

Galleon had about $200 million of investor assets at Bear: Ibid.

Had Bear been forced to file for bankruptcy protection, Galleon would have been one company in a long line of creditors: Ibid.

Rajaratnam had heard that Goldman might be shopping for a commercial bank and subsequent conversation between him and Gupta: *US v. Rajaratnam*, Government Exhibit 534-T-R.

Just a month earlier, Goldman's twelve-person board of directors was in St. Petersburg: *US v. Gupta*, Blankfein testimony, June 4, 2012.

Gupta's corporate board seats and the $3.2 million he earned from them: Duff McDonald, "Rajat Gupta: Touched by Scandal," *Fortune*, October 1, 2010.

The conversation between Gupta and Rajaratnam about Goldman's board debating buying a bank or an insurer like AIG: *US v. Rajaratnam*, Government Exhibit 534-T-R.

Chapter Twenty-Nine: A Tragic Call

It was Thursday, September 11, 2008, and Raj Rajaratnam was starting to feel like a boxer fighting the legend Muhammad Ali: *US v. Rajaratnam*, Government Exhibit 616-T, Transcript of a wiretapped conversation between Rajaratnam and Anil Kumar, September 11, 2008.

The conversation between Rajaratnam and Kumar: Ibid.

He was actually calling from Dublin, where he was huddled in a retreat with members of the Young Presidents' Organization: Ibid.

"Anand Mahindra's got fifty people meeting in Montauk...he's invited me to it": Ibid.

Kumar was constantly "scheming" and subsequent remarks by Rajaratnam to Gupta: *US v. Rajaratnam*, Government Exhibit 534-T-R, Transcript of a wiretapped conversation between Rajaratnam and Gupta, July 29, 2008.

Rajaratnam's tsunami appeal at the Stone Rose Lounge: Anita Raghavan, "Power and Pleasure," *Forbes*, October 11, 2010.

"I asked my guy if KDB is gonna buy" and subsequent conversation between Rajaratnam and Kumar: *US v. Rajaratnam*, Government Exhibit 616-T.

Kumar conversation with Rajaratnam on August 15: *US v. Rajaratnam*, Government Exhibit 553-T-K, Transcript of wiretapped conversation between Kumar and Rajaratnam, August 15, 2008.

"Have you spoken to Hector?" and subsequent conversation between Rajaratnam and Chiesi: *US v. Rajaratnam*, Government Exhibit 554-T, Transcript of wiretapped conversation between Rajaratnam and Chiesi, August 15, 2008.

"Alright, thanks a lot man" and subsequent conversation between Rajaratnam and Rengan: *US v. Rajaratnam*, Government Exhibit 559-T, Transcript of wiretapped conversation between Rengan and Raj Rajaratnam, August 15, 2008.

Rengan relaying his conversation with Palecek to Raj: *US v. Rajaratnam*, Government Exhibit 563-T, Transcript of wiretapped conversation between Rengan and Raj Rajaratnam, August 15, 2008, 5:41 p.m.

Galleon's Technology funds had quadrupled their position in AMD: *US v. Rajaratnam*,

Government Exhibit 22, Galleon Technology and Diversified Daily Closing Position in AMD Stock (AMD), April 1, 2008, through October 8, 2008.

"It's not September 15th": *US v. Rajaratnam*, Government Exhibit 616-T.

Geetanjali Gupta's memory of her father's agitated state on the weekend of September 21, 2008: *US v. Gupta*, Testimony of Geetanjali Gupta, June 11 and 12, 2012.

Geetanjali Gupta's wedding on June 21, 2008: Described by Suzanna Andrews in "How Rajat Gupta Came Undone," *Bloomberg Businessweek*, May 19, 2011, and in several sentencing letters.

"Many Indian parents (mine included) forbade dating": Letter written by Rajat Gupta's niece, Nandita Gupta, on behalf of her uncle before his sentencing.

What would Geetanjali think: Letter written by Gupta's daughter's friend Bhakti Mirchandani before Gupta's sentencing.

Gupta's wondering if his lack of emotion was rooted in the early death of his parents: Gupta's taped remarks at Creativity and Personal Mastery class, taught by Srikumar Rao at Columbia Business School, April 2004.

Geetanjali met Rajaratnam when he came to pitch New Silk Route: *US v. Gupta*, Geetanjali testimony.

Chapter Thirty: "Buy Goldman Sachs, Buy Goldman Sachs"

Byron David Trott's actions on the morning of September 23, 2008: *US v. Gupta*, Testimony of Byron Trott, May 23, 2008.

Trott's conversation with Buffett: Ibid.; Andrew Ross Sorkin, *Too Big to Fail* (New York: Penguin, 2009).

The call from Jon Winkelried and subsequent conversation: *US v. Gupta*, Trott testimony.

Trott's conversation with Goldman's executives in New York and the overture to Buffett: Trott testimony; Sorkin, *Too Big to Fail*; Chris Blackhurst, "Billionaire Buffett and the Only Banker He Trusts," *Evening Standard* (London), September 25, 2008.

Buffett going to the Dairy Queen: Sorkin, *Too Big to Fail*; Trott testimony.

Subsequent meetings on the thirtieth floor: *US v. Gupta*, Trott testimony.

One of Rajaratnam's cardinal rules was that he not be disturbed during the first half hour and last half hour: *US v. Gupta*, Testimony of Caryn Eisenberg, May 22, 2012.

Rajaratnam's instructions to Eisenberg on how to handle calls at the start and the end of the trading day: *US v. Gupta*, Eisenberg testimony.

Rajat Gupta's presence on Eisenberg's important people list: *US v. Gupta*, Government Exhibit 2300, the second page from Eisenberg's notebook detailing the list of important callers.

Rajaratnam would sometimes instruct Eisenberg to lie: *US v. Gupta*, Eisenberg testimony.

The description of Rajaratnam's office with floor-to-ceiling glass walls and a sliding panel: *US v. Gupta*, Eisenberg testimony; Galleon trader Ananth Muniyappa testimony, May 22, 2012.

Will Keaten's email on Goldman: *US v. Gupta*, Government Exhibit 9094, Email from Will Keaten to Galleon's Tech and Trading Group, September 16, 2008.

Shortly after 3:54 p.m. on Tuesday, September 23, Gomes, Gupta's secretary, dialed Rajaratnam's direct line: *US v. Rajaratnam*, Testimony of Carol Ann Shields, an information technology security program manager, March 29, 2011.

It was the only call to Rajaratnam's direct line since 2:27 p.m. that day: *US v. Gupta*, Eisenberg testimony.

Eisenberg's recollection of the caller and her move to find Rajaratnam: Ibid.

It lasted thirty-five seconds at most: *US v. Gupta*, Government Exhibit 50 says the duration of the call from the McKinsey conference room to Rajaratnam's direct line was 30 to 35 seconds.

Rajaratnam summoning Rosenbach and Rosenbach reappearing after less than a minute in Rajaratnam's office to say "Buy Goldman Sachs": *US v. Gupta*, Eisenberg testimony.

At 3:56:44 p.m., Rosenbach managed to buy almost $25 million of Goldman stock: *US v. Gupta*, Testimony of Ananth Muniyappa; Government Exhibit 53, a chart showing trading by a portfolio code associated with Rajaratnam in Goldman stock on September 22 and 23, 2008; Government Exhibit 1622, an instant-message communication between Muniyappa and a Deutsche Bank salesman at the market close on September 23, 2008, where the salesman says he bought 200,000 shares of Goldman for Galleon portfolio manager and trader Rosenbach at a price of $124.8368 each; Government Exhibit 1619, an instant-message exchange between Muniyappa and Rosenbach at 4 p.m. on September 23, 2008, where Rosenbach tells Muniyappa to allocate 150,000 shares to Rajaratnam's portfolio and keep 50,000 shares for his fund.

Ananth Muniyappa's position at Galleon, his location on the trading floor, his duties, and the portfolio managers he traded for: *US v. Gupta*, Testimony of Ananth Muniyappa, May 22, 2012.

Rajaratnam turned to Muniyappa and ordered him to buy 100,000 shares of Goldman stock: Ibid.

Muniyappa's phone conversation with Ted Backer: Ibid.

"bgt 67,200 GS @ 124.0343, fyi," instant-messaged Backer: *US v. Gupta*, Government Exhibit 1620, instant message from Ted Backer at Morgan Stanley to Muniyappa on September 23, 2008, at 4:01 p.m.

Muniyappa allocated 217,200 shares of Goldman stock to Rajaratnam's portfolio: *US v. Gupta*, Muniyappa testimony.

The physical state of Leon Shaulov, who ran the Buccaneers fund, when the Buffett news came out: Ibid.

"Thx for the heads up": Government Exhibit 1629, Email from Leon Shaulov to Gary Rosenbach on September 23, 2008, at 6:16 p.m.

First conversation between Ian Horowitz and Rajaratnam on September 24, 2008: *US v. Gupta*, Government Exhibit 21-T, Transcript of a wiretapped conversation between Rajaratnam and Horowitz on September 24, 2008, at 7:09 a.m.

An hour later, Rajaratnam telephoned Horowitz: *US v. Gupta*, Government Exhibit 22-T, Transcript of a wiretapped conversation between Rajaratnam and Horowitz on September 24, 2008, 7:56 a.m.

Chapter Thirty-One: Trading at the Setai

Lloyd Blankfein's practice in dealing with the Goldman Sachs board and the events of October 23, 2008: *US v. Gupta*, Testimony of Lloyd Blankfein, June 4, 2012.

Blankfein's more palatial pad at 15 Central Park West: Max Abelson, "Viva 15 C.P.W.! Goldman C.E.O. Lloyd Blankfein Closes for $26M," *New York Observer*, January 18, 2008.

Securities analysts were calling for Goldman to earn $2.76 a share: *US v. Gupta*, Government Exhibit 1653, Goldman Sachs weekly investor relations report showing analysts' consensus earnings estimates for the fourth quarter in the week of October 17, 2008.

The *Wall Street Journal* reported that Goldman was going to lay off 10 percent of its workforce: Susanne Craig, "Goldman to Cut 10% of Jobs as Downsizing Wave Grows," *Wall Street Journal*, October 23, 2008.

Of Goldman's nine external board members, only one, Stephen Friedman, definitely could not

make the call: *US v. Gupta*, Government Exhibit 433, Goldman Sachs 4:15 p.m. Board Posting Call—Status on Attendance.

Gupta's schedule on October 23 and details of his flight from Barcelona, Spain, on American Airlines Flight 151: *US v. Gupta*, Government Exhibit 3600, Gupta's calendar from October 23 to October 27, 2008.

Gupta and his wife were headed to Providence on October 24 and his activities there: Ibid.

At 4:16 p.m., Gomes dialed into the Goldman call: *US v. Rajaratnam*, Testimony of Carol Ann Shields, March 29, 2011; Government Exhibit 75, Certain communications on October 23, 2008, and October 24, 2008.

Blankfein's report to the board: *US v. Gupta*, Testimony of William George, May 25, 2012; Blankfein testimony, June 4, 2012.

The debate about why Goldman was suddenly going to lose money: *US v. Gupta*, George testimony.

Twenty-three seconds later, Gupta's secretary telephoned Rajaratnam's direct work line: *US v. Gupta*, Shields testimony, May 24, 2012.

"Raj is one of the most outstanding hedge fund managers": *US v. Gupta*, Government Exhibit 1922, Email signed by Gupta but sent by Renee Gomes to Marshall Lux, February 15, 2007.

Gupta's disclosures to Kumar about his investment in Voyager: *US v. Gupta*, Testimony of Anil Kumar, June 4, 2012.

On October 5, before flying to Europe, Gupta lobbed a call to Rajaratnam: *US v. Gupta*, Government Exhibit 24-T, Transcript of a wiretapped conversation between Gupta and Rajaratnam on October 5, 2008.

"I know it must be an awful and busy week": *US v. Gupta*, Government Exhibit 25-T, Transcript of a wiretapped message from Gupta to Rajaratnam on October 10, 2008.

For twelve minutes and thirty seconds, the two were connected: In *US v. Gupta*, Shields said the two were connected for twelve minutes and up to thirty-five seconds.

The next morning, Rajaratnam's technology portfolio sold 50,000 shares and then 100,000 shares: *US v. Rajaratnam*, Government Exhibit 76, Galleon Tech Trading in Goldman Sachs Stock (GS) from October 21, 2008, through October 24, 2008.

The sales saved Galleon $3.8 million in potential losses: *US v. Rajaratnam*, Government Exhibit 77, Galleon Tech Losses Avoided by Selling Goldman Sachs Stock (GS) on October 24, 2008.

The conversation with David Lau: *US v. Gupta*, Government Exhibit 29-T, Transcript of a wiretapped conversation between Rajaratnam and Lau, October 24, 2008.

"How does it make you feel that your agency is absolutely incompetent?": Monica Langley, Kara Scannell, Susan Pulliam, and Susanne Craig, "SEC Chief's Big Bet on Goldman," *Wall Street Journal*, May 15, 2010.

"If we don't get serious about this process": Kara Scannell, "Assured of SEC's Survival, Schapiro Now Fights to Keep Regulatory Teeth," *Wall Street Journal*, June 11, 2009.

In December 2008, the wiretaps on Rajaratnam's phone ended: *US v. Rajaratnam*, Testimony of Diane Wehner.

Far divulged that Atheros will do "98, 99 million" in revenue: *US v. Ali Hariri*, complaint, MAG 09 2436, November 4, 2009.

The FBI approach to Far: *US v. Rajaratnam*, Franks hearing, Government Exhibit 89 shows that Far was interviewed by the FBI on April 21 in the presence of his lawyers, suggesting an approach was made earlier.

Walia mention of Far: In the Matter of Sedna Capital Management, NY-7665, Apjit Walia voluntary testimony, August 1, 2007.

The approach to Lee and the sit-down with his lawyer: First reported by Susan Pulliam, "The Network: The Feds Close In: Fund Chief Snared by Taps, Turncoats—Prosecutors Stalk Galleon's Rajaratnam After Finding a Revelatory Text Message," *Wall Street Journal*, December 30, 2009.

Closing of Spherix: Ibid.

Stopping off at the Setai and the tip Rajaratnam got on Cisco buying Starent: *US v. Rajaratnam*, Testimony of Anil Kumar, March 15, 2011.

"You know Anil, I am really disappointed": Ibid.

Kumar's purchase of 300 Starent shares: Ibid.

On October 13, Cisco unveiled a $2.9 billion deal for Starent: *US v. Rajaratnam*, Government Exhibit 945, Press release entitled: "Acquisition of Starent Networks Expands Cisco's Mobile Internet Offerings for Service Providers," October 13, 2009.

Chapter Thirty-Two: Handcuffs for Breakfast

The description of Rajaratnam on Thursday, October 15, 2009, and the size of Galleon: Anita Raghavan, "Power and Pleasure," *Forbes*, October 11, 2010.

Galleon outlasted the Bowman Technology fund and Andor Capital: Katherine Burton and Saijel Kishan, "Raj Rajaratnam Became a Billionaire Demanding Edge," Bloomberg News, October 19, 2009. Andor has since reopened, according to Alistair Barr, *MarketWatch*, March 2, 2011.

One of nearly fifteen hundred funds to close its doors: According to Hedge Fund Research Inc., 1,471 funds liquidated in 2008.

"It is our investors' money and they have the right: Letter from Lukasz Sito, May 5, 2011, quoted in *US v. Rajaratnam*, Sentencing Memorandum on behalf of Raj Rajaratnam.

By 2009, Galleon was on track to earn 20 percent in performance fees, and some big investors were close to pouring money: Raghavan, "Power and Pleasure."

He and his wife, Asha, were set to leave for London: Ibid.

"I am the last man standing": Ibid.

In the wee hours of the morning, B. J. Kang was talking with a member of the Office of Customs and Border Protection: *US v. Raj Rajaratnam, Rajiv Goel, and Anil Kumar*, 09 Mag 2306, Complaint, October 15, 2009.

When Streeter secured a guilty plea from Marc Dreier in May 2009: Benjamin Weiser, "Lawyer Gets Twenty Years in $700 Million Fraud," *New York Times*, July 13, 2009; John Ryan, "The 500 Lawyer Limelight: Jonathan Streeter," Lawdragon, August 5, 2012.

The two complaints, efforts to get Chiesi to cooperate, and her arrest: *US v. Danielle Chiesi*, 09 CR 1184, Miranda hearing, Testimony of FBI agent Kathleen Queally, November 22, 2010. Queally testified that there were two complaints. If the FBI had succeeded in getting Chiesi to cooperate, the complaint naming Chiesi and two other individuals, believed to be Robert Moffat and Mark Kurland, would "probably not" have been filed that day. The reason the FBI was trying to get Chiesi to cooperate was that it thought she could engage in a covert operation. "There were other people we were looking to obtain information on," Queally said, adding that Rajaratnam was part of a separate complaint. Chiesi sought the Miranda hearing after her arrest, saying that she was questioned for about ninety minutes without being advised of her right to remain silent.

Chiesi's affair with Moffat and her longtime lover Kurland: James Bandler and Doris Burke, "Dangerous Liaisons at IBM," *Fortune*, July 26, 2010.

The description of the arrest of Chiesi: *US v. Chiesi*, Miranda hearing, Queally testimony, November 22, 2010.

Chiesi thought it was a joke with Halloween being around the corner: *US v. Chiesi*, Miranda hearing, Testimony of Danielle Chiesi, November 22, 2010.

"Is my mom okay?": Ibid.

She was actually worried there might be a marijuana joint lying around: Susan Pulliam and Chad Bray, "Key Plotter Pleads Guilty in Galleon," *Wall Street Journal*, January 20, 2011.

All they found was Chiesi's pet cat and her fish: *US v. Chiesi*, Miranda hearing, Chiesi testimony.

The conversation between Chiesi and the agents regarding cooperation and Rajaratnam's arrest: Based on testimony from Wehner, Queally, and Chiesi at the Miranda hearing.

Rajaratnam was on his exercise bike and his arrest: Suketu Mehta, "The Outsider," *Newsweek*, October 23, 2011.

Two FBI agents, one playing good cop: Ibid.

They asked her to write a telephone number: *US v. Chiesi*, Miranda hearing, Chiesi testimony.

Chiesi confessed that she didn't have a bra on: Ibid.

"Well your sweater's big enough," Chiesi remembers Wehner replying: *US v. Chiesi*, Miranda hearing, Chiesi testimony.

The 7:30 a.m. deadline: *US v. Chiesi*, Miranda hearing, Queally testimony.

The story of Dominic Barton learning of Kumar's arrest while at a client meeting in Madrid: Joanna Pachner, "McKinsey & Co.: The Man Behind the Curtain," *Canadian Business*, April 7, 2011.

His wife lived in Shanghai and his children were in boarding school in Singapore: Ibid.

Barton's personal experience with the company's "up or out" management style: Ibid.

Kumar's collapse when agents first came to arrest him: First reported by George Packer, "A Dirty Business: New York City's Top Prosecutor Takes on Wall Street Crime," *New Yorker*, June 27, 2011. Kumar's fainting was confirmed in *US v. Anil Kumar*, 10 Cr. 13 (DC), Government's sentencing memo.

Chapter Thirty-Three: "Why Is It So Quiet Around Here?"

In November 2002, Rajaratnam delivered a rousing appeal for Prabhakaran's cause: David Rose, "Crouching Tiger, Hidden Raj," *Vanity Fair*, September 30, 2011.

Rajaratnam referenced as "individual B" in federal complaint in 2006: Evan Perez and Matthew Rosenberg, "Rajaratnam Wasn't Charged in Terrorism Probe," DowJones Newswires, October 17, 2009.

Walden's remarks to the *Wall Street Journal*: Evan Perez and Eric Bellman, "The Galleon Case: Officials Say Investor's Donations Wound up with Sri Lanka Rebels," *Wall Street Journal*, October 19, 2009.

One investor who had seen Rajaratnam led out in handcuffs: Susan Pulliam, "The Network: The Feds Close In: Fund Chief Snared by Taps, Turncoats—Prosecutors Stalk Galleon's Rajaratnam After Finding a Revelatory Text Message," *Wall Street Journal*.

The lyrics of "The Good Ship Galleon" song: Reported by Clemente Lisi, "Hip-Hop Track of the Trade," *New York Post*, October 17, 2009.

Rajaratnam was charged with trading on inside information in Akamai, AMD, Clearwire, and Google, and details of the complaint: *US v. Raj Rajaratnam, Rajiv Goel, and Anil Kumar* complaint, 09 Mag 2306, October 16, 2009.

The cooperating witness also known as Tipper A in the SEC action: Securities and Exchange Commission against Galleon Management LP et. al, 09 CV 8811, October 16, 2009.

They visited Michael Cardillo in the lobby of his building in November 2009: *US v. Gupta*, Testimony of Michael Cardillo, May 30, 2012.

Cardillo, who burst into tears after Raj's arrest: Susan Pulliam and Michael Rothfeld, "Plea Deals Ramp Up Pressure in Galleon," *Wall Street Journal*, January 27, 2011.

Cardillo's recording of calls with Michael Fisherman: *US v. Gupta*, Cardillo testimony.

Shortly before noon, Adam Smith saw Rengan walk "dramatically" into his brother's office: David Glovin, Patricia Hurtado, and Bob Van Voris, "Rajaratnam's Brother Took Notebooks After Arrest, Smith Says," Bloomberg, March 29, 2011, cited March 27 court papers, in which Smith is said to have told prosecutors that he saw Rengan remove the notebooks after his brother's arrest.

Smith's receiving inside information on Nvidia and trading on it: *US v. Adam Smith*, 11 Cr. 79 (JSR), Government sentencing memo (hereafter Government's Smith memo).

Rengan sought to confirm that the reference in a May 2008 call was not to the Morgan Stanley source: Glovin, Hurtado, and Van Voris, "Rajaratnam's Brother Took Notebooks After Arrest, Smith Says"; *US v. Rajaratnam*, Memorandum of Law in Support of Defendant Raj Rajaratnam's Motion to Exclude Testimony Concerning Certain Events After Mr. Rajaratnam's Arrest, March 27, 2011.

Adam Smith's destruction of his laptop and other actions he took after Rajaratnam's arrest: *US v. Rajaratnam*, Testimony of Adam Smith, March 30, 2011.

The presentment of Rajaratnam and Kumar before US magistrate judge Douglas Eaton: *US v. Rajaratnam*, M-09-2306, Transcript of Proceedings, October 16, 2009.

"I'm sorry": George Packer, "A Dirty Business: New York City's Top Prosecutor Takes on Wall Street Crime," *New Yorker*, June 27, 2011.

When he was first arrested he was not allowed to use the bathroom: Glovin, Hurtado, and Van Voris, in "Rajaratnam's Brother Took Notebooks After Arrest, Smith Says," cite the remark from a February 1 FBI interview summary of Smith.

Kumar's bail package secured by his $2.5 million home: Revealed at the presentment on October 16, 2009.

Rajaratnam's $5 million bail package: Ibid.

About a week after his arrest Rajaratnam brought over a fax to Smith: *US v. Rajaratnam*, Smith testimony, March 30, 2011.

Morvillo's career and his contribution to the white-collar defense practice: Peter Lattman and Benjamin Weiser, "Robert Morvillo, 73, Legal Pioneer, Dies," *New York Times*, December 25, 2011.

Government prosecutors had recently learned that she and her husband, Sakhawat, had submitted a doctored work schedule: *US v. Whitman*, Testimony of Roomy Khan, August 7, 2012.

It took prosecutors only two in-person meetings: *US v. Anil Kumar*, 10 Cr.13 (DC), Government Kumar Sentencing Memo, July 16, 2012.

Chapter Thirty-Four: "He's a Bad Man"

Gupta got on the board of trustees for the University of Chicago in 1995: *University of Chicago Chronicle*, August 17, 1995.

Rajaratnam, Gupta said, he later learned had taken his money out: *US v. Gupta*, Defense Exhibit 2105r showed that Rajaratnam had taken about $25.2 million out of Voyager; in Defense Exhibit 4015-T, Transcript of a wiretapped conversation between Rajaratnam and his lieutenant Sanjay Santhanam, Rajaratnam says in connection with Voyager, "I hope Rajat is a big boy. You know?...I didn't tell him I took that equity out."

The SEC was preparing to file civil fraud charges against Goldman: Alistair Barr, "Goldman Had Nine Months Warning from SEC—Report," DowJones Newswires, April 17, 2010.

"He's a bad man": Patricia Hurtado, "Goldman's Dahlback, Berkshire's Jain May Be Gupta Witnesses," Bloomberg News, January 29, 2012.

Alok "Rodinhood" Kejriwal's observations of Gupta at HBS: Interview with Alok Kejriwal, August 10, 2012.

In mid-April, the *Wall Street Journal* reported: Susan Pulliam, "Goldman Director in Probe; Prosecutors Examine Trades by Galleon in Bank's Shares as Investigation Widens," *Wall Street Journal*, April 13, 2010.

Chapter Thirty-Five: The Gupta File

The agency was still struggling to get its hands on the fourteen thousand hours of recordings: Zachery Kouwe, "Judge Allows S.E.C. to Add Galleon Case Charges," Dealbook, January 25, 2010.

Naftalis's representation of Muriel Siebert: See http://www.kramerlevin.com/gnaftalis/.

Just a month before, *Fortune* magazine had run a devastating piece: Duff McDonald, "Rajat Gupta: Touched by Scandal," *Fortune*, October 1, 2010.

George Canellos joined the SEC the summer before from Milbank, Tweed: See http://www.sec.gov/news/press/2009/2009-125.htm

"The government's unprecedented use of electronic surveillance": David Scheer, Joshua Gallu, and David Glovin, "Rajaratnam Slams Wiretaps, Cites Analysts in Defense," Bloomberg, November 24, 2009.

On May 7, 2010, Rajaratnam's lawyers filed a motion to suppress the recordings: *US v. Rajaratnam and Danielle Chiesi*, S1 09 CR.1184 (RJH), Defendant Raj Rajaratnam's Memorandum of Law in Support of His Motion to Suppress Evidence Derived from Wiretap Interceptions of His Cellular Telephone, May 7, 2010.

On August 12, 2010, Judge Holwell decided to hold a hearing to rule on the wiretaps: "Galleon Founder Wins Hearing on Wiretaps," Dealbook, August 13, 2010.

Lindi Beaudreault told the court: *US v. Rajaratnam*, Franks hearing, Testimony of Lindi Beaudreault, October 4, 2010.

But Michaelson painted a different picture: *US v. Rajaratnam*, Franks hearing, Testimony of Andrew Michaelson, October 4 and 5, 2010.

"It does not take a rocket scientist to understand": Bharara's remarks at the New York City Bar Association, October 20, 2010. See http://www.nycbar.org/44th-street-blog/2010/10/21/preet-bharara-on-the-future-of-white-collar-enforcement-a-prosecutors-view/?option=com_wordpress&Itemid=6.

Only a month later, on November 24, did Judge Holwell issue an opinion: US District Court, Southern District of New York, Memorandum Opinion and Order, November 24, 2010.

"I heard yesterday from someone who's on the board of Goldman Sachs": *US v. Rajaratnam*, Government Exhibit 678-T, Transcript of a wiretapped conversation between Rajaratnam and Lau, October 24, 2008.

On January 21, the US attorney's office unveiled a new indictment: Jonathan Stempel, "Rajaratnam Got Information Leaked by MS banker: Prosecutors," Reuters, January 21, 2011.

On Tuesday, March 1, 2011, the SEC filed a civil administrative action against Gupta: John Helyar, Carol Hymowitz, and Mehul Srivastava, "Gupta Secretly Defied McKinsey Before SEC Tip Accusation," Bloomberg, May 17, 2011.

"I am stunned and shocked by the proposed action": Email on March 1, 2011, from Rajat Gupta to business associates and friends.

Chapter Thirty-Six: Kumar Sings

"Greed and corruption": *US v. Rajaratnam*, Assistant US attorney Jon Streeter's opening argument, March 9, 2011.

The youngest son of a Cleveland lawyer: Kaja Whitehouse, "Going After Galleon: Low-Profile Prosecutor Is Thrust into Spotlight," *New York Post*, March 25, 2011.

By the time the trial started, of the forty-seven conspirators the government had charged, twenty-three had pleaded guilty: George Packer, "A Dirty Business: New York City's Top Prosecutor Takes on Wall Street Crime," *New Yorker*, June 27, 2011.

On the afternoon of Thursday, January 7, 2010: Zachery Kouwe, "Guilty Plea in Galleon Insider Trading Case," Dealbook, January 7, 2010.

The details of Kumar's plea and the maximum sentence: *US v. Anil Kumar*, Transcript of Kumar's guilty plea before then federal judge Denny Chin, January 7, 2010. Judge Chin is now an appeals court judge.

"You had an understanding or agreement with Mr. Rajaratnam" and following exchange: Ibid.

A year after Kumar's plea, Chiesi pleaded guilty: Justice Department, "Hedge Fund Employee Danielle Chiesi Pleads Guilty in New York to Insider Trading Charges," press release, January 19, 2011; Susan Pulliam and Chad Bray, "Key Plotter Pleads Guilty in Galleon," *Wall Street Journal*, January 20, 2011.

Streeter and Alex Chiesi had at one time literally lived next to each other: Alex Chiesi, when contacted about being a neighbor of Streeter's, said, "That is completely false." However, city property records show that Chiesi resided at the same Upper West Side address as Streeter in 2009.

Raj Rajaratnam knew "tomorrow's business news today": *US v. Rajaratnam*, Streeter opening argument.

Sat Rajaratnam, flanked by six lawyers, at the center of the defense table: Peter Lattman, "It's Greed vs. a Picture of Solid Research in Galleon Trial," Dealbook, March 9, 2011.

All of his previous convictions—Anthony Cuti, Marc Dreier: Whitehouse, "Going After Galleon."

His unsuccessful bid in 1974 to convict Meyer Lansky: Grant McCool, "Rajaratnam's Lawyer Dowd—A Man for Big Cases," Reuters, February 18, 2011; Daniel E. Ginsburg, *The Fix Is In: A History of Baseball Gambling and Game Fixing Scandals* (North Carolina: McFarland, 1995).

Dowd's expletive-filled email to Chad Bray: Packer, "A Dirty Business."

The "New Sheriff of Wall Street": William D. Cohan, in "Preet Bharara: The Enforcer of Wall Street—Term Sheet," *Fortune*, August 2, 2011, cites the *Washington Post* as dubbing Bharara the "Sheriff of Wall Street."

Bharara as one of *Time*'s 100 Most Influential People: "The World's 100 Most Influential People," *Time*, April 30, 2012. See http://www.time.com/time/specials/packages/completelist/0,29569,2111975,00.html.

Bharara's evenhanded approach in the Senate investigation: Benjamin Weiser, "For Manhattan's Next U.S. Attorney, Politics and Prosecution Don't Mix," *New York Times*, August 9, 2009.

The Senate confirmed Bharara in August 2009: On its website, the Manhattan US attorney's office says that Bharara was nominated for the job by President Obama on May 15, 2009, confirmed by the Senate on August 7, and sworn in on August 13, 2009. See http://www.justice.gov/usao/nys/meetattorney.html.

Bharara's daughter called his office "humongo": Bharara's remarks at swearing-in ceremony, October 13, 2009.

"My mother is the kindest, and most forgiving person": Ibid.

The government said Rajaratnam pocketed as much as $75 million from his illegal trades: Prosecutor Reed Brodsky said at Rajaratnam's sentencing that Rajaratnam pocketed between $70 million and $75 million through outright gains and losses avoided from his illegal trades. Judge Holwell said a "reasonable estimate" of the total gains arising from Rajaratnam's offenses are "greater than $50 million but less than $100 million."

Rajaratnam's net worth of $1.3 billion at one time: *Forbes* in March 2009 listed Rajaratnam as having a net worth of $1.3 billion.

"Disturbingly, many of the people who are going to such lengths to obtain inside information": Bharara's remarks at the New York City Bar Association on October 20, 2010.

Preetinder means the "one who loves God": Alisa Chang, "Meet Preet Bharara: New York's Highest-Profile Prosecutor," WNYC News, January 27, 2011.

Bharara's birth in Ferozepur in 1968 and his parents' journey to America: Weiser, "For Manhattan's Next U.S. Attorney, Politics and Prosecution Don't Mix."

"My dad was more of a tiger dad": Sarah Jacob, "Preet Bharara on Insider Trading, Rajat Gupta and Wiretaps," NDTV.com, August 1, 2012.

Bharara's education at the Ranney School: Chang, "Meet Preet Bharara"; Cohan, "Preet Bharara: The Enforcer of Wall Street."

Vinit went on to found a business called Diapers.com: Ibid.

"Look what Preetie did": Interview with Christine Gasiorowski, June 16, 2011.

Chip Clark's recollections of Preet: Interview with Chip Clark, September 21, 2011.

His friendship with Viet Dinh: Cohan, "Preet Bharara: The Enforcer of Wall Street."

The couple live in Westchester County: Peter Lattman, "The Bruce-Bharara Bromance," Dealbook, November 1, 2012.

"The evidence will show that the government has it wrong": John Dowd opening argument, March 9, 2011.

Kumar's definition of a hedge fund and "That would be a very big mess": *US v. Rajaratnam*, Testimony of Anil Kumar, March 10, 2011.

"Ahhh...like a baby treats a diaper": *US v. Rajaratnam*, Government Exhibit 692-T-R, Transcript of a wiretapped conversation among Rajaratnam, Horowitz, and Smith.

"I think you are being very generous": *US v. Rajaratnam*, Government Exhibit 534-T, Transcript of a wiretapped conversation between Rajaratnam and Gupta, July 29, 2008.

A few days before, Gupta took a leave of absence from his own private equity fund, New Silk Route: Saijel Kishan and Cristina Alesci, "Gupta Takes Leave from New Silk Route Amid SEC Charges," Bloomberg, March 10, 2011.

Stepped down as adviser to the Bill and Melinda Gates Foundation: Andrew Jack, "Gupta Resigns from Gates Foundation," *Financial Times*, March 27, 2011, quotes a statement of the Gates Foundation saying that "Rajat has stepped down from his role on the Foundation's Global Development advisory panel until these matters are resolved."

"You wrote here it was going to be tricky": *US v. Rajaratnam*, John Dowd's cross-examination of Kumar, March 15, 2011.

Presence of Bharara, Sorkin at Blankfein testimony: Packer, "A Dirty Business."

Holwell rhymed the last syllable of Blankfein's name with "bean": David Glovin, Bob Van Voris, and Patricia Hurtado, "Rajaratnam Jury Candidates Ask 'Lloyd Who?' on Insider Trial's First Day," Bloomberg, March 9, 2011.

"My sense of it, yes" and following remarks by Blankfein: *US v. Rajaratnam*, Testimony of Lloyd Blankfein, March 23, 2011.

Dowd's questioning of Blankfein and his responses: Ibid.

Blankfein shaking Rajaratnam's hand: Basil Katz and Lauren Tara LaCapra, "Blankfein Extends Hand to Rajaratnam Defense Team," Reuters, March 24, 2011.

"To do your homework but to still cheat on the test" and "have two torpedoes in the water": *US v. Rajaratnam*, Testimony of Adam Smith, March 29, 2011.

Schutte cast the research effort at Galleon as disciplined and Rajaratnam as well prepared, knowing "what questions to ask": *US v. Rajaratnam*, Testimony of Richard Schutte, April 12, 2011.

Brodsky's cross-examining of Schutte on SpotTail: David Glovin, Patricia Hurtado, and Bob Van Voris, "Rajaratnams Invested $25 Million in Fund Run by Defense Witness," Bloomberg, April 15, 2011; Kaja Whitehouse, "Raj's High Wires, Sent Hedgie $25M," *New York Post,* April 15, 2011.

"He could level the playing field for kids": *US v. Rajaratnam*, Testimony of Geoffrey Canada, April 13, 2011.

Jarrell had been paid $200,000 by the defense: Chad Bray, "Witness Cites Public Data," *Wall Street Journal*, April 16, 2011.

"Conquer the stock market at the expense of the law": Reed Brodsky closing argument, April 19, 2011.

"the greediest man": John Dowd closing argument, April 19, 2011.

As to count one, "Guilty": *US v. Rajaratnam*, Transcript of verdict, May 11, 2011.

Chapter Thirty-Seven: An Unhappy Diwali

"It bothers me a little bit when people suggest": George Packer, "A Dirty Business: New York City's Top Prosecutor Takes on Wall Street Crime," *New Yorker*, June 27, 2011.

At first, P&G asked if it would be sufficient for prosecutors to question one director: A P&G spokesman said the firm cooperated fully with the government and made available both current and former directors and senior executives.

Brodsky's discovery of Rajaratnam's investment in Schutte's fund and Smith's role: Kaja Whitehouse, "Broadway Brodsky Pit Bull Crime Fighter's Next Target: Rajat Gupta," *New York Post,* May 21, 2012; Government's Smith sentencing memo.

It took two FBI agents showing up at his home at 6:42 a.m.: *US v. Gupta*, Testimony of Ayad Alhadi, May 31, 2012.

Kumar met with the government more than ten times, making seven trips from California to New York: *US v. Anil Kumar*, 10 Cr.13 (DC), Government's Submission Pursuant to Section 5K1.1 of the Sentencing Guidelines (hereafter government's Kumar sentencing memo), July 16, 2012.

Prosecutors were asking for a prison sentence of as many as twenty-four and a half years for Rajaratnam: Peter Lattman, "US Is Seeking Maximum Prison Term in Galleon Case," *New York Times*, August 9, 2011.

Rajaratnam declined to take the opportunity to speak at his sentencing: Ibid.

On October 13, Judge Holwell sentenced Rajaratnam to eleven years in prison, the longest ever in an insider trading case: *US v. Rajaratnam*, Transcript of sentencing, October 13, 2011.

It reflects "a virus in our business culture": Ibid.

The SEC's dismissal of its administrative proceeding against Gupta and the original suit by Gupta: Peter Lattman, "SEC Drops Proceeding Against Rajat Gupta," Dealbook, August 4, 2011.

Judge Rakoff ruling that Gupta's lawsuit could proceed: *Rajat K. Gupta v. Securities and Exchange Commission*, 11 Civ. 1900 (JSR), Opinion and Order, July 11, 2011.

Kanchan Gupta was driving from work when his brother called: Kanchan Gupta letter written on behalf of his older brother before his sentencing.

Gupta paid $1.65 million in 2000 for his pied-à-terre at the Century: City Register, County of New York, Deed for purchase of residential unit 22K in 25 Central Park West; purchase price is from LexisNexis.

15 Central Park West is home to Dan Loeb, Blankfein, and Weill: New York City property tax records for Loeb, Blankfein, and Weill.

Chapter Thirty-Eight: Et Tu, Kumar?

Seven months earlier, he had been arraigned on charges of one count of conspiracy to commit securities fraud and five counts of securities fraud: Michael Rothfeld, Susan Pulliam, and S. Mitra Kalita, "Gupta Case Targets Insider Culture," *Wall Street Journal*, October 27, 2011.

In February 2012, the government unveiled a new indictment: Peter Lattman, "New Charges Filed in Insider Trading Case Against Ex-Goldman Director," *New York Times*, February 1, 2012.

The new indictment charged that in March 2007 Gupta called in to a Goldman audit committee meeting: *US v. Gupta*, S 1 11 Cr. 907 (JSR), Superseding indictment, February 1, 2012.

Gupta recommended each of Zainulbhai's children for the University of Chicago: Adil Zainulbhai letter written on behalf of Gupta before his sentencing.

"During these times, you get to know your real friends": Copy of email sent by Rajat K. Gupta (hereafter Gupta email) to friends, May 18, 2012.

On May 16, federal judge Rakoff said he would allow three wiretaps: Peter Lattman, "Judge May Permit Wiretaps as Evidence in Insider Case," Dealbook, May 16, 2012.

"Today is Friday, May 18th": Gupta email.

The SEC civil case filed in federal court on October 26, 2011: See http://www.sec.gov/litiga tion/litreleases/2011/lr22140.htm.

Rakoff's indomitable presence in the courtroom: First reported in "Judge Rakoff: A Hot Bench," *Economist*, June 9, 2012.

"You look so much taller than Napoleon": *US v. Gupta*, Judge Rakoff, May 21, 2012.

Brodsky dubbed Napoleon by the *Wall Street Journal*: Reed Albergotti, "Napoleon of Courtroom Next Takes on Gupta," *Wall Street Journal*, May 21, 2012.

"Your Honor, just to be clear, he won't mention AIDS, malaria or tuberculosis" and the subsequent exchange: *US v. Gupta*, Reed Brodsky, May 21, 2012.

In 2009, Judge Rakoff presided over the wedding of one of Naftalis's sons: Azam Ahmed, "A Litigator Known as Colombo with a Law Degree," Dealbook, October 27, 2011.

Rakoff's representation of Martin Siegel and his crime: Chronicled in James Stewart, *Den of Thieves* (London: Simon & Schuster, 1991), 416–23.

The composition of the Gupta jury: Peter Lattman, "Jury Is Seated in Rajat Gupta Trial," Dealbook, May 21, 2012.

"This is a case about illegal insider trading" and following remarks by Brodsky: *US v. Gupta*, Reed Brodsky opening argument, May 21, 2012.

The government was offering a "cropped photo" of Gupta: *US v. Gupta*, Gary Naftalis opening argument, May 21, 2012.

Caryn Eisenberg's list of VIP callers: *US v. Gupta*, Government Exhibit 2300, List of important callers from page 2 of Eisenberg's notebook.

Eisenberg's testimony of the events on September 23, 2008: *US v. Gupta*, Testimony of Caryn Eisenberg, May 22, 2012.

Loeb was under investigation for passing information on Intel, Apple, and Hewlett-Packard: Patricia Hurtado and David Glovin, "Goldman's David Loeb Passed Tip to Rajaratnam,

US Says," Bloomberg, May 23, 2012, quotes prosecutor Reed Brodsky as saying Loeb passed information on these three stocks.

He was "extremely friendly": *US v. Gupta*, Eisenberg testimony, May 22, 2012.

Ananth Muniyappa took the stand wearing a plaid shirt: Peter Lattman, "Rajaratnam's Goldman Trade a Focus at Gupta Trial," Dealbook, May 23, 2012.

Naftalis's exchange with Judge Rakoff about Buffett: Sidebar between lawyers in *US v. Gupta*, Trott testimony, May 23, 2012.

George's testimony that Goldman was losing money: *US v. Gupta*, Testimony of William George, May 25, 2012.

Heather Webster's notes: *US v. Gupta*, Government Exhibit 5516, Webster's contemporaneous notes of her meeting with Rajat Gupta and his wife at their Westport home on April 23, 2008.

Kumar testimony on Gupta's $10 million loss in Voyager: *US v. Gupta*, Testimony of Anil Kumar, June 4, 2012.

Told the government that Gupta said Rajaratnam had not kept a straight book: Ibid.

Paris Hilton had arrived for a settlement conference in a dispute with an Italian lingerie company: Peter Lattman, "Blankfein Takes the Stand in Insider Trading Case," Dealbook, June 4, 2012.

"I am sure you want to hide the fact this witness is a lawyer": *US v. Gupta*, Judge Rakoff during Testimony of Lloyd Blankfein, June 4, 2012.

The one area Blankfein shed new light on was Gupta's conversations with KKR: Ibid.

His daughter was graduating from Fieldston: Lattman, "Blankfein Takes the Stand."

"I am going to a restaurant in Yonkers": *US v. Gupta*, Blankfein testimony, June 4, 2012.

Naftalis cross-examination of Blankfein: *US v. Gupta*, Blankfein testimony, June 7, 2012.

After the jury left, Naftalis said it was "highly likely" his client would testify: Kara Scannell, "Gupta Likely to Testify in His Own Defense," *Financial Times*, June 8, 2012.

By Sunday, Gupta had decided against testifying: *US v. Gupta*, Letter from Naftalis to Judge Rakoff, June 10, 2012.

Geetanjali is a graduate of Harvard Law School and Harvard Business School and received a bachelor's in applied math from Harvard College: Peter Lattman, "Gupta's Daughter Testifies at His Insider Trading Trial," Dealbook, June 12, 2012.

The weekend of September 21 at the Guptas: *US v. Gupta*, Testimony of Geetanjali Gupta, June 11, 2012.

Suprotik Basu's call from a businessman "who wanted to end all childhood deaths from malaria" and his subsequent remarks: *US v. Gupta*, Testimony of Suprotik Basu, June 11, 2012.

"When you take leverage you know": *US v. Gupta*, Defense Exhibit 4015-T, Transcript of a wiretapped conversation between Sanjay Santhanam and Raj Rajaratnam, October 2, 2008.

Internal Galleon document showing Rajaratnam took $25.2 million out of Voyager: *US v. Gupta*, Defense Exhibit 2105r, An analysis of Voyager.

Tarlowe's summation: *US v. Gupta*, June 13, 2012.

"One of the unluckiest men in the world": *US v. Gupta*, Brodsky, June 13, 2012.

Gupta "never did any insider trading" and remainder of Naftalis summation: *US v. Gupta*, Naftalis, June 13, 2012.

The note from juror number 6: *US v. Gupta*, Jury note 10, May 25, 2012.

Geetanjali was at the Starbucks: Email from Peter Lattman, *New York Times*, June 15, 2012.

"On Count 2 ... not guilty": *US v. Gupta*, Transcript of verdict, June 15, 2012.

The man she knew did not emerge in the trial: Anita Gupta sentencing letter.

Chapter Thirty-Nine: A Family Secret

The summer between Gupta's conviction and sentencing: Drawn from author interviews and sentencing letters.

His second daughter, Megha, spotted an unfamiliar look: Letter written by Megha Gupta on behalf of her father ahead of his sentencing.

"As I listened to the evidence": Letter written by Purnendu Chatterjee on behalf of Gupta before Gupta's sentencing.

The Gupta sentencing letters: Michael Rothfeld, "Dear Judge, Gupta Is a Good Man—Bill Gates, Kofi Annan Among Those Writing in Support of Inside Tipster Ahead of His Sentence," *Wall Street Journal*, October 13, 2012.

Aman Kumar's recollections of "Rajat uncle": Letter written by Aman Kumar on behalf of Gupta ahead of his sentencing.

A week after the jury verdict, Gupta headed to Boston: Letter written by Geetanjali Gupta on behalf of her father ahead of his sentencing.

Goldman had advanced money to pay legal bills, which by the end of the trial amounted to $30 million: Peter Lattman, "Goldman Stuck with a Defense Tab, and Awaiting a Payback," Dealbook, June 18, 2012.

But a week before his sentencing Gupta learned Goldman was seeking to recoup $7 million: Chad Bray, "Gupta Opposes Goldman's Bid for Probe Reimbursement," *Wall Street Journal*, October 22, 2012.

The slights faced by his third daughter, Aditi: Letter written by Aditi Gupta on behalf of her father ahead of his sentencing.

"I think it is fair to say Rajat Gupta's life has been an extraordinary one" and subsequent remarks by Naftalis and Judge Rakoff: Sentencing of Rajat K. Gupta, October 24, 2012.

Remarks of Naftalis and Rakoff: Ibid.

"A great deal of sensation" has "prevailed over this case": "Professor and Pupil's Case, Defense Arguments Concluded," *Amrita Bazar Patrika*, November 26, 1935.

The incident on April 9, 1935: "Professor and Pupil on Trial, Impersonation Charge, Incident at BA Examination Hall," *Amrita Bazar Patrika*, May 9, 1935; "Story of False Mustache, Professor on Trial, Personation Charge at the B.A. Examination," *Amrita Bazar Patrika*, June 1, 1935.

On December 4, 1935: "Professor Sentenced to Six Months R.I., Impersonation Case Judgment, Pupil Given Benefit of Doubt, Bail Granted by High Court," *Amrita Bazar Patrika*, December 5, 1935.

In April 1936, his sentence was upheld by the Calcutta High Court: "Conviction Upheld by High Court, Professor's Case, Echo of Impersonation in Exam Hall," *Amrita Bazar Patrika*, April 23, 1936.

"The last eighteen months have been the most challenging" and subsequent remarks by Gupta: *US v. Gupta*, Gupta's remarks at sentencing.

Rakoff's sentence: *US v. Gupta*, Sentencing Memorandum and Order, October 24, 2012.

Afterword

Details of Rajaratnam's surrender and new life in prison: Bob Van Voris, "Rajaratnam's Prison Trades May Run from Postage Stamps to Mackerel Packets," Bloomberg, December 5, 2011.

"The Americans stood their ground": Suketu Mehta, "The Outsider," *Newsweek*, October 23, 2011.

Millett's remarks: *US v Rajaratnam*, 11-4416, US Court of Appeals for the Second Circuit, October 25, 2012.

"My ability to return to my prior": *US v Anil Kumar*, 10-cr-13, Anil Kumar's statement at his sentencing on July 19, 2012.

The incident with Baylor College: *US v Kumar*, Sentencing Memorandum submitted on behalf of Anil Kumar, footnote 5.

Kumar's work for Max India: Ibid.

Goel's troubles since his arrest: *US v. Goel*, No. 10 Cr. 90 (BSJ), Sentencing Memorandum on behalf of Rajiv Goel, September 7, 2012.

Whitman's conviction on two counts of conspiracy: Patricia Hurtado and Bob Van Voris, "Whitman Capital Founder Guilty of Insider Trading," Bloomberg, August 20, 2012.

Khan's one-year prison sentence and Judge Rakoff's remarks: Patricia Hurtado, "Roomy Khan Gets One Year in Prison in Insider Trading Case," Bloomberg, January 31, 2013.

The bringing of civil and criminal charges against Mathew Martoma: Bob Van Voris and Patricia Hurtado, "Ex-SAC Manager Martoma Charged in Record Insider Scheme," Bloomberg, November 20, 2012.

Bloomberg News reported that Martoma was born Ajai Mathew Mariamdani Thomas: Katherine Burton, Saijel Kishan, and Bob Van Voris, "Cohen's 'Elan Guy' Martoma Dropped Ethics for Hedge Fund," Bloomberg, November 23, 2012.

"He has stained the India story": Email interview with Gurchuran Das, July 26, 2012.

The India Way: Peter Cappelli, Habir Singh, Jitendra Singh, and Michael Useem, *The India Way: How India's Top Business Leaders Are Revolutionizing Management* (Boston: Harvard Business Press, 2010).

In order for Israel to be counted among the nations of the world, it has to have its own burglars and prostitutes: Variations of the quotation are widely attributed to the Jewish poet Chaim Nachman Bialik, though, without any source. Though some authors such as Donna Rosenthal have attributed the quote to Ben-Gurion without citing a source, it is more likely that if Ben-Gurion made the remark, he was drawing on Bialik.

Every store on Oak Tree Road is owned by an Indian-American: Monte Burke, "The Secret to Immigrant Entrepreneurial Success Can Be Found in Edison, NJ," *Forbes,* June 25, 2012.

INDEX

ABOUT THE AUTHOR

ANITA RAGHAVAN was born in Malaysia but came to the United States as a young girl. She attended Cheltenham Ladies College in England. A graduate of the University of Pennsylvania, she spent eighteen years at the *Wall Street Journal* and became the London bureau chief for *Forbes* in 2008. Currently she is a contributor to *New York Times* Dealbook and *Forbes*.